Philip Perlmutter

Legacy of Hate

**a short history of ethnic, religious,
and racial prejudice in America**

M.E. Sharpe
Armonk, New York
London, England

Copyright © 1999 by M. E. Sharpe, Inc.

All rights reserved. No part of this book may be reproduced in any form
without written permission from the publisher, M. E. Sharpe, Inc.,
80 Business Park Drive, Armonk, New York 10504.

Library of Congress Cataloging-in-Publication Data

Perlmutter, Philip.
Legacy of hate : a short history of ethnic, religious, and racial prejudice in America / Philip
Perlmutter.
p.   cm.
Includes bibliographical references and index.
ISBN 0-7656-0406-X (hardcover : alk. paper)
1. Hate—United States. 2. Prejudices—United States. 3. Racism—United States.
4. Discrimination—Religious aspects—United States. 5. United States—Race relations.
6. United States—Social conditions. I. Divided we fall. II. Title.
BF575.H3P47   1999
305.8′00973—dc21
99-11648
CIP

Printed in the United States of America

The paper used in this publication meets the minimum requirements of
American National Standard for Information Sciences—
Permanence of Paper for Printed Library Materials,
ANSI Z 39.48-1984.

BM (c)   10   9   8   7   6   5   4   3   2   1

To my darling wife Rosanne,
children Jeff and Cathy,
son-in-law Alan,
and
grandchildren Eli and Riva

Contents

Dwell on the past and you will lose an eye.
Forget the past and you will lose both eyes.
—Old Russian Proverb

Preface to Revised Edition

The focus of this revised and updated edition of my earlier book, *Divided We Fall: A History of Ethnic, Religious, and Racial Prejudice in America,* continues to be on ethnic, religious, and racial groups, but with greater attention given to Asians, Hispanics, and women. Also new is a chapter on how to measure progress, or the lack of it, in minority-group relations.

Throughout, I continue to use *prejudice, discrimination,* and related synonyms somewhat loosely because I feel their behavioral manifestations are more important and obvious in dealing with history and minority-group life. No psychological or sociological words or theories can convey the pain caused. My desire to highlight that pain, as experienced by many groups, led me to drop some of the psychosocial material from the earlier edition.

Of course, I have made many corrections, have added new information, and have rewritten or discarded sentences and paragraphs that, upon rereading, I did not fully understand or could not defend. The result, I hope, is a tighter, more objective, and more helpful book for students, teachers, community relations practitioners, and readers interested in minority-group history.

Preface

There is an apocryphal story about a minister telling his Sunday congregation, "There are many prejudiced people here." All the parishioners nodded in agreement, but looked accusingly at those seated next to them. Outside of religious centers, too, it is always the other person who lacks virtue, has no sense of humor, or is bigoted. "I" or "We" are really nice, except when made not nice by others.

History does not reveal who the first bigots were, but we do know that bigotry in America preceded the first European White invaders and that, after their arrival, it expanded between and among people as more and more arrived, vanquished the Indians, and moved across the country.

For example, before Columbus, some Indians enslaved one another and practiced cannibalism. The early European settlers, though fervently religious, were wantonly bigoted, justifying their conquests, enslavements, massacres, and witch hunts in the name of a godly or manifest destiny. Furthermore, contrary to popular perception, though most early settlers were English and Spanish, a few were Poles, Norwegians, Scots, Jews, Slavs, Finns, Swedes, Dutch, French, Africans, and others. Whatever their religion, race, or ethnicity, each displayed or experienced some kind of prejudice, which general history rarely recorded, but which its victims did—in memory if not in print.

Such limited attention also comes from the Anglo-Saxon centrism of much American historiography, in which until recent decades "others" are looked down upon, resented, or considered insignificant, except as exotica or footnotes; the socioeconomic class, race, and philosophic outlook of historians, who ignored or slighted whatever did not conform with their values and expectations; the absence, if not destruction, of writings and records of aboriginal groups; the concentration on the sufferings of a few highly visible racial and ethnic minorities (Blacks, Native Americans, Jews), as if they had no other experiences; the awesome difficulty of dealing with a multiplicity of groups, many of whom were relatively small in number; the scarcity of writers interested in ethnicity or adept in foreign languages; the passive acceptance by some minority groups of being excluded from history books or, when included, inadequately, inaccurately, or insensitively so; and lastly, the ethnocentric writings of minority groups themselves, as if no other minorities had similar experiences.

True, much has been written about the psychological and sociological "here and now" of bigotry. Books and articles galore have credited its psychological dynamics to asocial behavior, deemed curable by education or psychological treatment. At the same time, a plenitude of sociological literature has claimed that bigotry results from the process and structure of society, wherein massive reform, if not revolution, is the prescribed solution. In either case, it was often naively, or conveniently, assumed that by studying one group, the prototype, people would learn that there but for the grace of color, creed, or culture go they. Unfortunately, neither history nor life is that rational or moral. People do not readily identify with other groups and, their capacity to tolerate or ignore the sufferings of others is almost unlimited, particularly when they have forgotten or never knew their own historical anguishes.

I have therefore attempted to depict bigotry as it affected many groups, and when dealing with any one group, to do so against a background of injustices to others. Only then can the pervasiveness of bigotry be fully understood. In doing so, my hope is that readers will say "I didn't know that" and will want to know more about themselves and others.

A plurality of historical illustrations will show that no minority group in America was immune to some form or degree of intolerance. Sometimes it was mainly religious, as in anti-Catholicism, anti-Mormonism, and anti-Semitism. Or it was specifically racial, as with Indians, Blacks, and Asians. Or it was ethnic—directed against such specific groups as the Portuguese, Armenians, French Canadians, and the British. Moreover, bigotry frequently manifested itself in various combinations of religion, ethnicity, and race so that tension and distrust existed between Protestant Irish and Catholic Irish, Swedish Lutherans and Norwegian Lutherans, West Indian Blacks and American-born Blacks, as well as Japanese and Filipinos. Within specific groups, too, there were prejudices, involving the region they lived in or came from, their generation in America, their socioeconomic status, or their level of education.

How much racial, religious, or ethnic bigotry existed in the past is difficult, if not impossible, to assess because of the absence of trained observers, sociological tools, or even a common standard of inhuman behavior. No Gallup or Roper poll measured people's feelings, beliefs, or knowledge about others. Political leaders and writers did comment on what was happening, but often from different and contradictory perspectives. Most victims never recorded their sufferings, either because they could not or would not write, were too intent on surviving, or felt it would not matter. Those who did tell their stories were all too often disbelieved or ignored by other groups, or forgotten by their own succeeding generations. The result is that most histories are those of the victors, whose self-proclaimed conquests and monuments obliterated the anguish they had caused.

Though America has been rightfully portrayed as born of democratic principles, to no less extent was it born of undemocratic ones. On the one hand, the plenitude of religious, racial, and ethnic groups generated intergroup suspicion, tension, and hostility, but it also inspired a structure and way of government wherein no one group could gain or maintain hegemony over all others and the rights of all individuals would be guaranteed, regardless of religious, ethnic, racial, and most recently, sexual background.

America is thus a living contradiction of many dimensions—historical, sociological, and psychological—that have manifested themselves on every level of society—individual, communal, and national. Here, too, instead of focusing solely on one or another of these dimensions, as most writers have done, I interrelate them in one presentation, sacrificing depth of research for breadth of presentation.

I hope to show the following:

Historically. There was a simultaneity, accretion, and pluralism of victimizers and victims throughout American history, wherein different groups always had or added a new target for their bigotry. For example, early Quakers, Catholics, Lutherans, and Huguenots were hated at the same time that Blacks and Indians were disdained and brutalized. These were replaced or added to, in varying degrees, with subsequent immigrant groups from Europe, Asia, South America, and Canada. No immigrant group—new or old, large or small—was without some victims or victimizers. So it was with the Scotch-Irish and Quakers, Mormons and Gentiles, Anglicans and Congregationalists, and all White groups against Blacks. Moreover, neither being conservative, liberal, progressive, or radical, nor being religious, areligious, or antireligious, prevented individuals, groups, institutions, unions, or political parties from practicing some form of bigotry.

Sociologically. There was an acculturation of people who struggled to transcend the bigotry heaped upon them. If immigrants were "nobodies" in Europe or elsewhere, they and particularly their children became "somebodies" in America, where they assumed an *American* national rather than an Old Country provincial identity.

Psychologically. Newcomers and old-comers faced problems of defining and defending themselves ethnically and culturally. Who am I? How do others define me? How do I want them to view me? How shall I respond to prejudice and discrimination? The answers have always been complex and painful, with some groups fiercely opposing bigotry and others fatalistically accepting it.

Economically. Whatever the minority, it usually started on the bottom of the socioeconomic ladder, replacing and often competing with those who came before them. It was a dynamic that employers often exploited to keep wages low, profits high, and unions out. At the same time, a process of "deproletarianization" and "embourgeoisement" took place, wherein, contrary to Marx, many workers and laborers—and especially their children—could and did become middle- and upper-class citizens.

Educationally. From the beginning of schooling in America, ethnocentrism, xenophobia, and Anglo-Saxon superiority prevailed, as did indifference and hostility to the needs of racial, religious, and ethnic groups. Not until the civil rights movement did lessons and lectures, as well as segregation and exclusion, stop generating and validating bigotry against Blacks, Native Americans, Mexicans, Asians, and eastern and southern Europeans.

Politically. Throughout American history, various groups were accused of disloyalty, dual loyalty, or no loyalty. The early colonists feared rebellion, revolt, or revolution by Indians and Blacks, separately or together. Anglophobes, Francophobes, Hispanophobes, and Germanophobes were convinced that immigrants from England, France, Spain, and Germany were plotting to destroy America. Protestant nativists saw a Catholic conspiracy at work, with Rome as the command center and local churches as operational cells. Anti-Semites believed that the forged "Protocols of the Elders of Zion" were a true blueprint for world domination by Jews. The bigoted, including many recently arrived immigrants, dreaded an Asian invasion and takeover of America by Chinese and Japanese. Supposedly enlightened intellectuals, social scientists, and patriots argued that culturally and genetically certain immigrants—particularly those from southern and eastern Europe—were corrupting the vitality and bloodstream of American democracy.

Religiously. Colonial America was not only an outpost of, and haven from, Old World prejudices and conflicts, but it was also the spawning ground for New World tolerances and freedoms, in which neither Catholic pope nor Protestant archbishop would control the thoughts and behaviors of any or all citizens. Today's religious freedom is the result of a complex movement from the military triumphalism of Portuguese and Spanish Catholicism to the stern exclusiveness of English Protestantism, to the pragmatic pluralism of dissenting religious and irreligious Americans, who declared that government shall make no law respecting the establishment of religion or prohibiting the free exercise thereof.

In dealing with so many groups and developments, contradictions, ambiguities, and paradoxes are always present. Similarities, dissimilarities, and total differences characterize our multivaried population.

Though prejudice and discrimination were pervasive, their intensity, form, and duration varied, depending on the time, location, and people involved. Anti-Semitism never provoked the mob violence that anti-Catholicism did, and both never equaled in duration and degree the slavery and bloodshed inflicted upon Blacks and Indians. Furthermore, however small or benign the minority group, its members were subject to the accusation of being inferior, clannish, pushy, or unpatriotic.

As America grew older in years, larger in size, denser in population, and wealthier in natural and material resources, it became less suspicious, restrictive, and intolerant and more respectful, expansive, and protective of the right to be racially, religiously, and ethnically different. Such meliorism was accretive, not only because of those who believed in the equality or egalitarianism of all people, but also because many of the victims of bigotry sought surcease of abuse and a clear implementation of basic constitutional rights. What could not be obtained by petition, protest, lawsuit, or fight was obtained by political coalitions or individual group strength and voting. Taken together, America's diverse groups helped create and keep America the freest country in the world, supporting the ideal, if not always the reality, that all people are created equal and possess the same inalienable rights and opportunities for life, liberty, and the pursuit of happiness.

Underlying all my thoughts is a conviction that whatever America's shortcomings, it is the least bigoted country in the world and will continue to be so, but only if we hold to some simple Founding Father wisdom. For our nation to flourish, said George Washington, there not only must be a strong union of states, a respect for justice and good government, but also a "pacific and friendly Disposition, among the People . . . which will induce them to forget their local prejudices and policies, to make those natural concessions which are requisite to the general prosperity, and in some instances, to sacrifice their individual advantages to the interests of the Community."

To that I say, "Amen."

Acknowledgments

Grateful acknowledgment is made to the following magazines and newspapers in which articles I wrote were published while I was writing or revising this book.

"Ethnicity and the Public Schools," *Journal of Intergroup Relations,* November 1975.

"Ethnicity, Education and Prejudice," *Ethnicity,* March 1981.

"The Decline of Bigotry in the United States," *Christian Science Monitor,* 5 March 1981.

"Prejudice, Politics and Patriotism," *Christian Science Monitor,* 28 October 1981.

"Immigrants Keep Making It, Despite Stereotypes," *Boston Globe,* 8 September 1985.

"I Think the Indians Discovered America," *New York Times,* 10 October 1987.

"From Prejudice to Pride: How Parochial Schools Became Respectable," *Catholic Twin Circle,* 21 February 1988.

"A Proliferation and Pollution of Standards," *The Social Critic,* Spring 1998.

"Saying You're Sorry Just Isn't Enough," *The Journal of InterGroup Relations,"* Summer 1998.

Chapter One

The Seeds of Contempt

Although rightfully hailed as a land of opportunity, freedom, equality, and justice, America has also been criticized as a nation born, bred, and nurtured in interracial, interethnic, and interreligious rivalries and conflicts, wherein one group's well-being was often achieved at another's expense. Rarely were the conflicts a matter of absolute right or wrong, though each group claimed to be the injured party and utilized varied means to advance or protect itself, including invidious rules and regulations, murder, and war.

From the time of America's discovery to the nineteenth century, Old and New World conflicts were replicated and magnified. Immigrants from the same region or country tended to form colonies, outposts, settlements, and communities, as well as a variety of group-specific religious, ethnic, social, and fraternal organizations. Few were the groups not in contention with one another because of differing beliefs or competing ambitions.

Intergroup conflicts often involved problems of ethnicity and race: Indians versus Indians, Whites versus Whites, Whites versus Indians, Whites versus Blacks, and Blacks versus Indians. Religion also provided a focus of conflict, pitting Protestant against Protestant, Catholic against Catholic, Protestant against Catholic—and all of these against other religions. The profusion and polarity of European Christians—Catholics, Lutherans, Calvinists, Quakers, Anglicans, and Anabaptists—were carried over to the New World, where at varying times Catholic Spain, Portugal, and France vied with each other or with Protestant Holland and England.

Finally, geopolitics created conflict as each European power sought to establish its private territory: the English, Dutch, Swedes, and Scotch along the East Coast; the French in the north and south central areas; the Spanish in the Southwest, Southeast, and Far West; and the Russians in the Pacific Far Northwest. Far from home, they encroached on each other's territories and particularly on those of the Indians, who in their own intertribal differences made alliances with one or another European power.

The most successful European invaders, of course, were the English, whom the Sieur d'Iberville, in 1699, accurately predicted would expel all others because however much they enriched themselves, they "do not return to England but stay and will flourish by their riches and their great efforts; while the French abandon them and retire as soon as they have gained a little wealth."[1] Slowly but surely, the other European powers were forced to withdraw, first by the English and then by the Americans.

If in the nineteenth century a clear pattern of group pluralism, prejudice, succession, and exploitation existed, its early forms were seen in the seventeenth and eighteenth centuries. Poor Whites—indentured servants, redemptioners, and convicts—were encouraged to immigrate to America to do menial labor. Cervantes labeled America a refuge for the scum of all Spain.[2] What White people could not or would not do, Indians were compelled to do, and failing that, indentured Europeans, convicts, and Black slaves were brought over to do. In the pursuit of profits and power, the early immigrants and colonizing companies, like later industrial employers, stimulated Black-White and Indian-Black rivalries. Ethnic prejudice was widespread, with Germans, Scotch Irish, Irish, and Scots the least liked and often assigned or encouraged to settle in areas that served as buffers to the Spanish in the South, the French in the West and North, and Indians wherever they were. Throughout the time, the European colonists feared uprisings, attacks, or rebellions by those indentured, enslaved, or confined to the frontiers.

Some early writers went so far as to claim that America's very discovery was a mistake, which led to the extermination of Indians and their civilization, the provocation of imperialist wars, the extension of slavery, the spread of fatal diseases, and the depopulation of Europe's talented and enterprising young men. "All strength and all injustice were on the side of the Europeans," said Holland's Abbe Corneille De Pauw in 1768, who argued that because the natives in America had only weaknesses, "they were therefore bound to be exterminated, and exterminated in an instant's time ... the conquest of the New World, so celebrated and so unjust, has been the greatest of all misfortunes to befall mankind."[3]

Other commentators romanticized America as a New World to which only people of goodwill and courageous heart fled in search of freedom and the peaceful pursuit of happiness. They were portrayed as benign discoverers and explorers, who brought religion, morality, and civilization to an illiterate, savage, and sinful native population. To such observers from afar, America was synonymous with liberty and an opportunity to start a new life, free of religious, political, and economic taboos and tyranny. The military brutality, religious intolerance, and ethnic prejudice of the time were ignored or played down, however, except for the memories and folklore of their victims.

A fair reading of American history will show that though there was evil in America, all was not so. The distinction is both logically and historically crucial for understanding American intergroup relations. Just as America was a land of Indian dispossession and Black enslavement, so was it one of refuge and opportunity for countless religious, political, and economic émigrés. And just as scoundrels, criminals, and killers came here, so did good and compassionate people, who decried the injustices about them and demanded their compatriots conform to a standard of behavior that would make the New World better than the Old World and closer to the ideals of the Promised Land.

Indian-Indian Relations Before Columbus

If contemporary American is a pluralistic wonderworld, the same was true before Columbus landed. For millennia, Asian nomads, hunters, and explorers settled the lands from the Bering Sea to Cape Horn. Not until man occupies another planet, wrote one scholar, will he explore so vast a domain. Siberian immigrants allegedly came to America in 22,000 B.C. and reached South America by 9400 B.C. In Brazil, recent archeological findings suggest that human life existed at least 32,000 years ago.[4]

At the time Columbus set sail, estimates on how many natives lived in the Americas range from some 8 million to more than 75 million. What is fairly certain is that they developed some 160 language families, with at least 1,200 dialect subdivisions, totaling more native-language families than in the rest of the world. Moreover, contrary to stereotypes of Indians as high-cheeked, hawk-nosed, and red-skinned, they reflected more variations in height, face, and color than in the whole White racial stock.[5]

With such diversity, it is not surprising that before the first Europeans came, there were native-native conflicts that involved torture, murder, scalping, cannibalism, and slavery. Because they had no guns or horses, the Indians fought on foot with bows and arrows, stone-tipped spears, and clubs. In one form or another, slavery was practiced by the Aztecs, Incas, Mayans, the Cuna of Central America, Northwest coastal tribes, and various tribes in Louisiana, Florida, and northward up the coast to Virginia. Male Indian slaves were often subject to harsher treatment than females and children. Tlingit Indians killed slaves and used their bodies as foundations for house posts or totem poles. The Kwakiutl sometimes killed their slaves on the beach so that their bodies could be used as rollers for incoming canoes of esteemed guests. In the Southeast, the feet of slaves were often mutilated to prevent their running away. At times, powerful tribes (such as the Tsimshians and Chinooks) raided weaker ones for prisoners, who were then sold as slaves to wealthier but less powerful tribes. Even among the Eskimos, blood feuds, quarrels, and wars abounded over women or hunting and fishing boundaries.[6]

A few Indian tribes practiced scalping and head taking as wartime rituals, particularly the Tunicas and Muskogeans in the Southwest. The practice of scalping spread to many tribes when the White settlers provided bounties for the scalps of enemy Indians.

Cannibalism was also practiced by such tribes as the Aztecs, Tupinamba, Guarani, and the Caribs, after whom the word *cannibalism* was coined. The Guarani of South America killed some 60,000 Arawakan Chane and enslaved the remainder, a few of whom were slaughtered when their captors felt hungry. One demographer estimated that the Aztecs alone sacrificed 250,000 people a year, eating their limbs and feeding their torsos to animals. Forced tribute and labor were common practices, even among the highly advanced Indian societies, so that when the Spanish took over, it meant little more than a change of masters.[7]

Farther north, the Iroquois, Hurons, Algonquins, Montagnais, and Ottawas frequently cannibalized captured Indian and European enemies after ceremoniously torturing them. In describing Iroquois practices, one observer wrote, "Then, they tear the heart from the breast, roast it upon the coals, and, if the prisoner has bravely borne the bitterness of the torture, give [it] seasoned with blood, to the boys, to be greedily eaten, in order, as they say, that the warlike youth may imbibe the heroic strength of the valiant man."[8]

Throughout North America, intertribal warfare, slave taking, and plunder were common. The early-seventeenth-century French missionary Gabriel Sagard reported scarcely any Indian "nation which is not at war and dissension with some other, not for the purpose of possessing their territory and conquering their country, but solely to exterminate them if possible and take revenge for some slight wrong or unpleasantness."[9]

At their worst, Indians were no different from Europeans back home or in America. Both Catholics and Protestants tortured and killed each other and dissenters within their ranks. Martin Luther favored burning witches, and John Calvin had no hesitancy in having his theological opponent, Michael Servetus, burned alive. Depending on who was in power in England, Protestants or Catholics were tortured, hanged, burned, or beheaded. In a four-year period, "Bloody Mary," the daughter of Henry VIII, burned 300 Protestants.[10]

When Europeans confronted Indians, both discovered the other's savagery, "but in the inevitable conflict of a culture of iron with Neolithic cultures, the sword was bound to sharpen itself on the stone."[11] By introducing horses, metal knives, hatchets, and especially guns and rum, the Europeans consciously and unconsciously intensified inter-Indian disunity and warfare. Unfortunately for the Indians, they never foresaw the destruction that was to befall them.

The "First" in America

From the earliest days of America's recorded history, a profusion of claims and theories existed about who the first residents and "discoverers" were. One Norse saga told of how some seamen, in 1029, driven off course on the way to Iceland, touched land somewhere south of the Chesapeake Bay, where they met people who "appeared to them that they spoke Irish." Another saga referred to the area as *Irland-it-Mikla,* that is, Great Ireland.[12]

Some early Spanish writers said that the Indians probably descended from such groups as Carthaginians, Jews, Chinese, Tartars, Romans, Japanese, Koreans, Egyptians, Moors, Canary Islanders, Ethiopians, French, English, Irish,

Germans, Trojans, Danes, Frisians, or Norsemen. Father Gregorio Garcia, in the sixteenth century, saw similarities between Indians and Jews because both were cowards, lacked charity, and did not believe in Jesus, which also explained why Jews were dispersed and Indians persecuted. Another Spanish writer claimed that western Indian languages contained many Hebrew and Yiddish words and that the natives, like Jews, had long noses, spoke gutturally, wore side curls, and were circumcised.[13]

Sixteenth- and seventeenth-century Europeans projected biblical explanations. For having dared build the Tower of Babel, God had punished the residents, scattering them throughout the world, with those farthest from Creation's center the most fallen from Grace. In England, in 1650, the Reverend James Thorowgood published a book, *Jews in America or Probabilities that those Indians are Judaical.* In *An Historical and Geographical Account of Pennsylvania,* published in 1698, the first inhabitants were said to resemble "the Jews very much in the Make of their Persons, and Tincture of their Complexions . . . and have a kind of Feast of Tabernacles, laying their Altars upon Twelve Stones."[14]

On the other hand, to the famed Dutch scholar and statesman Hugo Grotius, Indians in the North were descended from Norwegians, those in the Yucatan from Ethiopians, and those in Peru from Chinese. Some Indians were thought to be of Welsh descent because of their fair skins, blue eyes, blond hair, and Welsh-sounding words. A young English Methodist was sent to America to find and reconvert them, only to report, "I could not meet such a people, and from intercourse I have had with Indians from latitudes 35 to 49, I think you may safely inform our friends they have no existence."[15]

By the late eighteenth century, a belief grew that the thousands of mounds of earth in the Mississippi Valley were not built by Indians but by a more intelligent race, probably White and possibly Jewish, who, though no longer there, proved a White racial ownership and a justification for displacing Indians. Early-nineteenth-century American men of science proffered a number of explanations: the "first" Americans were Malays conquered by Tartars from northwest Asia, who in turn became Indians; they were descendants of Noah, who had come after the Flood or had migrated from North Africa via the West Indies, to be followed by Romans, Egyptians, Norwegians, Welsh, Greeks, and others; or they were indeed Indians, but related to Egyptians who had developed the civilizations of Mexico and Peru.[16]

By the century's end, priority of discovery became saturated with Anglo-Saxon and Teutonic pride, leading many a nativist and New England patrician to oppose the creation of a Columbus Day holiday because Columbus was Catholic, never set foot on the continent, and was usurping credit due Leif Ericson.

In the twentieth century, with the rise of pluralism as a valued way of American life, many minority groups used archeology to support their claims of ancestral presence in America, which was not the sole legacy of a Spanish (or Italian) Columbus or of a Norse Leif Ericson. Nor was it a God-given inheritance of Puritans, Pilgrims, and other Protestants. Minorities boasted of how members of their groups had been in America long before Columbus set sail or Martin Luther and Henry VIII broke away from the church. Indeed, for some such claims, there is evidence, debatable as it may be:

About 3,000 years ago, Celtic mariners reached New England and established the kingdom of *Idragalon,* meaning Land Beyond the Sunset. Inscriptions on stones in Tennessee and Georgia were made by ancient Jews. Artifacts in Brazil belonged to Romans who arrived seventeen centuries before Portuguese explorers.[17] Art designs in Ecuador and Mexico suggest Japanese and Chinese contact or presence some 5,000 years ago. And terra-cotta figures of Japanese-appearing sailors and a wrestler found in Mexico are believed to have been left by Japanese 500 years before Columbus.[18]

Similarities of physiques, agricultural proficiencies, religious beliefs, housing construction, or words and sounds suggest pre-Columbian contacts of North Dakota Mandan Indians with Swedes and Norwegians; Poles with Hopis; Libyans with Zuni Indians; Welsh with Indians in Alabama; Basques and Norsemen with Algonquins; Phoenicians and Egyptians with the Wabanaki tribe in New England; and Jews with Delaware and Wyandotte Indians. An Afghan priest and four Chinese Buddhist monks are said to have reached northwest Canada, which they called "The Great Han Country," in A.D. 458 and then traveled to Mexico, as evidenced by Chinese-Aztec similarities in linguistics, myths, and numismatics.[19]

More speculative are claims by Mormons that in pre-Columbian times their ancestors came in three successive migrations and that today's Indians are descended from the two evil sons of Lehi, whom God had cursed with dark skins. Arab accounts of a strange, far-off land have been said to refer to South or North America, which Arab sailors reached from Casablanca. Claims have also been made that a Pole and a Hungarian, as well as some Blacks and Venetians, were in North America long before Columbus.[20]

If not "before" Columbus, then being "with" him also became a source of pride for many groups: that he sailed in Basque-built ships with a mostly Basque crew; that one of his pilots, Pedro Alonso Nino, was a Black; that he and some crew members were former Jews; that a Polish roving seaman, Franciszek Warnadowicz, was with him; that two of his seamen were Ragusans; that an Irishman helped row him ashore; that he was Portuguese; and that in addition to possibly being Greek himself, he had some Greek crew members.[21] Regardless of which lost seamen, explorers, invaders, or settlers came first, they were all Johnny-come-latelies in the history of the continent.

White-Indian Conflict

Misunderstandings, conflicts, and wars were inevitable between Europeans and Indians, not only because of their differences in language, religious belief, social behavior, and physical appearance, but also their outlook on land and possession.

The first Europeans arrived accidentally. The North American continent was simply in the path of their search for a new route to the Far East's gold, precious stones, spices, woods, dyes, and perfumes. For the Indians, the Europeans were unexpected and, as they quickly learned, destructive of their way of life. Though thousands of miles away, African Blacks became the victims of greedy Europeans, brought in chains to do the work that Europeans thought below their dignity and that Indians refused to do.

Preceding Columbus by some 500 years, the Norsemen came for a variety of reasons: loot, land, barter—and accident of wind and tide. As brutal as they were on the European continent, so with the natives they encountered, who were pejoratively labeled *Skraelings,* meaning wretched, savage, despised inferiors. To them goes the dubious honor of being the first Europeans in North America to manifest Christian triumphalism. As recorded in the Icelandic "Saga of Eric the Red," Leif Ericson landed on the continent and "found men upon a wreck, and took them home with him [to Greenland], and procured quarters for them all during the winter. In this wise he showed his nobleness and goodness, since he introduced Christianity into the country." By the fifteenth century, however, the Norse disappeared from the continent, either because voyages were no longer profitable, living conditions too difficult, or native hostility too life-threatening.[22]

The large-scale movement from Indian-Indian conflict to White-Indian conflict started with Christopher Columbus persuading Spain's Ferdinand and Isabella to fund his ill-planned expedition to the Indies (which meant India, China, East Indies, and Japan). There he hoped to obtain precious metals and spices, convert everyone to Catholicism, and make an alliance with the Great Khan—a mythical sovereign allegedly favorable to Christianity who would agree to attack "the abominable sect of Mohomet" from the east while Spain attacked from the west. Among his crewmen were a number of prison inmates from Palos and Cadiz, a practice that other European powers expanded.[23]

Little is actually known about his personal life or appearance, which helps explain the many claims about Christoforo Colombo (Italian). Though probably born in Genoa, his exact birthday is unknown. English-speaking countries know him by his Latinized name Christopher Columbus, though in France, it is Columb; in Portugal, Colom; and in Spain, Colón. None of the more than eighty extant portraits of him, all made after his death, have been authenticated for accuracy.[24]

Contrary to popular impression, Ferdinand and Isabella were not poor when they looked to the West for a safe and short way to the East. In truth, they possessed vast wealth, which they lavishly spent to extend their royal status. As small as their investment was in Columbus, estimated at $16,000 to $75,000, they hesitated to make it, just as the kings of France, England, and Portugal had, because most experts of the time believed (and correctly so) that the Indies could not be where Columbus had claimed. By the most optimistic computations then, he had underestimated the breadth of the Atlantic Ocean by 25 percent, and by today's reckonings, by 75 percent.[25]

When he bumped into the Bahama Islands, he insisted he was in the Indies and called the natives *los Indios,* which, although not as odious as *Skraelings,* was no less inaccurate. On reaching Cuba, he thought it Japan, or at least an island close to it, though there were none of the riches, buildings, or populations to which legend ascribed. Columbus recorded how the natives had no metal weapons, but were "marvellously timorous . . . so guileless and so generous with all they possess, that no one would believe it who has not seen it. They never refuse anything which they possess, if it be asked of them; on the contrary, they invite anyone to share it, and display so much love as if they would give their hearts." Nevertheless, he was certain that if they themselves did not possess wealth, they knew where it was. It was simply a matter of earning their trust, which he sought by giving them red caps and glass beads, "which they hung on their necks, and many other things of slight value in which they took much pleasure."[26] The natives, in turn, quickly learned that the best way to get rid of him was to say gold could be found on the next island, or on the one after it, or somewhere beyond the horizon. And off he went.

In his hunger for wealth and religious purity, as well as knowledge that Ferdinand and Isabella had approved of an inquisition in their kingdom, Columbus urged a policy of preventing "any stranger, except Catholic Christians, to trade here or set foot here."[27] Equally audacious was his claim of discovering a new land, with rivers teeming with spices and gold, though the islands were as old as the land from which he had sailed and contained none of the wealth he swore existed. To ensure his claims, he left a small group of crewmen on Hispaniola before returning home.

As news spread of his voyage, Portugal accused Spain of trespassing on its claims. Pope Alexander VI resolved their differences by dividing the unexplored world between them, without any thought to the possible reactions of their residents, the legendary Emperor of Japan, or the Great Khan—or the actual rulers of France, England, or Holland.

Meanwhile, all did not go well for Columbus's men in Hispaniola. The natives slaughtered them because of their oppressive rule, lust for native women, and insatiable demands for gold. Ethnic Iberian animosities contributed to their defeat, with commentators of the time noting that "certain Vizcayans joined together against the rest," causing "a division among the Christians."[28]

After island hopping and gift giving failed to bring the desired results, Columbus and his crews in subsequent voyages took more drastic actions. They established quotas for natives bringing them gold dust, failure of which led to having their hands cut off or being killed. In 1494, Columbus introduced New World slaves to Europe by sending more than 500 to be sold in Seville, the profits of which, he suggested, would offset the Crown's investment in him. His brother, Don Bartholomew, likewise sent 300 Indian prisoners in

1496. By the time of Columbus's fourth voyage, Ferdinand and Isabella had stopped the practice.[29]

A worse fate awaited the remaining natives, for while Spain in the early Middle Ages had been "the most tolerant land in Christendom," it had by now become "the most fanatically intolerant," at home and abroad. In the first two years of Spanish occupation of Hispaniola, one-third of the estimated 300,000 natives died, and by 1548, only 500 natives were alive. As a result, African slaves were imported to do the hard mining and plantation work. King Ferdinand approved such importations so that "all of these be getting gold for me," subsequently ordering still larger shipments because one Black could easily do the work of four Indians. The Spanish throne also authorized in 1497 the colonization of the New World with male and female convicts—except for those guilty of heresy, treason, or sodomy.[30]

Though four voyages never brought the wealth he had hoped for, they did inspire others to go west to reach the East. Columbus's legacy is not only that of fierce ambition, pride, greed, and seamanship but of transplanting to the New World European war technology, Christian triumphalism, racial intolerance, and massive land robbing—while back home his patrons carried on inquisitions, expelled Jews and Muslims, and dreamed of further ways of crushing Islam.

The enormity of the devastation was noted by some writers of the time. Bartolome de Las Casas, "the Apostle of the Indies," accused Spanish colonists of having "behaved like ravening wild beasts, wolves, tigers, or lions that had been starved for many days . . . afflicting, torturing and destroying native peoples." Similarly, in 1511, a Dominican priest asked congregants in Hispaniola to tell him "by what right or justice do you hold these Indians in such cruel and horrible slavery? By what authority do you wage such detestable wars on these people, who live mildly and peacefully in their own lands, in which you destroy countless numbers of them with unheard of murder and ruin . . . ?"[31]

The great sixteenth-century defender of Spanish conquest Juan Gines De Sepulveda wondered how anyone could doubt that the Indians, "so uncivilized, so barbaric, contaminated with so many impieties and obscenities—have been justly conquered by such an excellent, pious, and most just king as was Ferdinand the Catholic and as is now Emperor Charles, and by such a most humane nation and excellent in every kind of virtue?"[32]

Underlying Spanish greed and cruelty was a religious contempt for others and truculent pride in one's own beliefs. After all, the natives were a dispersed and despised people, whose art, language, and writing deserved destruction and whose land belonged to the Catholic church, which had retained title to it through successive popes, going back to Jesus, who obtained it from God. Thus, before the Spanish engaged in battles with any "Indians," one of their notaries read a statement to them explaining the origins and rights of the church to "judge and govern all Christians, Moors, Jews, Gentiles and other sects. . . . Therefore as best we can, we ask and require you . . . that you acknowledge the Church as the Ruler and Superior of the whole world and the high priest called Pope, and in his name the King and Queen Dona Juana our lords, in his place, as superiors and lords and kings of these island this Terra-firma."[33]

If the Indians agreed, all would be well. If the Indians refused, however, the notary was enjoined to say that "with the help of God, we shall forcibly enter into your country and shall make war against you in all ways and manners that we can, and shall subject you to the yoke and obedience of the Church and of their Highnesses; we shall take you and your wives and your children, and shall make slaves of them, and as such shall sell and dispose of them as their Highnesses may command; and we shall take away your goods, and shall do all the harm and damage that we can, as to vassals who do not obey, and refuse their lord, and resist and contradict him; and we protest that the deaths and losses which shall accrue from this are your fault, and not that of their Highnesses, or ours, nor of those cavaliers who come with us."[34] More appalling than the statement itself, which the natives could not understand, was the practice of reading it even when no Indians were about to hear it. In their self-righteousness, the conquistadors believed their behavior good and moral, whether in taking Indian lands or lives, or forcing them to convert.

Similar values were applied to sexual relations. Short of Spanish women, the invaders readily took Indian women, if not by force than by purchase or gift from Indian chiefs. Although mating with Indians was frowned upon, particularly if they had not been converted, "the service rendered to God in producing mestizos is greater than the sin committed by the same act," said one footloose conquistador. Santo Domingo's governor was instructed in 1503 to have "some Christians marry some Indian women and some Christian women marry some Indian men, so that both parties can communicate and teach each other and the Indians [to] become men and women of reason." To win the favor of the Spanish, some Indian girls whitened their skin.[35]

Indian deaths and resistance to enslavement led to Emperor Charles's authorization of a large-scale purchase in 1518 of Black slaves from Portuguese traders. What the Indians would not do, it was believed Blacks would, as illustrated in the plea of a sixteenth-century Hispaniola official for permission "to buy Negroes, a race robust for labor, instead of natives, so weak that they can only be employed in tasks requiring little endurance." At times, Blacks were used as overseers of Indian laborers. Even then, the Spanish opposed Black-Indian marriages and liaisons, fearing that Blacks would reinforce Indian paganism or, equally repugnant, infect them with Islamic beliefs.

While such religious and cultural triumphalism was being enforced in the New World, Emperor Charles back in Europe was denouncing the rise of Protestantism and particularly Martin Luther, vowing to give all his "dominions, friends, body, blood, life, and soul" to destroy both, thus engendering the seeds of Catholic-Protestant hatred in both continents.[36]

French, English, Dutch, and Swedish Invasions

After the Spanish, other Europeans—French, English, Dutch, Swedes, and Russians—invaded the continent, with no less hubris and greed, each believing in their right of conquest and resenting those of differing religious beliefs or nationalities. Less numerous and for the most part short-lived were Scottish colonies in Nova Scotia (1620), eastern and northern New Jersey (1683), and South Carolina (1684), with the latter two also serving largely as refuges for religious dissidents: Quakers in New Jersey and Presbyterians in South Carolina.[37]

Each major power sought to replicate itself, and so "New" England, France, Netherlands, and Sweden were created, though all had difficulty in attracting voluntary settlers, except for those greedy for wealth or land or anxious to escape religious bigotry. Whether as soldiers, settlers, traders, pirates, convicts, or missionaries, the European powers forsook their Old World rivalries and prejudices only when people of their "own kind" refused to settle among them or when overwhelmed by war.

In defiance of the 1493 Spanish and Portuguese division of the world, Francis I, of France, epitomized the envious side of European imperialism when he sent ships to Canada, declaring that "the sun shines for me as well as for others. I should very much like to see the clause in Adam's will that excludes me from a share of the world."[38] Under his reign, Verrazano in 1523 and then Cartier in 1534 hoped to find a northwest passage to the Orient, but instead of gold and silver, found fish, lumber, and plenty of fur-bearing animals. Being more interested in trade than in permanent settlements, the early French posed less of a threat to the Indians than their European counterparts.

Not until decades later did they seek to create a New France, when furs became a major source of revenue because of the great demand for them in Europe. Quebec was established in 1608. Père Marquette and Joliet (a fur trader) paddled down much of the Mississippi, to be followed by LaSalle, who claimed both sides of the river for France and named the area "Louisiana" in honor of the king. To ensure their holdings and protect their growing fur trade, they exploited inter-Indian rivalries, allying with the Hurons against the Iroquois and inciting Indian raids against English colonists in New England.

In that the Indians were believed to be living "without a knowledge of God and the use of reason," they were to be converted into Catholics and Frenchmen. At least, so it was hoped. Some were sent to France as prospective missionaries, galley slaves, or curios. French missionaries, like Spanish ones, often found themselves at odds with their military and commercial kinsmen, who wanted only loot and gold.

French enthnocentrism required the banning of all non-French Catholics from overseas territories, except Protestant Huguenots, who had lost their religious and civic rights with the revocation of the Edict of Nantes in 1685. Their emigration to Holland, Germany, England, and America prompted the coining of the word *refugee*. France allowed them to settle in the New World, but mainly to rid itself of them, challenge Spanish claims, and, if they found gold, to obtain an effortless royal share. Most of the early French traders in Canada were Huguenots, who cynically viewed Jesuit and Franciscan attempts to convert Indians as merely a replacement of one kind of idolatry with another.[39]

In the French West Indies, planters first utilized *engagés* (similar to English indentured servants), and then Black slaves, purchased mainly from the Dutch. By the end of the seventeenth century, the French formed their own company to supply African slaves for their West Indies colonies.

A similar pattern of behavior evolved in the Louisiana area, where the French established a permanent settlement in 1699, which attracted few settlers and to which many soldiers and sailors deserted. To meet the need for laborers, France and Canada sent assorted miscreants. One shipment, as described in 1719, consisted chiefly of females—"murderesses, prostitutes, thieves, knife experts, and female criminals branded on the shoulder with the fleur-de-lys, associates of coiners or of the bands of brigands infesting the forest of St. Germain."[40]

In order to obtain respectable settlers, immigrants were recruited from Switzerland, England, and Germany. Jews, however, were excluded, just as in the Caribbean. Louisiana's *Code Noir* of 1724 enjoined officials to expel "all Jews who may have established their residence. . . . These, as declared enemies of the Christian name, We command to leave in three months." Marriages between Whites and Blacks were banned, as well as "concubinage of whites and manumitted or free-born blacks with slaves." Unfriendly Indians were oppressed, particularly the Natchez, while friendly ones were catered to, hopeful they would become allies against the English or hostile Indians. Intra-French tensions also surfaced between those coming from France and Canada, with those from the latter disdainfully referred to as "the Canadian clique."[41]

The Dutch and Swedes were no less exclusionary or greedy. As early as 1606, Dutch ships penetrated the St. Lawrence River, trading with Indians for furs. In their avarice, some Hollanders robbed Indian graves for the beaver skins in which corpses were wrapped. In 1609, Dutch merchants commissioned Henry Hudson to find a non-Spanish, non-Portuguese passage to the Orient. Failing that, but reaching the Delaware Bay and river that was to bear Hudson's name, the Dutch formed the West India Company twelve years later. Its purpose was to promote "the honor of God by the proclamation of the Holy Gospel, and desiring also to provide that the inhabitants of the United Netherlands should benefit not only from their previous shipping and commerce but also, so far as possible, from an increase in that welfare and trade."[42]

By the time of the first Dutch settlement on Manhattan in 1624, with about thirty French-speaking Walloon families, the company was earning great profits by raiding Spanish settlements in the Caribbean, capturing Spanish treasure-laden ships, and monopolizing Dutch trade with Africa, whose gold, spices, and slaves rendered the furs of New Netherland relatively insignificant.[43]

Like the Spanish and French, the Dutch believed theirs was the only true church, stipulating that "no other religion shall be publicly admitted to New Netherland except the Reformed, as it is at present preached and practiced by public authority in the United Netherlands." But because few Dutch immigrated and more people were needed to ensure the company's profits, Germans, Swedes, and Finns were encouraged to immigrate. And records of the time indicate the presence of some Ukrainians.[44]

Dutch wealth did not escape the envy of Sweden. The prospectus of the Royal Swedish General Trading Company noted in 1627 that the Dutch had "become so powerful by . . . voyages to the East Indies, Guinea and other distant places, that it has already been able to resist the king of Spain. . . . And in all this time Sweden had until the present day lost or not shared in all the aforesaid profits." Eleven years later, New Sweden was established in Delaware, just south of a Dutch settlement. As with the Dutch, few Swedes voluntarily settled, and those who did specialized in fur trading, while committing themselves to maintaining religious purity "according to the true confession of Augsburg, the Council of Upsala, and the ceremonies of the Swedish church." Also present were petty criminals, including some Finnish ones.[45] When taken over by the Dutch in 1655, the total population of New Sweden was only 500.

The English, too, felt their economic rights should not be denied. "Money is the principal part of the greatness of Spain," said Francis Bacon to Queen Elizabeth, who eagerly sent Sir Humphrey Gilbert in search of a northern passage to the Indies, enunciating the principle of "first discovery," whereby he could settle all "territories not actually possessed by any Christian prince or people."[46] Captains John Hawkins and Francis Drake captured Spanish treasure ships and plundered their American settlements (with the occasional aid of escaped slaves). Drake had no compunction about looting Catholic churches and property, justifying his behavior as retaliation for prior Catholic abuse of Protestants. It was Hawkins, in 1652, who initiated England's slave trade in Sierra Leone, where he captured, or purchased from the Portuguese, some 300 Black Africans and then sold them to the Spanish in Hispaniola.

Greed motivated all early English expeditions. Captain John Smith complained that among his colonists there was "no talke, no hope, no worke, but dig gold, wash gold, refine gold, loade gold," forcing him to declare that "he who doth not work shall not eat" and that anyone not liking his regime and running away should be shot, hanged, or broken on the wheel.

Just as the Spanish had thought of finding a Great Khan who would be their ally against Islam, so some Englishmen hoped the Indians would join with them against Catholicism and Spain, both of which were causing them problems in Ireland. Richard Hakluyt wrote in the 1580s that if his fellow Englishmen "would either join with these Savages, or send or give them armor as the Spanish arm our Irish rebels, we should trouble the King of Spain more in those parts, then he hath or can trouble us in Ireland, and hold him at such a bay, as he was never yet held at." Nevertheless, the very hostility and aggression the English directed against the Irish was soon turned against the Indians, who were believed a similar people—wild, unkempt, unintelligible, and requiring force to civilize.[47]

Native inability to recognize English-professed magnanimity sometimes bewildered their would-be benefactors. In one of their early confrontations, a group of Eskimos on Baffin Island preferred suicide to submission. As one of Martin Frobisher's captains described the scene, in the 1570s, a "company" of Eskimos had been "environed by our men on the top of a high cliff, so that they could by no means escape our hands, finding themselves in this case distressed, chose rather to cast themselves headlong down the rocks into the sea, and so be bruised and drowned, rather than to yield themselves to our men's mercies."[48]

Demographic needs and religious triumphalism were also at work. To William Vaughan, the establishment of overseas colonies would relieve England's overpopulation and crime. Hopefully, he wrote, "our extortioners, perjurers, pettifoggers at law, coney-catchers, thieves, cottagers, inmates, unnecessary ale-sellers, beggars, burners of hedges to the hindrance of husbandry and such like . . . might perhaps prove profitable members in the New Found Land."[49]

Robert Gray was more idealistic, saying that "it is everie man's dutie to . . . bring the barbarous and savage people to a civill and Christian kinde of government, under which they may learne how to live holily, justly, and soberly in this world, and to apprehend the meanes to save their soules in the world to come."[50]

To ensure survival against attacks by foreign powers, Indians, pirates, and rebellions, the early English settlers included or were sometimes led by professional soldiers, usually veterans of England's various wars back home. In Massachusetts, 20 percent of her early leaders had been military commanders before immigrating. Living conditions were harsh. In Virginia, between 1607 and 1624, some 13,000 of the 14,000 immigrants died of disease, starvation, exposure, or attacks by Indians. The shortage of women prompted the London Company's plan to ship and sell virgins for a price of 100 to 200 pounds of tobacco each.[51]

The growing need for immigrants, particularly artisans, made the company less choosy about who came, which created new problems. The first "ethnic strike" against disfranchisement took place in 1619 in Jamestown, in which a small number of German, Slovak, Armenian, and particularly Polish artisans had been encouraged to settle to help make glass and manufacture clapboard, resin, frankincense, and potash. As one Virginia company correspondent noted, "Upon some dispute of the Polonians . . . it was agreed (not withstanding any former order to the contrary) that they shall be enfranchised and made as free as any inhabitant there whatsoever." The strike succeeded because the company needed the non-English workers and did not want a reputation that would discourage artisans from settling. Other ethnic tensions are hinted at by the colonial secretary's criticism of four Italian craftsmen being so difficult that "a more damned crew hell never vomited."[52]

Religious purity, as defined by the Anglican church, was to become the prescribed way of life. Catholics were disfranchised and priests were expelled from Virginia. Quakers were banned and the ships transporting them heavily fined. In his passion for religious orthodoxy, Governor Berkeley thanked "God there are no free schools nor printing; and I hope we shall not have these hundred years: for learning has brought disobedience and heresy and sects into the world and printing has divulged them and libels against the best government. God keep us from both!"[53]

Religious orthodoxy was particularly strong in Massachusetts, where the more separatist Pilgrims settled. Though hailed for its democratic consensus, the Mayflower Compact actually reeked of restriction, chauvinism, and provincialism. Its signers stated that they undertook their voyage for "ye glorie of God, and advancement of ye Christian faith, and honour of our King & countrie" in order to "covenant and combine our selves togeather into a civill body politik, for our better ordering & preservation."[54]

The Puritan settlers sought to establish a way of life difficult to lead in Holland and denied them in England, where the very term *Puritan* had at first been used as a slur. Theirs was to be a church free of Catholic or Anglican ritual, in which the Sabbath would be strictly upheld. They were the newest saints in a world of multiplying sinners. The very concept of democracy was odious. "If the people be governor who shall be governed," asked John Cotton. Only Puritans were "freemen," fit to vote, and be called "Mister." A nonvoting resident was called "Goodman" and his wife, "Goodwife."[55]

Those not conforming to Puritan standards were either sent back to England "as persons unmeete to inhabit here," put on probation for a month, or allowed to remain for no longer than three weeks. In Providence and Portsmouth, Rhode Island, a town vote was required before anyone could settle, and in New Haven, strangers and newcomers not receiving townsmen approval were subject to whipping and expulsion.[56]

Catholics and Quakers were especially resented. Like the Dutch in New York, the Puritans viewed the Quakers as a "cursed sect of heretics," agents of Satan, and secret Catholics who were part of an international papal plot. With the exception of Rhode Island and then Maryland, they were not wanted, and if present, oppressed or expelled. In 1659 alone, over forty Quakers were whipped, sixty-four imprisoned, forty banished, one branded, three had ears cut off, and four killed. One victim's flesh was recorded as "beaten Black, and as into Gelly, and under his Arms the bruised Flesh and Blood hung down, clodded as it were in bags." In the Northwest, in the 1740s, the Aleuts were brutalized by Russian merchants and entrepreneurs, who had no hesitancy in shooting them and destroying their villages.[57]

"Immigrants Wanted"

Absent accurate figures, estimates suggest that in the entire American hemisphere in 1700, Indians represented 80 percent (9,650,000), Whites 11 percent

(1,330,000), and Blacks 6.5 percent (780,000). In Anglo-America (the territory generally between the Allegheny Mountains and the Atlantic), however, of a total population of 450,000, Whites represented 67 percent, Blacks 22 percent, and Indians a mere 7 percent.[58]

It was a time when relatively few Europeans immigrated to America, especially when their economic conditions were stable or prosperous. The few skilled workers who did leave home were criticized. "The ruinous numbers of our men daily flocking to the American plantations, whence so few return . . . will drain us of people as new Spain is, and will endanger our ruin as the Indies do Spain," warned an Englishman in 1674. Frederick the Great proscribed immigration from his realm and established a special agency in Hamburg to prevent any residents from sailing for America.[59]

Almost all colonies tried to attract immigrants through some combination of advertising, land grants, travel payments, and guarantees of rights and freedoms. Although northern colonies appealed to religious dissenters and purists, southern ones sought the more economic minded. Virginia was "abundantly stored with what is by all men aimed at, viz, Health and Wealth," bragged William Bullock in 1649. North Carolina touted itself as the "best established Government in the World," where land was cheap and opportunity great "to purchase a Plantation by which means many are become as wealthy and substantial Planters, as any in the Government."[60]

Among those immigrating were morally questionable characters, by today's or yesteryears' standards: wealth seekers, runaways, whores, religious zealots, playboys, convicts, thieves, in addition to merchants, traders, and shippers who bought and sold slaves or servants, whether White, Black, or aboriginal. Included among such people were clergymen, leading the Virginia legislature in 1632 to decree, "Ministers shall not give themselves to excess in drinking, or riot, spending their time idly by day or night playing at dice, cards, or any other unlawful game. . . ." As in earlier times, America continued to be a "last resort of scoundrels," where contrary to immigration promotions, sexual code violations were widespread and per capita consumption of alcohol greater than that of Europe.[61]

So extensive was man stealing or "spiriting" that in 1670 alone there were some 10,000 cases, and in the following year, one kidnapper testified that for twelve years he had shipped 500 persons annually to the colonies, while another kidnapper confessed that he had sent 840 persons in one year.[62]

Except for those forcefully brought over, the early immigrants shared a unique sense of risk taking. Usually, no established person would "voluntarily abandon a happy Certainty, to roam after imaginary Advantages, in a New World," wrote Robert Beverley, in 1705. "Besides which incertainty, he must have propos'd to himself, to encounter the infinite Difficulties and Dangers, to terrifie any Man, that cou'd live easy in England, from going to provoke his Fortune in a strange land." As one immigrant advised prospective immigrants in

1629, they should bring everything they need with them because there were no "taverns nor alehouses, nor butchers, nor grocers, nor apothecaries' shops to help" them.[63]

Indentured servants and redemptioners were treated harshly, working four to seven years before being freed, but only if they paid their debts in full and were well behaved. Before the 1730s, an estimated half of the yearly English immigrants and practically all of the non-English ones came under some form of servitude. As with Black slaves, they were bought and sold in America, the West Indies, and even in their homelands. Most desirable were English, Scottish, and Welsh servants, followed by Irish ones; least desirable were convicts, Jews, and Quakers. By the end of the eighteenth century, as many as 250,000 indentured workers were said to have arrived in America.[64]

Some immigrants voluntarily indentured themselves after arriving, though for scant gain. In Kentucky, wrote a late-eighteenth-century observer, "They are treated by their masters in a similar manner to the felons formerly transported from England to Virginia. Instead of being put in possession of portions of land, and quickly discharging their engagements, they sink deeper into debt, and this by the means of being obliged to purchase on credit at the most extravagant charges from their masters the stores and necessaries of which they stand in need. Thus situated they are never free from the landholder who is an absolute tyrant, while his miserable indented servants are likely to remain slaves forever." And yet, some indentured immigrants succeeded socioeconomically. As early as 1629, seven former indentured servants had become members of the Virginia legislature.[65]

At times, indentured Europeans were treated more harshly than Black slaves. "Negroes being a property for life," noted another eighteenth-century writer, "the death of slaves in the prime of youth or strength is a material loss to the proprietor; they are, therefore, almost in every instance, under more comfortable circumstances than the miserable European, over whom the rigid planter exercises an inflexible severity. They are strained to the utmost to perform their allotted labour; . . . they groan beneath a worse than Egyptian bondage."[66] Still, they began being replaced by Black slaves, who were considered more economical to maintain, easy to replace through breeding, and kept for a lifetime. The obvious difference between the two groups is that most Whites volunteered for servitude because that was the only way they could pay for their passage and eventual homesteading; for Blacks there was no promise or hope of surcease in their involuntary enslavement.

Whoever the immigrants, their tribulations often began with setting sail for the New World, which involved overcrowding, disease, cruel captains, disabling storms and calms, and food and water shortages, so that about one-third of the passengers died en route. With good fortune, seventeenth-century crossings took anywhere from five to twelve weeks, and sometimes longer. Immigrant ships leaving England had to guard against a variety of pirates and privateers—English, French, Dutch, Irish, Flemish, Spanish, and Algerian.[67]

In describing his fifteen-week voyage from Rotterdam to Philadelphia on a boat with mainly German and Swiss redemptioners, Gottlieb Mittelberger, in 1750, wrote that "the ship is full of pitiful signs of distress—smells, fumes, horrors, vomiting, various kinds of sea sickness, fever, dysentery, headaches, heat, constipation, boils, scurvy, cancer, mouth-rot, and similar afflictions, all of them caused by the age and the highly-salted state of the food, especially of the meat, as well as the very bad and filthy water, which brings about the miserable destruction and death of many. Add to all that shortage of food, hunger, thirst, frost, heat, dampness, fear, misery, vexation, and lamentation as well as other troubles."[68]

Throughout much of the seventeenth and eighteenth centuries, England also sent prisoners of war to the colonies, where they were sold into servitude. Some 150 Scotch Royalist prisoners of war, taken by Oliver Cromwell, were shipped to Boston in 1650, where they became ironworkers or were sold as bonded servants. Other prisoners of Cromwell—Irish, Scots, and Quakers—were shipped to the West Indies. When part of the United Kingdom, Scotland also sent some 200 jailed Presbyterian dissenters, rebels, and criminals. Francis I authorized Jacques Cartier and Sieur de Robeval to bring "criminals and malefactors detained in our prisons" to New France, where they would hopefully acknowledge God and "mend their lives."[69]

Bad as regular sailing conditions were, they were worse for convicts, who were confined below deck, amid filth and disease. A visitor to one ship described a prisoner "chained to a board in a hole not about sixteen feet long . . . a collar and padlock about his neck, and chained to five of the most dreadful creatures I ever looked on."[70]

Georgia was founded as a "convict colony" for inmates of England's debtor prisons. The governor of Pennsylvania, in 1728, feared the rise of a "Colony of Aliens [through] an importation of Irish Papists and Convicts." In Virginia, in 1751, the *Gazette* lamented "the most audacious robberies, the most cruel murders, and infinite other villanies, perpetuated by convicts transported from Europe." In all, England sent an estimated 50,000 convicts to at least nine of her continental colonies, prompting Benjamin Franklin to recommend that rattlesnakes be sent to England in exchange for such "human serpents."[71]

In vain, attempts were made to stop convict importation. When Virginia and then Maryland passed laws barring trade with anyone bringing "jailbirds" by land or sea, the Parliament overruled them.[72] To England, it was far better and cheaper to dump them in America than to keep them imprisoned at home.

European Introduction of Black Slavery

Slavery was no mere happenstance or slip of the moral conscience, but a premeditated, enormously profitable, politically desirable, and religiously sanctioned action, particularly when Christians were not the victims. "Blessed is the slave whom his master, returning, finds performing his charge," said Jesus. To Saint Augustine, slavery was imposed "by the just sentence of God upon the sinner," and Thomas Aquinas believed it the result of Adam's sin. A number of fifteenth-century popes and high churchmen readily used slaves as entertainers, servants, or oddities. Church of England leaders and parishioners behaved likewise, with one bishop owning 655 slaves.[73]

It was Portugal that initiated the mass European transportation of African slaves in 1441, when some of its adventuring exploiters presented a dozen to Prince Henry the Navigator, who then received the pope's permission to launch further raids, with "complete forgiveness" of all sins.[74] So profitable did they prove that within a few years the prince ordered the building of a trading post and fortress on Arguin Island off Africa's Cape Blanco.

Slavery soon attracted the envy and competition of other countries. While Europeans focused on the west coast of Africa—shipping slaves to Europe and then to the New World—Arabs concentrated on the east coast—shipping slaves to Arabia, Persia, and India. By the late 1700s, England established ten slave-trading posts in Africa; the Dutch, fifteen; and the Danes, four. In time, American slavers from Rhode Island and Massachusetts entered the trade, though to a lesser extent than the above countries. Just as the slave takers came from different countries, so did slaves. Some 25 percent came from Angola, while another 25 percent came from the Bight of Biafra. The Gold Coast, Senegambia, and the Windward Coast, each provided between 10 to 15 percent. The Bight of Benin, Sierra Leone, and Mozambique-Madagascar each provided 5 percent or less.[75]

As with American Indians, conflicts and wars between Africans facilitated their conquest and enslavement. Arab and European entrepreneurs eagerly exacerbated intra-African hostilities by supplying arms and equipment to favored tribes. Moreover, on both African coasts, Blacks themselves captured, kidnapped, enslaved, and sold others, with their European purchasers only regretting that when "the natives were everywhere at peace," they could not purchase many slaves.[76]

From the very beginning, no qualms were had about taking and selling African slaves. As one early Portuguese defender of the practice wrote, Africans were "heathen," and "more than those of any other nation, act on the principle of 'long live the winner,' and as Negroes they fear nothing save only corporal punishment and the whip. . . . It is only in this way that the former governors and conquerors kept them in subjection, and only in this way can we keep what we have won by force of arms."[77]

Before and during their transoceanic voyage, many tried to escape. Between 1690 and 1845, one historian found specific records of some fifty-five slave revolts aboard ship and reference to another hundred.[78] Moreover, an estimated one-third of those enslaved died in Africa on the march to ports of departure and another third died crossing the ocean. The very ill were thrown overboard. A glimpse of the horror of their ocean passage is provided by an observer of the time:

The sense of misery and suffocation was so terrible that in the 'tweendecks—where the height was sometimes only eighteen inches, so that the unfortunate slaves could not turn around, were wedged immovably in fact, and chained to the deck by the neck and legs—that the slaves not infrequently would go mad before dying or suffocating. In their frenzy some killed others in the hope of procuring more room to breathe. Men strangled those next to them and women drove nails into each other's brains.[79]

With the growth of the African slave trade in America, a fourth dimension of intergroup conflict developed—Black-White relations, which, though it involved less than 5 percent of the Blacks brought to the Western Hemisphere, provoked the longest animosity and bloodshed. John Smith of Pocahontas fame recorded their introduction to English America in 1619, when a Dutch man-of-war ship sold the Virginia colony twenty "Negars."[80]

Though historians disagree on whether specific racial discrimination existed before slavery was legalized in the early 1660s or whether it was slavery that brought about discrimination, it is rather clear that Blacks—free or slave—were viewed with disdain. Similarly, whether self-interest determined their morality, or vice versa, it is also clear that White Christians defended slavery by selective biblical rationalizations.

The abolitionist-minded stressed Exod. 21.16: "And he that stealeth a man, and selleth him, or if he be found in his hand, he shall surely be put to death." The slavery defenders pointed to Lev. 25.44: "Both thy bondmen, and thy bond-maids, which thou shalt have, shall be of the heathen that are round about you; of them shall ye buy bondmen and bondmaids. Moreover, of the children of the strangers that do sojourn among you, of them shall ye buy, and of their families that are with you, which they begat in our land: and they shall be your possession. And ye shall take them as an inheritance for your children after you, to inherit them for a possession; they shall be your bondmen for ever."

In America, slavery was defended economically, socially, and religiously. The Dutch West India Company considered it most important to increase the slave population in New Netherland because "the agricultural laborers who are conveyed thither at great expense to the Colonists, sooner or later apply themselves to trade, and neglect agriculture altogether." Governor Winthrop, in 1645, urged war against Indians so that captives could be exchanged for Blacks, who worked hard and cost less to maintain than English servants. Inevitably, White artisans soon resented the training and hiring out of Black slave laborers, who deprived them of jobs and, according to New York's governor, George Clarke, in 1737, forced White artisans "to leave us and seek their living in other countries."[81]

Socially, too, Black slaves were believed a natural, if not God-ordained, part of the world, wherein some people were born "to be Low and Despicable; some to be Monarchs, Kings, Princes and Governors, Masters and Commanders, others to be Subjects, and to be Commanded . . . yea, some to be born Slaves, and so remain during their lives." Even those masters permitting slaves to be baptized believed it "doth not alter the condition of the person as to his bondage or freedom," a belief Virginia incorporated into its laws in 1667.[82]

Baptized or not, slaves were expected to behave in a scriptural manner. After all, Saint Paul did admonish Ephesian servants to "be obedient to them that are your masters according to the flesh, with fear and trembling, in the singleness of your heart, as unto Christ." Somewhat less stern, one Maryland minister advised a group of slaves to serve their "owners with cheerfulness, respect, and humility, not grumbling, or giving any saucy answers, but doing your work with readiness, mildness, and good nature; because your sauciness and grumbling is not so much against your owners, as it is against God himself, who hath placed you in that service, and expects you will do the business of it as he hath commanded you."[83]

The greater the number of Black slaves, the more they were feared and oppressed, particularly those suspected of being rebellious. In the early 1700s, such slaves were beheaded and their heads placed on poles as a warning to other slaves. In South Carolina, in 1739, rebellious slaves were disemboweled and then hanged. In vain, the English Crown repeatedly urged its governors to enact laws preventing slave owners from practicing "inhuman severitys," which included whippings, torture, maiming, and murder. Even slave children were subject to being sold or given away when their upkeep proved too expensive. As one not uncommon advertisement read, "A Negro child soon expected of a good breed, may be owned by any person inclining to take it away."[84]

White brutality invariably contributed to fears of Black retribution. One New Englander compared White violence against suspected Black plotters to that of the Salem witch hunters, wherein "Negro & Spectre evidence will turn out alike" to be of no substance, and he urged New York colonists "not to go on to Massacre and destroy your own Estates by making Bonfires of Negroes." In Georgia, in 1735, slaves were banned lest the Spanish in Florida incite them to rebel and kill the English settlers. In the French West Indies, a series of decrees barred those of slave ancestry from entering professions, holding public office, or marrying interracially.[85]

Such attitudes and behaviors, however, did not prevent miscegenation, which started almost as soon as the first Blacks and Whites, Whites and Indians, and Indians and Blacks began to live alongside each other.[86]

In Virginia, legislation was passed in 1662 fining "any Christian" committing "fornication with a Negro man or woman." In one form or another, other colonies followed suit. In 1664, Maryland banned marriages between White women and Black slaves, as did Massachusetts in 1705, South Carolina in 1717, North Carolina in 1718, Delaware in 1721, and Pennsylvania in 1725. Over and over, lawmakers referred to interracial sexual relations and their offspring as an "abominable mixture," "spurious issue," "disgrace of the nation," and "dishonor of God," imposing fines, whippings, banishment, or servitude on the White partner.[87] What was the "Promised Land" of milk and honey to the English settlers was the "Egypt" of bondage and degradation to Blacks.

Spiritual and Physical Ruination of the Indians

When Europeans needed Indians to provide them with food, to trade with them, to find gold and silver, or to help defend themselves against other European powers or hostile Indians, they admired their friendliness and resourcefulness. As Europeans became more self-reliant and more interested in expanding their land base, however, their attitudes toward Indians changed. Indians began being viewed as barbarian, idolatrous, and superstitious.

In the name of *vacuum domicilium* and God's transcending ownership, which the British (like the Spanish) claimed to represent, all unoccupied lands were subject to confiscation. What Indians did not do to improve the land, the English settlers would. "Where there is a vacant place," wrote John Cotton, "there is liberty for the son of Adam or Noah to come and inhabit, though they neither buy it, nor ask their leaves." In Milford, Connecticut, in 1640, a town meeting resolved that the earth belonged to "the Lord," who gave it to "the Saints," and that they were "the Saints."[88] Even when colonists obtained land by purchase or treaty, they knew—or quickly learned—that Indians did not realize what they had agreed to, namely, not ever returning to their traditional fishing and hunting grounds (a right still sought today by some tribes).

Such behaviors did not preclude European efforts to mold Indians in their image. Spain, with large holdings and few immigrants, sought to integrate them into a new form of western Catholic culture. Many Indians resisted. Some defiant Indians in 1597 complained of Spanish clergy condemning their "dances, banquets, feasts, celebrations, fires, and wars ... they always reprimand us, oppress us, preach to us, call us bad Christians, and deprive us of all happiness." New France, which had relatively few settlers, sought to transform the Indians into Frenchmen and Catholics, but within their tribal situations. To the Swedes of New Sweden, the Indians were filthy and wild, not "because we believe them to be mad and insane, but on account of their idolatry and error in religion." New England, which had the largest number of settlers, treated the Indians as independent nations or wards, who hopefully would accept "the onlie true God and Savior of Mankind, and the Christian faith." Pacific Northwest Russians were largely indifferent to the spiritual well-being of the natives, though a few Aleuts were taken to Siberia, baptized, given Russian names, and taught Russian so they could serve as translators.[89]

Throughout this process few socialized with the Indians or bothered to learn any of their languages or spiritual beliefs; though, unlike the British, the French were more given to living with or marrying Indian women. "The Americans, or men of English and German blood," wrote one early French traveler, "have a natural antipathy to the savage, which is increased by their cruelty toward their prisoners. The Americans have a repugnance to the savage women, the Canadians [French] the contrary."[90]

A few English colonists advocated intermarriage, but for self-serving reasons. "The natives could by no means persuade themselves that the English were heartily their friends, so long as they disdained to intermarry with them," said William Byrd of Virginia. Another colonist wrote that if "we had taken Indian wives in the first place, it would have been some compensation for their lands. . . . We should become the rightful heirs to their lands."[91]

Not surprisingly, the French exploited their closer relationship. Sir William Johnson complained in 1749 that they were telling Indians that the British looked upon them as "slaves or Negroes." Chief Pontiac, a strong supporter of the French, told his warriors that the English were "dogs dressed in red, who have come to rob you of your hunting grounds, and drive away the game. . . . The children of your great father, the King of France, are not like the English. . . . They are very dear to me for they love the red men, and understand the true mode of worshipping me."[92]

Though not in love, all was fair in war for Europeans and Indians, except that the former warred to protect and expand their new small holdings while the latter did it to defend and retain their large ancestral homelands. Also, as the colonists increasingly learned that they must cooperate to protect themselves against hostile Indians or other European powers, the Indians generally failed to do so, though a few tribes formed a loose confederation to maintain peace among themselves, such as the Iroquois League of Seneca, Cayuga, Mohawk, Oneida, Onondaga, and Tuscarora.

Indian disunity and behavior in war, whether among themselves or against colonists, were seen as further evidence of their being savages, for only non-Christians would kill women and children, burn down homes and villages, and launch surprise attacks and ambushes. "We may as well goe to War with Wolfs and Bears," lamented a South Carolina official.[93] That colonists did the same or worse (e.g., giving smallpox-infected blankets to hostile Indians) posed no moral dilemma, for they were convinced that God had given them the right and might to so act.

The seventeenth and eighteenth centuries were replete with intra- and interracial brutality. As a result of a quarrel in the 1630s, Connecticut and Massachusetts colonists, with the help of Mohican and Narragansett allies, launched a dawn attack on a large Pequot Indian village in Connecticut, setting it afire and burning alive or shooting more than 500 natives, losing only two soldiers. As a colonist at the time described the scene: "Down fell men, women, and children; those that [e]scaped us, fell into the hands of the Indians that were in the rear of us. . . . It may be demanded, Why should you be so furious? . . . Should not Christians have more mercy and compassion? . . . We have sufficient light from the Word of God for our proceedings." Nearly forty years later, during the bloody and brutal King Philip's War, the colonists rounded up and interned some

500 innocent "Christian Indians" on a small, desolate island in Boston Harbor. As was feared of Japanese Americans during World War II, the colonists believed the latter might join their Wampanoag, Narragansett, Nipmuck, and Pocumtuck enemies. The Dutch in New Netherland also did not hesitate to massacre Indians, as when Governor William Kieft in the early 1640s launched an all-out war against the Algonquins, from whom he had sought tribute and taxes. In one major surprise attack, the governor's troops wantonly burned down an entire village and ruthlessly killed some 700 Indians, without suffering a single fatality.[94]

Both sides engaged in scalping for prowess, revenge, and profit. Though Indians had done so long before the Europeans arrived, the Europeans expanded the practice by offering bounties for scalps of European or Indian enemies with prices varying according to the time, place, and victim. To stop a developing racket in scalps, the Massachusetts disburser of bounties was directed "to bury the several Indian scalps now in his custody in some private place so as not to be discovered or produced again."[95] In South Carolina, English colonists paid Indians for scalps of runaway Black slaves, but both ears had to be attached lest Indians presented two scalps from one head.

Peaceful attempts were also made to win Indian souls and favor by gift giving, ranging from rather harmless blankets, hats, waistcoats, needles, pots, and threads to harmful guns, gun powder, bullet molds, scalping knives, and rum. In some cases, Indians adopted Christianity after experiencing or witnessing a cure by a missionary. Still others simply did so in the hope that the White men would not devastate their homes, relocate them, kill them, or—at least— would reward them with supplies, medicines, or the land of their enemies.

More extensive were the diseases that Europeans brought with them—smallpox, measles, and typhus, the "shock troops of conquest," whose rear troops were famine and scurvy. From Africa, ships and personnel had transported malaria and yellow fever. Indians succumbed to the diseases "so easily that the bare look and smell of a Spaniard cause[d] them to give up the ghost," wrote a seventeenth-century Germany missionary. A Yucatan Indian recalled pre-Spanish times when there was "no sicknesses . . . no aching bones . . . no high fever . . . no smallpox . . . no burning chest . . . no abdominal pain . . . no consumption . . . no headache." In New France, a Jesuit reported that Micmac Indians were "astonished and often complained that, since the French mingle and carry on trade with them, they are dying fast and the population is thinning out." Similarly, after the Russians settled in the Pacific Northwest, thousands of Aleuts, Eskimos, and Tlingits died of disease.[96]

When not by European gun, Bible, guile, or disease, Indians helped destroy themselves by allying with one or another European power, either to defend themselves against another tribe or to exact revenge or plunder. Killing, torturing, or enslaving other Indians was not unusual. For example, in the western plains, Apaches often raided Wichita villages, trading captured women and children for horses and weapons from the Spanish in New Mexico and Mexico. In South Carolina, English settlers and their Indian allies often raided hostile tribes, shipping their captives off as slaves for sale in Virginia, Boston, Rhode Island, Pennsylvania, New York, and the Caribbean.[97]

Without Indian allies, the Puritans could not have defeated King Philip, nor could Hernando Cortes have vanquished the Aztecs. Cortes was pleased to discover "discord and animosity" between native groups in Mexico because, he said, it would ease "subduing them more quickly, for, as the Scripture has it, 'divided they fall.'" Many colonists thought that war was the usual intertribal relationship, not realizing how they exacerbated those relations by their own presence and by supplying Indians with more deadly weapons.[98]

There are writers who claim that the past must be understood in terms of the cultural values of the time and their relativity. Thus, if missionaries were bigoted toward Indian beliefs and mores, destructive of Indian communal life, and exploitive of Indian labor, they were "much more humane and considerably less destructive" than the Anglo-Saxon pioneers who came after them. Moreover, if Whites and Indians were brutal, they were simply acting in accordance with their respective values and traditions. Remember, we are told, it was an age of brutality, with people doing what came culturally to them. Just as Indians practiced torture, decapitation, and cannibalism, Europeans used racks and wheels, thumb screws, rat-infested prisons, witchcraft, public beheadings, autos-da-fé, and launched wars in which soldiers and crusaders looted, raped, and massacred their enemies. Even in tolerant Amsterdam, in 1535, the hearts of a number of Anabaptists were publicly cut out.[99]

Such rationalizations often ignore the existence of a past morality that decried certain wrongs, regardless of who was involved. Neither European colonists, African slaves, nor native Indians believed it was right to be murdered, tortured, or dispossessed by strangers, particularly by those whom they had not invited to settle among them or whom they had at first helped. Montaigne, in the sixteenth century, argued that the Indians might well be called barbarians by the rules of reason, but not in comparison to the French, who surpassed them in every kind of barbarity.[100]

In America, men like Bartolemé de Las Casas, Roger Williams, and John Eliot spoke out against injustices to Indians. Williams wrote a treatise denying that King James had any right to give Indian lands away. Realizing what was being done to the Indians, an Englishman indignantly asked, "By what right or warrant can we enter into the land of these Savages, take away their rightful inheritance from them, and plant ourselves in their places, being unwronged or unprovoked by them?"[101]

Unfortunately, such views were in the minority. The dominant behavior of Europeans was at best benign condescension and at worst wanton ruthlessness toward Indians, who never realized what was to befall them all—complete surrender to the will and power of European-born and then American-born Whites.

Expanding White-White Conflict

As more and more European invader-settlers arrived, relations worsened not only between them and the Indians but also among themselves. White-White conflicts over imperial rivalries, land claims, and Indian trade were aggravated by transplanted ethnic and religious conflicts. For example, within a few years after founding New Spain, inquisitions of Indians, Englishmen, and Jews were introduced. In Mexico, in 1522, Indians were tried for concubinage, idolatry, and sacrificing humans. Indian berdaches were condemned and frequently burned as "sodomites"; in Panama, Balboa ordered the bodies of forty of them fed to his dogs. In Mexico, Peru, and Colombia, dozens of Jewish converts to Catholicism were jailed, garroted, or burned at the stake for allegedly or actually practicing Judaism. By 1635, Chinese barbers in Mexico City were so resented by Spanish barbers that they were banished from the city. In Spanish New Orleans, which France had ceded in 1762, the governor reportedly ordered "the English to a man and all protestants and Jews" driven out.[102]

To escape religious oppression from French Catholics, Protestant Huguenots fled to America and established colonies in Florida, South Carolina, North Carolina, New York, and Virginia. Yet in Florida, Spain's Pedro Menendez (the founder of Saint Augustine) brutally tortured and killed most of them in 1564, declaring that "I do this not as to Frenchmen but as to Lutherans." A few years later, Dominique de Gourges reciprocated by having his French soldiers slaughter an entire Spanish garrison in Florida, claiming that "I do this not as to Spaniards and pigs, but as to traitors, thieves and murderers." No less gruesome were English soldiers who, with Indian allies, attacked Spanish missions in Florida in 1702 and 1704, leaving a scene of "indescribable horror: scalped and mutilated bodies of men, women, and children lay about the ground, or hung from stakes."[103]

Huguenots in France, meanwhile, continued to be persecuted when not massacred, consigned to being galley slaves, or sold as servants to Catholic planters in the French West Indies. Said one French government official in the 1680s, "If it happen again to be possible to fall upon such [Huguenot] gatherings, let orders be given to the dragoons to kill the greatest part of the Protestants that can be overtaken, without sparing the women, to the end that this may intimidate them and prevent others from falling into a similar fault."[104]

Interethnic imperial rivalries led to the Dutch conquest in 1655 of New Sweden, which had some 500 men, women, and children. Formed seventeen years earlier in Delaware, the Swedish colony was continually underfinanced, undermanned, and overburdened with interethnic and interreligious differences. Small as it was, New Sweden had a variety of settlers, including Swedes, Dutch, and Finns, as well as expelled prisoners from the motherland.[105] Because of Swedish reluctance to emigrate, half of the colony's population were Finns, who had originally moved to Sweden, where as punishment for violating Swedish laws they had been compelled to settle in New Sweden.

As with other imperial powers, the Swedes sought the material and spiritual rewards of Indian trade and conversion. Their hopes ended in 1655, when they were forced to surrender to the Dutch of New Netherland, who in 1664 likewise surrendered to the English, giving rise to New York. From then on, Swedish customs began eroding. In 1749, a Swedish scholar traveling among the descendants of the first settlers in New Sweden wrote that there had been "two Swedish smiths here, who made hatchets, knives, and scythes, exactly like the Swedish ones," but that the "hatchets now in use are often the English style. . . . Almost all the Swedes had bath-houses and they commonly bathed every Saturday, but now these bath-houses are done away with. They celebrated Christmas with several sorts of games, and with various special dishes, as is usual in Sweden; all of which is now, for the greatest part, given up."[106]

It is to the Dutch that credit and criticism go for probably producing the first proclamation of religious freedom in North America as well as the first anti-Semitic high official. In the former case, as the Dutch were planning to capture Pernambuco in northern Brazil from the Portuguese in the late 1620s, they issued regulations on how the area would be governed, including the following clause:

> The liberty of Spaniards, Portuguese and native, whether they be Roman Catholics or Jews, will be respected. No one will be permitted to molest them or subject them to inquiries in matters of conscience or in their private homes; and no one should dare to disquiet or disturb them or cause them any hardship—under the penalty of arbitrary punishments or, depending upon circumstances, of severe or exemplary reproof.[107]

After conquering Pernambuco, they generally enforced the clause, except when it came to Jesuits, whom they immediately expelled. Their victory, however, was an uneasy one. As with French-British and British-American struggles in North America, both the Dutch and Portuguese engaged in slavery and had different native groups as allies, who did not hesitate in fighting each other. It was a matter of the enemy of their enemy being their friend, even though they did not really care for them. Thus, though the Dutch had Indians as allies, they felt demeaned that the bulk of their Portuguese victors consisted of lesser breeds: mulattoes, Blacks, Indians, and half-breeds of various kinds.[108] At the same time, whether under Dutch or Portuguese control, Black slaves in Brazil were oppressed, some of whom took advantage of their warring European captors and fled to northeastern Brazil, where they established the Republic of Palmares, which lasted almost seventy years before being destroyed.

As a result of Dutch-Portuguese warfare, twenty-three Jewish political refugees, mostly children and women, fled Brazil for New Amsterdam, where Peter Stuyvesant sternly governed the area for the West India Company, which had some of the "most selfish, greedy and profit-seeking businessmen in Holland."[109]

Not only did he resent Jews, Lutherans, and Quakers, but all who did not subscribe to his Calvinist views. As soon as the Jewish group arrived, he wanted them expelled. Bureaucrat that he was, however, he first sought permission from his home office that "the deceitful race—such hateful enemies and blasphemers of the name of Christ—be not allowed further to infect and trouble this new colony, to the detraction of your worships and the dissatisfaction of your worships' most affectionate subjects."[110]

Stuyvesant's "worships," however, responded that Jews had helped them earlier in Brazil against the Portuguese, that Jewish shareholders in the company would not favor such an action, and that the West India Company needed immigrants to develop the land since relatively few Dutch were willing to leave their homeland. Ergo, Jews were allowed to remain, "provided that the poor among them shall not become a burden to the company or to the community, but be supported by their own nation."[111]

Stuyvesant was more successful in persecuting Quakers, whom he considered an "abominable Heresy," filled with "seducers of the people, who are destructive unto magistracy and ministry." After imprisoning, torturing, and expelling one of their ministers, he proclaimed in 1657 that any ship bringing Quakers into the province would be confiscated and anyone harboring them overnight would be fined. Lutherans, too, were denied the right of public worship, fearful that if they were allowed to worship publicly, "the Papists, Mennonites and others would soon make similar claims." When a few resident Lutherans, who had been attending services at the Dutch Reformed Church, petitioned Stuyvesant to have their own minister, he indicated "he would prefer to lose office than to permit this." When they defiantly held their own service, he imprisoned some of them.[112]

Stuyvesant's zealousness was somewhat tempered when the West India Company reminded him in 1663 that "although we heartily desire that these [Quakers] and other sectarians remained away from there, yet as they do not, we doubt very much whether we can proceed against them rigorously without diminishing the population and stopping immigration, which must be favored at a so tender stage of the country's existence. You may therefore shut your eyes, at least not force people's consciences, but allow every one to have his own belief, as long as he behaves quietly and legally, gives no offense to his neighbors and does not oppose the government."[113]

By 1664, the Dutch administration of the city had grown so harsh that even the Netherlanders welcomed the English takeover. Even then, Calvinist-Lutheran tensions continued. As one Anglican clergyman noted in 1680, the Lutheran and Reformed ministers "behaved themselves one towards the other as shyly and uncharitably as if Luther and Calvin had bequeathed and entailed their virulent and bigoted spirits upon them and their heirs forever."[114]

In the English colonies, Old World Catholic-Protestant, anti-Jewish, and intra-Protestant bigotry continued. Each colony had its own immigration policy, preferring immigrants of the same religious beliefs and excluding strangers, criminals, paupers, and the poor. As in England, the Welsh were considered devious and unstable, the Scots mean and money-oriented, Quakers heretics, Irish violent and animal-like, and Catholics of any kind unwanted.

Blasphemy laws were common, with heavy penalties for those denying the sanctity of the Bible or divinity of Jesus. In Connecticut, "direct, express, presumptuous, and high-handed blasphemy" meant the death penalty. In Delaware, it resulted in "thirty-nine lashes well laid on." In Catholic-founded Maryland, "reproachful words or speeches concerning the blessed Virgin Mary, the Mother of our Savior" led to a heavy fine, public whipping, and imprisonment or expulsion. Many a God-loving colonist readily imposed castration, flogging, earclipping, or branding for adultery, seduction, rape, bastardy, homosexuality, bigamy, and miscegenation. Books and pamphlets, too, were punished by public hangmen; in one Connecticut case, a disapproved book was given thirty-nine lashes before being burned.[115]

As in Europe, but to a lesser extent, witch hunts led to at least eighty-three trials between 1647 and 1691, mostly in New England, in which twenty-two people were executed and others whipped, fined, or banished. In 1688, the first, if not only, Catholic—Ann Glover—was hanged as a witch in Boston. The most infamous trial took place in Salem, in 1692, resulting in 13 women and 6 men being hanged, and another man pressed to death. An additional three women and an infant of one of the executed women died in jail, fifty were freed after pleading guilty, and 150 awaiting trial were released from jail. Racism and Francophobia surfaced in the trial when one defendant was charged with selling power and shot to the Indians and French, sleeping with Indian women, and fathering Indian babies.[116]

Though immigrants were needed for buying and settling lands taken from Indians, developing natural resources, providing increased revenues, and populating frontier areas as buffers against French, Spanish, and Indian attacks, certain immigrants were abused, not wanted, or strongly disliked.

One of the largest immigrant insurrections occurred in British East Florida, when some 300 Greeks and Italians futilely revolted against the cruel treatment of their British overlords. In Boston, the Protestant Irish Charitable Society, founded in 1737, barred Catholics from joining.[117] Though comprising less than 1 percent of the population, Catholics loomed large in the Protestant mind. Newspapers, pamphlets, and sermons depicted the pope as a Devil and the church as a monstrous beast, dedicated to barbarism, ignorance, press control, and religious bigotry.

Many colonies levied discriminatory head taxes on ship captains bringing Catholics. Once here, Catholics were subjected to everything from outright discrimination to expulsion. Various colonies passed laws barring Catholics from settling or holding public office. In New Hampshire, in 1696, all inhabitants were required to take an oath against the pope and Catholic doctrine. In New York, Catholic schools could not be started, and fines were levied on Catholic fathers employing anyone other than a Protestant to teach their children.[118] By 1700, Catholics enjoyed civil and religious rights only in Rhode Island, but then, in 1719, they were excluded from public office.

Almost equally disliked were the fiercely independent Protestant Scotch-Irish, who numbered some 250,000 in the early eighteenth century. As in England and Ireland, their strict Calvinist beliefs and ethnic customs were resented by their Anglican and Irish-Catholic neighbors. Benjamin Franklin believed them a barbaric people. To Quakers, they were quarrelsome, rebellious, bigoted, and makers and drinkers of bad whiskey, who wanted to establish a religious tyranny; in turn, the Scotch-Irish thought Quakers un-Christian, effeminate, self-indulgent, hypocrites, and inciters and abetters of Indian raids against them.[119]

New Englanders opposed their establishing Presbyterian churches, while compelling them to contribute to the upkeep of Puritan ones. In Boston, they could not serve in the militia, and in Worcester, a mob destroyed one of their newly built churches. In Delaware, in 1723, an Anglican priest described them as "the bitterest railers" against the Church of England that "ever trod upon American ground." In Stirling, Connecticut, officials declared them "not wholesome inhabitants." So intense were Scotch-Irish and German animosities in Pennsylvania that land agents in 1743 were instructed not to sell the former any more land in the predominantly German counties of Lancaster and York. Similarly, the frontier areas of Pennsylvania, New Jersey, Maryland, the Carolinas, and Virginia were called a "Mac-ocracy," ruled by "banditti of low Scotch-Irish whose names usually began with Mac."[120]

Though also less than 1 percent of the population, Jews were viewed with ambivalence. On the one hand, the colonists admired Jewish history and patriarchs and gave children and towns Old Testament names. Some even studied Hebrew. As neighbors, however, Jews were taboo—unless they converted, which many Puritans believed a necessary prelude for Christ's second coming. Cotton Mather prayed "for the conversion of the Jewish nation, and for my own having the happiness, at some time or other, to baptize a Jew." New York's royal governor denied them the right of public worship, which was reserved for Christians only.[121] In 1737, the winner of a close election to the state legislature was disqualified because Jews—contrary to English law—had allegedly voted for him.

Throughout the colonial period, Jews, like other nonestablishment groups, had to obey prevailing religious laws and pay taxes for the upkeep of churches. Even so, they were not physically attacked or intimidated as were some Christian dissenters or their Jewish kinsmen in Europe.[122] By the time of the American Revolution, small numbers resided in each of the colonies, with congregations in Charlestown, Newport, Philadelphia, and New York City.

Baptists were scorned by Puritans and Anglicans for opposing church-state union and infant baptism. As early as 1647, Massachusetts passed a law banishing Baptists as "incendiaries of commonwealths and infectors of persons in main matters of religion." To John Bulkley, in 1729, they brought "an Odium on the

Ministry in the Land" and spread "Senseless Opinions," which led good Christians to criticize their ministers and "forsake our Assemblies, neglect Family Prayer, Prophane the Sabbath, etc." In Massachusetts and Virginia in particular, their ministers were denied licenses to preach, and in many cases subjected to fines, lashing, imprisonment, and expulsion. In vain, a Baptist emissary went to England to plead for surcease of oppression. So intense were anti-Baptist actions that 1768 to 1774 has been called the "period of Great Persecution." Sympathetic to their plight, James Madison wrote that the "diabolical, hell-conceived principle of persecution rages. . . . There are at this time in the adjacent county not less than five or six well-meaning men in close jail for publishing their religious sentiments, which in the main are very orthodox." It was in a letter to persecuted Baptists that Jefferson, in 1802 coined the phrase "wall of separation between church and state."[123]

Various groups of Germans arrived in the later seventeenth century—sectarians from the Rhineland and then Lutherans from the Palatinate, whom the English colonists (particularly Anglicans and Scotch-Irish) soon avoided as neighbors. By 1790, Germans comprised almost 9 percent of the colonial population, residing mainly in Pennsylvania, where Governor Patrick Gordon said they were "ignorant of our Language & Laws," and by settling close together, made themselves a "distinct people from his Majesties Subjects." Benjamin Franklin called them "Palatine Boors" and "generally the most stupid of their own nation," who endangered the colony by their inferior non-English customs. Such views contributed to his slim defeat in the 1764 election for the General Assembly.[124] In vain, in 1762, the publisher of the *Philadelphische Staatsbote* tried to improve intergroup understanding by printing English lessons in his publication.[125]

To the eighteenth-century Acadians in Canada goes the sorry distinction of being the first European-rooted group to be interned and deported. Unlike French Huguenots, they were Catholics, deemed "perfidious," with an "inveterate enmity" to the British, under whose rule they had been living for some four decades. The British resented their refusal to swear allegiance to the Crown, and much in the manner that Americans later exhibited toward Indians, issued military orders in 1755 imprisoning and then deporting more than 6,000 men, women, and children. To do so expeditiously and economically, the British military first lured males into their posts, thereby leaving Acadian women and children helpless to resist. The British confiscated their property as compensation for the costs of expelling them to colonies from Massachusetts to Georgia. Large numbers trekked to Louisiana, where they were to be called "Cajuns," and where Spanish and French residents welcomed them as hard workers and ready fighters against any British incursion.[126]

In their journey south, they confronted suspicion and hostility. In Massachusetts, Acadians were confined to restricted areas. Most of those shipped to New York were later sent to the French West Indies, while half of those sent to Pennsylvania died of smallpox. In some colonies, all those under twenty-one were separated from their parents or guardians and indentured. In Charleston, they were accused of encouraging a slave rebellion, and the very poor among them were compelled to become indentured servants. Catholic Maryland welcomed them somewhat; Virginia prohibited their disembarking; and Georgia literally sold them into slavery. Cajuns refer to their tribulations as "Le Grand Dérangement"—a time of woe, anguish, death, and bigotry, which Longfellow partially recounted in *Evangeline,* and which historian George Bancroft considered "the greatest forcible dispersion of people of European extraction in the history of the New World."[127]

As in England and Dutch New Amsterdam, Quakers were often persecuted in the British colonies, particularly in Massachusetts, where they were subject to hanging, imprisonment, flogging, fines, expulsion, and even deportation to England or the British West Indies. Though admired by some for their peaceful and industrious ways, they were more resented for their fervent opposition to religious ceremony and authority, friendliness toward Indians, refusal to serve in militias or pay taxes for their upkeep, and their opposition to slavery, though some were slave traders and owners. By the late seventeenth century, Quaker settlements had developed in New Hampshire, New York, Maryland, Virginia, the Carolinas, New Jersey, and Rhode Island, which was the most tolerant, though Roger Williams considered their beliefs heretical.[128]

The Seeds of Tolerance and Democratic Pluralism

The above intergroup prejudices and hostilities should not becloud the existence of many people who came and created laws and regulations for civility and community peace. This was particularly true of those English Protestant colonists who had brought with them political ideals and values born of the struggle in England for limited monarchy and parliamentary government, including protections relating to judicial due process, freedom from unfair taxation and arbitrary imprisonment, religious toleration, and freedom of assembly, petition, and speech.

Though Virginia was reported to be "an unhealthy place, a nest of Rogues, whores, dissolute and rooking persons," according to John Hammond in 1656, it was not

> without divers honest and virtuous inhabitants, who observing the general neglect and licensiousnesses there, caused Assemblies to be call'd and Laws to be made tending to the glory of God, the severe suppression of vices, and the compelling them not to neglect (upon strickt punishments) planting and tending such quantities of Corn, as would not onely serve themselves, their Cattle and Hogs plentifully, but to be enabled to supply *New-England* (then in want) with such proportions, as were extream reliefs, to them in their necessities.[129]

In both Dutch and English New York, as well as in English Rhode Island, Pennsylvania, and Maryland, the seeds of tolerance, pluralism, and harmonious intergroup relations were planted, though largely at first for believers in the divinity of Jesus. In opposition to Peter Stuyvesant's harshness to Quakers, thirty-one townsmen presented him with a document, known as the Flushing Remonstrance, which stated their desire not to offend anyone,

> in whatsover forme, name or title hee appears in, whether Presbyterian, Independent, Baptist or Quaker; but shall be glad to see anything of God in any of them; desiring to doe unto all men as wee desire all men should doe unto us, which is the true law both of Church and State; for our Saviour saith this is the Law and the Prophets; Therefore, if any of these said persons come in love unto us, wee cannot in Conscience lay violent hands upon them, but give them free Egresse into our Towne and howses as God shall perswade our Consciences.[130]

Though Stuyvesant repudiated the remonstrance, it nevertheless reflected a growing moderation in the Dutch colony and "the most important piece of theorizing about religious liberty that New Netherland produced." By 1687, New York's governor noted the existence of "firstly a chaplain . . . of the Church of England; secondly, a Dutch Calvinist; thirdly, a French Calvinist; fourthly, a Dutch Lutheran. Here be not many of the Church of England; few Roman Catholics; abundance of Quaker preachers, men, and women especially; Singling Quakers; Ranting Quakers; Sabbatarians; Anti-Sabbatarians; some Ana-baptists; some Jews; in short, of all sorts of opinion there are some, and the most part none at all."[131]

In Pennsylvania, thanks to William Penn, a convert to Quakerism, religious freedom for Quakers and Catholics was established, for which he was accused of being a Jesuit in disguise. Founded in 1681 as a "Holy Experiment," Quakers were assured it was a place to live in peace and brotherly love, where freedom of worship would prevail for all believers in God, especially Protestant ones. "No man," he wrote, "nor number of men upon earth hath power or authority to rule over men's consciences in religious matters."[132] Penn first wanted the area called New Wales, but after an objection by a Welsh member of England's Privy Chamber, who thought it inappropriate for such an idealistic venture, it was changed to its current name.

The first large contingent of settlers were Welsh, followed by German and English Quakers, Scotch-Irish Presbyterians, French Huguenots, and Dutch Calvinists. By 1702, Justus Falckner described Pennsylvania Christians as being "divided among almost countless sects . . . such as the Quakers, Anabaptists, Naturalists, Libertines, Independents, Sabbatarians, and many others. . . . According to their confession the Protestants here . . . are either Evangelical Lutheran or Presbyterian and Calvinist. So the Protestants are also divided here into three nationalities, an English Protestant church, a Swedish Protestant Lutheran church, and people of German nationality who are of the Evangelical Lutheran or the Reformed churches."[133]

In Roger Williams's Rhode Island, all settlers were assured that they "may walk as their conscience persuade them," free to elect their own governor, with no one barred from political life because of religion. In 1654, ten years after Williams obtained his patent to consolidate various settlements, he wrote, "We have long drunk of the cup of as great liberties as any people we can hear of under the whole heaven. We have not only been long free . . . from the iron yoke of wolfish bishops, and their popish ceremonies. . . . We have not felt the new chains of Presbyterian tyrants, nor in this colony have we been consumed with the over zealous fire of (so-called) godly Christian magistrates."[134]

Maryland was originally founded as a refuge for Catholics where they and Protestant immigrants would live in peace. Lord Baltimore required the colony's governors to swear:

> I will not myself or any other, directly or indirectly, trouble, molest, or dis-countenance any person professing to believe in Jesus Christ, for or in respect to religion: I will make no difference of persons in conferring offices, favors, or rewards, for or in respect of religion: but merely as they shall be found faithful and well deserving, and endured with moral virtues and abilities: my aim shall be public unity, and if any person or officer shall molest any person professing to believe in Jesus Christ, on account of his religion, I will protect the person molested and punish the offender.[135]

In 1649, the famed Maryland Act of Toleration was passed, which applied, however, only to believers in Jesus Christ and the Holy Trinity, and wherein penalties were prescribed for those who defamed others as "an Heritick, Schismatic, Idolater, Puritan, Independent, Presbyterian, Popish, Priest, Jesuits, Jesuited papist, Lutheran, Calvinist, Anabaptist, Brownish, Antinomian, Barrowist, Round head, Separatist, or any other name or term in a reproachful manner relating to matters of Religion."[136]

Unfortunately, as more Protestants settled, their relations with Catholics worsened; and in the 1690s and early 1700s, Maryland passed laws restricting the rights of Catholics, including one to prevent "the Growth of Popery" by Jesuit missionaries. In protest, a group of Maryland Catholics signed a petition complaining of being "almost reduced to a Levell with our Negroes" and deprived "of all the Advantages promised our Ancestors on their Coming into this Province."[137]

The vast distance of the colonies from Europe's strongly centralized religious institutions, as well as the increasing ethnic and religious diversity of people, also contributed to the growth of intergroup tolerance. The Great Awakenings in the early eighteenth century not only stimulated religiosity but also facilitated religious decentralization, division, and pluralism. Anglican and Congregational primacy in the South and North respectively weakened as other groups expanded. For example, Baptist congregations rose from about 400 in 1780 to 2,700 in 1820; Lutheran congregations increased from 225 to 800; Presbyterians, from nearly 500 to 1,700; Methodists, from some 50 to 2,700; Roman Catholics, from 50 congregations and missions to 120. As a whole, from 1780 to 1820 Christian congregations dramatically climbed from 2,500 to 11,000.[138]

Intergroup Differences and the Revolutionary War

By the time of the American Revolution, the colonists represented a relatively small, prosperous, and well-armed British outpost, confined by the Appalachians on the west, the Atlantic on the east, and large numbers of Indians as well as Spanish and French domains just beyond their settlements. To kinsmen in England, they were uncouth, ungrateful, and lacking respect for their betters.

Throughout the colonies, social and political inequality were rife, but not central to igniting the revolution. Except for Blacks, people could much more easily rise socioeconomically than in Europe. Of a population of almost 3 million (excluding Indians), more than 500,000 were Black slaves. Some 300,000 were White indentured servants, and about 50,000 were White former convicts from abroad. The million or so women had limited legal standing—denied the right to sue, serve on a jury, and, if married, unable to own property in their own name. Dr. Benjamin Rush, a prominent physician and supporter of the revolution, epitomized the male attitude toward women in a letter to a prospective bride: "From the day you marry you must have no will of your own. The subordination of your sex is enforced by nature, by reason, and by revelation. . . . The happiest marriages I have known have been those when the subordination I have recommended has been most complete."[139]

Though more than one-third of the White population was of non-English descent, an "Anglification of American life" was occurring. English values, mores, and language became dominant as publications, scientific apparatuses, and medical journals freely passed between America and England.[140] As with Englishmen back home, the colonists valued the reforms of the Magna Carta and "Glorious Revolution" of 1688. Still, fears—if not paranoia—grew of England's moving from a policy of relatively salutary neglect to determined enforcement of new taxes and rules governing exports.

Just as nineteenth-century immigrants had a variety of loyalties and prejudices, so most colonists maintained strong attachments to their local areas of residence, distrusted those from other colonies, and were reluctant to combine military forces to fight the Indians or the French (as when on the eve of the French and Indian War delegates from New England, New York, Pennsylvania, and Maryland roundly rejected Benjamin Franklin's "Plan of Union" to deal with mutual defense, the Indians, and western land settlements).

In religion too, they clung to their different Protestant views. North Carolina's governor noted the long-standing "distinctions and animosities" between Anglicans and Presbyterians. Farther north, Puritans believed that England was plotting to impose an autocratic Anglican episcopacy, which they considered no less odious than a Catholic one. Many feared both churches were colluding to enrich themselves at their expense and that England, rife with popish priests, wanted to send an Anglican bishop as a Trojan horse from which the pope would emerge and conquer all of North America.[141]

More ominous was the Quebec act of 1774, whereby England granted French Catholics religious freedom and transferred land to the Quebec province that many colonists wanted. Although the act was a "Magna Carta" to French Canadians, to American colonists it was seen as an immediate threat to their Protestant religion and civil rights, and rumors circulated that a Catholic bishop was en route to Canada carrying "a cargo for relicks, indulgences, and other popish valuables."[142]

Those not affiliated with either denomination, as well as nonbelievers, resented having to pay for church upkeep and, as never before, criticized England's escalating demands for religious conformity, political obedience, and taxes.

Lastly, many colonists deplored England's immigration policies and respect for Indian title to western lands, which had been denied them by the royal Proclamation of 1763. In the Declaration of Independence, they accused George III of endeavoring "to prevent the population of these States," thereby exposing frontier settlers to "mercilous Indian savages, whose known rule of warfare is an undistinguished destruction of all ages, sexes, and conditions." There were also expansionists who believed they had a God-given right to the entire West, Florida, and Canada.

Until the Declaration of Independence, many colonists considered themselves English subjects whose rights were being violated by the king and Parliament rather than as revolutionaries seeking national self-determination, and they hoped that differences with their "British brethren" would be resolved. Even two months after the Battle of Bunker Hill, Thomas Jefferson was looking with fondness toward a reconciliation. Many believed the war would not last more than a year, and it was opposed by one-third to one-half of the population. At one point, almost as many Loyalists served with the British as men in Washington's army.[143] Distrust of each colony for the other and a strong centralized government continued, even in the Articles of Confederation, wherein each state retained its sovereignty and power, rendering the government entirely dependent upon them for funds and manpower.

Though many Revolutionaries came from families of three or more generations in America, eight of the fifty-six signers of the Declaration of Independence were first-generation immigrants from England, Wales, Scotland, and Ireland. Except for one Catholic (Charles Carroll) and a few Deists, all were Protestants, who in spite of their internal religious differences felt compelled to seek the help of Blacks and Indians, as well as of foreign countries. Many army recruits were foreign-born, almost 40 percent in Maryland.[144]

To England, the Revolutionaries were a "hotch-potch medley of foreign, enthusiastic madmen," and New Englanders were "Goths and Vandals of America," who had formed a "monstrous and an unnatural coalition" with Virginians. It was ridiculous of Americans to talk of oppression, wrote John Witherspoon, because "British liberty" had enabled their settlements to advance far beyond those of other nations.[145]

Various colonies passed legislation requiring public oaths of allegiance to the Revolution. Those who refused the oath were subject to removal from office and disenfranchisement, and were denied the right to collect debts, sell or buy land, or practice their profession. To prevent the return of Loyalists who had fled, Massachusetts passed confiscation and banishment legislation, declaring that if any came back without court permission, they could "suffer the pains of death without benefit of clergy."[146]

As the war intensified, revolutionary passions spawned the first display of American nativism and violence. Calling themselves "Patriots," the revolutionaries damned those loyal to England as traitors, some of whom were tarred and feathered, imprisoned, branded, or even shot or hanged. A Loyalist, said the *New York Journal,* was "a thing whose head is in England, and its body in America, and its neck ought to be stretched." Accusations were also made that all prostitutes in New York City were Loyalists.[147]

"Oppressions multiply & it seems determined to make this country intolerable," wrote Loyalist James Allen in 1777. "The most discreet, passive & respectable characters are dragged forth & tho' no charge can be made, yet a new idea is started (which like all other beginnings of oppressive schemes soon became general) of securing such men as hostages. . . . If necessity is a plea, who created it, or where will it stop? Massacres, proscriptions & every species of iniquity may be justified by necessity."[148]

Many Loyalists, though born in America, decided to leave the country, becoming the first, and certainly the largest (approximately 200,000), group of political refugees. Such departures broadened the definition of refugee, which the 1796 edition of the *Encyclopaedia Britannica* credited to the expelled Huguenots, but now applied to all people who leave their country in times of distress, noting that "since the revolt of the British colonies in America, we have frequently heard of American refugees."[149]

Only after the war had been going on for a little more than a year did Congress define an act of treason as levying war against the colonies, being loyal to England's king, or giving aid and comfort to the colonists' enemies. The Constitution refined the definition, but provided safeguards against unjust accusations; there had to be a confession of treason in an open court or two people testifying to having witnessed the same act of treason.

Allegiance divisions within families, economic classes, religions, national origins, and regions were common, with many backcountry colonists changing sides several times, depending on which army was in control of the area and how much pressure it put on residents to join them. Under the leadership of Benjamin

Franklin's son, some pro-British colonists organized a military unit that engaged in guerrilla activities so savage that the British commander eventually had it disbanded. In Vermont, some political leaders negotiated with the British to establish neutrality and form an independent British colony. In Pennsylvania, nearly all Scotch-Irish supported the Revolution, though a few formed a Loyalist regiment; in the South, they fought on both sides. Germans in Pennsylvania supported the Revolution, but in Georgia, most were Loyalists because the British protected them against Indian raids. Though some Scots, such as John Paul Jones, served the Revolution with distinction, most remained solidly Loyalist, with the British army promising those joining them free land, exemption from taxes for twenty years, and remission of owed quitrents. A Loyalist Irish regiment, Volunteers of Ireland, was formed in Philadelphia, but most Irish supported the Revolution, which had some nine Irish-born generals. Small numbers of Poles served in the American, French, and British armies. Huguenots, Dutch, and Swiss were also divided.[150]

Religiously, Congregationalists and Presbyterians generally favored the Revolution, while Anglicans generally opposed it, particularly in the North. To Judge Thomas Jones, a New York Loyalist historian, the term *Rebel* was synonymous with Presbyterian. The British maligned Presbyterian churches as "sedition shops" and readily set some afire. Because of Revolutionary passions in Boston, the Anglican priest and lay leaders of Kings Chapel either fled or were deported.[151]

There was a Revolutionary "Jew Company," and while Haym Solomon helped finance the Revolution, a minority of Jews opposed it. The royal governor of Georgia wanted all Jews banned from the colony, claiming they were "violent rebels and persecutors of the king's loyal subjects" and provided "no peace or security in the province." In spite of the prevailing anti-Catholicism, the vast majority of Catholics supported the Revolution.[152]

With few exceptions, such as Dunkards (German Baptists), Baptists overwhelmingly supported the Revolution once it began, with many pastors volunteering to serve as chaplains. French Acadians also supported it, hoping the British would be defeated so they could return to Nova Scotia. All Methodist ministers, save one, went over to the British side, opening their laity to the suspicion of being Loyalists. In Virginia, Methodists were charged with preaching "passive obedience," preferring to die rather than kill because men could not "serve Mars and Christ at the same time."[153]

Blacks and Indians were in a no-win situation, though they were sought as allies by Americans and British. At first, some colonists advocated recruiting Blacks, but Washington and his military command rejected the idea, knowing that slave owners did not want to lose their workers and that other White Revolutionaries feared Blacks being armed and trained militarily. In contrast, the British urged Blacks to revolt and offered freedom to those joining them, thereby further angering the rebelling colonists, particularly in the South. As was to be done with the Japanese during World War II, the Virginia Committee of Safety, in

April 1776, ordered all Blacks more than thirteen years old to be relocated inland, away from the coastal British forces. In many areas, local patrols were established to prevent runaway slaves from reaching British land or naval forces.[154]

In response to British successes in enlisting Blacks as well as the need for additional troops, Washington approved recruiting free Blacks, as did most states, some of whom accepted slaves. At that time, the ranks were not segregated, and both Massachusetts and Rhode Island raised all-Black battalions. New York passed a law allowing slaves to be substituted for White recruits. Most Revolutionary Black troops came from the northern colonies, while South Carolina and Georgia refused to have any, though they used them as auxiliaries for construction and general help. "No regiment is to be seen in which there are not Negroes in abundance," wrote one Hessian officer, "and among them there are able-bodied, strong and brave fellows."[155]

Both sides actively sought the support of Indians or at least their neutrality. For Indians, the unhappy choice was picking the lesser evil or the more probable winner. Resentful of the brutal expansionism of frontier colonists, most Indians sided with the British, who had tried to protect them and enforce the Proclamation of 1763, in which settlers were proscribed from crossing the Appalachian Mountains. Others preferred the new promises of colonists, as well as their gifts, army commissions, and regular army pay for their braves, which were reinforced by threats of harsh reprisals should they help the British. Whatever the side, their military actions took place largely on the frontiers, where they made no distinction between soldiers and civilians, and were referred to as the "hell hounds of death." Savagery, however, was also practiced by the White colonists, who one British official said had butchered Cherokee women and children in cold blood or burned them alive.[156]

Generally, the Tuscaroras, Oneidas, and Delawares sided with the colonists, and the Iroquois, Mohawks, Onondagas, Cayugas, Senecas, and Cherokees aided the British. Throughout the war, many Oneidas served the colonists as soldiers, messengers, diplomatic representatives, guides, interpreters, informers, and spies.[157] One Indian, Louis Atayataronghta, became a lieutenant colonel.

There were also outright pacifists, such as Quakers, Brethren, Mennonites, Rogerenes, Schweckenfelders, and recently arrived Shakers. Pennsylvania Quakers abjured the war: "We are out of the whole business and will give aid and comfort to neither party." Fearful that Quakers might help the approaching British army, Pennsylvania revolutionaries arrested twenty in late 1777 and relocated them to Virginia, where some died in captivity. The pacifist dilemma was reflected in North Carolina's Moravians, who kept "trying to persuade the Whigs that they were not loyalists and the loyalists that they were not Whigs."[158]

Even among those who fought for the Revolution, problems of morale and discipline were widespread. Military personnel turnover was high, with many recruits returning home after completing their one-year enlistment. Shortages of military supplies and medical attention, plus deaths from illness, further de-moralized soldiers. Desertion involved at least one-third of the regular troops, and General Washington felt compelled to ask the Continental Congress for permission to increase the number of disciplinary lashes that could be given a soldier from the biblical 39 to 500. From 1777 to 1783, twenty-eight mutinies took place, ranging in size from a squad to a regiment. Some American soldiers, with British funding, actually plotted to assassinate Washington, for which one was hanged and thirteen imprisoned.[159] Major General Benedict Arnold not only turned traitor (largely for money), but led British troops against his former countrymen.

Each side included foreigners as volunteers, allies, mercenaries, or turncoats. The British continually encouraged foreign-born troops to desert, promising par-dons, land, reimbursement for turned-in weapons, and if they desired, free pas-sage home. By March 1778, English statistics showed that 1,134 soldiers and 354 sailors (mostly natives of Ireland, England, and Scotland) had deserted and joined British forces. Although denouncing such behavior, Washington told the Congress that he hoped "some means would be devised to cause more frequent desertions of their [British] troops," and in 1776 Congress adopted a policy of encouraging Hessians and others "of whatever nation or religion" to leave the British forces. Convicts were enlisted by both sides, particularly by the British and Hessians, who gave pardons to prisoners in England or indentured servants of colonists. Some Hessian units enrolled runaway slaves, but restricted them to noncombatant duties.[160]

Better known are the foreign officers in the Revolutionary ranks: the Marquis de Lafayette of France, Baron de Kalb of Prussia, Michael Kovats of Hungary, and Count Casimir Pulaski and Thaddeus Kosciusko of Poland. In all, eleven major generals and sixteen brigadier generals were foreign-born. Many foreign-ers had come solely in search of adventure and a higher military rank than they had at home, and their ambitions so irritated Washington and the Congress that in 1777 all unassigned military aspirants were ordered to return to Europe.[161]

Aiding the British were some 30,000 Germans, largely Waldecker, Braun-schweiger, and Hessian troops, whom the Declaration of Independence said were employed by George III to "compleat the works of death, desolation and tyr-anny." Earlier, the British had futilely sought to hire soldiers from Russia and Holland. Nevertheless, some English officials opposed using German mercenar-ies for fear that once in America they would be "offered lands and protection" and that the 150,000 Germans already in America would encourage them to desert.[162]

And indeed, such happened. Congress printed broadsides in German, offering deserters free land, cows, pigs, and oxen, according to their rank. Hundreds accepted. Hessian Major Carl Baurmeister blamed the desertions on "the scatter-ing of printed invitations and previous persuasion on the part of the inhabitants, who have resorted to every possible inducement." In all, German mercenaries suffered some 2,000 casualties in twenty engagements, and after the war's end, about one-half decided to remain.[163]

The need to win favor with religious and ethnic groups was also recognized. To gain American-German support, the Congress published documents in German, such as the *Artikel des Bundes und der immerwaehrenden Einstracht zwischen den Staaten* (the Articles of Confederation). Others were published in French in the hope French Canadians would rebel against their British rulers. One broadside boasted of Protestant and Catholic amity and urged French Canadians to join them in "resolving to be free."[164]

To further attract French Canadian support, Washington banned the burning of effigies of the pope on Guy Fawkes Day, declaring the custom "so monstrous, as not to be suffered or excused; indeed instead of offering the most remote insult, it is our duty to address public thanks to these our Brethren, as to them we are so much indebted for every late happy Success over the common Enemy in Canada." Such outreach facilitated the recruitment of three companies of French Canadians. Some years later, in a letter to a group of American Catholics, Washington expressed admiration for their wartime patriotism, as well as the important assistance of Canadian ones.[165]

The Revolution evoked wide support overseas, from where Benjamin Franklin reported that "all Europe is on our side . . . as far as applause and good wishes can carry them." Of course, European self-interest and hatred of England also benefited the colonists. In spite of English opposition, Belgian, Dutch, Swedish, Spanish, Italian, and particularly French officials and merchants secretly sold or gifted military supplies to the Revolutionaries, who could not produce sufficient quantities. Dutch loans helped avert colonial bankruptcy. As the British minister in the Hague wrote, "America would have had to abandon their revolution if they had not been aided by Dutch greed." A French shipment of some 21,000 muskets and 100,000 pounds of gunpowder contributed to American victory at Saratoga in 1777. The following year, France openly allied itself with the colonists and sent huge amounts of military and material—18,000 soldiers, 31,000 sailors, and 67 warships, among whom were several scores of Swedish officers and Italian and Corsican sailors and soldiers.[166]

Spain, too, entered the war, but as an ally of France, which promised to help her regain Gibraltar and the island of Minorca, as well as safeguard her colonial empire from British expansionism. General Washington at first was suspicious of France's motivations, saying that "hatred of England may carry some into an excess of confidence in France. . . . But it is a maxim found on the universal experience of mankind that no nation is to be trusted farther than it is bound by its interest, and no prudent statesman or politician will venture to depart from it."[167] Soon Francophobia turned to Francophilia.

A similar reversal of feelings took place in France, where American Revolutionaries were hailed, particularly among intellectuals, thanks largely to Franklin's lobbying efforts. American Loyalists, however, were horrified that the

Revolutionaries could prefer a "treacherous and cruel" France over England, which was "a faithful and loving mother, even though at times a severe one." Even Benedict Arnold, now a British officer, denounced his former countrymen for joining with France, "the enemy of the Protestant faith."[168]

In Ireland, the Revolution inspired residents to threaten rebellion against England unless granted home rule. More out of hatred of England than love of revolution, Spain in 1779 and Holland the following year entered the war. As England searched and seized neutral vessels trading with America, other European countries, such as Russia, Denmark, Prussia, Portugal, the two Sicilies, and Sweden (which became the first neutral country to recognize the new United States) adopted a policy of "armed neutrality."

After war's end, Patriot-Loyalist ill feelings continued to fester in some families, as epitomized in Benjamin Franklin's letter to his son, who had sought a reconciliation:

> Indeed nothing has ever hurt me so much and affected me with such keen Sensations, as to find myself deserted in my old Age by my only Son; and not only deserted, but to find him taking up Arms against me, in a Cause, wherein my good Fame, Fortune and Life were all at stake. You conceived, you say, that your Duty to your King and Regard for your Country requir'd this . . . *there are Natural Duties which precede political* ones, and cannot be extinguished by them.[169]

No matter which side the Indians had helped, they were losers, without any European protector or benefactor—French or English—and more than ever vulnerable to the hostility, acquisitiveness, and westward movement of American frontiersmen and land speculators. Pro-British Iroquois never recovered their power, and many of them, as well as Mohawks, fled with Loyalists to Canada. Pro-Patriot Oneidas had their crops and orchards destroyed, and became "a divided people . . . living in horrid conditions." In the South, Indian allies of the British—Cherokees, Choctaws, and Creeks—were treated as defeated enemies, and the North Carolina legislature laid claim to all Cherokee lands, upon which Indians could continue living, but only until they were relocated to a reservation.[170]

Blacks fared no better. Some 5,000 served in the Revolutionary army and another 1,000 with the British, who had an Ethiopian regiment, whose emblem on the uniforms read, "Liberty to Slaves." Many more fled behind British lines, hopeful a Loyalist victory would gain them freedom. Willingly or not, by war's end, thousands left with the British for East Florida, West Indies, Canada, or Britain. However, the subsequent peace treaty specifically prohibited British troops from "carrying away any Negroes, or other property of the American inhabitants."[171] Though some Blacks were freed because of their military service with the British and Americans, and the northern states gradually abolished slavery, the plight of most Blacks remained unchanged, particularly in the South, where the majority lived.

Renewed fears of an aristocratic class and standing army arose, this time by Americans who believed that in times of peace the nation is best defended by a citizens' militia. When disbanding army officers formed the Society of Cincinnati, with membership restricted to the eldest male descendent (including those of French officers), rumors spread of a conspiratorial, promonarchist military caste. Though headed by men like Washington and Lafayette, it was denounced by Franklin. Pennsylvania condemned it; Rhode Island disenfranchised its resident members; and Massachusetts declared it "dangerous to the peace, liberty and safety of the Union." Such fears were part of the debate on establishing a standing army, which anti-Federalists claimed would be "in the hands of an elite office corps." As a result, the new Congress ordered the disbanding of the army, except for less than 100 soldiers to guard military stores, with no officer above the rank of captain.[172]

Just as many of today's business leaders claim that what is good for them is also good for the country, so with Federalists, whom the working class and Republicans accused of wanting to establish an American aristocracy. In the first Congress, debate erupted over how the president and other governmental officers should be called. Suggestions included "His High Highness the President of the United States and Protector of Their Liberties," "His Patriotic Majesty," and, as John Adams recommended, "His Elective Majesty." Anti-aristocracy sentiment prevailed, with the use of simple titles for government officials and the Constitution's prohibiting the granting of titles of nobility or allowing elected officials to receive such from a foreign power, unless approved by Congress. Similar public opposition was increasingly expressed about the titles, wealth, pride, and arrogance of clergymen.[173]

Though well aware of the need for unity, the rebelling colonists preferred their local governments and militias rather than a central, all-powerful one, which they feared would weaken their geographic sense of being and violate their individual political rights. As a result, the Founding Fathers deliberately included provisions in the Constitution for the separation of governmental powers and maintenance of state rights. They also laid the conceptual basis for equal political rights and opportunities in the "Comity" and "Guarantee" clauses, which required states to grant citizens of other states the same privileges their own have and that all newly formed states not be incompatible with republican principles. Then, because of continuing fears of a centralized government, a federal Bill of Rights was created to protect individual freedom of speech, assembly, petition, and religion, as well as to protect any citizen from hasty prosecution for treason.

For all the religious, ethnic, racial, regional, and class differences, the war helped unify the population. Not only did the colonists transcend their differences but also those of their foreparents, regardless of whether the latter were religious or political refugees, criminals or debtors, adventurers or malcontents, or idealists in search of a better world. Reinforcing that unity was anger at the

British for employing German mercenaries, as well as enlisting and inciting Blacks and Indians to rebel against them. Now, too, at the urging of the Congress in 1788, the states began passing laws barring the importation of convict labor, prompting England to find other areas to dump its criminal population.

More enduring was the vision of the kind of society the Founding Fathers wanted for themselves and posterity. Their emphasis was on a society free of arbitrary rules, whether by the executive, legislative, or judicial branches of government. In less than fifty words, the preamble to the Constitution identified goals that remain true today: forming a more perfect Union, establishing justice, insuring domestic tranquility, providing for common defense, promoting the general welfare, and securing the blessings of liberty. Unlike changes of government elsewhere in the world, no military dictatorship, rampant terrorism, political assassinations, or attempted coups followed.

Moreover, a sense of civic mission and destiny took root, which Washington reflected in one of his last messages to the states in 1783. America, he wrote, "seemed to be peculiarly designated by Providence for the display of human greatness and felicity. Heaven has crowned its other blessings by giving the fairest opportunity for political happiness than any other nation has even been favored with and the result must be a nation which would have a meliorating influence on all mankind."[174]

Existing prejudices did not prevent native- or foreign-born minorities—Irish, Scotch-Irish, Dutch, Germans, French Huguenots—from serving in high positions in the Continental Congress or in the newly established government, neither of which thought it necessary to make English the nation's official language. In fact, after some debate, the Congress said that any naturalized citizen could vote as well as be elected to high office—except that of the presidency.

As one foreign visitor, in 1788, evaluated the war's impact, "Americans came into contact with men from many countries and, as a consequence, broke loose from their old habits and prejudices. When they saw that other men with religious opinions different from their own could none the less be virtuous, they understood that it was possible to be a good man whether one believed or not in transubstantiation or in the divinity of Christ. So they concluded that they should tolerate one another, and that this was the kind of worship most agreeable to God."[175]

By 1790, when the first census was taken, of an estimated White population of 3 million, two-thirds lived within fifty miles of the ocean, 60.9 percent of whom were English; 14.3 percent, Scotch and Scotch-Irish from Ulster; 8.7 percent, German; 5.4 percent, Dutch, French, and Swedish; 3.7 percent, Southern Irish; and 7 percent unidentifiable and varied. Most people of English descent lived in Virginia and Massachusetts, where religious exclusiveness was strongest. Pennsylvania had the largest number of Germans. The Dutch concentrated in the "zone of tolerance"—New York, New Jersey, and Pennsylvania. Jews resided mainly in New York and Maryland. The largest group of Irish lived in New Jersey, where the fewest English lived.[176]

As White residents gained power and property, Indians lost theirs, though their names were retained on many rivers and regions. The Constitution merely said that Congress would regulate commerce with Indians and that all Indians not taxed would be excluded from being counted in the apportionment of congressional representatives. More ominous, Indians confronted a government victorious in war, with a reservoir of battle-seasoned veterans.

Still, promises of peace and security were given Indians. The Northwest Ordinance of 1787 was not only the first federal document to contain a bill of rights but also affirmed that "the utmost good faith shall always be observed toward the Indians, their land and property shall never be taken from them without their consent; and in their property, rights, and liberty, they shall never be disturbed, unless in just and lawful wars authorized by Congress."

Contrary to such assurances, various settlers, traders, and speculators killed Indians with impunity, stole their lands, sold them huge quantities of alcohol, and made illegal land and trade deals with them. In vain, President Washington reminded Congress in 1795 that "we should not lose sight of an important truth which continually receives new confirmations, namely, that the provisions heretofore made with a view to the protection of the Indians from the violences of the lawless part of our frontier inhabitants are insufficient . . . unless the murdering of Indians can be restrained by bringing the murderers to condign punishment, all the exertions of the Government to prevent destructive retaliations . . . will prove fruitless.[177]

While the conviction grew that Indians would assimilate with the majority culture or be destroyed by it, it was believed that Blacks would survive, but only as an enslaved people.

The Trivialization of Slavery

The hypocrisy of seeking independence while maintaining slavery was not unnoticed during the Revolutionary War. As one colonist chided his neighbors:

> Blush ye pretended votaries for freedom! ye trifling patriots! who are making vain parade of being advocates for the liberties of mankind, who are thus making a mockery of your profession by trampling on the sacred natural rights and privileges of Africans; for while you are fasting, praying, nonimporting, nonexporting, remonstrating, resolving, and pleading for a restoration of your charter rights, you at the same time are continuing this lawless, cruel, inhuman, and abominable practice of enslaving your fellow creatures.[178]

Some ministers urged large-scale colonization of Africa by Black Americans, who would convert the natives into "a civilized, Christian, happy people." Such an exodus, wrote Samual Hopkins, would also "gradually draw off all the Blacks in New England, and even in the Middle and Southern States," so that "this nation will be delivered from that which, in the view of every discerning man, is a great calamity, and inconsistent with the good of society."[179]

Some slave-holding colonists were torn between economic self-interest, political expediency, and religious principle. "I abhor slavery," said Henry Laurens, a prominent South Carolina slave dealer, but "I am not the man who enslaved them; they are indebted to Englishmen for that favor; nevertheless I am devising means for manumitting many of them. . . . Great powers oppose me—the laws and customs of my country, my own and the avarice of my countrymen. What will my children say if I deprive them of so much estate? . . . I will do as much as I can in my time, and leave the rest to a better hand."[180]

The contradiction between the colonists' claims of being oppressed by England while they oppressed others was readily evident to many British and French observers. Samuel Johnson asked, "How is that we hear the loudest *yelps* from liberty among the drivers of negros?" The French paper *Mercure de France* told readers that "the friends of justice and humanity will be perhaps astonished to learn that in the United States, in that asylum of peace, happiness and liberty, which has so often reechoed to those sacred words 'All men are created equal,' there still are today nearly seven hundred thousand slaves."[181]

Many colonists had no pangs of conscience, not even those who had opposed slavery. In welcoming the safe arrival of a slave ship, a colonist wrote that "a gracious overruling Providence had been pleased to bring to this land of freedom another cargo of benighted heathen to enjoy the blessing of a Gospel dispensation." More pragmatic was General Charles Cotesworth, South Carolina's delegate at the Constitutional Convention in 1787, who declared, "While there remained one acre of swampland uncleared in South Carolina, I would raise my vote against restricting the importation of Slaves."[182]

Though all states north of Maryland had abolished slavery by 1786, most Blacks remained enslaved because 90 percent lived in the South, where their chances for freedom were stymied by the invention of the cotton gin and the expansion of cotton planting. To inhibit organized resistance or rebellion, many plantation owners purchased slaves of different tribal origins, just as later manufacturers would do with European immigrants.[183] Only by inference does the Constitution refer to *slaves* and *slavery*. While *persons* free and indentured, as well as Indians not taxed, were to be counted for direct taxation and congressional representation, only "three-fifths of all other persons," meaning Black slaves, were to be so counted. In that way, the founding slave states that favored a full-bodied count were prevented from having 50 percent of the congressional seats.

Also, instead of banning the importation of slaves, the Constitution forbade Congress from interfering with the practice for twenty years (until 1808), much to the pleasure of Georgia and South Carolina. More pleasing to the South was a constitutional clause requiring extradition of all runaways. As stated in Article IV, "No person held to service or labor in one State, under the laws thereof, escaping into another, shall, in consequence of any law or regulation therein, be discharged from such service or labor, but shall be delivered up on claim of the party to whom such service or labor be due." Only in the Northwest Ordinance of 1787 was slavery barred in the huge territory it encompassed. Three years later, when the first census was taken, Blacks totaled 757,000, representing 19.3 percent of the population.

Black-Indian Conflict

The maintenance of slavery also generated Black-Indian conflict, as Whites sought to keep both groups divided lest they jointly rebel against them. Unlike the English, the early Spanish and Portuguese sometimes approved of marriages with Indians, but usually opposed them with Blacks, as well as between Indians and Blacks. Invidious appellations were given the offspring of interracial unions, such as *zambos* for the children of Blacks and Indians, *mestizos* for Europeans and Indians, and *mulattoes* for White colonists and Blacks.

In spite of the historiographical differences over how Indians viewed Blacks, some tribes, like the Seminoles, were clearly friendly and intermarried with them, while others, like the Cherokees, resented and exploited them. In fact, to some Cherokees, the Spanish were not "real white people" because, as one chief said, they "looked like mulattoes, and I would never have anything to say to them."[184]

To safeguard their outposts against Indian-Black alliances, colonial French, Spanish, English, and Americans exploited the fears of both groups. Indians were employed to crush slave rebellions or catch runaway slaves and were told that the latter caused diseases. Conversely, Blacks were told gory stories of Indian cruelty and were used to fight hostile Indian tribes.

Some Indians became "bona fide slavetraders," stealing Blacks from one group of slaveholders and selling them to another. The Cherokees developed their own slave codes, in which tribal members were prohibited from teaching "any free Negro or Negroes *not of Cherokee blood* or any slave belonging to any citizen or citizens of the nation, to read or write." In fact, in 1730, when competition with the English over slaves arose, a seven-man Cherokee delegation journeyed to England and signed a treaty with King George II, stipulating that if any Black slaves ran away from their English masters, "the Cherokee Indians shall endeavor to apprehend them, and either bring them back to the Plantation from whence they run away, or to the Governor." In the next century, some northern missionaries, fearful of undermining their effectiveness among the Cherokees and Choctaws, opposed demands of their superiors that they condemn slavery.[185]

In short, for uprooted and enslaved Blacks, and for vanquished and dispossessed Indians, there was no escape from White oppression or cunning.

The Revolution, Church-State Separation, and Pluralism

Barely a year after emigrating to America from England, Thomas Paine said, with some exaggeration, "This new world hath been the asylum for the persecuted lovers of civil and religious liberty from every part of Europe."[186] And, indeed, the Revolution laid the basis for the freest country in the world. Not only did it loosen the ties of church and state without provoking anticlerical violence, but, equally important, it projected a set of ideals that progressively outlawed all injustices based on race, religion, and national origin. Laws and blindfolded justice were to rule, not potentates, prelates, or people.

Whether as religious idealists, political theorists, or victims of prejudice, more and more individuals advocated toleration of other beliefs, though not necessarily their equality. By the Constitution and Bill of Rights, the realms of state and church were to be separated. Article VI, Section 3, of the Constitution specifically banned any religious test for federal office (which was not applied to the states until the Fourteenth Amendment in 1866), and the Bill of Rights precluded government from establishing any religion or preventing its free exercise.

The Revolution also helped escalate religious identity, expression, dissension, and democracy, as increasing numbers of clergy and laity believed they could communicate directly with God, without the need of a centralized authority or government, and that people should have the right to practice their beliefs as long as, in Jeffersonian terms, they did not "break out into overt acts against peace & good order."[187]

Nevertheless, for all of its differing groups, Protestantism continued to be specified as the sole privileged religion in many new state constitutions. Some establishment Protestants wanted the right to continue taxing people for church upkeep and bitterly deplored the absence in the federal Constitution of any acknowledgment of God, Jesus Christ, or the country's being "Christian" in creation and fact, warning that the prohibition of a religious test would one day allow Jews, Catholics, Unitarians, Turks, Mohammedans, Atheists, or Deists to hold federal office.[188] (Such beliefs were to appear time and again, but fortunately with ever-diminishing public support.)

In New Jersey, no Protestants were to be denied civil rights, and only they could be elected to office. North Carolina's new constitution prohibited civil office to all denying "the being of God or the truth of the Protestant religion or the Divine Authority, either of the Old or New Testament, or who ... hold religious principles incompatible with the freedom and safety of the State." The 1780 Massachusetts constitution assured equal protection to all Christians, but prescribed an oath of office that devout Catholics could not take with integrity— a repudiation of papal authority in civil, ecclesiastical, and spiritual matters.[189] New Hampshire's constitution held on longest to Protestant exclusivity, with Catholics and Jews not eligible for election to state legislature or governorship until 1876. Only New York's 1777 constitution did not prevent Jews from holding office, though it did Catholics. At their worst, compared to European practice, such restrictions were mild and unaccompanied by religious wars.

Under Jefferson's initiative, Virginia's constitution unequivocally stated that "all men shall be free to profess, and by argument to maintain, their opinions in matters of religion, and that the same shall in no wise diminish, enlarge, or affect their civil capacities."[190] Only four states, from 1789 to 1792, amended their constitutions to match Virginia's and the government's in religious freedom: Delaware ended a requirement for a Trinitarian oath; Pennsylvania deleted all references to the New Testament; and South Carolina and Georgia abolished all religious references. Eight other states delayed taking action, making it impossible for a Jew or Catholic to hold office.

Unlike their coreligionists abroad, many Catholics favored church-state separation, and so in 1784, when the Maryland state assembly considered a bill taxing all residents for the support of religious groups, most Catholic delegates opposed it, fearful of a reestablishment of the Protestant Episcopal church. "[W]e have all smarted heretofore under the lash of an established church and shall therefore be on our guard against every approach towards it," said John Carroll.[191]

Though Catholics could vote, political parties and organizations generally refused to nominate them for office lest Protestant voters be alienated. Moreover, some states barred ministers from holding public office (a practice finally declared unconstitutional in 1978). Throughout the eighteenth century, the franchise was usually limited to those free, White, male, and twenty-one, whose finances and real estate holdings were deemed respectable.

Whether domestic or foreign, tyranny was repudiated and its victims not to be denied sanctuary or humanitarian help. Thus, when thousands of Santo Dominicans fled in 1793 to America from revolutionary turmoil, various cities and states raised funds to help them; even Congress voted an appropriation.[192]

Citizenship requirements were minimal, with each state having its own procedures for naturalization, but all requiring a public oath of fealty to the state and to no foreign country. When Congress debated a bill in 1790 to create a uniform citizenship process, some congressmen argued that the recommended two-year period was too harsh because it would be inconsistent if,

> after boasting of having opened an asylum for the oppressed of all nations, and establishing a Government which is the admiration of the world, we make the terms of admission so hard as is now proposed. It is nothing to us, whether Jews or Roman Catholics settle among us, whether subjects of kings, or citizens of free States wish to reside in the United States, they will find it in their interest to be good citizens, and neither their religious or political opinions can injure us, if we have good laws, well executed.[193]

Nevertheless, a two-year residency was enacted, as well as requirements that applicants be free and White, and willing to pledge to support the Constitution. Five years later, in order to diminish immigrant political support for Jeffersonians, Congress raised the residency requirement to five years and stipulated that immigrants had to reject "absolutely and entirely all allegiance and fidelity to any foreign prince, potentate, state, or sovereignty of whom or which he was before a subject or citizen" and specify the name of the power they had left.[194]

No less reflective of the ideals of freedom was the letter George Washington wrote to a Jewish group in 1790:

> All possess alike liberty of conscience and immunities of citizenship. It is now no more that toleration is spoken of, as if it was by the indulgence of one class of people, that another enjoyed the exercise of their inherent natural rights. For happily the government of the United States, which gives to bigotry no sanction, to persecution no assistance, requires only that they who live under its protection should demean themselves as good citizens, in giving it on all occasions their effectual support. . . . May the children of the Stock of Abraham, who dwell in this land, continue to merit and enjoy the good will of the other inhabitants, while every one shall sit in safety under his own vine and fig-tree, and there shall be none to make him afraid.[195]

Washington's allusion to the Bible was no act of ethnic ingratiation, but rather one of religious understanding and symbolic identification. Just as the Puritans considered themselves latter-day chosen people, so did those who came after them, but in a pluralistic rather than exclusive manner. Deeply versed in the Jewish and Christian Bibles, the Revolutionary leaders often referred to their political condition as Egyptian slavery, to King George III as the pharaoh, to the Atlantic Ocean as the Red Sea, and to Washington and Adams as Moses and Joshua. Jewish biblical figures and experiences also inspired Blacks, who believed that just as Jews were slaves in Egypt, so were they in America; and just as God had delivered the Jews, so He would them. Such "philo-Judaism" did not preclude a hope by some Protestants that Jews would convert, which could be achieved by being more accepting of them. The "unlimited toleration of them," wrote the Reverend Charles Crawford, in 1784, "is the cause of God."[196]

Some Founding Fathers well realized the impact of their reforms on people abroad. A "perfect equality of religious privileges" would probably cause immigrants "to flock from Europe to the United States," predicted Alexander Hamilton, and, with equal insight, James Madison said that those areas that most encouraged immigrant settlements "advanced most rapidly in population, agriculture and the arts."[197]

Although each Christian group still believed it alone represented the one true faith, the war had caused many to realize that a plurality of groups assured their individual well-being. Instead of being a threat, a "multiplicity of sects was the best and only security for religious liberty in any society," said James Madison, arguing that civil rights also consisted of a "multiplicity of interests" that "must be the same as that for religious rights." To Edmund Randolph, of Virginia, a multiplicity of sects prevents "the establishment of any one sect, in prejudice to the rest." And Patrick Henry argued that "no particular sect or society ought to be favored or established, by law, in preference to others."[198]

Aiding the growth of diversity was the disaffiliation of religious institutions from parental churches abroad, which often supplied the colonists with clergy, Bibles, and books. As a Lutheran minister in New York wrote to a colleague, "If the mother church in Europe does not have mercy on us, then the Christian religion in America in general, and the Evangelical Lutheran in particular, is done for."

Even before the Revolution, Presbyterians and Dutch Reformed resented control by Scotland and Holland respectively. After the Revolution, the Methodist Conference in 1784 and the Dutch Reformed church in 1806 excluded any foreign preacher not acceptable to its local leaders. As the first Roman Catholic bishop in America, John Carroll favored an independent national church, which would elect its own bishop, be answerable only to the pope on spiritual matters, and replace Latin with English in liturgy: "America may come to exhibit a proof to the world that general and equal toleration . . . is the most effectual method to bring all denominations of christians to an unity of faith." Still largely unwelcomed in White churches, Blacks increasingly organized their own, particularly Baptist, Episcopalian, and Methodist churches, as well as benevolent and fraternal organizations.[199]

No less significant were the irreligion, a-religion, and secularism of many colonists, particularly among the more educated. In New England, where religious organization was strongest and non-English settlers fewest, not more than one in seven persons was a church member; farther south, it was less than one in fifteen; and in the Far South, the ratio was still greater. Such large numbers of unchurched people represented "a constant deadweight" on those who felt everyone should be a church member.[200]

The country's vastness of land also affected intergroup relations. Great distances separated the settlers, with contact limited to foot, horse, boat, and mail, via few roads and waterways. Though such isolation contributed to xenophobia, it also forced people who lived close to each other and had similar hopes to cooperate. Equally important, for immigrants and migrants alike, the opportunity to own land and create communities served to dissolve the prejudices and preferences they had brought with them.

For all the religious bigotry of those times, it was more in attitude, harsh as that was at times, than in physical abuse of others. A ban on religious tests was incorporated in the Constitution, and state constitutions were rewritten to provide greater tolerance and, in a few cases, equal treatment of religious believers. Although the test ban was included to protect government against a religious group gaining dominion over the country, the Bill of Rights' First Amendment protected religion from manipulation by government and other religious groups. Whatever their shortcomings (from today's perspective), the documents were radical advances, not existent in any other country, whose immediate impact abroad was on the French. "Every eye today is fixed upon North America," wrote a French reporter in 1783. "The philosophers of all Europe see in the new constitutions . . . the noblest, and perhaps the last, hope of the human race."[201]

With all the advances in religious and political freedom went an ambivalence, if not xenophobia, about the further diversification of people. As Alexander Hamilton wrote:

> In the composition of society, the harmony of the ingredients is all important, and whatever tends to discordant mixture must have an injurious tendency. The United States has already felt the evils of incorporating a large number of foreigners into their national mass; by promoting in different classes different predilections and antipathies against others, it has served very much to divide the community and to distract our councils. . . . The permanent effect of such policy will be, that in times of great public danger there will always be a numerous body of men of whom there may be just grounds of distrust; the suspicion alone will weaken the strength of the nation; but their force may be employed in assisting an invader.[202]

Those desires for homogeneity intensified feelings of nationalism and nativism, just as the growing heterogeneity spawned pluralism and cultural relativism. Both sets of desires were to grow and clash still more in the decades that followed.

Postrevolutionary Paranoia and Plots

Victory in war and government building did not end class, ethnic, and religious differences or fears of foreign intrigue, which intensified as Federalists and Republicans opposed each other. Just as Federalists favored the propertied, English-speaking citizens and good relations with England, Republicans appealed to the average citizen, small shopkeepers, immigrants, religious and nonreligious independents, and those favoring improved relations with France. Religiously, too, Congregationalists, Episcopalians, Lutherans, German Reformed, Dutch Reformed, and Quakers voted for the Federalists, while rural Baptists, Methodists, and Presbyterians, as well as town Irish Catholics, backed the Republicans.[203]

In Massachusetts, class differences led to Shays' Rebellion in 1786 when armed rebels futilely tried to halt imprisonment for debts and mortgage foreclosures. The rebels believed they were upholding the spirit of 1776 against the propertied classes and governing officials, who, in turn, believed they had to protect the Revolutionary principles of life, liberty, and property.[204]

Particularly repugnant to the administrations of Washington and Adams was the formation of Democratic-Republican societies by city workers and western farmers who, together with France, were blamed for the Whiskey Rebellion in 1794 (sometimes called the Scotch-Irish Rebellion). The Federalist imposition of an excise tax on distilled spirits, though generally resented in the West and South, was most bitterly opposed by Pennsylvania's Scotch-Irish farmers, who still remembered the harsh excise laws in Scotland and Ireland, where homes had been invaded and property confiscated. Their resistance led President Washington to order a militia force of 15,000 men into the area to quell the rebellion. Hamilton justified the action, lest there be "a CARTE BLANCHE to ambition, licentiousness and foreign intrigue."[205]

Other Federalists pointed to Frenchmen, Irishmen, and Jews in the Democratic-Republican societies. Printer and editor James Rivington said that French agents of a supposed "Metropolitan See of Sedition and Murder" in Paris were in collusion with the societies, one of whose vice-presidents was Jewish. Such conspirators, he wrote, could be easily recognized by their physical appearance. "They all seem to be, like their *Vice-President,* of the tribe of Shylock: they have that leering underlook, and malicious grin, that seem to say to the honest man— *approach me not.*"[206]

In the war between France and England, America wanted to be neutral, though each of the combatants sought it as an ally, particularly France, who felt that just as it had helped America during the Revolutionary War, so the favor should be returned. In violation of Washington's Proclamation of Neutrality, France outfitted privateers in American harbors to raid British shipping and colonies, while back home it initiated a "Reign of Terror," accelerating the flight of royalists and political liberals, of whom some 10,000 to 25,000 fled to America.[207]

Simultaneously, hostility to England resurfaced as it seized American ships bound for French ports and impressed our seamen. After the Jay Treaty, in which America and England agreed to resolve their differences, France angrily recalled its minister from Washington, D.C., and America found itself in an undeclared war, in which France also seized American ships. When President John Adams sent a delegation to France in the hope of establishing peace, a few French officials offered to help on condition a huge loan and bribe be given, to which one of our delegates allegedly said, "Millions for defense, but not one cent for tribute."

Federalists eagerly exploited the tensions by labeling France and its admirers as enemies. Fears now spread of a French plot to invade America with the help of armed Blacks from Santo Domingo, whose alleged goal was the establishment of republics in the trans- and cis-Appalachians. Patriotic Americans were urged to arm themselves against "outlandish sans-culotte Frenchmen" who would "fire, plunder and pillage" their homes and farms, as well as ravish and murder their wives and sweethearts.[208]

Against such a setting, Congress rejected the adoption of the French metric system, and then, in 1798, passed the Alien and Sedition Acts. Though nominally designed to protect America from foreign agitators and revolutionaries, the acts also reflected a Federalist attempt to strike at Republicans, who were accused of being *Frenchmen* in all their feelings and wishes." Residency requirements for citizenship were extended from five to fourteen years; the president was given power to deport aliens considered dangerous; and fines and imprisonment were provided for those speaking or writing false, scandalous, and malicious statements against the Congress or president. The enemies were Republicans and French, Irish, and British immigrants who favored the French Revolution. The Sedition Act's first victim was Ireland-born Congressman Matthew Lyon, of Vermont, who was imprisoned for writing a letter to a Federalist newspaper allegedly libeling President Adams. Before and after its passage, dozens of ships filled with frightened French left for home or Santo Domingo, much to the delight of public opinion, whose pro-French sympathies were now effectively destroyed. "Would to God the immigrants would be collected and retransported to the climes from whence they came," wrote one New York correspondent.[209]

To paranoid Federalists and others, the Irish rebellion, Irish immigrants, and French revolutionaries were part of a world conspiracy, particularly by the Illuminati of Bavaria, who together with Freemasons and atheists wanted to destroy all religion and government. Its members were said to have infiltrated the Republican Party, and Jefferson was accused of being "the very child of *modern illumination,* the foe of man, and the enemy of his country." The Reverend Jedidah Morse accused them of being under France's direction in their "increasing abuse of our wise and faithful rulers; the virulent opposition to some of the laws of our country . . . the baneful and corrupting books, and the consequent wonderful spread of infidelity, impiety, and immorality . . . and lastly, the apparently systematic endeavor made to destroy, not only the influence and support, but the official existence of the Clergy."[210]

Fortunately for democracy, when elected president, Thomas Jefferson repealed the Alien and Sedition Acts and pardoned all convicted under them, saying, "If there be any among us who wish to dissolve this Union, or to change its republican form, let them stand undisturbed, as monuments of the safety with which error of opinion may be tolerated where reason is left free to combat it." Not until the Civil War period did federal restrictions on free speech again become a major national issue. Jefferson also abolished presidential ceremonials and speeches to the Congress believed imitative of English custom.[211]

Federalists, particularly in Massachusetts, continued to blame their loss of political power on foreigners and their conspiracies, which they said threatened their representatives with becoming "drowned amid the discordant jargon of French, Spanish, German and Irish delegates, chosen by slave owners, in a disproportionate ratio."[212] In the decades to follow, the politics of prejudice and nativism were to resurface with each major influx of immigrants, economic downturn, war, or threat of war.

Summary

From the time before Europeans invaded America to the end of the eighteenth century, a pluralism and accretion of intergroup conflicts took place between Indians and Indians, Whites and Indians, Whites and Whites, Whites and Blacks, and Blacks and Indians. Protestants opposed Protestants; Catholics opposed

Catholics; and Protestants opposed Catholics, Jews, and all others deemed untrue believers. The ethnic dimension to many of the conflicts revolved around imperial claims. Contrary to contemporary sermonizing, the closer some groups came to each other, the greater was their mutual distrust.

There were also a number of concurrent salutary developments: an ending of European imperial wars on continental America; increasing numbers of immigrants and offspring who rejected Old Country allegiances; an extraordinary revolution after which no intrarevolutionary bloodshed followed; an emergence of some truly exceptional political leaders and laws ensuring the rights of all male citizens (except Blacks and Indians); and a growing awareness that the very diversity of people and beliefs was good for the country, if for no other reason than it prevented any one group from dominating all others.

A unique nation was in the making, different from and more bountiful than those from which immigrants and their offspring had come. America was a land of opportunity for many and varied people, who wanted a government incapable of tyrannizing them and, while at the same time, guaranteeing them protection and equality of treatment. *E pluribus unum* was both a fixed ideal and evolving reality—a model for those abroad who sought and fought for a republican, rather than imperial, form of government.

In the process, Americans displayed good and evil, altruism and greed, and idealism and oppression, in which no group was immune from becoming a victim or victimizer. Some groups suffered more than they benefited, while others benefited more than they suffered. All too often, a group's well-being depended upon numbers and might, and woe unto those who lacked either or both.

To be sure, the melioristic making of America was painful. The interethnic, interracial, and interfaith prejudice and discrimination of the late eighteenth century not only contradicted the ideals of the Declaration of Independence and Bill of Rights but also served as social, economic, and emotional breeding grounds for the intergroup bigotry to follow. As individual rights and group freedoms expanded, Black-White conflict intensified, and new forms of tensions emerged between native-born Americans and foreign-born Asians and Europeans, as well as between various immigrant groups themselves.

Chapter Two

The Weeds of Contempt

Just as the first Europeans in America bathed themselves in self-righteousness and triumphalism, so with their nineteenth-century descendants and successors. Recalling his early-nineteenth-century education, T.L. Nichols wrote, "Geography was chiefly American, and the United States was larger than all the universe. . . . We despised monarchical countries and governments too thoroughly to care much about their histories and if we studied them, it was that we might contrast their despotisms with our own free happy institutions. We were taught every day and in every way that ours was the freest, the happiest, and soon to be the greatest and most powerful country in the world."[1]

And in many ways, the superlatives were true, not only because of the millions of people who voluntarily migrated to this country, but also because they remained, with relatively few returning home or leaving for other countries. As one historian pointed out, the whole of America had become the frontier of the whole of the Old World.[2]

With the superlatives went racial, religious, and ethnic bigotry, rooted in ethnocentrism and xenophobia. As old and new Americans moved west and overseas, they transplanted their various bigotries onto others through territorial purchase, squatter occupation, and military conquest, lording over allegedly lesser peoples—Mexicans, Alaskans, and Caribbean and Pacific Islanders.

Throughout the nineteenth century, when America was at peace and prosperous, intergroup tensions and calls for immigration restriction and exclusion subsided. When economic depression, labor strife, war or the threat of war developed, however, Americans struck out against the supposed enemy within—alien or radical.[3] Generally, the worse the conditions, the more the vituperation against religious, racial, and ethnic groups, each of whom was charged with inability to assimilate, lowering wage standards, strikebreaking, and taking jobs away from the native-born. Not only did the latter oppose the foreign-born but various immigrant groups themselves distrusted each other, accusing subsequent immigrant groups and resident Blacks and Indians of the very faults they were accused of having. The result was an ever-repeating pattern of majority-group members disliking minority ones and the latter disliking each other.

Although prejudice and discrimination are rightfully blamed on the practices and beliefs of dominant groups, institutions, and government, they also resulted from minorities who brought their own bigotries with them to America and for the most part confronted each other for the first time under a government that both tolerated differences and provided a freedom to act out those differences. All, however, was not gloom and doom. The very conditions that spawned bigotry also fostered solutions for combating its many forms. How these processes played themselves out in the nineteenth century is the thrust of this chapter.

Immigrants, Migrants, and Motivations

Since the nation's founding, a rather permissive policy of admitting immigrants from more and more countries evolved, with all eligible for citizenship—except those not "free white persons," which for decades meant Blacks, Indians, and Asians. Whether on a state or federal level, such permissiveness embraced a constellation of competing humanitarian, selfish, and bigoted attitudes and policies.

Pragmatism usually prevailed. When needed to level forests, dig mines, fight Indians, inhabit uncultivated land, extend frontiers, guard boundaries, buy land, or work for low wages, business interests and state governments carried on extensive promotional campaigns for immigrants. When insufficient numbers arrived, assorted felons and Black slaves were forcibly brought over, though many criminals and ex-convicts arrived on their own.

The increasing populating of America could not have taken place without an abundance of land—free for the taking or inexpensive—as well as the continuous building of roads, waterways, railroads, and low-cost transatlantic travel. As early as 1817, a British visitor noted that "Old America seems to be breaking up, and moving westward" and that between Baltimore and Pittsburgh one is "seldom out of sight . . . of family groups behind and before us."[4] The only people going directly to the Pacific Coast were small numbers of Russians who established military and trading posts from Alaska to California, as well as a small group of Americans hired by John Jacob Astor to establish a fur-trading center in Oregon.

The first federal immigration statute, in 1819, was enacted because of unsafe and unsanitary transoceanic conditions. Regulatory rather than restrictive, it established rules on how many passengers in relation to a cargo a ship could carry and led to official immigration statistics being compiled. Even then, the early numbers were largely inaccurate because of careless record keeping by customs officials, lack of review by State Department officials, and nonrecording of many European immigrants coming from Canada.[5] As in colonial days, each state, particularly those with large ports, had its own immigration policies, over which the federal government gradually asserted primacy. In 1849, the Supreme Court declared New York and Massachusetts state laws taxing immigrants unconstitutional.

Unlike today, the total number of immigrants was relatively small, with fewer arrivals for the entire 1820–30 decade (some 150,000) than for almost every year since 1846. Even then, America was not the only country to receive immigrants. Far larger numbers left for other countries—250,000 Germans to Russia from 1818 to 1828 in contrast to 10,000 to America; and by the 1850s, almost as many Irish went to England as to America.[6]

The nineteenth century experienced two major westward transplantations of people—one from Europe and the other from America's East Coast to the Mid- and Far West. Though migrations within Europe and Asia involved large groups forced to move by a ruler or tyrant, migration to America was composed mainly of individuals and families who voluntarily uprooted themselves for a much-heard-of but unknown land.

Toward the century's end, European immigrants began being classified as the "old" or "new." The former referred to those coming before the late nineteenth century from the British Isles, Germany, Holland, and northwest Europe gener-ally, and were benignly defined as "permanent settlers."[7] By the 1870s, over two-thirds of the immigrants were still from those areas. Next came the new immigrants, mostly from Russia, Austria-Hungary, Poland, Italy, Greece, and the Balkans, representing some 70 percent of those coming between 1901 and 1910, with less than 15 percent from northwest Europe. Though often uncertain about remaining, eastern European immigrants arrived in ever-increasing numbers and percentages, so that although Austria-Hungary, Italy, and Russia supplied about 1 percent of the total immigration in 1869, they constituted 10 percent in 1882, and then 87 percent in 1907.[8]

Bridging both movements were a variety of smaller immigrant, migrant, so-journer, and gold-seeking groups. French Canadians came from Quebec in the 1840s and by 1900 numbered more than 500,000 in New England.[9] The 1848 discovery of gold in California triggered a multinational movement of tens of thousands of fortune seekers: Americans from the East and foreigners from Europe, Central America, South America, Asia, and Australia. Thousands of Mormons kept moving westward until they reached the Salt Lake Valley in the late 1840s. Icelanders arrived in the 1850s, and by 1900 numbered about 30,000—or 43 percent of Iceland's total population.[10] After the Civil War thou-sands of young men from the East went west. Chinese and Japanese from their respective homelands or Hawaii settled mainly in California.

A number of factors affected where immigrants settled: the ocean routes they took and their ports of arrival, the skills they brought with them, the locales of job recruiters and opportunities, the availability of land, the areas where kinsmen or family lived, the amount of money they brought with them, and the availability of riverboats, canals, or railways. For example, Yankee whaling ships determined the ports of arrival and settlements of the first wave of Portuguese immigrants in the early nineteenth century, particularly New Bedford and San Francisco. As the whalers followed the prevailing winds, they stopped at various ports in the Madeiras and Cape Verde to hire seamen to replace Yankees who had either not signed on in New England or had jumped ship en route, after which the newly hired often settled on the East or West Coasts.[11]

The movement of Germans to the Mississippi Valley and the Irish to New England followed, respectively, the cotton and timber trade routes across the ocean. The cotton trade channeled Germans to New Orleans, from where they moved north via inexpensive riverboats to such cities as St. Louis and Cincinnati. Many Irish went on lumber ships offering cheap transportation to Canada and then boarded gypsum ships sailing to New England, where land was easier to acquire and greater opportunities existed for year-round employment.[12] Within a few years after the Cunard Line made Boston a terminus in the 1840s, the Irish Catholic population zoomed to about one-third of the city, making it probably the highest proportion of all East Coast port cities.[13]

Although every major northern state doubled or tripled its foreign-born population in the last three decades of the nineteenth century, the percentage declined in the South from 4 percent in 1870 to less than 3 percent in 1900, with some states having only 1 percent.[14] Fewer immigrants settled in the South because the area preferred Black slaves and then cheap Black laborers, offered less employment and land opportunities, and generally proved more difficult to reach.[15] The one exception was New Orleans, which attracted a variety of immigrants—in addition to Acadians, Spanish, French, Italian, and Portuguese.

John Quincy Adams reflected the general attitude toward immigrants, saying:

> The multitude of foreigners who yearly flock to our shores, to take up here their abode, none come from affection or regard to land to which they are total strangers, and with the very language of which those of them who are Germans are generally unacquainted. We know that they come with views, not to our benefit but to their own—not to promote our welfare, but to better their own condition. We expect therefore very few, if any transplanted countrymen from classes of people who enjoy happiness, ease, or even comfort, in their native climes. The happy and contented remain at home, and it requires an impulse, at least as keen as that of urgent want, to drive a man from the soil of his nativity and the land of his fathers' sepulchres.[16]

And indeed, for the most part, the less-well-off came and often did so with unreal expectations and little, if any, knowledge of American government, laws, geography, or way of life. As early as 1784, Benjamin Franklin warned prospective immigrants that America was not a land where a fortune could easily be earned, nor a land where equipment, Black workers, and stocks of cattle were provided free of charge. "These are all wild imaginations," he wrote, "and those who go to America with expectations founded upon them will surely find themselves disappointed."[17]

Still, they came, rejecting Old Country economic, political, and/or social burdens and hoping for a new world of opportunities. Unlike the first Pilgrims, nineteenth-century immigrants did not come in highly organized groups, protected by compacts, but were largely on their own, carrying their possessions in satchels, backpacks, or pockets, always prey to robbers and corrupt officials. To a journalist in the 1840s, Bavarian immigrants were "a lamentable sight" traveling on the Strassburg road, with "long files of carts . . . every mile, carrying poor wretches, who are about to cross the Atlantic. . . . There they go slowly along; their miserable tumbrils—drawn by such starved, drooping beasts, that your only wonder is, how can they possibly hope to reach Havre alive—piled with scanty boxes containing their few effects. . . . One might take it for a convoy of wounded, the relics of a battlefield, but for the rows of little white heads peeping from beneath the ragged hoods."[18]

Early-nineteenth-century immigrant sailing ships could delay leaving port for weeks because of unfavorable weather or tides or lack of a full complement of passengers. Ever present were unscrupulous venders, boardinghouse proprietors, ship personnel, ticket agents, and money changers. In fact, some ship agents misled immigrants to board ships destined for countries other than America. For example, it has been suggested that the Syrian communities in Australia, South America, Mexico, the Caribbean, and Canada were started by immigrants who thought they had arrived in America.[19]

Once aboard ship, immigrants were confronted with filth, overcrowding, disease, and ruthless seamen. One observer of immigrant voyages noted that "it was a daily occurrence to see starving women and children fight for the food which was brought to the dogs and the pigs that were kept on the deck of the ship." A Welsh newspaper advised immigrants to "watch over your things on the last day aboard because there is every kind of creature here. Consider every man a thief until he proves the opposite."[20]

After surviving a voyage, which could last six weeks, immigrants had to face unscrupulous earlier immigrants, who flocked to the ports to steal their money, luggage, and possessions or lead them to hotels and boardinghouses that overcharged them. Hundreds of wharf thieves were known to board a single ship and prey upon unwary immigrants. In New Orleans and New York City, Irish societies sought city help in protecting single Irish females from procurers and dishonest employment agents and tried to encourage them to settle in the West where they would be safer.[21]

As *Harper's Weekly*, in 1858, described the pitiable situation of the arriving immigrant:

> Federal, State, and municipal authorities regarded him with as much indifference as if he had been a bale of cheap goods. Scoundrels of the very lowest caliber—emigrant runners—seized him, and made him their own. If he had any money, they robbed him of it. If he had a pretty wife or daughters, they stole them too, if they could. If he had neither money nor daughters, they merely took his luggage. It was well for him if, after having been robbed of all he had, he was not beaten to death, or entrapped into committing crimes which transferred him almost directly from the emigrant vessel to Blackwell's Island or the State Prison.[22]

Beyond port, months could pass before immigrants settled in an area, started to work, and accumulated sufficient money to lead a stable life. Longest in time to overcome were the attitudes of their new neighbors, which ranged from noblesse oblige to outright xenophobia. Even among those welcoming them, there was ambivalence or change of mind about their presence. At first, Jefferson feared they would "warp and bias" free government and "render it a heterogeneous, incoherent, distracted mass," but after becoming president, questioned whether we should "refuse to the unhappy fugitives from distress that hospitality which the savages of the wilderness extended to our fathers arriving in his land. . . . Shall oppressed humanity find no asylum on this globe?"[23]

Nevertheless, newspaper stories, letters, and word of mouth inspired poorer immigrants to go to America, particularly those with large families, which in Europe were a burden but in America an advantage because of the relative abundance of jobs and land. Their optimism was also related to their age, health, skills, marital status, friendliness of destination, and, above all, ability to adjust preemigration expectations with settling-down realities. Then, as now, the family that came and stayed together usually had the greatest chance of succeeding.

From the Pacific, a growing "Coolie traffic" was developing, in which Chinese laborers in debt, promised jobs, and/or given small advances were transported to America, South America, and the Caribbean. Voyages could last four months, on ships manned by brutal crewmen, where food and water were frequently inadequate.[24]

For political and religious refugees, it was better to be free and struggling in America than repressed or oppressed back home. For economic emigrants, opportunities were greater in America than in the Old Country, where jobs were fewer and class distinction greater. For the famished (particularly the Irish during the 1840s), food could be obtained and land cultivated. For criminals or ex-criminals, a new life could be begun, within or outside of the law.

Servants could become independent citizens or even masters. In fact, a visiting Scotswoman advised friends not to bring servants because within a "few weeks—nay, not unfrequently, a few days . . . finding themselves in a country where all men are placed by the laws on an exact level . . . they are transformed from the servants of their employer into his companions, and at one and the same moment lay aside obsequiousness and array themselves in insolence."[25]

For some women suffering discrimination, America offered freedom of professional choice; for example, after studying and working in a Berlin hospital, Marie Zakrzewska immigrated to America in 1853 "to show to those men who had opposed me so strongly . . . that in this land of liberty, equality, and fraternity, I could maintain that position which they would not permit to me at home."[26]

For most immigrants, optimism outweighed the pragmatic difficulties of moving, which were considerable, especially for adults who had to forfeit the security of friends and familiar places, overcome guilt feelings about having left aged parents or uprooting family members, learn a new language, and cope with the uncertainty of living in a strange land. "We have become strangers," wrote O.E. Rőlvaag, in 1911, "strangers to the people we forsook, and strangers to the people we came to. . . . The people we forsook, we remain apart from, and the people we came to, we also remain apart from. We have thus ceased to be an integral part of the larger whole; we have become something by ourselves, something torn off, without any organic connection either here or there."[27] For many, such strains and pains intensified their determination to succeed. Better in a new, though unknown, world than in the old and too-well-known one.

European governmental and church leaders frequently opposed any mass exodus of people. In the 1790s, would-be French immigrants were warned about phony land ventures and told that Americans were a vile, disease-ridden people, given to selling their daughters into prostitution. To a Swiss pastor, nothing seemed as grievous "as the headlong, irresponsible emigration of those heartless parents with their many little innocent children . . . as if under a spell and a desperate resolution since most of them were poor and had barely gotten together enough travel money." In Austria, local officials were told to prevent foreigners from recruiting laborers; and in Greece, the government ordered publication of warnings about the dangers of transatlantic voyages. A number of English immigrant guidebooks recommended going to English colonies rather than to America, where people were of "low cunning" and hated England, and where to be successful, immigrants had to bow "to the idol of Democracy, and vow eternal hatred to all hereditary rights."[28]

Such activities did not dissuade multitudes from flocking to America, where land was cheap, food plentiful, and jobs everywhere. More in keeping with their desires was the advice of an 1891 immigrant guidebook:

> Forget your past, your customs, and your ideals. Select a goal and pursue it with all your might. No matter what happens to you, hold on. You will experience a bad time but sooner or later you will achieve your goal. If you are neglectful, beware for the wheel of fortune turns quickly. You will lose your grip and be lost. . . . A final virtue is needed in America—called cheek. . . . Do not say, "I cannot; I do not know."

Another immigrant guidebook, published in Greek in 1908, advised arriving immigrants to bathe regularly, talk softly, and become dentists, who would prosper from repairing the teeth of Americans who ate too much candy.[29]

And so it was with countless people. Neither physical hardship, family separation, strange surroundings, nor bigotry stopped the pluralistic peopling of America. With the exception of foreign officers in search only of glory during the Revolutionary War, most came for existential reasons unrelated to any ancestral ties to the land or understanding of American values, geography, or government.

In stark contrast, Blacks were brought here against their will and had to struggle more than any other group to obtain their rights as citizens. They were a stigmatized group—segregated from and by White society with the blessings of social custom and state or federal law. "The ethnic group that was a way station, a temporary resting place for Europeans as they became Americans," wrote John Hope Franklin, "proved to be a terminal point for Blacks who found it virtually impossible to become American in any real sense."[30]

Ethnic and Racial Colonies

In addition to individuals and families immigrating on their own, various entrepreneurs (legal and unscrupulous), idealists, and ethnic groups came to establish communities, most of which never started or failed shortly afterward. Equally futile proposals and plans were launched to have American Blacks settle in the Far West or abroad.

In the late eighteenth century, New Smyrna was founded in Florida, where Greek immigrants hoped to cultivate vines, cotton, tobacco, silk, and other products, and where—because of their alleged prowess as rowers—they "might be of greatest service to the inland navigation of America." Instead of the hoped-for 500 Greek immigrants, only a small number came, as well as some Italians, and soon afterward, the colony dissolved.[31]

Nineteenth-century communalists—English, German, Swiss, French, Polish—had to obtain United States governmental permission and cooperation before settling, which at first was given ambivalently and then clearly denied. For example, in 1816, Franco-Americans concerned with their kinsmen in France asked Congress to sell them some land in Alabama on easy credit terms, promising to develop wine orchards and olive trees, thereby ending the need to import such products from Europe. Congress sold some land, but the project colony failed because of the inexperienced and underfinanced French immigrants who came.[32]

Hearing of the French project, Irish societies in New York, Philadelphia, and Baltimore also asked Congress for land under equally favorable terms. This time, however, Congress refused, believing that the Irish should not be given easier terms than Americans in acquiring land and that the establishment of ethnic enclaves would slow down the desired Americanization process. "The general law prescribes an open sale" of land, wrote Jefferson in 1817, "where all citizens may compete on an equal footing for any lot of land which attracts their choice. To dispense with this in any particular case requires a special law of Congress, and to special legislation we are generally averse, lest a principle of favoritism should creep in and prevent that of equal rights."[33]

It was in response to an inquiry from Baron von Furstenwaerther that John Quincy Adams, as secretary of state, in 1819, outlined the first formal expression of immigration policy, saying that America has never adopted any measure to *encourage* or *invite* emigrants from any part of Europe. It has never held out any incitements to induce the subjects of any other sovereign to abandon their own country, to become inhabitants of this. From motives of humanity it has occasionally furnished facilities to emigrants who, having arrived here with views of forming settlements, have specially needed such assistance to carry them into effect. . . . But there is one principle which pervades all the institutions of this country, and which must always operate as an obstacle to the granting of favors to new comers. This is a land, not of *privileges,* but of *equal rights.*[34]

A partial policy deviation occurred in 1834 when Congress agreed to allot some land in Illinois or Michigan to a few hundred Polish refugees of the 1830 insurrection against Tsar Nicholas I, but only on condition they pay $1.25 per acre, an offer not available to other Poles. Because of procedural delays in the granting process, however, as well as dissensions and rivalries among the immigrants themselves, the plan for a Polish colony was abandoned.[35] Twenty years later, however, the first Polish colony was established in East Texas, named Panna Maria in honor of the Virgin Mary.

Generally, any ethnic group wanting to settle and live together in one geographic area had to do so on its own. Secretary of State William H. Seward rejected a request to establish a Welsh colony on western lands as a constitutional part of the United States, and some years later, President Grant told a Russian Mennonite delegation exploring the possibility of settling in America that he would not exempt them from any possible military service because of their pacifist beliefs.[36] Indians, however, were often compelled as a group to live elsewhere. Between 1820 and 1844, some 100,000 were forced to leave their ancestral homes for resettlement west of the Mississippi.

Though individual Europeans were generally encouraged to enter America, their governments were told, indeed warned, by President Monroe not to establish settlements in Latin America or on the West Coast, where Russian expansionism from Alaska to Oregon and California was feared. In what came to be called the Monroe Doctrine, the president said that "the American continents . . . are henceforth not to be considered as subjects for future colonization by any European powers."[37]

Just as Europe fumed at the declaration, Latin America rejoiced and distributed it, only to have its requests for alliances and material aid rejected. Put simply, America was more interested in keeping Europeans out of the region than in helping those living in its bounds. Three years later, when invited to participate in a conference of Latin American countries, southern congressmen protested that it would be attended by "Negroes from Santo Domingo—where a great slave revolution had succeeded."[38]

At the same time, efforts continued to encourage freed Blacks to leave America, even in the South, where in 1827 the American Convention for Promoting the Abolition of Slavery (formed in the 1790s) had 130 local branches. Another organization, the American Colonization Society, formed in 1816, proposed the establishment of a colony of only free Blacks in Africa, with the financial help of government and citizen contributions. Deeply patriotic, the society attracted the support of slaveholders, missionaries, negrophobes, and abolitionists, each for its own reasons. Slaveholding members felt that repatriation would rid the country of free Blacks who might otherwise foment slave revolts or that it would increase the price of their slaves. Missionaries hoped Black colonizers would bring Christianity to the "Dark Continent" and make "her soil ready for the seeds of knowledge and piety." And a few abolitionists believed that not until all freed slaves were out of the country would slavery end. Meanwhile, according to the society's secretary, Elias B. Caldwell, Blacks should be kept "in the lower state of degradation and ignorance," because education would merely excite ambitions that could not be fulfilled.[39]

By then, some American Blacks began identifying with the accomplishments of ancient Africa, particularly Egypt, believing that they, as the world's most enlightened of their race, had a responsibility to help their homeland. One wealthy New England Black shipowner actually took thirty-eight free Blacks at his expense to Sierra Leone where he hoped they would Christianize the natives and help destroy the slave trade. Nevertheless, more White people than Black ones believed in colonization, and few Blacks volunteered to leave America. By 1830, the society resettled only 1,420 free Blacks to Liberia, and a decade later began declining (finally ceasing operation by 1912).[40]

There were also Whites and Blacks who urged that slaves be sent to Haiti, Canada, Mexico, South America, or the American West. As governor of Virginia, James Monroe urged Jefferson to adopt a plan to purchase land abroad where unruly Blacks would be shipped. Though Jefferson liked the idea and believed Blacks racially inferior, he felt they should not be sent to any area that might one day become part of the country, such as South and Central America. On becoming president, Monroe thought Blacks should be transferred at government expense to vacant territory in the West, but Henry Clay dissented, saying those areas would soon be overrun by "a wave of European races."[41]

For many freemen and abolitionists, colonization was repugnant. William Lloyd Garrison believed it "a libel upon humanity and justice—a libel upon republicanism—a libel upon the Declaration of Independence—a libel upon Christianity." Writing to the American Colonization Society, a group of Black freemen said, "Many of our fathers and some of us have fought and bled for the liberty, independence, and peace which you now enjoy, and surely it would be ungenerous and unfeeling in you to deny us a humble and quiet grave in that country which gave us birth."[42]

The irony of encouraging Blacks to leave while encouraging Europeans to enter was not unnoticed. "We are NATIVES of this country; we ask only to be treated as well as FOREIGNERS," proclaimed Peter Williams in an 1830 July Fourth celebration. "Not a few of our fathers suffered and bled to purchase its independence; we ask only to be treated as well as those who fought against it. We have toiled to cultivate it, and to raise it to its present prosperous condition; we ask only to share equal privileges with those who came from distant lands to enjoy the fruits of our labor."[43]

Also criticized was the hypocrisy of some abolitionists, such as groups that excluded Blacks as members, White abolitionists who invited Blacks to their home without introducing them to family members, or, as the *Colored American* wrote in 1837, those who "imagine they are free from prejudice against color, and yet are content with a lower standard of attainment for colored youth, and inferior exhibitions of talent on the part of colored men."[44]

In short, only Blacks were denied equal rights and only they were encouraged to leave, and only Indians were forcibly confined and relocated, while all European powers were warned not to intrude themselves into the Western Hemisphere.

Increasing Forms of Prejudice and Discrimination

The greater the diversity and numbers of immigrants, the closer they lived to other groups, and the more they competed for jobs and an equal access to the country's bounties, the more resident Americans feared what was happening to the country. Each group brought its own prejudices, which frequently clashed with those of earlier immigrant groups as well as native-born Americans. To defend the American—namely, Protestant—way of life, a host of national and local associations were created, such as the American Bible Society in 1816, the American Sunday School Union in 1824, the American Tract Society in 1825, the American Home Missionary Society in 1826, and the Society for the Promotion of Collegiate and Theological Education in the West in 1843. What they could not achieve by faith and persuasion, more militant and aggressive associations would try to achieve through force.

Also taking form were a number of pseudo sciences of phrenology, craniology, physiognomy, and ethnology, all of which divided people into races, which determined their attitudes, behaviors, intelligence and morals, and warned against any racial mixing of native-born Americans with Blacks, Indians, or immigrants, particularly the Irish.[45]

As in prior decades, immigrant criminals and their countries of origin were resented. In 1836, an American consul reported that the city of Hamburg periodically deported criminals "either condemned for life or a long period; they give them the choice either to endure their time or to emigrate; in which case the Government pays their passage." The consul in Basle noted that he had successfully put a stop to deportations of criminals by Switzerland and Baden.[46]

Poor immigrants were no less disliked. An 1838 congressional investigation described those arriving as a "most idle and vicious class; in their personal appearance the most offensive and loathsome; and their numbers increasing with such rapidity by emigration, as to become burdensome to the American people; our own citizens being obligated to contribute largely from their own earnings to support them in idleness."[47]

Just as recent Asian, South American, and Caribbean Island immigrants have been accused of criminality and causing diseases, so with past European immigrants. "They have brought the cholera this year, and they will always bring wretchedness and want," noted an early-nineteenth-century diarist. "The boast that our country is the asylum for the oppressed in other parts of the world is very philanthropic and sentimental, but I fear that we shall before long derive little comfort from being made the almshouse and refuge for the poor of other countries." To one hostile journalist, were it not for the "lazy and vicious emigrants from England and Ireland," almost all of "our prisons, our penitentiaries, and our almshouses" could be dispensed with. According to a government surveyor, French Canadians "have no more manners than the Indians—care nothing for schools—and are kept in ignorance by their Romanish priesthood."[48]

Such feelings did not preclude the United States Army from recruiting immigrants because native-born Americans were not enlisting in adequate numbers, and many of those who did were given to alcoholism or desertion, of which immigrants were less likely. Between 1821 and 1823, nearly one-fourth of the recruits were foreign-born. To an English visitor in the West, "The most worthless characters enter the army, which consists of a *melange* of English deserters, Dutch, French, Americans &c. Five dollars are the monthly pay of a private, and many laborers in the States earn a dollar per day."[49]

Politically, immigrants were relatively few in number and without any significant political power. In the early 1800s, Manhattan's Tammany Society was still anti–Irish Catholic, excluded immigrants from membership, and urged Americans to purchase only goods made in America. Their nascent associations, communities, and political activity generated fears of a mobocracy; James Fenimore Cooper accused immigrants of lacking "convictions of liberty" and the ability to "read the great social compact, by which society is held together."[50]

Behind the various criticisms was a "stranger anxiety"—an instinctive fear of strangers, particularly those speaking a foreign language. Catholic immigrants were charged with plotting to seize the country, undermine Protestantism, and destroy religious freedom. Anti-Catholic books, pamphlets and magazines proliferated. Differences over state aid to parochial schools and over whose Bible should be read in public schools helped trigger mob attacks and the burning of Catholic churches and convents. Boston's *Atlas* urged every "true American" employer to immediately "refuse to employ the miscreants, on any terms," forcing them to return "to their own benighted and miserable country." Not unusual was the *New York Evening Post* ad in 1830: "Wanted. A Cook or Chambermaid . . . must be American, Scotch, Swiss or African—no Irish." To avoid being identified as Catholics, Protestants from northern Ireland adopted the term *Scotch-Irish* in the 1840s; before then, they had called themselves *Ulstermen, Irish Presbyterians,* or simply Irishmen.[51]

In actuality, Catholics were still a minority, though a growing one, with little or no political power. In Boston, a diocesan paper castigated Protestant critics as "mendacious tract-mongers, mercenary Bible-mongers, peculating missionaries, and modern Pharisees . . . foul libelers, scurrilous scribblers and unprincipled calumniators." To charges of being unpatriotic, Boston's *Pilot* reminded readers that Benedict Arnold was not a Catholic and that during the Revolutionary War, "All of our foreign generals were Catholics," who "taught our fathers how to handle arms."[52]

Similar hostility was directed against Mormons and Masons, who were respectively considered more tyrannical and secret than the despised Roman Catholic church. Though developed in England and condemned by the pope as early as 1738, many Protestants denounced Masonry as "subversive of the laws of the country," an instrument of British intrigue, and an "infidel society" of French atheists, Jesuits, Jews, Mohammedans, and deists plotting to destroy Christianity and government.[53]

Such feelings, plus public outrage at the mysterious murder of a Masonic defector, led to the establishment of an anti-Masonic party in 1828 in New York, and three years later, to a national party and large number of anti-Masonic papers, particularly in New England, where Masons were excluded from Vermont town offices and juries. Though basically a New England phenomenon, anti-Masons also attracted rural supporters, who readily accepted wild stories about secret rituals and plots by Masons and Catholics.[54]

Intergroup conflict was frequent from the 1830s to 1850s, with at least thirty-five major riots in Baltimore, Philadelphia, New York, and Boston. In one three-year period, 1834–37, some 157 acts of mob violence occurred. In Philadelphia, in 1844, Protestants invaded an Irish-Catholic neighborhood and burned down over thirty homes and two churches, killing or injuring some fourteen people. A few months later, a similar clash left thirteen dead and more than fifty wounded. In areas like Kentucky, Maryland, New Jersey, and Ohio, German Americans were damned as godless and Hessians, and at times physically attacked for their alleged self-segregation and opposition to slavery, temperance, and Sabbatarian laws.[55] Such feelings did not prevent the election of Martin Van Buren, the first president of non-English descent, who spoke Dutch and was born after the Declaration of Independence had been signed.

The Development of Prejudice in the West

Meanwhile, in the West, other forms and combinations of intergroup hostility erupted against Mormons, Mexicans, Indians, and "gold rushers."

Latter-Day Saints, or Mormons

From its inception by Joseph Smith in 1830, the Church of Jesus Christ of Latter-Day Saints (Mormon) was subjected to religious persecution and forced flight by those it termed *Gentiles*. Most Mormons were as native-born as their oppressors, who accused them of clannishness, sexual promiscuity, sadism, wanting to free slaves, being too friendly to Indians, and seeking political domination. Their industriousness and intense religious convictions, particularly about polygamy, added to their being disliked. In New York, Ohio, Missouri, and Illinois, mobs frequently burned their homes, dispersed their cattle, and tarred and feathered their leaders.

"The Mormons must be treated as enemies," declared the governor of Missouri, in 1838, "and must be exterminated or driven from the state, if necessary, for the public good." And indeed they were, with thousands leaving for Illinois, "the old and young, the sick and feeble, delicate women and suckling children, almost without food and without clothing . . . compelled to abandon their homes . . . farms were sold for a yoke of oxen, an old wagon or anything that would furnish means of transportation."[56]

As harassments and attacks continued, Mormons became more defiant. In what became known as the Mormon Declaration of Independence, they said, "We are weary of being smitten, and tired of being trampled upon . . . from this day and this hour, we will suffer it no more. And that mob that comes on us to disturb us, it shall be between us and them a war of extermination; for we will follow them until the last drop of their blood is spilled; or else they will have to exterminate us."[57]

In 1844, after Joseph Smith ordered his followers to destroy a newspaper critical of him, he and his brother were arrested and brutally killed by a raging mob in Carthage, Illinois. Shortly afterward, Brigham Young led some 16,000 Mormons into what was still Mexican territory—the Salt Lake Valley—where they began building their New Zion, far from Gentile persecution.

Though generally friendly to the Indians, whom they considered remnants of a lost tribe of Israel, Mormons knowingly trespassed and settled on their lands, believing they were bringing a higher civilization. Strong efforts were made to convert them, and Mormon settlements set aside land for them on which to live and work. In fact, to some Indians, Mormons were preferable to other White people and other Indians, who raided their camps and sold their captured or kidnapped children to White traders from New Mexico, or to anyone who wanted them. Artist Solomon Nunes Carvalho described one such sale to Brigham Young: "They were prisoners, and infants of the Snake Indians, with whom the Utahs were at war. . . . They were almost living skeletons . . . Young intended to send them to Salt Lake City, and have them cared for and educated like his own children."[58]

Mormon isolation from Gentiles eroded after America took possession of the Salt Lake Valley through the Treaty of Guadalupe-Hidalgo, which ended the Mexican War. Meanwhile, they continued to seek converts and settlers from all parts of the world, particularly from England, Scandinavia, and Germany. Attempts were even made to attract Jews and Chinese, and missions were sent to

Jerusalem and China, only to be aborted. Through their Perpetual Emigrating Fund, some 50,000 European immigrants were brought to Utah between 1850 and 1887.[59]

Like seventeenth-century New England Puritans, Mormons insisted upon orthodoxy of belief. "They will not extend to others the privileges which they claim for themselves," wrote a visiting journalist at the time. "They assert the right to worship God after their own fashion, yet do their best to exclude from Utah all who reject the Book of Mormon." In disgust, Sven Aarestad wrote his brother, a newly converted Mormon, "If you have become a Catholic, Methodist or Baptist I could have given you my blessing . . . but these horrendous Mormons who do not deserve to be called Christians! It makes my hair stand on end."[60]

Mainline Protestant churches—particularly Baptist, Presbyterian, Methodist, and Congregationalist—joined in the criticism. One leading Baptist evangelist denounced Mormonism as un-American and anti-America, "based on a bogus book, rotten revelations, tricky translations, a profligate prophet, a counterfeit creed . . . propagated by a profiting president, abetting apostles, bigoted bishops and plundering priests."[61]

Anti-Mormon passions culminated in 1857, when President Buchanan ordered 25,000 troops in Utah to affirm federal rule. In a blistering proclamation, he told Mormons,

> The land you live upon was purchased by the United States and paid for out of their Treasury; the proprietary right and title to it is in them, and not in you. Utah is bounded on every side by States and Territories whose people are true to the Union. It is absurd to believe that they will or can permit you to erect in their very midst a government of your own, not only independent of the authority which they all acknowledge, but hostile to them and their interests. . . . The Constitution and laws of this country can take no notice of your creed, whether it be true or false. That is a question between your God and yourselves, in which I disclaim all rights to interfere.[62]

As tensions escalated, Mormons not only fought United States troops, but some of them, in collusion with local Indians, in 1857, committed what has been called, "the Mountain Meadows Massacre," wherein 120 civilian men, women, and children were slaughtered as they were passing through the area on the way to California. Mormon ethnocentrism more frequently reflected itself in not selling land or water rights to Gentiles, not patronizing Gentile stores, and threatening to expel any Mormon who associates with Gentiles or sends his children to Gentile schools.[63]

Relations softened somewhat during the Civil War, though Brigham Young damned both sides, saying that if the Lincoln administration asked him "for a thousand men, or even five hundred," he "would see them damned first and then they could not have them."[64] Uncertain about their loyalty, the Union established Fort Douglas outside Salt Lake City.

In the following decades, the Congress passed various laws outlawing bigamy and plural marriages, which resulted in hundreds of Mormons being fined, arrested, and imprisoned, in addition to those who fled the reach of lawmen. The 1887 Edmunds-Tucker Act went so far as to disenfranchise Mormon voters, disincorporate their church, and confiscate church property; moreover, courts frequently denied Mormon immigrants citizenship. Finally, in 1890, yielding to governmental pressure and harassment, the Mormon church officially renounced polygamy, and six years later, Utah was admitted as the forty-fifth state.

Mexican Americans

Farther south, a longer-lasting pattern of intolerance evolved as American settlers gradually took over an entire Mexican area and people, just as the latter's ancestors had done to the Indians. Even before the Anglo invasion from the north, the residents born in Spain (Gachupines) discriminated against Mexican-born residents (Creoles), and both groups discriminated against the Indians and the offspring of Creoles and Indians (Mestizos). By the 1820s, Spain had sold Florida to the United States and had been dethroned in the Southwest by rebellious Mexicans, thereby ending her imperial presence in continental America.

Whether under Spanish or Mexican rule, Indians were treated as serfs, ever subject to the religious intolerance and brutality of their Spanish-speaking overlords. Raids on Indian villages were frequent, as were forced baptism and labor. As one early-nineteenth-century observer wrote:

> The process is, to raise a posse and drive in as many of the untamed natives as are requisite, and to compel them to assist in working the land. A pittance of food, boiled wheat or something of the kind, is fed to them in troughs, and this is the only compensation which is allowed for their services. Their condition is worse than that of the Peons of Yucatan, and other parts of Mexico.[65]

The first Americans came to the Southwest after the War of 1812, when New England traders established ties with the Spanish in California and Mexico and with the Russians in Alaska. Texas, however, attracted the largest number of immigrants and squatters.

At first, Mexican immigration policies encouraged their coming. Though mainly southerners, Protestants, and slaveholders or advocates, they had to swear loyalty to Mexico, convert to Catholicism, or, at the very least, refrain from practicing Protestantism. By 1834, Anglo numbers grew to some 35,000—ten times that of the resident Mexicans, whom they felt were inferior. Conflict was inevitable as Americans bought or illegally took over large amounts of acreage, sought local self-government, practiced or advocated slavery in contravention of Mexican law, and resented Mexico's denying non-Catholics the right of public worship.

When Mexico sent troops into the area to strengthen its control, the Americans rebelled, resulting in brutality and bloodshed on both sides. The Mexican army defeated and killed all the defenders of the Alamo and then, two weeks later, executed more than 300 Americans who had surrendered in the belief that their lives would be spared.

Because the Americans were either legal immigrants or intruders, their vaunted revolution in 1836 was actually a foreign insurrection, which gave birth to the Lone Star Republic, whose first laws validated slavery. Passions, prejudices, and hostilities, however, did not cease. The Alamo was remembered and American expansionism—including slavery—did not end. When President Polk futilely sought to purchase the New Mexico and California territories, Representative David Wilmot also futilely introduced a resolution prohibiting slavery, utilizing the language of the 1787 Northwest Ordinance.

With the outbreak of war in 1846 between Mexico and America, resident Mexicans were attacked, robbed, and generally treated as enemies by American soldiers and settlers. Indians in the area were treated no better.

The *New York Evening Post* editorialized in 1847 that "the Mexicans are *Aboriginal Indians,* and they must share the destiny of their race." To the *New Englander,* the war would "result in a great good to the world—to this country— to Mexico herself—to the cause of learning, good government, and religion." To Albert Gallatin, however, an octogenarian at the time, such argumentation was a "shallow attempt to disguise unbounded cupidity and ambition." The reality of what was taking place was noted by a few military officers. To Ulysses S. Grant, a lieutenant in the invading army, the war was the "most unjust ever waged by a stronger against a weaker nation."[66]

At the same time, anti-Catholicism reached into the military, in which Catholic soldiers were subjected to bitter prejudice, so much so that President Polk appointed Catholic military chaplains to service their needs, much to the further resentment of nativists who denounced Mexico for being a Catholic country and plotting to poison American soldiers. Well aware of such bigoted attitudes, Mexican officials encouraged American Catholics (as well as others) to desert, offering them money and acreage and saying that American Protestants were part of a Masonic plot to destroy the Catholic church. Written in English, a Mexican propaganda broadside asked the "Sons of Ireland" how they could "fight by the side of those who put fire in your temples in Boston and Philadelphia? Come over to us! May Mexicans and Irishmen, united by the sacred ties of religion and benevolence, form only one people." In all, some 250 soldiers, mostly recent immigrants, defected to the Mexican army, where they formed the San Patricio battalion, all of whom were killed—or captured and hanged—during the last days of the war.[67]

On the home front, many Americans thought the war cruel and motivated by a desire to extend slavery. Protestant churches differed, with Congregationalists, Unitarians, and Quakers strongly opposing the war, while Baptists and Methodists strongly supported it. Other denominations were lukewarm or neutral, as were Episcopalians and Lutherans. In protest, Henry Thoreau refused to pay his town taxes and willingly went to jail, declaring that Americans "must cease to hold slaves and to make war on Mexico." Southerners like John Calhoun opposed the war and the annexation of Mexico, but only because the territory was economically unsuited for slavery and its Mexican, Indian, and Mestizo residents were racially inferior. Resenting charges of disloyalty, a Boston Irish newspaper began publishing the official list of deserters, many more of whom were native-born than foreign-born.[68]

The war ended with the Treaty of Guadalupe-Hidalgo in 1848, whereby America obtained land enough subsequently to form five states and parts of two others, with no restrictions on introducing slavery. Just as the Spaniards had rendered the Indians outcasts and kept Mexicans in peonage, American expansionists now treated them with no less contempt or cruelty. Furthermore, rights that Indians had had under Mexican rule were abrogated when California became part of the United States.[69] After Mexico and America signed their peace treaty, gold was discovered in California, intensifying the bitterness of the former Mexican owners and attracting a new onslaught of greedy Americans.

Indians

No sooner had the Revolutionary Army been disbanded than Congress realized that a regular army was needed to protect the frontiers against Indian incursions and resentments, as well as against British and Spanish maneuverings to limit American expansionism. Now, the surrounding western and southern areas—like the Revolution itself—served as a major military training ground, national unifying force, and political springboard for a number of army officers, such as Andrew Jackson and William Henry Harrison.

Though treaties and formal address continued to call Indians "friends and brothers," "red brethren," and "members of the great American family," and though almost 350 treaties with 53 tribes were made between 1778 and 1837, government troops and civilians had few qualms about violating agreements and victimizing signatories. As a Moravian missionary noted in 1818, Mohicans and related tribes were "destroyed by wars, and carried off by the small pox and other disorders, and great numbers have died in consequence of the introduction of spirituous liquors among them."[70]

It was the Indians, however, who continued to be blamed for what befell them—their inability to recognize the White man's higher civilization, their intertribal feuds and wars, their filth and alcoholism, and their refusal to work the land. Indians, of course, viewed their plight differently—and correctly so. The *Cherokee Phoenix* (published in Georgia) stated that the blame was neither theirs nor "the will of Heaven, nor simply in the intercourse of Indians with civilized man; but they were precisely such causes as are now attempted by the state of

Georgia; by infringing upon their rights; by disorganizing them, and by circumscribing their limits."[71]

In his first message to Congress, President Monroe rationalized the taking of Indian land, declaring that "the earth was given to mankind to support the greatest number of which is capable, and no tribe of people have a right to withhold the wants of others more than is necessary for their support and comfort."[72] Nevertheless, he believed that Indians should not be relocated against their will.

Political philosophy became cruel law when, in 1823, Chief Justice Marshall nullified the right of Indians to "complete sovereignty, as independent nations," because of the "fundamental principle that discovery gave exclusive title to those who made it. However extravagant the pretension of converting the discovery of an inhabited country into conquest may appear," he said, "if the principle has been asserted in the first instance, and afterwards sustained; if a country has been acquired and held under it; if the property of the great mass of the community originates it, it becomes the law of the land and cannot be questioned."[73]

This led to further discriminatory laws. In 1830, Congress passed the Indian Removal Act, enabling the president to exchange land west of the Mississippi for land in the east. Removal rather than conversion, and exclusion rather than assimilation, became government policy as tens of thousands of Indians were compelled to give up homes, farms, and livestock.

As with the sixteenth-century Spanish, a few governmental and religious leaders opposed such actions. John Quincy Adams said that relocation violated government obligations to protect Indians. Edward Everett rejected assurances that in the fertile West, far from White people, Indians would flourish, saying that if the land were that good, settlers would soon immigrate there and displace them; and instead of having a "permanent home," Indians would have a "mere holding-place—half-way house on the road to the desert."[74]

Might, however, transcended right. For those hesitating or refusing to leave, United States Army troops, militias, and local White bigots resorted to intimidation, bribery, and violence. First to go were the Choctaw in Alabama and Mississippi. By 1834, close to 13,000 were relocated west of the Mississippi River. Though most White people were delighted, the *Vicksburg Daily Sentinel* compassionately noted:

> They are going away! With a visible reluctance which nothing has overcome but the stern necessity they feel impelling them, they have looked their last on the graves of their sires—the scenes of their youth, and have taken up their slow toilsome march with their household goods among them to their new homes in a strange land. They leave names to many of our rivers, towns, and counties, and so long as our State remains the Choctaws who once owned most of her soil will be remembered.[75]

Next were the Creeks, whose lands White speculators wanted. When they resisted (the Creek War of 1836), the United States Army forced them to relocate—their warriors handcuffed and chained. The following year, the Chickasaws were forced to leave. The most resistant were the Cherokees, most of whom lived on Georgia land where gold had been discovered. Though the Supreme Court had upheld their ancestral land rights, President Jackson defiantly ordered their relocation. Harassed by White greedy Georgians and surrounded by army troops, some 16,000 Cherokees, including their Black slaves, were directed west on what became known as the Trail of Tears, where at least one-fourth died of disease, hardship, and starvation, much in the manner of French Acadians a century earlier. A soldier participating in the removal observed:

> Men working in the fields were arrested and driven to the stockades. Women were dragged from their homes by soldiers whose language they could not understand. Children were often separated from their parents and driven into the stockades with the sky for a blanket and the earth for a pillow. And often the old and infirm were prodded with bayonets to hasten them to the stockades.[76]

The Seminoles in Florida, which America purchased from Spain in 1819, refused to be relocated and fled to the swamplands. Unlike the prior relocations, the presence of Blacks among the Seminoles intensified resistance. Not only were there Blacks who had fled White masters but also those whom the Seminoles had purchased as slaves. The Seminoles did not want to lose their possessions, nor move to the area allocated them—among the Creek Indians.[77]

With the help of other Indian troops (including a few Seminoles), it took the army some six years to vanquish and transport the Florida Indians to the West, except for a small number who hid in the Everglades, where a few of their descendants still reside. Excluded from the forced relocation were Seminoles of Black descent, who were sold as slaves. In Texas, some two decades after winning independence from Mexico in 1836, every major Indian tribe had been driven out. As Waco Indian chief Kakakatish lamented, "The soil I now stand upon was once mine; it is now the land of the Texans. I am now here on this soil, where in my young days I hunted the buffalo and red deer in peace, and was friendly with all, until the Texan came and drove me from my native land."[78]

Legal efforts were also made to dispossess Indians believed to be Blacks because of intermarriage and miscegenation. In a petition to the Virginia legislature in 1843, the White inhabitants of King William County argued that the land claims of the Pamunkies no longer existed because their blood had "so largely mingled with that of the negro race as to have obliterated all the striking features of Indian extraction. Your petitioners . . . protest this dangerous and anomalous condition, for it has assumed all the feature of legally established body of free negroes . . . the harbor for runaway slaves. . . . They could be easily converted into an instrument of deadly annoyance to the white inhabitants by northern fanaticism."[79]

The net result was that while in 1820 some 125,000 Indians lived east of the

Mississippi, by 1844 less than 30,000 remained.[80] No matter where they lived, surcease of oppression was assured them only in the next world, but only if they became Christians.

Just as with earlier European clergy, so now American Protestant missionaries competed among themselves (and with Catholic missionaries) "to christianize the Heathen in North America, and to support and promote Christian Knowledge" in the new western settlements. As early as 1819, the government established a federal Civilization Fund to enlighten Indians, which was believed best done by Christian missionaries, such as Baptists, Moravians, Episcopalians, Presbyterians, and Roman Catholics, who all promptly applied for funds.[81]

In describing missionary activities in the Northwest Territory, Alexander Ross, who had married an Indian, wrote that it was not uncommon

> to see the pious and persevering evangelist, after undergoing every hardship to open a new field for his labors among the heathen, followed after by some weak zealot of another sect who had not energy or courage of himself to lead, but who no sooner reaches the cultivated vineyard of his precursor than he begins the work of demoralization and injustice by denying the creed and labors of his predecessor, clothes some disaffected chief, and infuses animosity and discord among all parties, in order to get a footing and establish himself.[82]

At times, Protestant missionaries accused their Catholic counterparts of conspiring with Indians against white Protestant settlers to gain control of the West for Rome.

Indian dislocation and destruction were not all due to the Spanish movement north from Mexico and the colonial American movement west, but also to French Canadians moving south into the Ohio Valley region down the Mississippi; to Americans moving into the southeast and then southwest into Texas, New Mexico, Arizona, and California; and to Russians edging down from Alaska to California. The American movement from the East Coast was more massive in numbers of people and military force, and ultimately more devastating.

Creeping Expansionism and Prejudice

Whether as British subjects, revolutionaries, or newly independent people, Americans longed for the lands of others. Neither rivers, valleys, or mountains were too wide, deep, or high to stop them, nor could any Indian, Mexican, or European power or combination of powers. If not by purchase, then by encroachment, fraud, conquest, and missionizing, they moved forward, taking their values and prejudices with them and denying those in their way the very freedoms, equality, and self-rule for which they themselves had fought.

During and after the Revolutionary War, they hungrily eyed Florida, Canada, and Nova Scotia, claiming they were needed for national security, economic well-being, and ordained destiny. After stressing the value of Canada and Nova Scotia for American fisheries, Samuel Adams said that "these, say some, are not Part of the United States, and what Right should *we* have to claim them? The Cession of those Territories would prevent any Views of Britain to disturb our Peace in future and cut off a Source of corrupt British Influence which issuing from them, might diffuse Mischiefe and Poison thro the States."[83]

When Spain ceded the vast Louisiana Territory to Napoleon in 1800, Jefferson and others became alarmed, wanting neither country to control the Mississippi, along which Americans were settling and prospering. "It belongs *of right* to the United States to regulate the future destiny of *North America,*" commented a *New York Evening Post* writer. "The country is *ours; ours* is the right to its rivers and to all the sources of future opulence, power and happiness, which lay scattered at our feet; and we shall be the scorn and derision of the world if we suffer them to be wrested from us by the intrigues of France." Federalists, however, feared that obtaining the territory would further diminish their political power by opening it to "the Gallo-Hispano-Indian *omnium gatherum* of savages and adventurers."[84] To Napoleon, who needed funds to maintain his war with England, it was better to sell the area to America than have it possibly taken over by the British.

With our purchase for a mere $15 million, almost doubling America's size and ending French influence in continental America, came a multiplicity of different people. New Orleans, wrote an observer at the time, was "a confused mixture, a shapeless composition of people of all countries and of all professions: Creoles of the country, French, Spanish, English, Americans, Germans, Italians, etc., a veritable tower of Babel. Here one can scarcely be understood by his neighbor; and the only language intelligible here to these diverse beings is that of self-interest."[85]

Although Americans had fought the Revolutionary War to establish a government with powers derived "from the consent of the governed," they quickly denied the same to Louisiana Territory residents, who were, as Jefferson said, "as yet as incapable of self-government as children." Absolute rule was to prevail, which one critic termed a "complete despotism." In defense of such behavior, a congressman argued that "the principles of liberty can not suddenly be ingrafted on a people accustomed to a regimen of a directly opposite hue. The approach of such a people must be gradual." To the French residents, however, the incoming Americans were a rootless, self-seeking "peuple sans loix ni discipline."[86]

Farther north, New Englanders settling in the Detroit area viewed French residents as "generally poor wretches . . . a lazy, idle people" and those living in the nearby marshes, "muskrat Frenchmen," who disgracefully lived with Indian women. Reciprocally, the French complained that the "age of the practical, hardworking, money-getting Yankee is upon us, and the careless, laughter-loving Frenchman's day is over."[87]

American territorial ambitions were temporarily thwarted during the War of 1812, which for England was secondary to her fierce conflict with France in Europe. Both England and France blockaded each other and opposed any third parties supplying the other. For a second time, Americans were in a state of war, fueled by Britain's seizing of American merchant ships and sailors, by Britain's and Spain's arming and encouraging Indians' belligerence toward American frontier settlements, and by congressional War Hawks desiring to acquire Canada, Florida, and western territories.

With the outbreak of hostilities, all British males over fourteen years old were required to register with the nearest United States marshal, with whom some 10,000 did, while others were interned, particularly in New York City and Charleston, South Carolina. The Shawnees, Creeks, Seminoles, and some others sided with the British, whom they continued to prefer to encroaching Americans. Reciprocal brutality was common. In one battle, General Andrew Jackson's forces massacred more than 500 Creeks, whose dead were tabulated by cutting off their noses and placing them in a pile, while their bodies were skinned and tanned for the production of souvenirs. On the western frontier, more Indians than Whites served the British, whose appointment of Shawnee Chief Tecumseh as a brigadier general further embittered Americans, who saw a redcoat behind every redskin.[88] His defeat and death at the Battle of Thames ended all possibility of an Indian sovereign territory in the Ohio Valley region.

As during the Revolutionary War, racial, ethnic, and religious factors were at work, as well as inter-Indian rivalries and warfare. Unlike many other tribes, Cherokees enthusiastically helped General Jackson, though, as noted earlier, that did not stop him as president from ordering their relocation to Oklahoma. Blacks were again reluctantly enrolled in the army and navy, and New York authorized the creation of two Black regiments; others fled to join the British, who promised them freedom. In Louisiana, Jackson mustered the support of local French, Creoles, pirates, and free Blacks, to whom (much to local White resentment) he offered equal pay and benefits in forming a Battalion of Free Men of Color. To Jackson, it was better to have Blacks in his ranks than in the ranks of the enemy.[89]

Religiously, Congregationalist and Presbyterian church leaders opposed our entering the war, believing that to do so would help Catholic France and the anti-Christ Napoleon. "It seems to be morally impossible that any man of real piety ... should pray for the downfall of England ... or that France might get ascendency over her," said Isaac Brahman. Methodist and Baptist clergy, reflecting frontier settlers and lower-income levels of society, generally supported the war.[90]

Anti–Irish Catholic and anti-immigrant passions and charges of group disloyalty escalated at the Federalist convention in Hartford, where New England delegates demanded constitutional amendments expanding state powers and barring naturalized citizens from holding federal office. Elsewhere, Federalists and other war opponents accused President Madison of being a tool of the French, and some New England governors refused to allow their militias to serve beyond their respective state boundaries.

With the Treaty of Ghent, in 1814, relations with England returned to the antebellum status quo. Though the war was unpopular and brought no new land for America, it made life less dangerous for those living on the frontiers, trading with the Indians, or wanting to take over Indian, British, and Spanish lands. Indian power was sharply reduced, as was the influence of their British and Spanish allies, who now had to confront a growing American standing army. At best, the war contributed to a rising sense of nationalism and armed might and inspired the writing of the "Star-Spangled Banner" (which in 1931 became our official national anthem). For the Federalist Party, it marked the beginning of its end, four years later.

In the Southeast, in 1819, America intimidated Spain into ceding East and West Florida. England, too, succumbed to American pressure, ceding Oregon Territory up to the 49th parallel, though American expansionists had demanded much more territory.

As more and more people, including New Englanders and European immigrants, moved south to Mississippi and Alabama, west to Indiana and Illinois, and northwest to Oregon, they overwhelmed, if not killed, all Indian and animal life in their path, creating seventeen new states between 1812 and the outbreak of the Civil War. By 1830, almost 25 percent of the population lived west of the Appalachians, and by 1850, about half. America's westward movement was unstoppable, and by the time of the Civil War, about one-fourth of the population lived in a state other than the one in which they were born.[91]

In the Far Northwest, which was under Russian control, the plenitude of whale oil and baleen attracted a variety of American traders and seamen, including Portuguese, Scandinavians, Germans, Spaniards, Englishmen, and Irishmen. American expansion there was by sea, not by train or wagon as to the West. The Russian minister in Washington, D.C., hoped that after the Americans had invaded the Southwest, the lack of resources in Alaskan colonies "would keep them safe from the greed of freebooters, but it was not so. Although the fish, the furs, some other comparatively insignificant products of our possessions certainly did not measure up to the rich valleys of the Mississippi and Rio Grande, nor to the gold-bearing plains of California, they did not escape the covetousness of the Americans." And, indeed, once Alaska was purchased in 1867, large numbers of Americans entered it in pursuit of land, fur, fish, and minerals, and treated the natives with almost the same harshness as had the Russians. There, too, various American missionizing groups competed with each other and with remaining Russian Orthodox clergy for native members.[92]

In short, a process of creeping occupation and incorporation of other people's lands was taking place, which many Americans defended as "Manifest Destiny," a phrase coined in 1845 by the editor of the *Democratic Review,* who claimed the entire continent had been "allotted by Providence for the free development of our yearly multiplying millions." Such self-righteousness and lust for neighboring lands did not dampen traditional American sympathy for revolutionary movements. The presence of tens of thousands of European immigrants from despotic governments intensified public support for Polish and Hungarian attempts to free themselves respectively of Russian and Austrian rule. Aid committees were formed to collect funds to purchase arms for Polish fighters in the 1830s. Two decades later, public support for Hungary swelled when the revolutionary leader Louis Kossuth visited the country. As a congressman from Ohio declared: "If I was authorized to speak for the whole American people, and had the voice of ARTICULATE THUNDER, I would tell the despotic Governments of Europe that henceforth in contests for liberty ... there must be no such interference as there has been in the past."[93]

To many Europeans, however, Americans were not that gifted, idealistic, or credible—not when we ruthlessly took other people's lands, practiced slavery and lynchings, had citizens and legislators who fought duels, and were ignorant of European life. While touring America in 1857, the Norwegian jurist Ole Munch Raeder was dismayed that "three-fourths of the people in the East and ninety-nine hundredths of the people in the West are fully convinced that the other side of the Atlantic is nothing but a heap of medieval feudal states ... and have not enough vitality to rise from the abyss of misery and corruption into which they have fallen as the result of centuries of ignorance and despotism."[94]

Meanwhile, Protestant clergy and missionizing societies, convinced of their "chosenness," preached the Gospel abroad as at home. Envious of English missionizing in the Pacific Islands, they created in 1810 the American Board of Commissioners for Foreign Missions. Hawaii was believed part of the "promised land," though not possessed. Thus, at the ordination of two Hawaii-bound missionaries, the Reverend Heman Humphrey said, "As the nation of Israel was militant, so is the church now. As the land of Canaan belonged to Israel in virtue of a divine grant, so does the world belong to the church. And as God's chosen people still had much to do before they could come into full and quiet possession of the land, so has the church a great work to accomplish in subduing the world 'to the obedience of Christ.'" Some of the wives were missionaries, too, and when their children passed six years of age, they were sent back home on the mainland for schooling, rather than chance being contaminated by the values and behaviors of native Hawaiian children. Two decades later, the board established its first mission to Armenians in Turkey.[95]

Similar triumphalism led to the establishment in 1820 of the American Society for Meliorating the Condition of the Jews, which sought to convert Jews and establish a colony in America for European Jewish converts who had not been accepted by other Christians. Four years later, the society had more than 200 branches from Maine to Georgia, but few converts. Not only did Jews resent their activities, but so did some Christian groups, who feared successful missionizing might lead to the emergence of a powerful Jewish settlement that would menace their own faith.[96]

Admiration for ancient Israel did not preclude the State Department from engaging in anti-Jewish practices, though for political expediency. Some two years after being appointed consul to the North African Barbary States, Mordecai Noah, a prominent New York Jewish political and community leader, was summarily dismissed by Secretary of State James Monroe, who wrote him that when appointed, "it was not known that the religion which you profess would form any obstacle to the exercise of your Consular functions." President Madison's explanation was more explicit: "the ascertained prejudices of the Turks" against Judaism.[97]

The Gold Rush and Minority Crush

The discovery of gold in California initiated a rush of transcontinental migrants and transoceanic immigrants, broadening the area's pattern of intergroup bigotry. In large part it was a replay of the dishonorable cast of characters who had come to colonial America, only this time motivated solely by a desire for instant wealth. Among them, noted an observer, were "vagabonds from every quarter of the globe. Scoundrels from nowhere, rascals from Oregon, pickpockets from New York, accomplished gentlemen from Europe, interlopers from Lima and Chile, Mexican thieves, gamblers of no particular spot, and assassins manufactured in hell for the expressed purpose of converting highways and byways into theaters of blood." Smaller numbers of women and children came. About one-fourth of the women were prostitutes, either from the East Coast or Mexico, Chile, France, and even China.[98]

Books, pamphlets, newspaper stories, and word-of-mouth reports swept America and the world. For example, in Norway, stories multiplied of the profusion of available gold, with such how-to publications appearing as *An Account of California and Its Riches of Gold, Including a Map of California.* In Portugal, a booklet said California teemed with gold, precious metals, and "innumerable throngs of people . . . from every quarter of the globe . . . entirely employed in the exploitation of gold."[99]

Most were Americans who had crossed the continent either by horse and wagon, by boat to Panama and trudgery through the jungle to ships on the Pacific Coast to take them north, or by sailing from the east on the long voyage around Cape Horn to California. The most dangerous route was across Panama, where countless numbers died of cholera, dysentery, fever, or smallpox.[100]

In 1849, some 100,000 arrived, including some 8,000 Mexicans, 5,000 South Americans, and several thousand Europeans and Asians. By May of 1849, at least ninety abandoned ships were in San Francisco's harbor because their crews and captains had joined the passengers in search of gold. In the early half of 1852, twenty-eight boats of Chinese miners arrived from China and one from Mexico. "Every part of the State was overrun, as it were, in a day," wrote a commissioner of Indian affairs. "All, or nearly so, of the fertile valleys were seized; the mountain gulches and ravines were filled with miners; and without the slightest recognition of the Indians' rights, they were dispossessed of their homes, their hunting grounds, their fisheries, and, to a great extent, of the productions of the earth."[101]

People also came from far-off Australia, though the voyage took some two months. By the end of 1849, some 800 Australians and Tasmanians arrived, their numbers then increasing until gold was discovered in Australia two years later. Among them were escaped convicts, ex-convicts, and parolees whom the British allowed to settle anywhere except in Great Britain. Their neighborhood in San Francisco was called "Sydney Town," which one scholar labeled the most notorious criminal area in America's history. Lawless Aussie miners were subject to lynching, immigration restrictions, and reshipment back home, all of which prompted a Melbourne newspaper to urge similar restrictions against equally undesirable Californians who rushed to Australia when gold was discovered there.[102]

The French, too, aroused the animosity of native Americans, who resented their clannishness and pejoratively referred to them as "Keskydees," because when spoken to through an interpreter, they continually asked "Qu'est-ce qu'il dit?" Commenting on the plight of French immigrants in California between 1849 and 1851, a French journalist wrote, "merchants, workmen, clerks, women, old men, children, everyone, from the peasant to the man of the world and even ... the rentier, who hoped to triple his income and who is eating it up: all wanted to share this wealth which they would find so easily in this corner of the New World, but what they found, let us say it, is misery."[103]

As was done by the early European settlers in the East, so now was done in the West, as the greed of discovery and occupation became the right of possession and discrimination. The famed gold rush was in effect an infamous "minority crush," as "foreign miners," including Spanish and Indian residents, were subjected to discriminatory tax laws, physical attacks, lynchings, and expulsions.

Chinese miners, whose numbers increased from 323 in 1849 to 55,000 in 1855, were resented, harassed, terrorized, and robbed of their gold claims. As one Yankee miner noted, the "little yellow men were hated by most of the white miners for their ability to grub out fortunes which they themselves had left—for greener pastures." For a while there was even a plan to return them to China, but no one was able to muster the necessary funds and ships.[104]

Free Blacks, numbering close to 1,000 in 1850, were not welcome, particularly in the mining districts, where it was believed that they (as with the Chinese) had some mysterious power to locate gold. Unless barred from California, said delegates to the 1849 constitutional convention, "a black tide ... greater than the locusts of Egypt" would befall the state.[105]

The attitude toward Indians was more decisive and brutal. California's Governor Peter Burnett declared in his 1851 annual message that "a war of extermination will continue to be waged between the two races until the Indian race becomes extinct . . . while we cannot anticipate this result with but painful regret, the inevitable destiny of the race is beyond the power and wisdom of man to avert."[106]

In the rural areas, Indians were abducted, sold, and enslaved. In 1854, when the Yuki Indians of California were almost all murdered or sold into servitude, White settlers kidnapped and sold their surviving young girls to Mexican cowboys, built fences to prevent any Yukis from returning, and organized state-financed militia units to war against remaining Yukis. Mexicans, too, killed, captured, and enslaved Apaches.[107] The events in California were not unique. The Klondike gold discovery at century's turn triggered a scenario similar to the California one, attracting thousands of miners, including Chinese, Indians, and Blacks, particularly to Nome, which quickly became a center of robbery, murder, and disease.

Increased Immigration and Nativist Paranoia

By mid-century, America was still primarily rural and Protestant, with a population that had doubled since 1820 to some 23 million, 16 percent of whom were Black and 10 percent foreign-born, mostly from Ireland, Germany, and England. Only seven cities had populations over 100,000: New York, Baltimore, New Orleans, Philadelphia, Boston, Cincinnati, and Brooklyn (which was then independent).[108] Pride in colonial and revolutionary ancestry, as well as a rising contempt for immigrants, led to the creation of local and state historical genealogical societies and calls for more racially and ethnically restrictive citizenship naturalization qualifications.

Just as Americans were on a massive transcontinental move, so Europeans were on a transoceanic one. Though less than 10 percent of the total population, immigration kept rising from 143,439 in 1821–30 to 559,125 in 1851–60. Many settled in the big cities, and by 1860, the populations of Milwaukee, Chicago, and St. Louis were more than 50 percent foreign-born; New York, Cincinnati, Buffalo, and Detroit, more than 45 percent; Boston, Brooklyn, Pittsburgh, Louisville, New Orleans, and Newark, more than 35 percent; and Philadelphia and Baltimore, more than 24 percent. "The time of the Puritans and of William Penn is past," lamented an observer of the time.[109]

Many skilled Europeans left home because of economic hard times or the urging of American industry. In the 1830s, large numbers of unemployed English and Irish hand-loom weavers helped establish Philadelphia's fine cotton goods trade. After 1860, Cornish and Scotch miners, Belgian glassmakers, and German brewers left for similar jobs in America.[110]

With their increasing numbers and involvement in politics went old and new accusations of political corruption, wage lowering, alcoholism, poverty, criminality, disease, and naturalization fraud. This led to the creation of local and national groups calling for changes in naturalization laws so that immigrants could not vote before being residents for twenty-one years, just as with native-born Americans. Attitudes toward revolutions abroad also changed. President Millard Fillmore told the Congress that though America was sympathetic to the "unfortunate or oppressed everywhere in their struggle for freedom," the country had an "imperative duty not to interfere in the government or internal policy of other nations." Labor unrest and violence abroad generated fears that the same could happen in America. In 1850 the *New York Herald* protested the "vast importations of foreign socialists," and in 1853 the *Boston Daily Transcript* declared there was an international conspiracy originating in England. Protestant evangelicals urged early conversion of the young in order to get a head start in combating "error, infidelity, Socialism, anti-marriage, anti-property, anti-legal fanatism, anti-Sabbath and anti-Christ."[111]

Fears were even expressed that foreign countries were sending soldiers in the guise of immigrants to overthrow the country. Unlike in European countries, America had no requirements for foreigners to have a passport. Leaders of the American Republican Party, in 1844, accused Austria of exporting "the abject slaves of their country, who, bound in fetters of civil and religious serfdom, would be incapable in twice twenty-one years, of understanding the principles of civil and religious freedom which alone fit a man to become an American citizen." One Alabama representative said the czar could easily send 100,000 Russians to this country as emigrants without causing any excitement. "They would go and equip themselves with American rifles, furnish themselves with American powder, and American bullets, and go . . . to any portion of the country and be ready at any time, to exhibit themselves as an armed force, in the heart of the country."[112]

A few of the charges had some truth, just as those against earlier British immigrants. By 1850, the ratio of paupers among immigrants was much higher than for the native-born—1 for every 32 foreigners in contrast to 1 for every 317 native Americans. From 1854 to 1860, of the almost 45,000 recipients of relief aid from the New York Association for Improving the Condition of the Poor, 69 percent were immigrants from Ireland, in contrast to 10.8 percent for German immigrants.[113]

Similarly, in 1850, more than half of the convicted criminals were immigrants, though they represented only 11 percent of the population. Epidemics, too, were blamed on immigrants, who in St. Louis, Cincinnati, New York, and New Orleans suffered greatly during the 1832 cholera outbreaks; in New York City alone, more than 40 percent of the dead were Irish immigrants.[114]

More widely criticized was alcoholism, though native-born Americans had long practiced heavy drinking. As early as 1810, some 14,000 known distilleries produced over 25 million gallons a year. "You can go into hardly any man's house without being asked to drink wine, or spirits, even in the morning," said an early-nineteenth-century English tourist. "Even little boys at, or under, *twelve* years of ago, go into *stores,* and tip off their drams." Drinking was particularly heavy in mining towns and the West. The first local and national temperance societies were formed in Massachusetts in 1813 and 1826 respectively, followed by others, such as the Woman's Christian Temperance Union and Sons of Temperance. Support for temperance was weakest in the South.[115]

Organized opposition to hard drinking was strongest in New England and developed along religious, class, and political lines, led by well-to-do, old-line Federalists, Congregationalists, Presbyterians, Baptists, Methodists, and newly emerging Protestant sects. The Republican Party was home to many who favored abolition and prohibition and criticized immigrants, in contrast to the Democratic Party, which increasingly attracted the immigrant vote, particularly of the Irish and Germans.[116]

In the 1840s and early 1850s, anti-alcoholism was a major local and state political issue, and temperance conventions analyzed the positions of political candidates and organized to defeat those who disagreed with them. As a rising political figure, Abraham Lincoln in 1842 decried hard drinking and expressed the hope that the day would soon arrive when "there shall be neither a slave nor a drunkard on the earth." Resentful of the anti-immigrant bent of Protestant temperance societies, immigrants created their own, particularly the Irish, usually advocating moderate drinking habits rather than total abstinence or prohibition.[117]

To preserve American morality further, many Protestant spokesmen demanded that only the King James Bible be used in the public schools and that Sunday closing laws be enforced or instituted. In contrast, liberal Protestants, Seventh-Day Adventists, atheists, Quakers, and Jews vigorously opposed such measures, leading to more court cases between 1845 and 1854 than in any prior decade.[118] At times, Sunday-closing-law opponents differed among themselves: Jews saw such laws as denying their religious rights; Christian fundamentalists saw them as perversions of a biblical injunction; and liberal Protestants saw them as a threat to freedom of conscience.

The political implications of rising numbers of immigrant voters were no less disturbing. Like many southerners, the famed Alamo hero Sam Houston charged immigrants in the North with "diminishing Southern representation in the Councils of our Nation and increasing the proportionate ratio of the representation of [the] North and Western states. This gives the abolitionists more power. It is greatly to the interests of the South to stop it and increase the naturalization to twenty-one years." To some congressmen, Indians were preferable to immigrants. For example, during the debates on the Kansas-Nebraska homestead bills of the mid-1850s, some legislators argued against "bullying and browbeating" Indians to obtain their land and give it to "foreigners and immigrants," who were "worse than the Indian occupants."[119]

On the other hand, northerners feared that southern slavers and northern capitalists were conspiring to take over the country, destroy civil liberties, and establish a national economy based on Black and White slave labor, which would include immigrants. The *Cincinnati Freeman* asked, "What security have the Germans and Irish that their children will not, within a hundred years, be reduced to slavery in this the land of their adoption?"[120]

If immigrants were disliked, it was their "own causing." The Irish themselves generated "the ill-feeling that now exists among the Americans. . . . Such, too, is eminently the case with a very large class of German immigrants." To another commentator of the times, the old Scotch merchants and Dutch farmers were acceptable because they came "not only to adopt a country, but to help to build it up. But they that come *now* come to *live* upon the country."[121]

Such feelings spurred the creation of nativist clubs, such as the Order of the American Star, Black Snakes, Tigers, Rough Skins, Red Necks, Thunderbolts, Gladiators, Screw Boats, Hard Times, as well as the secret societies of the Order of United Americans and the Order of the Star Spangled Banner. The most prominent group was the American Party or, as it was popularly known, the Know-Nothing Party, with whose views Whigs and Republicans often allied themselves. Know-Nothing anti-Catholic and anti-immigration candidates won city, state, and national offices, particularly in New York, Massachusetts, Delaware, and Pennsylvania. In Connecticut alone, in 1854, some 169 Know-Nothing lodges and 22,000 members existed, much to the pleasure of the *Hartford Courant,* which editorialized: "The individual Catholic votes as the priest dictates; the priest follows the dictates of the prelate, and he so controls the elections as shall best serve the interests of the Pope, the establishment of the Church, and its subsequent complete rule over the country." In the Far West, gold rushers with Know-Nothing passions succeeded in running candidates for local offices. Many of San Francisco's vigilante groups in the mid-1850s included either Know-Nothing members or sympathizers.[122]

Know-Nothing became a common household word, so much so that there were Know-Nothing candy, tea, toothpicks, a clipper ship, and even a newspaper menu:

Catholic broth	Jesuit soup
Roasted Catholic	Broiled priest
The Pope's Big Toe, broiled	
Fried nuns, very nice and tender	
(Dessert) Rich Irish Brogue	Sweet German Accent[123]

A Belgian Catholic missionary, while in Kentucky, wrote his nephew in 1858 that "it might be supposed that in a country which boasts of unexampled tolerance and liberty, the Catholic Church would be, if not protected, at least spared from persecution. But it is not so. A party, whose only principle is a hostility to the Faith, has several times been formed. Now it flourished under the name of *Know-nothing,* and it might be termed, 'the ignorant and brutal.' "[124]

Just as Catholics were the constant foci of Know-Nothingism, Jews were occasionally targeted. During an 1855 debate on a Sunday closing bill in California, one Know-Nothing aspirant for governor accused them of having come to the area only to make money and then leave for their New Jerusalem. Such attitudes did not prevent the election of the first Jewish United States senator, David L. Yulee, of Florida and then the second Jewish senator, Judah P. Benjamin, of Louisiana, both of whom were criticized for being Jewish, though they did not practice the faith. A few Jews actually supported the Know-Nothings because of their anger at European Catholic anti-Semitism.[125]

Fortunately, as vocal as nativists were, they represented a small part of the population, most of whom had no or little contact with the Irish or Jews, except in popular literature and stereotypes. Before the decade ended, nativist groups lost much of their appeal, as the public became outraged by their violence, secret rituals, factional disputes, poor legislative record, and fervent calls for Prohibition.

Racism and Nativism

Throughout this time, America was uniquely racist, at least in comparison to other world powers. England had outlawed slavery in her colonies in 1833. Fifteen years later, France did the same. Sweden abolished slavery in 1846 and Denmark followed suit two years later. By 1850, slavery ended in Spanish America. Portugal and Holland outlawed the practice in 1856 and 1860 respectively. Even the serfs of central and eastern Europe were beginning to be set free.

Only America persisted as the major practitioner, defender, and extender of slavery, more so in the South and the newly acquired Louisiana Purchase territories than in the North, where various states were adopting laws for its gradual abolition. Out of a Black population of almost 3 million in 1840, only 14 percent were free.[126] Throughout those pre–Civil War years, debates intensified over what the racial nature of the territories should be, with the South wanting slavery extended and the North seeking its end.

Only through Henry Clay's compromise of 1820 was Missouri allowed to enter the union as a slave state, Maine (separated from Massachusetts) as a free state, and all other territory north of the 36° 30′ parallel closed to slavery. Again in 1850, Clay effected a compromise over the territory seized from Mexico: California was admitted as a free state, New Mexico and Utah territory residents were allowed to decide for themselves whether their areas would be free or slave, the slave trade (but not slavery) was banned in the District of Columbia, and a law was adopted making it easier for southern slaveholders to recover slaves who had escaped to the North.

Clay caught the historical irony of those wanting to extend slavery to the Pacific, telling the Senate in 1850 that "while you reproach, and justly too, our British ancestors for the introduction of this institution on the continent of America, I am, for one, unwilling that the posterity of the present inhabitants of California and New Mexico shall reproach us for doing the same thing which we reproach Great Britain for doing to us."[127] Though each compromise restricted the spread of slavery, it also extended it, resulting in a postponement rather than resolution of the problem. Four years later, the Kansas-Nebraska Act repealed the 1820 compromise and created the territories of Kansas and Nebraska, where the residents would decide whether or not slavery would prevail. This time, however, debate led to violence, particularly in Kansas, where slave owners (particularly from Missouri) and abolitionists (particularly from New England) rushed or sent money and arms to ensure a vote for their views. The result was massive bloodshed in Kansas and a further intensification of pro and con feelings and agitations, which in a few years culminated in civil war.

Racism, however, was not limited to geopolitics. Though declared illegal in 1807, the importation of slaves continued on ships built and owned by northerners who sold their human cargo in the South. President Madison decried the practice in 1810, telling the Congress that Americans were to blame for "carrying on a traffic in enslaved Africans, equally in violation of the laws of humanity, and in defiance of those of their own country."[128] So lax were laws that foreign slaving ships flew the Stars and Stripes in order to avoid search by other countries, while American slavers flew a foreign flag to avoid search by American warships.

In vain, President Van Buren also urged Congress to tighten the laws:

> Advantage has been taken of these defects to give the vessels wholly belonging to foreigners and navigating the ocean an apparent American ownership. This character has been so well stimulated as to afford them comparative security in prosecuting the slave trade—a trade emphatically denounced in our statutes, regarded with abhorrence by our citizens, and of which the effectual suppression is nowhere more sincerely desired than in the United States.[129]

In spite of such protestations, some 5,000 slaves per year were smuggled into the country between 1808 and 1860, while some 100,000 slaves in the South fled to the North, largely via Ohio.

Meanwhile, a profitable business developed in the deliberate impregnating of Black women and the selling of their children. "Slave-rearing was the surest, most remunerative and most approved means of increasing critical capital," wrote historian Frederic Bancroft. "It was advised and practiced by the wisest rural slaveowners."[130]

Many southerners defended slavery as being in the best interests of slaves and the principles of religion and morality. "I consider slavery one of the best evils that exists upon the earth—one of the best, because the Negro is benefited by it, because it keeps them out of houses of prostitution, out of jails and workhouses," declaimed one Louisianan. More extreme was George Fitzhugh, of Virginia, who held that a slave was better off than a free laborer, who was hated by his employer because "he asks high wages or joins strikes; his fellow-laborer hates him because he competes with him for employment. . . . As a slave, he will be beloved and protected. Whilst free, he will be hated, despised and persecuted."[131]

Small numbers of southern and northern Black freemen also bought, sold, and held other Blacks as slaves. As of 1830, more than 10,000 were held by an estimated 3,500 Black slave owners. In Louisiana, at least ten Black slave owners had 50 or more slaves; and in South Carolina, one man owned some 200 slaves. Some free Blacks even employed White workers. Not only did such Blacks seek wealth like other people, but by owning slaves, they believed they would not be regarded as insurrectionists. To their White counterparts, however, they were encouraging slaves to steal, run away, or even revolt.[132]

If in the South Blacks were valued and enslaved, in the North they were shunned, segregated, excluded, or attacked. Alexis de Tocqueville noted that "in the theatres gold cannot procure a seat for the servile race beside their former masters; in the hospitals they lie apart; and although they are allowed to invoke the same God as whites, it must be at a different altar and in their own churches, with their own clergy. . . . When the Negro dies, his bones are cast aside, and the distinction of condition prevails even in the equality of death."[133]

Early trade societies and unions implicitly or explicitly excluded Blacks, such as the Caulkers of Boston in 1724, the Shipwrights of New York in 1802, the Carpenters of New York in 1806, the Workingman's Convention in 1830, the General Trades Union of New York City in 1833, and the National Trades Union in 1835.[134]

In some cities, White mobs attacked Black neighborhoods, either in revenge for some real or imagined wrong by a resident or to drive all Blacks out of the city. Thus the "Hardscrabble" slum of Providence was invaded, as well as "Bucktown" in Cincinnati, and "New Liberia" in New Haven. White abolitionists were also attacked by mobs, which were often highly organized and included many "gentlemen of property and standing," such as doctors, lawyers, merchants, bankers, judges, congressmen, and Mayflower descendants.[135]

Church groups were not immune to racist beliefs, particularly Presbyterians, Methodists, and Baptists, who began seriously to debate the issue in the 1830s and, as the Civil War approached, to divide into northern and southern sections. Congregational and Unitarian churches held together, largely because they did not have a significant southern constituency. Before splits began taking place, many churchmen and churchgoers preferred silence or neutrality, citing Scripture on slavery's propriety and the value of obeying one's master. Thus, by 1843, more than 1,000 Methodist ministers and preachers owned 1,500 slaves, while their congregants owned some 208,000. In the North, too, there were clergy who justified slavery. To the famed evangelist George Whitefield, being a slave facilitated conversion to Christianity and "faith in Christ." And to Josiah Priest, had God not preferred a White complexion, He would not have given Jesus light hair and blue eyes. There were also Black slaves who believed their plight was God-ordained. Frederick Douglass told of how he had met such believers in the

South "who are under the delusion that God requires them to submit to slavery and to wear chains with meekness and humility."[136]

Abolitionists, too, had their own form of racism. Though believing slavery a sin, many viewed Blacks as children, gave them menial jobs, frowned upon interracial marriages, and, at times, barred them from membership in their organizations. If they had to associate with Blacks, hopefully it would involve light-skinned ones. Such duality of behavior was obvious to some members of both races. "We are culpably ignorant of, or shamefully indifferent to the wrongs which are inflicted upon our colored brethren," said one White abolitionist. "We are prejudiced against the blacks; and our prejudices are indurated . . . by the secret, vague consciousness of the wrong we are doing them. Men are adept to dislike those most whom they have injured most."[137]

In those early decades, the leaders of the women's rights movement were all abolitionists, but not all abolitionists supported them. In their founding statement in 1848, modeled after the Declaration of Independence, the women affirmed that "all men and women are created equal," and should have equal social, political, and economic rights. The suffragists often compared their plight to that of Black women. Elizabeth Cady Stanton wrote that a married woman "takes the name of her master, holds nothing, owns nothing, can bring no action in her own name; and the principles on which she and the slave is educated are the same. The slave is taught what is best for him to know—which is nothing; the woman is taught what is best for her to know—which is little more than nothing, man being the umpire in both cases. . . . Civilly, socially and religiously, she is what man chooses her to be . . . and such is the slave."[138]

It took the famed Frederick Douglass to clearly differentiate the injustices both groups endured.

> I do not see how any one can pretend that there is the same urgency in giving the ballot to woman as to the Negro. With us, the matter is a question of life and death. . . . When women because they are women are hunted down through the cities of New York and New Orleans; when they are dragged from their houses and hung upon lamp posts; when their children are torn from their arms, and their brains dashed out upon the pavement; when they are objects of insult and outrage at every turn; when they are in danger of having their homes burnt down over their heads; when their children are not allowed to enter schools; then they will have an urgency to obtain the ballot equal to our own.[139]

Anyone sympathizing with Blacks was viewed with contempt, particularly in the South where open discussion of slavery was suppressed for fear it would encourage slave revolts. Only Kentucky did not pass laws controlling and restricting speech, press, and discussion. Meanwhile, Whig and successor Republican opponents of slavery were maligned as the party of "niggerology." At times, those opposing slavery or violating the 1850 fugitive slave law were accused of treason. For example, in 1851 thirty-six Blacks and five Whites were indicted for armed resistance to a Maryland posse that sought to recapture runaway slaves in Pennsylvania; though found not guilty, they became the largest group of Americans ever simultaneously charged with treason.[140]

Unlike European immigrants who could become citizens after five years, Blacks born abroad or in America could not. They were simply property. Such was the ruling in the 1857 Supreme Court case of *Dred Scott* v. *Sanford*, in which Chief Justice Roger Taney said, Blacks were "a subordinate and inferior class of beings, who had been subjected by the dominant race, and, whether emancipated or not, yet remained subject to their authority, and had no rights or privileges but such as those who held the power and the Government might choose to grant them."[141]

The connection between nineteenth-century racism and nativism was well noted by Lincoln, who denounced Know-Nothingism in a letter of 24 August 1855: "How can anyone who abhors the oppression of Negroes be in favor of degrading classes of white people . . . as a nation we began by declaring that 'all men are created equal.' We now practically read it, 'all men are created equal except Negroes.' When the Know-Nothings obtain control, it will read: 'All men are created equal except Negroes, foreigners and Catholics.' "[142]

Three years later, he also upheld the constitutional rights of immigrants or those "whose ancestors have come hither and have settled here, finding themselves our equals in all things."

> If they look back through this history to trace their connection with those days by blood, they find they have none, they cannot carry themselves back into that glorious epoch and make themselves feel that they are part of us, but when they look through that old Declaration of Independence they find that those old men say that "We hold these truths to be self-evident, that all men are created equal," and then they feel that that moral sentiment taught in that day evidences their relation to those men, that it is the father of all moral principle in them, and that they have a right to claim it as though they were blood of the blood, and flesh of the flesh of the men who wrote that Declaration, and so they are.[143]

Nevertheless, as more people arrived and moved across the continent, prejudice and discrimination became more pluralistic, accretive, successive, and widespread.

The Civil War and Minorities

On the eve of the Civil War, the population was close to 31.5 million, including slightly more than 4 million foreign-born, over 85 percent of whom lived in the North, and almost 4 million slaves, more than half living in the South. The war was basically a White-White one between Northerners and Southerners, culminating decades of bitter debate and violence among Whites and between them and Blacks. At stake were the constitutional rights of states, the decision whether new territories taken or purchased from the Indians, French, Mexicans, or Spanish should be free or slave, and what the relations should be between the races anywhere in the country.

Just as Southerners favored extending slavery in the West to ensure economic well-being and federal influence, Northerners opposed doing so for fear of losing both, as well as land and jobs for White farmers, workers, and new immigrants, who were increasingly entering the country and moving to the West. Both justified their views and actions by the New and Old Testaments.

Before Lincoln took office, the South seceded, preferring the maintenance of slavery to that of the Union. Lincoln, of course, preferred the reverse, but like many opponents of slavery did not believe in absolute social or political racial equality or that Blacks could ever assimilate as readily as "Hans, Baptiste and Patrick." To him, it would be best for the country if all Blacks immigrated to Liberia, Central America, Haiti, or "any place or places" outside the United States.[144]

War passions and politics also evoked charges of disloyalty. Northern Republicans called Democrats "Copperheads," "Butternuts," or "Peace Democrats"— traitors all. In response, Democrats accused Republicans of "abolitionist fanaticism" and of subverting the Constitution and civil liberties in the name of racial equality. To some American religionists, the war was God's punishment for slavery and the omission of God's name from the Constitution.[145] Fears of treason led both Lincoln and Jefferson Davis to impose martial law in border states and suspend the writ of habeas corpus.

In the process of national division, regional self-interest and loyalty transcended religious and ethnic attachments. The North's greater variety of people was reflected in the composition of its military forces, which had significant numbers of ethnic soldiers and companies. As much as 25 percent may have been foreign-born, the largest groups being Germans (200,000), Irish (150,000), and French Canadians (40,000).[146]

Some regiments bore ethnic designations: the Swiss Rifles, Gardes Lafayette, Garibaldi Guard, Martinez Militia. In Chicago, a former captain in the 1848 Hungarian Revolution wrote Lincoln that a militia had been formed of "men of Hungarian, Bohemian & Slavonic origin," and requested permission to call it the "Lincoln Riflemen, of Slavonic origin," which Lincoln "cheerfully" granted. In the Southwest, a battalion of "Native Cavalry" (mostly Mexicans and South Americans) supported the North. A "Polish Legion" included Hungarians, Italians, Czechs, and Danes from Washington, D.C., and New York, led by Wlodzimierz Krzyzanowski, who after becoming a brigadier general was denied further promotion by the Senate because, as Carl Schurz recalled, "there was nobody there who could pronounce his name."[147]

The different ethnic accents, languages, and customs occasionally provoked fights and riots. One northern officer, a Yale graduate who served with Germans and Irish, complained of having "to eat their onions and drink their lager and very rarely to hear a word of musical English from American lips as I am almost the sole specimen of a Yankee in the Company."[148] Similarly, native-born soldiers resented having "greenhorn" officers.

Ethnic and religious attachments did not prevent northern and southern Methodists, Presbyterians, Lutherans, and Catholics from fighting each other, with the blessings of their respective regional leaders. "Sure it isn't a greater shame for an Irishman to fire on Irish colors than for an American to fire on American colors," said one Irishman. The New York *Jewish Record* editorialized that "fraternal blood has been spilled by violent hands, and, to our regret, we are compelled to add that the hand of the Southern Israelite has been found raised against his Northern brother." Just as Italians in New York joined the northern army, so Italians in Louisiana joined the South.[149]

Not all religious denominations divided into northern and southern sections, though they differed over slavery and the necessity of war, as in the cases of Lutherans, Quakers, Episcopalians, Jews, and Roman Catholics. The Episcopal bishop of Louisiana resigned to become a Confederate major general, while his Rhode Island counterpart prayed for the North's success "in saving our land from the ravages of sedition, conspiracy, and rebellion." Likewise, a Catholic bishop in Georgia defended slavery as "legitimate, lawful, approved by all laws, and consistent with practical religion and true holiness of all life"; an archbishop in New York City declared that "no state had a right to secede," except in the manner provided for in the Constitution.[150]

Northern and southern Blacks knew that the war did not start to free them, and were so told by many a Northerner. Nevertheless, the *Anglo-African*, a New York weekly, stated, "The South must be subjugated. . . . In aiding the Federal government in whatever way we can, we are aiding to secure our liberty." With a total population of some 4.5 million, nearly 180,000 Blacks served in segregated ranks in the Union army, most of whom were from slaveholding states. Almost 50,000 were in the navy. "The Negro loves freedom, and will fight to obtain it," said a Michigan Republican, while a Wisconsin Democrat confessed, "I never believed in niggers before, but by Jasus, they are hell for fighting."[151]

To a much lesser extent, free and slave Blacks hoping to better their situation and prove their equality to Whites served in the Confederate army, but mainly as teamsters, cooks, mechanics, hospital workers, and common laborers. They were not accepted for combat duty, lest they rebel. "Use all the Negroes you can get," said a former Georgia governor, "but don't arm them. . . . If slaves will make good soldiers our whole theory of slavery is wrong." In the closing months of the war, however, desperate for troops, the Confederacy began accepting Blacks for combat duty, without any promise of emancipation and only if they were "patriotically rendered by their masters," not exceeding 25 percent of a state's male slave population. Those Blacks who fled north to join the Union army were accused of "signal ingratitude and treachery," even to "the most considerate and kindest of masters," noted a wartime diariest. Captured northern Black soldiers (and their White officers) were subject to being killed or enslaved.[152]

Whether free in the North or enslaved in the South, Blacks continued to be demeaned and brutalized, even after Lincoln's Emancipation Proclamation, which freed slaves only in the rebelling states. Then, with the Thirteenth Amendment, slavery and involuntary servitude in any part of the country or place under American jurisdiction were outlawed, thereby rendering the *Dred Scott* decision null and void. Such freedom, however, was easier written than implemented, because racism had assumed a "halo of antiquity," which, according to the Reverend Increase Tarbox, Americans had inherited from parents "in the unquestioning period of childhood ... and which have been and are still firmly held by multitudes as undoubted truths."[153]

Similarly, after a mob of Irish workers torched a Brooklyn tobacco factory employing mostly Black women and children, the *Anglo-African* called "upon the world to bear witness to the dreadful effects which the system of slavery has had upon the Irish people. In their own country they are kind and hospitable to our poor and constantly abused race; but here, so dreadfully corrupted do some of them become that they are prepared for the vilest deed of diabolism. ... Americans! We charge you before high Heaven and the whole civilized world with being the authors of this great wickedness. It was you who first taught them to hate us."[154]

For the first time in American history, citizenship was not a prerequisite for conscription, with Congress declaring "all able-bodied male citizens ... and persons of foreign birth who shall have declared an oath their intention to become citizens ... liable to perform military duty." More than 700,000 immigrants arrived during the war, with many volunteering for service, particularly in the North where possibly 20 percent of the enlistments were foreign-born. In the South, the foreign-born also enlisted, though to a lesser extent. In New Orleans, a merchant noted that all foreigners were joining "and even the English have come forward en masse—it is a remarkable thing that no foreigners who have been here more than a month or two but sides heart and hand with the South."[155]

The conscription law allowed men to avoid military service by paying a commutation fee of $300, which enabled the rich to buy their way out and made the poor more likely to be drafted. Many fled the country, including aliens. When the elder son of Judge Thomas Mellon asked his father for permission to enlist, he was told, "Don't do it. It is only greenhorns who enlist. Those who are able to pay for substitutes do so, and no discredit attaches." Doing likewise did not prevent Grover Cleveland from later becoming our twenty-third president. The government soon ended the practice, but still allowed substitutes if they were aliens, veterans of two-year service, or boys under twenty years of age. This led to draft brokers advertising for substitutes, offering bounties of a few hundred to more than $1,000. Even poor aliens placed advertisements offering themselves to the highest bidder.[156]

Because of widespread opposition to the war, particularly in the North, many native-born Whites, Blacks, and newly arrived immigrants were forced into military service by being abducted, drugged, or intoxicated. For example, while some French Canadians voluntarily joined the Union army, others were tricked into doing so by recruiting agents promising them good-paying, "mostly outdoor work." The press and many foreign governments (France, Belgium, Italy, Denmark, Sweden, Germany, and England) deplored such practices, and in England, the aristocratic press ridiculed the "wretched" and "gibbering" mobs of "Irish and German mercenaries," who had been "drugged with whiskey" before enlisting.[157]

Confederate leaders as well as supporters in England charged the North with deceptively recruiting British residents in America and immigrants in Ireland. Southern agents went to Ireland where, with the help of local Catholic clergy, they told prospective immigrants that if they went to the North, they would be forced to serve in the army. "How will the liberation of the negro so benefit you or yours at home, that you should risk your life for his freedom?" Anti-British and anti-Protestant sentiments were exploited by claims that the North was inhabited by Cromwell's descendants, who shot Catholics in the streets and, since the war began, desecrated churches in Missouri, Mississippi, Virginia, Louisiana, and Florida.[158]

In New York, Black-White relations worsened after the government drafted some unemployed strikers, who felt they were being sent to war for the benefit of Blacks, who upon being freed would move North and take away their jobs. Shortly after some 3,000 striking longshoremen began being replaced by Blacks, four days of draft riots broke out in New York City in July 1863. A mob of "Irish rabble" assaulted draft headquarters and wealthy homes, and then beat, burned, or hanged Blacks in the streets, with casualties ranging from a few hundred to more than a thousand.[159]

Black-White competition also flared at major coastal and inland ports when Black longshoremen were hired as strikebreakers. The hiring of Black stevedores on Ohio riverboats in 1862 triggered the torching of Cincinnati's Black neighborhood, which led to the burning of some Irish homes in retaliation. As one visiting Englishman wrote in 1865, northern workers, though having "neither sympathy nor fellow feeling for the coloured race, make no objection to their emancipation providing they remain south of Dixie's line."[160]

The South's conscription law exempted owners of twenty or more slaves, provoking the resentment of many who owned none. To one disgruntled Alabaman, the Confederate slave owners wanted him and others to fight for the "infernal negroes and after you do their fighting you may kiss there hine parts for o they care." Some draft dodgers and army deserters fled to the Appalachians, the Ozarks, and German areas in Texas, where sympathy ran high for the North. Defiant German-American draftees in Austin County organized defense groups and threatened to kill fellow Germans loyal to the Confederacy, while their Wisconsin counterparts attacked a draft commissioner, destroyed records, and sacked homes of prominent Republicans.[161]

At times, Union and Confederate prisoners of war were enlisted, including some foreign-born ones. About 6,000 former Confederate soldiers agreed to be part of the United States Volunteers on condition they not fight their former comrades-in-arms but be sent to the West to fight hostile Indians.[162]

Though both sides provided military chaplains, legislation in the North restricted them to "regularly ordained [clergymen] of some Christian denomination," which meant Protestants. When Jewish and Christian leaders protested, the fundamentalist publication *The Presbyter* angrily replied that it was bad enough having Roman Catholic and Universalist chaplains without having to add "Jewish rabbis, Mormon debauchees, Chinese priests, and Indian conjurors."[163] In July 1862, however, Congress relented and allowed Jews to become official military chaplains.

Christian triumphalism intensified the following year when representatives of eleven Protestant denominations formed the National Reform Association, which sought a constitutional amendment declaring "the nation's allegiance to Jesus Christ and its acceptance of the moral laws of the Christian religion, and so indicate that this is a Christian nation." Those opposing such a measure, said one advocate, were free to "go to some wild, desolate land, and in the name of the devil, and for the sake of the devil, subdue it, and set up a government of their own on infidel and atheistic ideas; and if they can stand it, stay there till they die." Jews and Seventh-Day Adventists vigorously opposed it, as did many prominent figures and newspapers. Lincoln and the Congress avoided taking action on the measure (which the association continued to promote until 1945 when it ended its activities and the National Association of Evangelicals took up the cause).[164]

Meanwhile, wartime profiteering led to the amassing of great fortunes by such men as J.P. Morgan, Philip Armour, Clement Studebaker, John Wannamaker, Cornelius Vanderbilt, and the Du Ponts. President Lincoln removed Secretary of War Simon Cameron because of such involvement. In the North and South, military and civilian speculators, including members of General Grant's family, traded legally and illegally in cotton, which the North needed and in which the South abounded. As Charles Dana, of the *New York Tribune,* wrote of northern troops: "Every colonel, captain or quartermaster is in secret partnership with some operator in cotton; every soldier dreams of adding a bale of cotton to his monthly pay."[165]

Against such a background, the first United States official's action against Jews as a group took place when General Grant singled them out for illegal trading and ordered all to leave his military district within twenty-four hours. Some thirty men and their families vacated Paducah, Kentucky, as did other innocent Jews from Holly Springs and Oxford, Mississippi. Again, both Jews and Christians protested. Senator Lazarus Powell, of Kentucky, denounced the order as "atrocious," "illegal," "inhuman and monstrous," and as unworthy even of the "most despotic government in Europe." The *New York Times* declared the charges "contrary to common sense and common justice—contrary to Republicanism and Christianity." Soon afterward, Lincoln revoked the order, saying that to "condemn a class is, to say the least, to wrong the good with the bad. I do not like to hear a class or nationality condemned on account of a few sinners." (Some years later, while seeking the presidency, Grant repudiated his wartime order and then, as president, appointed a number of Jews to governmental posts, including the governorship of the Washington Territory and American Consul in Romania.)[166]

More extensive were the anti-Semitic stereotypes nationally of Jews being greedy, speculators, money changers, and killers of Christ. Judah Benjamin, Confederate secretary of war and then of state, was widely maligned for being a Jew, though as noted earlier, he never identified himself as such and was married to a Catholic. With Lincoln's assassination, new charges arose of a Catholic conspiracy, abetted by John Wilkes Booth, an alleged convert from Episcopalianism.[167]

Though Indians served and fought on both sides, the Civil War provided them no surcease of oppression. Most of the slave-owning five Civilized Tribes (Creek, Choctaw, Chickasaw, Seminole, and Cherokee) sided with the Confederacy, though some Indians within each tribe, particularly those of Black descent, joined the Union forces. In the North, an Indian Home Guard was organized and composed of three regiments. Army reports of the time reveal that though often heroic in battle, they were supplied with obsolete weapons, paid late, and treated condescendingly. Still, both sides were uneasy about using Indians in battle because of their practices of scalping or mutilating captives.[168] Both sides also readily broke their treaties with them. Navajos were ousted from their lands and relocated; Cheyennes and Arapahos were massacred; Nez Percés were forced to cede land; Sioux were decimated; and Apaches were slain and forced to flee to the mountains.

Anti-British feelings resurfaced in the North when England recognized the Confederacy as a belligerent rather than a mere group of rebels, built ships for the South, and demanded release of two southern diplomats forcibly taken by the North's navy from one of their ships. The latter action prompted Congressman Owen Lovejoy to say that though he never shared in the traditional American hostility against England, he now felt compelled to "record my inextinguishable hatred of that Government . . . and to bequeath it as a legacy to my children."[169] Members of the Fenian Brotherhood, formed in 1858 to help achieve an independent Ireland, exploited anti-British feelings, and recruited northern and southern soldiers to help train or fight alongside their compatriots in Ireland.

To a lesser extent, French attempts to mediate the war alone or with the cooperation of other European powers met strong criticism by Congress, which declared them unfriendly acts. In contrast, relations with Russia warmed. Just as America had favored the Russians during the Crimean War, so now Russia did with the Union. Fearful of a war with England and France, with her navy being blockaded in the Baltic, Russia sent two fleets in 1863 to visit America, where in

San Francisco and New York City they were enthusiastically received, with the Union's secretary of navy asking that "God Bless the Russians." Such actions so infuriated Poles in America and abroad that some schemed (in vain) to bring 20,000–30,000 Poles to join the Confederacy, but on condition they be granted land to build a colony of their own.[170]

By war's end, 360,000 Northerners and 260,000 Southerners had been killed, which in absolute numbers and proportion of the population of 30 million exceeded those during World War II (some 400,000 out of a population of 135 million). As happened after the Revolutionary War when many Loyalists fled the country, so now with thousands of Confederate soldiers. Irreconcilable in defeat and fearful of retribution on returning home, they fled, primarily to Mexico, as well as to Canada, Central and South America, Europe, and even Egypt and Japan. Some Indian tribes that had refused to take sides, such as the Kickapoo, also fled to Mexico, while others, regardless of which side they had supported, continued to be attacked by Whites, resulting in more than 200 battles between 1868 and 1876, including "Custer's Last Stand." Unhealed, too, were the schisms of northern and southern Baptists, Methodists, and Presbyterians (which for Methodists ended in 1939 and for Presbyterians in 1983); Black Baptist and Methodist denominationalism also expanded.[171]

In the years that followed, Andrew Johnson, like Lincoln, did not believe in racial equality, preferring a lenient reconciliation with the South. When Congress in 1865 became dominated by radical Republicans hostile to the South, Johnson vetoed their reconstructionist legislation. Nevertheless, in 1866 a Civil Rights Act and a Freeman's Bureau Act were passed, giving equal rights to Blacks and broadening the bureau's power to provide them with food, clothing, schooling, job counselling, and if necessary, military force to ensure their rights.

Johnson denounced such legislation as evil, saying it gave Blacks safeguards that went "infinitely beyond any that the general government has ever provided for the white race" and that the bill was "made to operate in favor of the colored and against the white race."[172]

Of more lasting significance was the passage of the Fourteenth Amendment in 1868 and the Fifteenth Amendment in 1870, whereby all people, including Blacks, born or naturalized in America were declared citizens whom no state could deprive of life, liberty, or property without due process of law; deny equal protection of the law; or disenfranchise because of "race, color, or previous condition of servitude." At the same time, Congress voted to allow aliens of African descent or nativity to become citizens, which in effect meant Hindus and Arabs from that continent, but not necessarily those from Asia. While the Civil Rights Act of 1870 made it a crime for two or more people to violate the right of Blacks to vote, it also implicitly protected the right of Chinese, whether citizens or not, to give evidence in court and to be protected against invidious taxes and fees that various western states had imposed on them.[173] Socially, the 1875 Civil Rights Act outlawed racial discrimination in public places, such as inns, buses, trains, theaters, and amusement parks. Now, Black men in large numbers could and did vote and hold public office in various states and legislatures. By Reconstruction's end in 1877, some had become congressmen.

Such reforms frightened many Whites, particularly those believing that "the negro exists for the special object of raising cotton, rice and sugar *for the whites,* and that it is illegitimate for him to indulge, like other people, in the pursuit of his own happiness in his own way." To one newspaper, Whites would be "thrown entirely upon their own resources" because, without Black labor, they will have "to begin where their fathers began." Many White woman suffragists, too, were upset, not that Blacks had obtained freedom, but that Blacks, Indians, and immigrants from Europe and Asia, though largely uneducated, were given the right to vote, but not women. In 1874, the Supreme Court unanimously held in *Minor* v. *Happersett* that the Constitution did not guarantee suffrage to "any" citizen, thereby upholding state laws that restricted it to males. Some Black suffragists were also dismayed that though many immigrants had fled to America in search of security, upon arriving they joined "in the hue and cry against native born citizens of this land."[174]

Though hard-gained, Black benefits were short-lived. Right after the war's end, a Union officer in Vicksburg wrote, "All the trickery, chicanery and political power possible are being brought to bear on the poor negro, to make him do the hard labor for the whites, as in the days of old." "Black Codes" multiplied, denying Blacks the right to own weapons, serve on juries, purchase or lease property, be idle, or behave disrespectfully toward Whites; at the same time, the institution of poll taxes and rise of terrorist acts deprived them of the franchise. Out West though, Black cavalry and infantry soldiers, who had helped fight the Indians, and protect mail and westward-bound settlers, threatened to retaliate against racism. In Texas, they posted a sign warning cowboys and others "to recognize our rights of way as just and peaceful men," and that if they not "received just and fair play . . . someone will suffer; if not the guilty, the innocent. . . ." Many northern states refused to pass legislation ensuring the right of Blacks to vote, prompting many White southerners to accuse them of hypocrisy. Scores of riots erupted in southern states as Blacks sought equal rights and treatment. To many visiting White South Africans and Englishmen, America was wrong in declaring Blacks equal to Whites. "The race problem of Southern America," said the *Rand Daily Mail,* "has been made more difficult by the well-meant, but unstatesmanlike, fifteenth amendment . . . which has produced nothing but bitterness and allegations of bad faith."[175]

With the reemergence of secret societies and the birth of the Ku Klux Klan, Blacks were subjected to floggings, house burnings, mutilations, shootings, stabbings, and hangings. In Louisiana, in 1868, 2,000 were killed or wounded in just a few weeks; in Florida, in a single county, more than 150 were murdered in a few months; and in Texas, murders became "so common as to render it impossible to keep accurate accounts of them," reported an army general.[176]

As with contemporary hate groups, such actions—and segregation—were believed necessary for preserving law and order. "The common white people of the country," said a North Carolina politician, "are at times very much enraged against the Negro population. They think that this universal political and civil equality will bring about social equality. . . . The white laboring people feel that it is not safe for them to be . . . working in close contact with the Negroes."[177]

In 1877, Reconstruction in the South ended when President Rutherford B. Hayes withdrew all occupying military troops, leaving the Black population without any protection. Because of intimidation and obstruction, Black voting declined between 1876 and 1884 by one-third in Louisiana, one-fourth in Mississippi, and one-half in South Carolina.[178]

Only abroad did Blacks have freedom. In supporting passage of the 1875 Civil Rights Act, Black Congressmen James T. Rapier of Alabama told Congress of his recent European trip, where for the first time he "could approach a hotel without the fear that the door would be slammed in my face." To call America "the asylum of the oppressed is a misnomer," he said, "for upon all sides I am treated as a pariah."[179]

As with no other group, laws and customs marked Blacks inferior. To avoid being singled out, White immigrants and particularly their offspring could change their names and even place of residence, but not Blacks, except for the few light-skinned, who "passed" into White society. Struggling immigrants also knew that though they were bad off, Blacks were more so, for neither in the Old nor New Country had they been slaves. No matter how disliked, they sensed or knew that Blacks (as well as Indians, Asians, and Mexicans) were more disliked. Like native-born Whites, some took to hating Blacks, and doing so with the same impunity.

Though Blacks could not easily vote or join unions, immigrants could and did, especially in large cities where they built community power bases that provided ambitious immigrants with numerous opportunities for election or political appointment. Ironically, just as immigrants were often damned for being socialists, Blacks were sometimes praised for not being ones, but only "as long as the dominant imposes its will on the servient and as long as they remain in the same relation to the whites as in the past."[180]

For all the benefits of being White rather than Black, or of being native-born rather than immigrant, both groups struggled for an unhampered right to vote. Well into the nineteenth century, White males were restricted in voting by poll taxes and property qualifications, as well as by invidious distinctions between native- and foreign-born. For example, in Rhode Island, as a result of the 1842 constitutional convention, native-born White males could vote only if they paid a dollar tax or if they served in the militia, but foreign-born White males had to be freeholders and possess $134 worth of land.

Promotion of Immigration from Abroad

Though the rights of Blacks and Indians were ignored, denied, or violated, and in spite of the festering xenophobia, federal and state governments (and certain businesses) continued to encourage the immigration of European laborers and settlers. President Tyler told Congress in 1841 that they should be welcomed for the blessings the country offered, in return for which they should view the country as theirs and "unite with us in the great task of preserving our institutions and thereby perpetuating our liberties." After President Lincoln urged the establishment of a "system for the encouragement of immigration," Congress passed a law in 1864 supporting importation of contract laborers. As with colonial indentured servants, such workers had to pledge their wages until the costs of the voyage had been paid off. Because some European countries were still pardoning criminals on condition they go to America, Congress officially condemned the practice in 1866.[181]

Unlike other foreign governments seeking immigrants (particularly South American ones and Canada), America did not offer free or subsidized transatlantic transportation, immediate citizenship, or funds for purchasing land or starting up homesteads. Instead, many states placed advertisements in foreign papers, distributed promotional pamphlets abroad, and established offices to encourage immigration.

In Hong Kong, in 1862, a flyer recruiting Chinese miners announced that Oregon welcomed them: "They will supply good houses and plenty of food. They will pay $24 a month and treat you considerately when you arrive. There is no fear of slavery. All is nice." Wisconsin promoted the availability of full political rights for all newcomers, and Minnesota boasted of its many ethnic newspapers. Colorado proclaimed itself the "Switzerland of America," where the poor "by industry and frugality better their conditions," the rich "more advantageously invest their means than in any other region," the young "get an early start on the road to wealth, and the old . . . a new lease on life."[182]

The advent of steamships shortened travel time across the Atlantic to under two weeks, and shipping lines and railroads employed thousands of legal and "secret" ticket agents, who frequently misrepresented conditions and opportunities in America. In the early 1900s, two leading steamship lines had some 5,000–6,000 agents in Galicia alone, and in Russia, agents helped immigrants secure passports to leave the country illegally.[183]

American railroads not only sought lucrative fares but also buyers for the millions of acres of western land they owned. The Northern Pacific had 800 agents in Europe. The Burlington and Missouri River Railroad Company appealed to European sportsmen to hunt buffalo and other game, distributing posters announcing, "THERE ARE NO HOSTILE INDIANS IN NEBRASKA WHATEVER," and assuring protection and help by friendly Indian chiefs. In

America, too, the railroads and land speculators advertised heavily, hoping to attract settlers, buyers, and tourists from the East.[184]

Many Europeans now came in groups to join family members or friends who had preceded them and who had loaned or given them money for the Atlantic passage. Though still not familiar with American life, they knew from letters and word of mouth about the areas in which their friends and family lived and about what kinds of jobs were available. Other groups of immigrants came with the help of immigrant companies, such as British farmers, who settled in Kansas, the Dakotas, and Oregon. The 1880 census reported that 73 percent of Wisconsin's population was of foreign parentage, 71 percent of Minnesota's, 66 percent of both Dakotas', and 44 percent of Nebraska's.[185]

For industry and business, free immigration meant keeping wages low, cowering freed Black plantation workers, intimidating native workers, and aborting unionization, all of which contributed to pitting native-born Whites against immigrants, immigrants against each other, and Whites and immigrants against Blacks and Asians.

In the North, when poor Irish laborers in New York City, in 1846, went on strike to gain a ten-hour day and an 87.5 cents per day wage, their employers, according to the *New York Weekly Tribune,* "hired a cargo of freshly landed Germans to take their places, and ordered the old laborers to quit the premises, which they refused to do, and resorted to the lawless, unjustifiable step of endeavoring to drive the Germans from the work by intimidation and violence. Of course the Military were called out, the Irish overawed, the Germans protected in their work, and thus the matter stands."[186] In the ensuing decades, the pitting of one minority against another intensified in all parts of the country. A synergetic relationship of bigotry and industrialization evolved, sustaining itself on Old and New World xenophobia, prejudice, and racism.

Anglo-Saxonism—Religious, Racial, and Social

As the French were building the Statue of Liberty and as the newly composed Pledge of Allegiance was gaining popularity, Anglo-Saxon chauvinism, Protestant triumphalism, and pseudo-scientific racism proliferated. Long gone were the days when Protestants were dissenters seeking freedom from their motherland. Now they were *the* establishment, whose values and mores dominated society. Politically, the Republican Party was theirs, and many of its leaders, such as Rutherford B. Hayes, Ulysses S. Grant, James G. Blaine, and Benjamin Harrison, were hostile to Catholics and immigrants. In large cities, however, they felt threatened by the growing political presence of southern, central, and eastern European immigrants, who were joining the Democratic Party.

As more immigrants arrived, priority of residence, purity of blood, and pride of Protestantism became benchmarks of social distinction and political legitimacy, which various intellectuals, businessmen, suffragists, temperance advocates, religious leaders, and nativists used to define others as biologically, psychologically, sociologically, or theologically unacceptable.

Literature of the day abounded in stereotypes and epithets for European and Asian immigrants. The following are just some that appeared in 1887: barbarians, polygamous relics of barbarism, half savages, human dregs of all the earth, diseased elements, the off-scouring of Europe and Asia, human and inhuman rubbish, heterogenous hordes, scum and riff-raff, filthy mendicants, and pauper populations of the Old World.[187]

Dictionaries and encyclopedias defined *race* in terms of physical characteristics or nationality. Each race was said to reflect a different stage of evolution, the most advanced being Anglo-Saxons and Teutons, and the lowest being southeastern Europeans, Indians, Blacks, and Moslems.

In the world of science, people's heads, brains, and facial features were measured, compared, and evaluated. Japanese brains, wrote one scholar, "although not growing quite so fast as those of Anglo-Saxons, grow more rapidly after puberty than do the Chinese brains," which "may account for the 'masculine' character of the Japanese compared with the relatively 'feminine' character of the Chinese."[188]

To another researcher, the new immigrants caused native-born Americans to become physically shorter, more darkly complected, entrepreneurally weaker, and have more abbreviated skulls. It was even argued that insanity among Whites was greater than among Blacks and Indians because the latter were less creative, sensitive, and civilized, and therefore too inferior to be insane, which a medical expert said was the price White people had to pay for being civilized.[189] Invidious distinctions were made between Indians and Blacks, with the latter held uncivilizable and dependent on White magnanimity for their survival, while the former were savages and doomed to extinction.

To other experts of the time, Portuguese were "volatile, impulsive, quick-tempered, rather obtrusive, suggestible, and poorly inhibited." Filipinos constituted "a race in an adolescent stage of development," with "super-sensitiveness, poor emotional control, and unstable moods." Bohemians were "depraved beasts, harpies, decayed physically and spiritually, mentally and morally, thievish and licentious." Slavs were "eaters of raw animal food, fond of drinking the blood of their enemies whom they slew in battle, and [men] who preserved as trophies the scalps and skins of enemies whom they overthrew." Greeks were said to be a greater tax on police courts than any other group in proportion to their total population.[190]

Equally ominous was the high immigrant reproduction rate. Studies showed middle-class Anglo-Saxon Americans having fewer children with each passing generation; while 13 percent of their marriages were childless, it was only 2.4 for Czechs, 2.5 for Russians, 2.6 for Poles, 3.9 for Germans, and 4.9 for Italians. To the secretary of the Missionary Society of Connecticut, in 1905:

> The birth and death rate constantly favor the new comer. These sturdy young people, with their large families are crowding to the front. The Pilgrim and

Puritan have had their day. Gregorian chants and Hebrew synagogues and sunny Italy have new meanings as we read the records of fifty different nationalities coming into our cities and towns, driving native help from our factories, buying up our "abandoned farms," holding the balance of power in political and moral questions, and making the future of not a few of our churches dependent upon these very "strangers and foreigners."[191]

Even people with the same nationality, ethnicity, or religion were invidiously compared. Southern Italians were considered inferior to northern ones, who were Teutonic and therefore capable of "great progress in the social organization of a modern society." To Burton Hendrick, the year 1881 marked the beginning of America's "Jewish problem" because the new eastern European Jewish immigrants represented "an entirely different type of Judaism from the staid Spanish Jew and the energetic German of the previous generations."[192] Among mainline Protestants, the smaller denominations were seen as obstacles to church unity.

Prominent historians, clergymen, and intellectuals credited America's uniqueness to Protestant, Anglo-Saxon, and Teutonic roots, which enabled the early colonists to clear the forests, fight the Indians, and settle the West. Hubert Howe Bancroft feared that if "the great unwashed" of Europe were allowed to settle in California, they would intermarry and pose a greater curse on the country's future than Asians and Africans combined. To Columbia University's John William Burgess, Teutonic Germans, Swedes, Norwegians, Danes, Dutch, and English had consciences and self-control that enabled them to enjoy civil and political liberty. Not so with Slavs, Czechs, Hungarians, and southern Italians, who "do not know our language and do not learn it. They are inclined to anarchy and crime. They are, in everything which goes to make up folk character, the exact opposite of genuine Americans." To the Unitarian social reformer Theodore Parker, the Irish were "ignorant . . . idle, thriftless, poor, intemperate, and barbarian," who "commit great crimes of violence."[193]

In spite of their many theological, denominational, and regional differences, many Protestant clergy and congregants espoused an Anglo-Saxon superiority, which viewed Roman Catholicism with disdain and "inimical to the best progress of society." To Southern Baptists, in 1890, the world's religious destiny was "lodged in the hands of the English-speaking people," to whom God had committed the enterprise of saving everyone. In such a world, Blacks were to be saved, but not integrated into White churches. A few Protestant clergy even espoused Anglo-Israelism, which originated in England and held that Anglo-Saxons were descendants of Israel's lost ten tribes, and that those living in England, Ireland, and America were the real "chosen people" and rightful heirs to God's blessings.[194]

The 1869 to 1870 Vatican Council's adoption of "Papal Infallibility" as dogma further intensified nativist demands for immigration restrictions, dismissal of Catholic workers, and defeat of Catholic political candidates. Many a

Protestant household was reluctant to hire Irish maids lest they be secret agents of the pope determined to convert their children or serve them poisoned food.[195]

Unlike the early nineteenth century when Catholics numbered less than 500,000, they now numbered in the millions, the largest Christian denomination, with growing big-city political power, churches, and parochial schools and were determined no longer to passively accept Protestant insult and discrimination. To historian John Gilmary Shea, it was contemptible to say New England Protestants established the principle of liberty of conscience. Rather, they were "narrow-minded, tyrannical, and intolerant in religious thought; cruel and unmerciful to white or red men who refused to submit to their ruling; grasping and avaricious in their intercourse with Indians; full of superstition and easily led by it into any excess."[196]

If in Ireland large numbers of people ensured continuing poverty, in America they increased opportunities for sociopolitical power. By 1890, New York City had twice as many Irish as Dublin and as many Italians as Naples. The first Irish American mayor was elected in Scranton in 1878, in New York City in 1880, in Boston in 1884, and in Chicago in 1893. On the federal level, Francis B. Spinola of New York became the first Italian American member of the House of Representatives in 1887. As Catholics advanced, cries arose of reverse discrimination, as in Albany in the 1890s, when a minister complained that in a construction workforce on the capital building, "of sixty 'orderlies' and cleaners, forty-two were Roman Catholics, two were Jews, two were nothings with Roman Catholic wives, and only four were Protestants. There were sixteen elevator-men, and all but one were Roman Catholics." Also, the fiercely anti-Catholic American Protective Association charged that civil service examinations favored Catholics and that "although only one-eighth of the population of the United States was Catholic . . . one-half of all the public officeholders were Catholic."[197]

Catholics and Jews alike were criticized for their respective opposition to the Protestant Bible in the public schools and Sunday closing laws. Accusations were made of a "conspiracy of Jesuit and Jew, infidel and atheist," who had "stricken hands like Herod and Pontius Pilate in the common work of crucifying Christ."[198]

Spurious Catholic documents—like the "Jesuit Oath of Secrecy" and the "Priest's Oath"—were widely distributed. Another, "Instructions to Catholics," urged believers to undermine the public schools. A supposed encyclical of Pope Leo XIII released all Catholics from any allegiance to the United States and urged them on or about the day of the feast of Ignatius Loyola in 1893 "to exterminate all heretics found within the jurisdiction of the United States." As a result, some people rushed to arm themselves, and the mayor of Toledo mobilized the National Guard to stop the rumored massacre.[199]

New anti-Catholic organizations and publications, such as *The Menace* and *Watson's Magazine,* viewed the recently formed Catholic Knights of Columbus as a secret advance guard of a papal conspiracy to persecute Protestants and end

American democracy. The American Protective Association, founded in 1887 as a secret membership organization, revived the anti-Catholicism of the defunct Know-Nothing Party and closely allied itself with the Republican Party. Among its members were Scandinavian, Canadian, British, and especially Scotch-Irish Protestants. Tracts were sent across the country, raising a cry that was repeated over and over—even in modern times against John F. Kennedy.

> Can a good Romanist be at the same time a loyal American citizen? . . . The Vatican claims absolute and supreme authority in all things, civil as well as spiritual, and every member of the church is bound to render to the Pontiff absolute and unquestioning obedience. This being true, is it not quite certain that whatever his personal opinions and feelings may be as an American citizen, he must support the Church against the State? . . . Can any person who is loyal to Romanism be true to Republicanism? Can a Romanist be a good citizen of America?[200]

The Guardians of Liberty, founded in 1911 by some retired military officers, opposed any political appointee or candidate "who owes superior temporal allegiance to any power above his obligation to . . . the United States." William C. Black, a Guardian lecturer, is credited with concocting the infamous "Knights of Columbus Oath" in 1912, wherein members swore:

> I will, when opportunity presents, make and wage relentless war, secretly and openly, against all heretics, Protestants, and Masons, as I am directed to do, to extirpate them from the face of the whole earth; and that I will spare neither age nor sex, or condition, and that I will hang, burn, waste, boil, flay, strangle, and bury alive these infamous heretics, rip up the stomachs and wombs of their women, and crush their infants' heads against the wall in order to annihilate their execrable race. That when the same cannot be done openly, I will secretly use the poisonous cup, the strangulation cord, the steel of the poniard, or the leaden bullet, regardless of the honor, rank, dignity, or authority of the persons, whatever may be their condition in life, either public or private, as I at any time may be directed to do so by any agents of the Pope or superior of the Brotherhood of the Holy Father of the Society of Jesus.[201]

Mormons were no less hated. To Congregationalist Josiah Strong, both Mormons and Catholics threatened the West, where "irreligion" abounded and "apostate Catholics" furnished the soil for socialism. "Mormonism also is doing a like preparatory work. It is gathering together great numbers of ill-balanced men, who are duped for a time by Mormon mummery." To Utah's governor, in 1889:

> That instinctive love of country, which is the distinguishing characteristic of the American people, does not find a responsive sentiment in Utah. The orthodox Mormon, in every political and business act, puts the church first, country afterwards. It cannot be otherwise, for the priesthood claims all government

but its own to be illegal, and claims a separate political destiny and ultimate temporal dominion, and by divine rights.[202]

As late as 1912, the former superintendent of Baptist missions in Utah termed Mormonism as "the Islam of America," whose adherents, though relatively small, were to be feared more than any other group. "No one else is trying to set up an *imperium in imperio* or to control either the state or national government. They are promising their followers nothing less than that they will in time control things politically in the United States."[203]

Though Jews numbered only 50,000 in 1850 (less than one-fourth of 1 percent of the total population), economic, social, and religious anti-Semitism grew with each decade, though not as intensively as in Europe. Unlike most other immigrant groups, they were a minority in their birthland and remained so in America. Jews were portrayed as mercenary, reprobate, and deicidal, superseded in "chosenness" by Christians.

"A rascally Jew figures in every cheap novel," wrote Rabbi Isaac M. Wise, "every newspaper printed some stale jokes about Jews to fill up space, and every backwoodsman had a few jokes on hand to use in public addresses; and all this called forth not a word of protest from any source." A few Christians noted, too, what was taking place. To Lyman Abbott, "The pictures which Shakespeare, Walter Scott and Robert Browning have afforded of the Christian's treatment of the Jew, of the prejudice in the Christian's heart against the Jew, are terribly realistic. Even in our own time and our own land, where legal restrictions and disabilities are impossible, the prejudice which has in times past wronged them, still continues, and has shown itself in exclusion from social intercourse, and even from public hotels."[204]

Rich or poor, Jews were increasingly "not wanted" in neighborhoods, resorts and private clubs, and universities, more so in the North than in the South. As a result of such discrimination, some Jews formed their own social clubs and organizations, such as the B'nai B'rith and the Young Men's Hebrew Association (YMHA). A few Reform Jewish rabbis advocated joining with Unitarianism, not only because of similar beliefs about God, humanity, and reason, but also because "we would then become part of the majority [Christianity] instead of remaining a powerless minority growing weaker."[205]

As the twentieth century approached, disdain for Jews expanded beyond that of Christ-killers and money lenders to social climbers and superfinanciers. Populists, silver advocates, and farmers blamed them (and banks and government) for the country's financial problems.

Wealthy German Jews in America and in Europe were accused of conspiring with England to cause money and credit problems. Grover Cleveland was labeled "the agent for Jewish bankers and British gold." Motivating the Jew, said a 1904 observer, was "his almost pariah-like exclusion from his surroundings, which, while it increases his energy and fighting instincts, must also free him, to some extent, from his scruples in dealing with Gentiles."[206]

As with the *Mortara Case* three decades earlier, which involved Vatican police kidnapping a Jewish child, the *Alfred Dreyfus Affair* in France, in the late 1890s, evoked strong protests by American Jews, Protestants, and Catholics, but for different reasons. Jews, of course, supported Dreyfus and decried the anti-Semitism behind his arrest and imprisonment. Protestants, however, did so more out of hostility to Catholics than sympathy for Jews. To the *American Monthly Review of Reviews:*

> France has remained till now a country on the side of authority, inheriting from its Latin civilization a superstitious respect for all who hold the smallest share of power, for every functionary, in a word, civil, ecclesiastical, or military. It is well known that Catholicism supports this idolatry. It exacts from the faithful absolute submission, complete surrender of the rights of reason, unqualified acquiescence not only in the word of God, but also, and especially, in that of his accredited representatives.[207]

Though aware of the anti-Catholicism about them, American Catholics reluctantly spoke up, but only in defense of the church and France. Reacting to Protestant criticism, the Catholic *Pilot,* in Boston, wrote:

> It requires only some crime of the Dreyfus character in one of the unhappy lands where English is not spoken to call forth an exhibition of that complacent self-righteousness, Pharisaism and cant, which seem to be all of the inheritance of Puritanism. . . . The fact that France, in the teeth of dangers that threaten her political existence, is striving hard to correct a judicial military crime appears to have no weight whatever with the British and American Pharisee.[208]

Being discriminated against did not stop some German Jews from criticizing new eastern European Jewish immigrants for their religious orthodoxy, social behavior, or poverty, and both the B'nai B'rith and the YMHA discouraged their membership. A few urged that "missionaries be sent to Russia to civilize the Russian Jews rather than have their backwardness ruin the American Jewish community." To Rabbi Wise, "We are Americans and they are not. We are Israelites of the nineteenth century and a free country, and they gnaw the dead bones of past centuries." Some Reform rabbis, believing Christian hostility toward Jews was traceable to their being different, ended the wearing of skullcaps, switched from traditional Saturday to Sunday services, and emphasized establishing close relations with their Christian counterparts.[209]

In spite of the anti-Semitism about them, Jews knew they were freer and more secure in America than in any other country in the world. American Jews did not experience the massive violence that Irish Catholics, Mormons, Mexicans, Asians, Indians, and Blacks had. American Christians neither called for nor initiated inquisitions, expulsions, pogroms, blood libels, or any of the other horrors that their European counterparts had or were initiating against other Christians or Jews. Between 1867 and 1914, more than a dozen trials of Jews took place in Germany and Austria-Hungary for their alleged ritual murder of Christians.[210]

America's racial, religious, and ethnic bigotry was not limited to a few educated or uneducated people (native-born or immigrant), but included some prominent reformers. To Elizabeth Cady Stanton, a leading suffragist and proud Anglo-Saxon, it was bad enough for native White women to be oppressed by "their own Saxon Fathers," but worse yet, by denying them the vote, America would be ruled by "Patrick and Sambo and Hans and Yung Tung."[211]

Though philosophically espousing the unity of the workingman, many Socialists and labor leaders wanted Asians excluded from immigrating to America and Blacks kept out of their unions. Daniel De Leon, chief ideologue of the Socialist Labor Party, said in 1900 that "the disfranchisement of the negro does not hurt the revolutionary party in the least." Victor L. Berger of the Socialist Party had "no doubt that the negroes and mulattoes constitute a lower race—that the Caucasian and indeed even the Mongolian have the start on them in civilization by many thousand years."[212]

The temperance and Sabbath observance movements also revealed strong strains of bigotry. "The saloon fosters an un-American spirit among the foreign-born population of our country," declared one teetotaler. "The influx of foreigners into our urban centers, many of whom have liquor habits, is a menace to good government . . . the foreign-born population is largely under the social and political control of the saloon." To the Presbyterian churches, in 1870, "with the growth of immigration from the nations of Europe, the desecration of the Sabbath was increasing with the playing of music, drinking, and feasting."[213]

Many philanthropic and reform organizations and leaders, particularly in New England, blamed open immigration for class conflict, group voting blocs, slums, and moral decline. Charity alone was keeping many immigrants alive, said a young social worker, "forcing down the standard of living among our poor, and complicating the problem incalculably at every turn." To the Associated Charities of Boston, in 1899, the city's Arabs "always find an excuse for refusing work, even when offered to them, as long as they can earn more by peddling and begging."[214]

The idea for a test barring illiterate immigrants first surfaced in Massachusetts in 1888, where the Immigration Restriction League was also formed six years later. Senator Henry Cabot Lodge, the test's most prominent advocate, proposed a bill to exclude all fourteen- to sixty-year-olds unable to "both read and write the English language or some other language." Admittedly, he said:

> The illiteracy test will bear most heavily upon the Italians, Russians, Poles, Hungarians, Greeks, and Asiatics, and very lightly, or not at all, upon English-speaking emigrants or Germans, Scandinavians or French. In other words, the races most affected by the illiteracy test are those whose emigration to this

country has begun within the last twenty years and welled rapidly to enormous proportions, races with which the English-speaking people have never hitherto assimilated, and who are most alien to the great body of the people of the United States.[215]

President Cleveland thought otherwise and vetoed the bill, saying it was more rational to "admit a hundred thousand immigrants who, though unable to read and write, seek among us only a home and opportunity to work, than to admit one of those unruly agitators and enemies of governmental control who can not only read and write, but delights in arousing by inflammatory speech the illiterate and peacefully inclined to discontent and tumult."[216]

Nevertheless, race, class, status, and sense of mission continued to pervade the country's socioeconomic elite, who considered acquisitiveness and entrepreneuralism virtues, with little regard to how they were carried on or their impact on the poor. Borrowing from Malthus and Darwin, railroad tycoon James J. Hill said, "The fortunes of railroad companies are determined by the law of the survival of the fittest," and John J. Rockefeller Sr. told a Sunday school class, "the growth of a large business is merely a survival of the fittest . . . merely the working out of a law of nature and a law of God." Jesus Christ was often recast to conform with their Protestant economic ethic. A best-selling book, *The Man Nobody Knows: A Discovery of the Real Jesus,* portrayed Jesus as Jerusalem's most popular dinner guest, an outdoor man, and an executive who "picked up twelve men from the bottom ranks of business and forged them into an organization that conquered the world."[217]

To avoid any confusion about who the "fittest" were, *Social Registers* came into being, which often included financial supporters of the anti-Catholic American Protective Association and other anti-immigration groups. At the same time, more and more patriotic groups formed, such as the Sons of the American Revolution, the Daughters of the American Revolution, the Colonial Dames of America, and the United States Daughters of 1812. In 1882, the first of many all-Protestant country clubs was established in Brookline, Massachusetts. Melvil Dewey, the famed inventor of the decimal classification of library books, organized a business club that excluded anyone whom its members deemed objectionable because of physical, moral, social, or racial condition and placed an absolute ban on Jews.[218]

In New England, many proud Yankees sought refuge in their English, Anglo-Saxon roots, which they had previously scorned because of the Revolutionary War and the War of 1812. In origin and essence, "American blood and English blood run from the same veins," said William Roscoe Thayer. To preserve that lineage, children were sent to private schools like Groton and St. Paul's, in which British names, manners, sports, and educational methods were imitated. In Boston's Back Bay section, English names were given to streets, hotels, and apartment houses—Clarendon, Exeter, Wellington, Hereford. In the South, racial and regional ideals (and myths) of the "Southern Gentleman" and "Southern Belle" flourished. Men were to be brave, courteous, and kindly, even to Blacks, while women were to be loyal, merciful, and sexually pure—unlike Blacks or poor Whites. Patriotism and military discipline were to be cultivated, and numbers of private military schools and state-funded military programs were established.[219]

Such chauvinism was not without critics. To James Russell Lowell, the "vague assertions of our Anglo-Saxon descent" were but a mere "cause or . . . apology of national oppression." Suffragist Carrie Chapman Catt cautioned women against displaying excessive pride in "Anglo-Saxon blood" because "we must remember that ages ago the ancestors of the Anglo-Saxons were regarded as so low and embruted that the Romans refused to have them for slaves." Boston's Isabella Stewart Gardner, irritated at a friend's continual references to her *Mayflower* descendants, responded, "Well, I understand the immigration laws are much stricter nowadays."[220]

For all the pious, patriotic, and paternal talk of roots, no clear Anglo-Saxon entity existed. Originally, the term described three large Germanic groupings— Angles, Saxons, and Jutes—and was used to distinguish the Saxons of Britain from those of Germany. After the Angles and Saxons spread through Britain in the fifth and sixth centuries, they were followed by Norsemen, Normans, Flemings, Walloons, Irish, Scots, and Welsh. By the time the English colonists came to America, they had no racial purity, but a hodgepodge of European backgrounds.

To big-city politicos, however, immigrants were to be befriended and valued, at least if they were to retain their power. In New York City, by 1870, 44 percent of the population were foreign-born, mostly Irish and German. By now, the Democratic Tammany Hall had abandoned its original nativism and actively nurtured immigrant voters.

As "Boss" Crocker told a reporter:

> Think of the hundreds of thousands of foreigners dumped into our city. They are too old to go to school. There is not a mugwump [Republican reformer] in the city would shake hands with them. They are alone, ignorant strangers, a prey to all manner of anarchical and wild notions. . . . Yes, and they are of value to Tammany. And Tammany looks after them for the sake of their vote, grafts them upon the Republic, makes citizens of them in short; and although you may not like our motives or our methods what other agency is there by which so long a row could have been hoed so quickly or so well? If we go down into the gutter it is because there are men in the gutter, and you have got to go down where they are if you are to do anything with them.[221]

Most Americans simply could not understand why immigrants did not assimilate as quickly as earlier northern Europeans. After all, immigrants should want to become good Americans, and good Americans did not act the way they did: not learning English; not joining existing churches but establishing their own; building parochial schools when public ones were available; crowding together in neighborhoods; and not learning and obeying the laws of the land. If immigrants liked the old ways so much, why did they leave home and why did they not return?

No less annoying were their religious and ethnic holidays, festivals, and parades, during which immigrants took the day or days off, reflecting a supposed greater loyalty to foreign homelands than to America. Polish weddings could last three to five days, and Greeks, Roman Catholics, and Jews celebrated many holy days. Absenteeism because of holy days, Sunday partying, or job resentment was common. When New York State, in 1909, declared 12 October a legal holiday in honor of Columbus, many newspapers protested that it subtracted "from the business energy of the State, from the earning power of its people, and . . . needlessly added to an already somewhat formidable list of idle days."[222] Major W. Shepherd summed up such attitudes well: "The American does not like foreigners, but he tolerates their presence if they will follow his example and adopt his institutions; but to be a separatist, to live in small national colonies, to appear or behave differently to the accredited type, not to care for local topics or the politics of the saloon—these are all crimes which the American cannot allow."[223]

Notwithstanding such feelings, many Protestant groups committed themselves to missionizing abroad, finding it easier to love and convert people far off than next door. The Student Volunteer Movement of the YMCA pledged to evangelize "the world in one generation," and its traveling secretary urged members not to stay at home "when a hundred thousand heathen a day are dying without hope because we are not there teaching the Gospel." Many American Black churches, too, engaged in missionizing in the West Indies, South America, and Africa, much to the displeasure of some White missionaries, who believed that White rule was being endangered by "Ethiopianism . . . under the guise of Christianity, of equality of black and white."[224]

In short, behind all the nativism, racism, restrictionism, xenophobia, anti-Catholicism, and anti-Semitism was a mindset of moral, social, intellectual, religious, and political superiority. For the most part, the carriers and proponents of such triumphalism did not consider themselves bigoted or cruel, but enlightened and concerned about the nation's well-being. They saw no contradiction between their high ideals and everyday behaviors. If it appeared so, it was due to the observers' own ignorance, lack of culture, racial inferiority, and Old World prejudices. The America they grew up in and loved was being transformed by the growth of large cities, rapid transportation, heavy industrialization, movement West, and increasing numbers of immigrants entering the political process and challenging their sense of wisdom and record of accomplishment. While in its best moods American Protestantism was capable of genuine charity, wrote Sydney Ahlstrom, "in its average performance and typical expression, it strengthened nativism, contributing in many ways to extreme manifestations of intolerance, and even providing leadership for nativist organizations."[225]

Chapter 3

Proliferation of People and Problems

Largely unskilled, anxious for work, and cheaper than machines, immigrants came in ever-increasing numbers at a time when no federal laws existed for minimum wages, working hours, safety conditions, or welfare. Paid lower wages than native-born or Black workers, their productivity could be increased by threats of dismissal or replacement by other minorities and their ethnic and religious rivalries inflamed to prevent unionization. The result was a multiple pattern of competition, exploitation, and succession, in which prejudice and discrimination were integral parts, reflecting old and generating new intergroup animosities.

In the last decade of the nineteenth century, the total number of immigrants more than doubled, rising from 3,687,564 to 8,795,386 for 1901 to 1910. Unlike pre-1870 decades when southern, eastern, and central Europeans represented less than 10 percent of those entering, they constituted 51 percent in 1891–1900 and 65.9 percent in the following decade. Though most were motivated by economic necessity, many came to avoid political or religious persecution (particularly Poles, Ukrainians, Ruthenians, and Jews), or to avoid conscription by the very countries that oppressed them. Usually late-nineteenth-century immigrants arrived with little and with less money than previous groups. For example, by 1910, 84 to 97 percent disembarked with less than $50, in contrast to earlier northwest European immigrants of whom only 50 percent arrived with less than $50.[1] Though poor, they were not the poorest of their homelands, but rather individuals or families who hoped to better themselves in America or help those whom they had left behind.

As in previous decades, a great deal of legal and illegal money was made in bringing and transporting immigrants across the ocean and country. As a turn-of-the-century scholar wrote, "The desire to get cheap labor, to take passenger fares, and to sell land have probably brought more immigrants than the hard conditions of Europe, Asia and Africa."[2]

Single immigrant women were particularly vulnerable to con men, who tricked or forced them into prostitution as they came off the boat or later at dances, movie houses, and beauty parlors. As a 1911 congressional immigration report noted, if the young immigrant "cannot be cajoled or enticed by the promises of an easy time, plenty of money, fine clothes, and the usual stocks of allurements—or fake marriage—then harsher methods are resorted to . . . intoxication and drugging as a means to reduce the victims to a state of helplessness. . . . Sheer physical violence is a common thing."[3]

Unfamiliar with American ways, unable to understand English, usually poor, but ever anxious to begin a new life, immigrants were prey to all kinds of swindlers offering to sell nonexistent jobs, the Brooklyn Bridge, or worthless land—as in the case of early Molokan farmers in Los Angeles, to whom unscrupulous real estate men sold desert land with no prospects for water or crops. Moreover, many employers readily slotted them into production lines requiring little or no ability to read or write English, where machinery lacked safety devices and accidents were high. If immigrants did not like such jobs, they were told they could leave because, as one foreman told complaining workers, "the emigrant steamers bring workmen enough."[4]

With the growing transoceanic immigration went two domestic ones. The first was to and from the East and West, which Ray Billington called "the greatest movement of peoples in the history of the United States," with a larger area settled than in all of America's past. While easterners went West, young western farmers headed for the growing cities, which offered greater economic opportunities. In fact, for every industrial worker turning farmer, twenty farmers became urban residents.[5] European immigrants frequently moved into their homes and farms, or settled in former campsites of railway and canal construction gangs.

"We gave the Americans a good life, we Swedes, Norwegians, Danes, and Germans, by settling the land when the rest of the colonists were running to the towns," said a turn-of-the-century Swedish immigrant. "We came in and did the rough pioneer work that had to be done if America was going to be more than a mushroom growth. Where would America be to-day if it were not for us in Minnesota, Wisconsin, Iowa? You can't keep up big cities unless you've got plenty of men working in the background on the land."[6]

To a lesser extent was the movement south of French Canadians. Though some had freely migrated to the English colonies or, as in the case of Acadians, had been forcibly relocated there before the American Revolution, large numbers kept arriving in the second half of the nineteenth century, settling mainly in New England. As in recent times, many traveled back and forth to their birthplaces in Canada. Although by 1840 there were only some 8,000 in New England, between 1870 and 1930 some 693,000 arrived. As with other foreigners, particularly Catholics, they were maligned and derided. In his history of Vermont, written in 1892, Rowland E. Robinson said their character "is not such as to inspire the highest hope for the future of Vermont, if they should become the most numerous of its population." Too many were "professional beggars . . . an abominable crew of vagabonds, robust, lazy men and boys, slatternly women with litters of filthy brats, and all as detestable as they were uninteresting."[7]

As wave after wave of immigrants arrived, a series of simultaneous successions took place in urban populations, labor force, landownership, crime, and prejudice. Though Chicago's first permanent settler was a West Indian Black, by the 1830s, some 4,000 people, largely Anglo-Saxons, French Canadians, and racially mixed Indians resided there. People came "from almost every clime, and almost every opinion," wrote one journalist. "We had Jews and Christians, Protestants and Catholics and Infidels. . . . Nearly every language was represented." By 1890, Germans represented 34 percent of the city, the Irish 17 percent, and Scandinavians over 14 percent. Thirty years later, Germans had declined to 11 percent and Scandinavians 7 percent, while Poles had risen to 12 percent, Italians to over 5 percent, and Blacks to 7 percent. Chicago now had the country's largest Scandinavian, Polish, Czech, Serbo-Croatian, and Lithuanian populations; the second largest German, Greek, Slovak, Jewish, and Black populations; and the third largest Italian community in the nation.[8]

In other large cities, too, the foreign-born increased in number and visibility. By 1900, they represented approximately one-third to one-fourth of the population in Boston, Buffalo, Cleveland, Detroit, Milwaukee, New York, Newark, Philadelphia, and Pittsburgh. In the West, immigrants and their American-born children were a majority in Minnesota, the Dakotas, Montana, Arizona, Wyoming, Utah, Nevada, and California.[9]

Similar transformations took place in smaller manufacturing towns. For forty years after an iron furnace was established in 1842 in Johnstown, Pennsylvania, the workers were predominantly native Americans, English, Welsh, Irish, and German; then, Slavs began moving in, followed by Italians and Syrians; by 1921, 60 percent of the population was foreign-born, largely from southeastern Europe. To realize how little manufacturers cared about American labor, lamented one Littleton, Massachusetts, resident in 1911, one needed only to stand outside a big mill at quitting time and see "Finns, Poles, Canadians, and a half dozen other nationalities, but mighty few Americans."[10]

As various groups dominated an area, street nicknames and official names changed, so that the Chicago area of "Kilgubbin" became "Little Hell," and then, as industry moved in, "Smokey Hollow." The earliest residents of Hamtramck in the Detroit area were French and named their main thoroughfares DeQuindre, St. Aubin, and Dubois. With the coming of Germans in the mid-nineteenth century, Faber, Leuschner, Geimer, Lehmann, Klinger, and Neibel streets came into being; then in the first decades of the twentieth century, as Poles settled in large numbers, streets were named Sobieski, Florian, Pulaski, and Poland.[11]

Religious buildings and worshippers, too, changed from indigenous Protestant to immigrant Catholic, Protestant, or Jewish. In Pittsburgh's south side, wrote an observer at the time, "The Servians bought out the church building used by the German Lutherans, the Slovaks bought out the church building of the Methodist

Protestants, the Croatians bought out the edifice of the Methodists, the Lithuanians bought out another building of the same denomination, the Greeks bought out the building of the Lutherans, while the churches of the Baptists and Congregationalists have been purchased by other peoples of southeastern Europe."[12]

Within a religious group, too, dramatic changes took place in numbers and ethnicity. For example, while the Catholic church had three foreign-language groups in 1820, a century later six nationalities—Irish, German, Italian, Polish, French Canadian, and Mexican—constituted at least 75 percent of the American Catholic population, which spoke some twenty-eight different languages.[13]

In the South, immigrants were at first welcomed, but only if they were northern Europeans and not, as the Georgia Immigration Association stated, "the lower-class foreigners who have swarmed into northern cities."[14] Northern immigration restrictionists encouraged Southerners not to admit European immigrants, warning them of "another race problem," pauperism, and illiteracy.

Reinforcing such fears were immigrant competition and friendliness with Blacks. "The mistake with us," said one Southerner, "has been that it was not made a felony to bring in an Irishman when it was made piracy to bring in an African." Among the undesirables, wrote the *Atlanta Journal,* were "the Latin elements, which in Cuba, Central and South America have gotten upon such free and easy terms with the negro population as to effect social equality." Czech and Slovak immigrants were harassed and dozens of Italians lynched or driven out of town. One group of sixty immigrants left for the North after being in the South for less than a year because they said they were treated worse than Blacks: "We work from early morning till night for low wages, are fed wretchedly, and are socially ostracized." If that was not enough to discourage or scare off immigrants, wild stories arose of Germans treated as slaves and of Jews being imprisoned in mines, working "like mules, under the lash of brutal negroes."[15]

By 1913, southern state immigration programs had ended, and southern congressmen were practically unanimous in opposing further southeastern European immigration. Except for New Orleans and a few other communities, a 1913 study acknowledged "intense race prejudice on the part of southern wage-earners of native birth has rendered impossible the extensive employment of southern and eastern Europeans in other branches of manufacturing in the South, and has consequently prevented the development of immigrant industrial colonies."[16]

Also taking place was a succession in jobs and professions and a de facto order of worker preferences. Generally, native-born workers were considered most desirable, followed by immigrants from the British Isles and Germany, then southern, central, and eastern Europeans. Least desirable were Blacks, Indians, and Mexicans. When employers wanted to keep wages low, speed production, or prevent unionization, however, finer distinctions were made. For example, in the mid-1800s, the Boston and Lowell Railroad hired only Irishmen as foremen, because they did not aspire to higher positions as did Yankees. Elsewhere, Poles were considered harder workers than Italians and Greeks. In Pittsburgh, Irish and

Italians were deemed better hod carriers than Hungarians. In Texas, Mexicans were preferred to Chinese as railroad workers. There were also Jewish clothing manufacturers who hired Italian rather than Jewish workers, whom they believed more prone to unionization.[17]

Newly arrived European immigrants, particularly the unskilled, usually started on the bottom, replacing earlier immigrant and native-born groups, and sometimes elevating them to higher positions. Edward Everett Hale, in 1852, said it was their inferiority that compelled them "to go to the bottom; and the consequence is that we are, all of us, the higher lifted." The same thing happened with Asians. "After we got Chinamen to work," said railroad builder Charles Crocker, "we took the more intelligent of the white laborers and made foremen of them. . . . They got a start by controlling Chinese labor on our railroad."[18]

Slowly, grudgingly, and increasingly, immigrants entered positions once held by native-born Americans and joined unions.

In Illinois, in 1886, only 21 percent of the trade union workers were American, but 33 percent German, 19 percent Irish, 12 percent Scandinavian, and about 5 percent each were Poles, Bohemians, and Italians. Nationally, by 1910, copper and iron mine workers were more than 65 percent foreign-born White males; clothing factories more than 75 percent; woolen and worsted mills, blast furnaces and steel rolling mills, tanneries, and bakeries more than 50 percent; coal mines, slaughter and packing houses, car and railroad shops, silk and textile mills, and street, road, sewer, and bridge construction and maintenance companies between 45 and 50 percent.[19]

The successions were multiple—ethnically, sexually, and racially. In the 1880s, the Irish constituted some 95 percent of New York City's longshoremen, but by 1912, some 33 percent were Italians; both groups were followed by smaller groups of Yugoslavs, Poles, Blacks, and other minorities. By century's turn, Italians were replacing French barbers, Black hotel workers, and German shoemakers. In the cigar-making industry, Bohemians succeeded Germans, who then were replaced by Russian Jews and Italians. In Chicago's stockyards, Upton Sinclair noted, "The Poles, who had come by tens of thousands, had been driven to the wall by the Lithuanians, and now the Lithuanians were giving way to the Slovaks."[20]

Although such successions and job proliferations benefited native-born workers, they provided immigrants with little opportunity to rise. Various studies of immigrant mobility reveal that for Dutch immigrants from 1841 to 1870, only some 31 percent improved their occupational status from their first to last job; Irish workers in Poughkeepsie in the later nineteenth century remained largely in unskilled jobs; only 14 out of every 100 Italian, Romanian, and Slovak immigrants starting blue-collar jobs rose to higher ones; and less than 5 percent of Mexicans in Santa Barbara in the early twentieth century were upwardly mobile. As John Bodnar noted, immigrants generally were likely "to find mobility horizontal rather than vertical or no mobility at all."[21]

In the process, some professions assumed distinct, but not exclusive, ethnic characteristics—Italians and Jews in the clothing industry; Italians and Portuguese in New England's textile manufacturing; Irish in the transportation field; eastern Europeans in the production of steel; Germans in printing and machine tooling; and Scotch-Irish and English in the skilled section of steel fabrication of by-products.[22]

In the early nineteenth century, 53 percent of Irish immigrants were women; 41 percent of German immigrants; 21 percent of southern Italians; 13 percent of Croatians; and 4 percent of Greeks. The only large immigrant group with almost equal percentages of male and female were Jews. Whatever their ethnicity, they were blamed for the decline of the family, the rise of juvenile delinquency, and not wanting to learn English.[23]

As their numbers and economic need grew, they too replaced native-born female workers, when the latter left to marry, have children, obtain better-paying jobs, or avoid being stigmatized for doing immigrant work. Not only did immigrant women have to deal with a job market that exploited or excluded them, but also with their own traditional group values, which opposed or discouraged wives, sisters, and daughters from working. A woman's place was at home, whether she was married or single.

Depending on the area, invidious religious and ethnic job preferences came into being. Many native-born White women refused to work alongside immigrant Europeans, Asians, or Blacks. At times, immigrant women were kept in separate workrooms and denied the use of dressing rooms used by American-born women. Those who became domestics were looked down upon. The Irish "are about the only race which can be said to prefer housework," said an early-twentieth-century Boston YWCA employment survey. "Italians do not take kindly to housework; they drift into the North End or into mills. Jews never do housework in any but their own homes." And, indeed, 1910 immigration statistics show that 54 percent of Irish immigrant women in the labor force were "servants and waitresses," compared to 9 percent of Italian women workers and 14 percent of Jewish ones.[24]

By 1920, foreign-born women workers over sixteen years old were one-third greater in percentage than that for all White women, largely because of their family's greater economic need for their earnings. Marriages across ethnic and religious lines were slight, and many intragroup marriages were arranged, either in America, during a visit back home, or through "picture brides."[25]

As in the labor and housing markets, crime and prostitution followed similar patterns of succession. By the early twentieth century, Italian and Jewish immigrants in New York City's Bowery district were replacing the Irish in criminal activity; a United States Industrial Commission claimed they had been influenced by "the corrupt remnants of Irish immigration which now make up the beggars, the drunkards, the thugs, and thieves of those quarters."[26]

As for prostitution, an 1859 study found that 60 percent of New York's prostitutes were immigrants, half of whom were Irish. By the early 1900s, surveys of immigrant and/or immigrant-descended prostitutes in the Lower East Side of New York City revealed a preponderance of Jews, following in descending numbers of French, Germans, Italians, Irish, and Poles. On the West Coast, high percentages of prostitutes were Chinese and Japanese.[27]

For most immigrant women, economic necessity was the propelling cause. "The horrors of the sweatshop," wrote New York City's police commissioner in 1906, "the awful sordidness of life in the dismal tenement, the biting, grinding poverty, the fierce competition, the pitiful wages for long hours of toil under unwholesome conditions, physical depression, and mental unhappiness are all allied with the temptation to join the better-clad, better-fed, and apparently happier [people]." Others were lured by "White Slavers" (mostly of French, German, and Polish origin), who promised them husbands, jobs, and payment to their families and then forced them into prostitution. At times, procurers escorted their victims across the ocean, telling port officials that the girls were their wives or relatives.[28]

As defendants or plaintiffs, immigrants received little justice in the courts, where they were subjected to judicial delays, high legal costs, and incompetent court officers. The New York State Commission of Immigration, in 1910, found "serious abuses in the interpreter systems, on which the alien's hope of justice depends; it found no instruction in our laws which would enable a well-meaning alien to remain law-abiding in the maze of our complex ordinances, department regulations, and state laws. It found few aliens able to appeal their cases, so their sentences were heavy and their situation was hopeless because of their financial inability to obtain a full review of their case."[29]

In some areas, immigrants found themselves competing with Black skilled and unskilled workers, who were few or nonexistent in their homelands. As they acculturated, many adopted the racist attitudes of native-born Americans, as if doing so would boost their standing by having another group below them. Gradually they replaced Blacks, thereby further restricting the latter's socioeconomic mobility. In New Orleans, Blacks first lost jobs building canals to Irish immigrants, and then to Chinese in the 1870s, and finally to southern Italians, who were labeled "black dagoes." In 1907, Samuel Scrotten wrote, "Negro waiters and hotel employees were giving way before the inroads of whites. Throughout the entire North and West most of the best hotels and restaurants [continued] to replace Negro waiters with whites. . . . The Italian, Sicilian and Greek foreign to America's institutions occupy what was confessedly the Negro's forty years ago. They [Greeks and Italians] have bootblack stands, newsstands, barbering, waitering, janitors, and catering businesses."[30]

Foreign- and native-born Whites readily supported Jim Crow laws particularly in the evolving local labor unions, which in spite of espousing worker solidarity excluded Blacks. As a result, Blacks formed their own, such as the Colored Caulkers Trade Union, the Colored Engineers Association, the Colored

Painters Society. In some cases, rather than have Black strikebreakers, unions permitted the formation of separate Black locals, and by 1887, the Knights of Labor had more than 400. As Samuel Gompers warned, "If we don't make friends of the colored man, he will of necessity be justified in proving himself our enemy. They will be utilized . . . to frustrate our every effort for economic, social and political improvement."[31]

Unable to enforce nondiscrimination on the local union level, the American Federation of Labor revised its constitution to read, "Separate charters may be issued to Central Labor Unions, Local Unions, or Federal Labor Unions, composed exclusively of colored workers where in the judgment of the Executive Council it appears advisable."[32]

For Blacks unable to join a union or obtain a job, strikebreaking was the only way to earn a living, much to the approval of Black leaders and organizations. Even then, jobs or promotions gained during a strike were lost when the White workers returned. More ominous for the future of the Black community, exclusion from jobs and unions led to a weakening and eradication of their skills, making it impossible to pass them on to their children. For example, in the South at the close of the Civil War, 100,000 out of 125,000 artisans and craftsmen were Black, but by 1900, the number had decreased to less than 10,000. In New York City, Jacob Riis wrote that trades which the Black "had practical control in his Southern home are not open to him here. Even the colored barber is rapidly getting to be a thing of the past." Organized labor was similarly hostile to Asians. After some West Coast agricultural workers formed the Japanese-Mexican Labor Association in 1903 and sought affiliation with the AFL, they were told they would be accepted only if Chinese and Japanese were excluded from membership.[33]

Of greater concern to unions was the willingness of new immigrants to work for less wages and help break strikes. The Knights of Labor lobbied hard—and successfully—for the 1885 Foran Act banning importation of contract labor, in which employers recruited unskilled workers from southern and eastern Europe, offering them prepaid passage. In 1888, further legislation made alien contract workers subject to deportation. Union labels were developed to distinguish products made by nonunion workers and to let purchasers also know they were not made by Chinese immigrants. Many socialists, too, resented the new immigrants. As Victor Berger complained to congressmen in 1911, "Slavonians, Italians, Greeks, Russians, and Armenians" had become "modern white coolies" of the steel industry, crowding out "Americans, Germans, Englishmen, and Irishmen."[34]

As with Blacks, established unions, particularly craft ones, often denied immigrants membership and opposed their forming separate unions; the International Hod Carriers and Building Laborers excluded Italians, and the American Federation of Labor denounced the formation of the United Hebrew Trades organization for "destroying the solidarity of organized labor by functioning along 'race' lines." Early-twentieth-century southern California unions excluded

Mexicans and Japanese, who went on to form their own.[35] When feeling threatened by immigrants forming separate negotiating groups or taking jobs away, some unions grudgingly admitted them.

Even then, intergroup bigotry remained. The Wood, Wire and Metal Lathers International Union, in 1918, established a rule requiring a minimum 50 percent of all lathers on jobs be "American," including those given by Jewish or Italian contractors who mainly hired immigrants; the rule, however, did not apply to jobs in which long-time native-born workers predominated. In a 1917 Montana mining strike, the workers—many of whom were immigrants—refused to have any Cornishmen on their grievance committee and intimidated recently arrived Finnish miners by telling them they had better join or the government would draft them into the army and ship them back to Europe to fight in World War I.[36]

An ironic consequence of the succession process was the criticism of new immigrants by previous ones, and both by native-born workers. Animosities and distrust among and between them were steeped not only in Old World learning or lack of such, but also in their competition for jobs and inability to understand each other linguistically and psychologically.

Late-nineteenth-century Armenian immigrants in Massachusetts were thought to be non-Christians, Muslims, or Turks, and were accordingly abused. As a Worcester physician recalled: "Beaten with clubs, stabbed with knives, wounded in various ways, almost without exception they needed and received help at the City Hospital." Such mistreatment did not stop some Armenians from harassing Turkish immigrants. In Providence in 1896, a group complained to the Turkish minister in Washington, D.C., that "Armenians use insulting language to us and maltreat us. Day and night we have no rest, either in the streets or at our homes."[37]

On the West Coast, Chinese and Japanese workers were resented for their industriousness, clannishness, and competitiveness. "When they come over to America," wrote one observer, "they underlive, underbid, and outwork us." With bitter irony, a Jewish correspondent wrote that the "Chinese have got the Jews by the horns, in the matter of cheap clothing, boots and shoes, and even shrewd Yankees . . . are apprehensive that John Chinaman will soon get the better of them. . . . The Yankees preached for and prayed with the Chinese lepers, and now they whine that they have been instrumental in improving a race that can outrank the shrewdest manufacturers of nutmegs and wooden hams."[38]

Japanese were accused of unfairly employing only their own kind and overcharging Americans for their products. Though early California Japanese farm workers were welcomed for doing work that White men refused, attitudes changed when they sought higher wages or started buying their own farms. Mr. A. Sharboro, president of the Italian Bank in California, wrote in 1908:

> Several Japanese firms have already engaged in fruit raising. It is useless to say that they can not only compete but drive away every one of our fruit-grow-

ers out of the State, if they are permitted to embark in large numbers in this industry. They will also learn to manufacture everything that we can make, and will soon drive our manufacturers and mechanics out of business by their unprecedented facilities of cheap living and long, patient working.[39]

In 1895, the *Chicago Tribune* noted, "The Greeks have almost run the Italians out of the fruit business in Chicago not only in a small retail way, but as wholesalers as well. . . . As a result, there is a bitter feud between these two races, as deeply seated as the enmity that engendered the Graeco-Roman wars."[40] In the Upper Midwest, Norwegian-Swedish and Scandinavian-Irish animosities were common, with one immigrant noting that "friction between Scandinavians and Irish settlers, caused in part by religious bigotry, was intensified by the fact that the bosses of railroad gangs were often Irishmen while the common laborers were Scandinavian immigrants."[41]

Just as "White flight" from Blacks and Spanish-speaking people has taken place in recent decades in many city neighborhoods, so native Americans fled from immigrants—native-born from Irish in New York City; Blacks from Poles in Detroit; and Irish, Jews, and Italians from each other. "As soon as one or two Hungarians move into a street," wrote a Hungarian priest in 1899, "the English residents leave because of the way the newcomers behave, and who can blame them? Who could tolerate the yelling, screaming and gallivanting about which goes on into the small hours of the morning?"[42]

Immigrants also brought their own intraethnic prejudices. Northern Italians resented southern Italians, German Jews resented eastern European Jews, Irish Catholics resented Irish Protestants, and Serbs and Croats from the Austro-Hungarian Empire resented each other. "The Germans, the Irish, and the Norse people were not received with open arms by those who preceded them, even those of related race or nationality," wrote Edward A. Steiner in 1909. "The Slav, if he is a Pole, would exclude his cousin, the Slovak, and both are united in thinking that the Ruthenian is a rather inferior being; while the Ruthenian would debar the Jews, Serbians and Croatians from the economic benefits of the land of his adoption."[43]

Feeling their status threatened by new arrivals, some prominent Italians, Germans, and Slavs joined in forming the National Liberal Immigration League in 1906, which though supporting free immigration advocated state-regulated dispersion of immigrants so as to "diminish and prevent" overcrowding in large cities. Some mid-nineteenth-century Irish Catholic leaders urged that Irish immigrants leave the large East Coast cities and settle in the West, thereby reducing their problems with poverty, crime, marital desertion, and alcoholism.[44]

In various work areas, pluralism was encouraged not to improve intercultural relations but to reduce or keep wages low or prevent unionization. "As rapidly as a race rises in the scale of living, and through organizations begins to demand higher wages and resist the pressure of long hours and over-exertion," wrote a turn-of-the-century scholar, "the employers substitute another race and the process is repeated."[45]

Such developments took place across the country, as well as in Hawaii. Because English immigrant workers were believed to be given to strikes, two carloads of Chinese workers from California were brought to Massachusetts, but when they proved inadequate to the work demands, French Canadians (called "the Chinese of the Eastern States") were encouraged to come. Some mining companies preferred the Slav because he "was willing to work for longer hours than the English-speaking laborer, to perform heavier work, to ply his pick in more dangerous places, and stolidly put up with inconveniences." In New York, a manufacturer frankly stated, "I want no experienced girls, they know the pay to get . . . but these greenhorns . . . cannot speak English and they don't know where to go and they just come from the old country and I let them work hard, like the devil, for less wages." In Texas, a White farmer refused to hire White workers because "We can't handle them as we do the Mexicans." In Hawaii, beginning in the 1850s, Chinese workers were brought to serve as role models for native Hawaiians, and when they grew in number, planters brought Portuguese and Japanese; and when the latter began demanding higher wages, Koreans and Filipinios were brought over.[46]

Union-busting had few moral restraints, as employers engaged in using lockouts, private police forces, spies, blacklists, and yellow-dog contracts, all promoting the "American Plan," which excluded unionizing. Striking workers (native-born or immigrant) were charged with engaging in un-American activities, inspired by socialists and communists. When "workmen were all Americans," said some Boston charity workers, "strikes . . . were unknown." More Machiavellian yet, some industries hired agents who planted rumors among ethnic strikers that others were planning to return to work. At times, agents tricked immigrants into being scabs. Jewish immigrants were taken directly from Castle Garden (an immigrant center) to New York City's waterfront, where after being attacked by striking workers, they realized they had been duped and quit in anger.[47]

Coal-mine owners tried to crush one strike by exploiting differences between Germans and Irish. Pamphlets written in German urged readers to act only on behalf of their own countrymen and families because "the Irish, the strike leaders, are always capable of turning against you." So intense were ethnic passions that IWW (Industrial Workers of the World) leader "Big Bill" Haywood warned striking mill workers in Massachusetts not to allow intergroup discord. "There is no foreigner here except the capitalists. . . . Do not let them divide you by sex, color, creed or nationality. . . . Billy Wood can lick one Pole, in fact he can lick all the Poles, but he cannot lick all the nationalities put together."[48]

Though employers usually had the power of government on their side, workers were on their own, with few unions and some radical ones that engaged in vandalism and assassinations. Historian James Ford Rhodes credited the violence to the workers' ethnicity: though English, Welsh, and Scotch minorities engaged in systematic violence only "in the intensity of conflict," the Irish needed little provocation because, true to their "Irish Roman Catholic blood," they "hated the capitalist and had a profound contempt for the law." The use of dynamite by extremist workers became so prevalent that the turn-of-the-century decades have been termed "the era of dynamite."[49]

Thus, we see a simultaneity of demographic, labor, and residential successions, together with a proliferation and expansion of ethnic, religious, and racial bigotry. Succession meant change, and change created uncertainty among and between the foreign- and native-born, thereby reinforcing old and creating new intergroup fears and hatreds. Throughout, immigrant sweat, blood, and tears, as well as prejudices, were ever present, with the most adaptable succeeding as never thought possible by themselves or others. Most immigrants simply endured the hardships of working and living conditions, hoping either to return home one day soon or that their children would have an easier time "making it" in America.

Immigrant Living and Working Conditions

Immigrants always confronted a number of overlapping conditions: their own patterns of behavior, the xenophobia of native Americans, a highly competitive and exploitative economic system, and an immediate need for money for food, shelter, and, if they had family abroad, helping them subsist or come to America. For still others, it was a matter of earning enough money in the shortest possible time and returning home. For most, a job—any job—was taken, no matter the salary, working conditions, or resentment of other workers.

To one degree or another, they all had a profound sense of family, community, daring, and desperation. Those who would not work could not survive, unless of course they engaged in criminal activities, which some did. Their fate was theirs to shape, and they knew that if they did not help themselves or help others of their group, no one else would, least of all the government.

"We work from morning to night without giving ourselves even one day a week for rest," wrote a Bulgarian Jewish immigrant about the Sephardic community in New York City. "Our economic condition is so bad that we cannot afford to spend several weeks in the country to get away from the oppressive heat of the New York summer. We are very frugal, saving our money to send to our relatives in the old country or just hoarding it away for a rainy day." Life among Greek immigrants was "hand-to-mouth," where time and money were of the essence and "urban employment and street vending, not farming, offered the best opportunities to obtain ready cash." Italians thought "primarily of saving money for a return to Italy, distrusting outsiders . . . willing to cross picket lines and to take whatever jobs they could find."[50]

Jobs were taken even if they differed from Old Country ones. According to a 1909 immigration commission study, 64 percent of immigrant workers in bituminous coal mines, almost 61 percent in oil and sugar refineries, 50 percent in furniture manufacturing, and 58 percent in leather and tanning had been farmers or farm laborers in the Old Country; another study indicated that while immigrants who were barbers, plasterers, and lumbermen practiced their professions here, 90 percent of those who were blacksmiths and practically all who were bookbinders, printers, shoemakers, and saddlers changed jobs. The Chinese laundryman was strictly an American phenomenon, there being no such laundries in China, and required little capital or knowledge of English. Similarly, few Greek and Italian proprietors of restaurants and barbershops respectively had engaged in such businesses in Europe.[51] Where immigrants worked was frequently influenced by a working family member or friend who told them of an opening, introduced them to the employer, and vouchsafed their reliability.

No less trying were living conditions. Immigrants crowded together and shared chores and expenses to live as cheaply as possible, and in the case of families, to accumulate funds for future purchases, supplement the earnings of the household head, or send some money home. Sections of New York City's Lower East Side in 1895 were more densely populated than Bombay or Paris. Many families accepted boarders to increase their income, particularly in cities where jobs were scarce, with the wife usually doing the shopping, cooking, and laundering for all. For example, a pre–World War I study of Johnstown, Pennsylvania, showed that less than one-third of all immigrant households had total incomes solely from the earnings of husbands, and nearly 50 percent had earnings from husbands and boarders.[52]

Crowding also resulted from greedy landlords and residential discrimination, which confined immigrants to the worst sections of town. Though native-born Whites did not want to live near them, some who had property readily charged immigrants higher rents than American-born tenants.

To one observer in 1921, Americans were largely to be blamed for the miserable living conditions of immigrants.

> The coal and iron mining regions of the country, to which so many of the Finns and Slavic peoples turn, show some of our worst housing conditions. Shacks are built both by individuals and by mining companies close to mine shafts, pits and coke ovens. Tin cans, tar paper, and old boards furnish building materials for crazy shelters. Into one or more small rooms crowd the large families of the workmen. Toilets are either absent, or else miserable privies are erected and neglected. Outdoor pumps furnish water and the ground surface serves as a sewer.[53]

Concurrent with the above was an expansion and compartmentalization of ethnic diversity. As in the eastern cities, so in the West. In the early 1870s, about one-third of the western settlers were foreign-born, representing more than half the male populations in Utah, Nevada, Arizona, Idaho, and California. Living conditions in various company towns and labor camps were less harsh than in the

East, though some companies provided inexpensive housing to attract workers. Friends encouraged immigrants to come directly from overseas, said the manager of the Albuquerque and Cerrillos Coal Company, "and in most instances with practically no funds whatever. If the mines were to work . . . somebody had to provide a place for them to live and finance them until such time as they produced coal."[54]

Nevada's mining towns had Indians, Germans, French, Mexicans, Chinese, Cornish, and Irish. As Richard Lillard portrayed the scene, the Indians were there from the start and "came in from their squatters' shacks or campoodies to do housework, buck wood, or scavenge. . . . The Cornishmen . . . were socially cohesive enough to be called punningly, 'Clannishmen.' The French had their Café de Paris. In their beer cellars the rotund Teutons sat and dreamed of the Vaterland amid banks of smoke from meerschaum pipes. Modest little signs, advising the public that L. Sam or Yee Lung did washing and ironing, pointed the way to hot, ill-ventilated rooms."[55]

Whether unionized or not, working conditions were frequently difficult, dangerous, and low paying. "My people do not live in America, they live underneath America," said a Ruthenian priest in 1907. "A laborer cannot afford to live in America." To sustain a family of three to four people, a worker had to earn $800 to $876 per year. However, a 1911 federal study of 10,000 male wage earners revealed that the average yearly income was some $413, with nearly half earning less than $400. Immigrant male workers and female workers generally earned less, with the newly arrived immigrants usually earning less than their predecessors.[56]

Working hours were long for union and nonunion members. In New York City, needle-trade workers put in fifty-six to fifty-nine hours per week, and during the busy season, they clocked as much as seventy hours per week. Transit carmen worked six days per week, ten hours per day. Imported Chinese contract laborers in Louisiana had to agree to working "from daybreak till dark with an intermission of one hour each, for breakfast and dinner, but no labor . . . on Sundays, except when necessary to secure the crop, feed stock, and customary household chores."[57]

Immigrant women workers had fewer job opportunities and lower pay scales than men. Irish, German, and Scandinavian immigrant women seemed to prefer domestic service, while French Canadian, Polish, Jewish, and Italian women entered factory work. In the early twentieth century, Slavic women were hired to do the least desirable work in the stockyards and foundries because such labor was believed physically too heavy for others. Few Asian women immigrated, not only because American employers did not want them, but also because they did not travel alone to distant areas and wives usually remained at home.[58]

Women worked as long as men, if not longer. In 1912, New York State limited the workweek to fifty-four hours. At one twine factory, a social worker noted, "The women came out. Pale, narrow-chested, from hand to foot they were covered with fibrous dust. . . . They were types of factory workers—pale, haggard feeders of machines—like those described in the days of a century past in England."[59]

Because the vast majority were young, single, lived with their parents, and usually worked until they were married, they were slower than men in organizing against their employers. Working daughters and mothers were discouraged from or reluctant to attend evening meetings or educational classes, either because of ethnic customs, household responsibilities, or fear of compromising their reputation. Moreover, women were expected to turn over their earnings to their parents or husbands. For Polish, Bohemian, Irish, and Slovak working women, economic independence was incomprehensible. "It follows that what the girl earns is easily appropriated by the parents, and, broadly speaking, obediently surrendered by the girl," wrote Louise Montgomery in her 1913 study. "Among the 300 girls between sixteen and twenty-four years of age, there are 290 who have no independent control of their own wages."[60]

Ethnic differences also existed among women who lived and worked independently of their families; according to a 1909 study, 25.7 percent were Russian Jewish, 18.6 were American-born natives, 14.3 were Irish, 11 percent were German, 5.1 percent were Bohemian, 5.1 percent were Austrian, 4.2 percent were Italian, and the remaining percentage was spread among Scottish, English, Romanian, Hungarian, Swedish, and others.[61]

Industrial accidents, child labor, and unsanitary and unsafe conditions were common, without benefit of health and accident insurance, employer liability laws, unemployment insurance, old age benefits, or resident medical facilities. Scores of Irish women were maimed or killed in New England mills. In Lowell, Massachusetts, in 1860, an entire mill of mostly Irish workers suddenly collapsed and caught fire, killing 88 and severely injuring 116. In the Triangle Shirtwaist Company fire in New York City in 1911, 146 workers died, mostly young Jewish and Italian women. Some five weeks later, at a large protest meeting, Rose Schneiderman mournfully noted: "This is not the first time girls have burned alive in the city. Every week I must learn of the untimely death of one of my sister workers. Every year thousands of us are maimed. The life of men and women is so cheap and property is so sacred. There are so many of us for one job it matters little if 140-odd are burned to death."[62]

Child labor, particularly by immigrants, was extensive. At the turn of the century, more than 1.7 million children under fifteen years of age were working long hours in fields, factories, mines, and workshops. A 1902 investigating committee found some 17,000 little girls working as long as twelve hours a day in Pennsylvania's silk mills and lace factories. Conditions were so bad in one Massachusetts mill town that a doctor found "a considerable number of boys and girls die within the first year after beginning work. Thirty-six out of every 100 of all men and women who work in the mill die before or by the time they are twenty-five years of age."[63]

Immigrants were particularly vulnerable to accidents because of their inability to speak or read English, desperation for work, and inexperience with industrial machinery. In New York, between 1884 and 1890, Irish males had more on-job accidents than any other group, having taken jobs no one else would. Generally, between 1903 and 1907, national accident rates reached new heights. A 1910 survey of industrial accidents in Pittsburgh indicated that every year the area produced "45 one-legged men; 100 hopeless cripples; . . . 45 men with a twisted useless arm; 30 men with an empty sleeve; 20 men with but one hand; . . . 70 one-eyed men—500 such wrecks in all." Foreign countries complained about what was happening. An Italian consul reported 500 Italian immigrants in Pennsylvania had lost their lives in one year, and an Austrian consul told of 82 men in the same area having been killed in a ten-month period. Even with the introduction of some safety equipment in 1913, fatal industrial accidents numbered 25,000 and industrial injuries reached close to 1 million.[64]

Accident compensation was minimal or nonexistent because of inadequate laws, indifferent industrial owners, or bigoted laws and courts. For example, until 1911, Pennsylvania courts prohibited compensation to the next of kin residing abroad, no matter the negligence of the employer. "The court is against the foreigner, and favors the corporation," said one foreign consul. "You cannot get a jury to give damages to foreigners. They say that too much money goes to Europe now, and they won't increase it by a verdict for the plaintiff."[65]

Nevertheless, immigrants worked on. Many had come only to earn a certain amount of money to send or take home to pay off a mortgage, buy land, or make life easier for themselves or family. "We'll only stay in America and work hard until we have (enough money for) twenty acres, and then we'll go home," said one Hungarian. After learning how much money two of his Syrian cousins were earning as peddlers in Fort Wayne, young Faris N. rushed home: "Mama, what do you think? I want to go to America and I will be away from you for two years."[66]

Home and family were very much on their minds. In the mid-nineteenth century, the Reverend John Francis Maguire noted that the great ambition of an Irish girl "to send 'something' to her people as soon as possible after she had landed in America. . . . To assist their relatives, whether parents, or brothers and sisters, is with them a matter of imperative duty, which they do not and cannot think of disobeying, and which, on the contrary, they delight in performing." Remittances by Swedish immigrants soared from 3 million dollars in the 1880s to near 10 million in the 1920s.[67]

Not everyone wished immigrants bon voyage. They were frequently discouraged from leaving—or encouraged to return—by friends, family, and governments. Ruthenians were implored by one newspaper not to "sell your land, so that you will leave something to come back to. Go for the sake of making money. Be thrifty and don't lose your savings on drinking. Return with the money earned and use it to improve your farms/households."[68]

Many governments feared losing skilled workers, diminishing their supply of cheap laborers, or reducing the number of people who could pay taxes or serve in the military. Unable to stop them, they encouraged immigrants to send remittances to their needy families and to maintain homeland allegiances, including service in the military. As described in 1912, Russia and Turkey regarded those who left "as little better than deserters. This was the attitude of Italy for a long time. . . . Hungary and Greece keep a watchful eye over their sons, and patriotic Magyars and Greeks in America influence their countrymen to retain their allegiance to the fatherland."[69]

Some returned home out of loneliness for family, broken health, inability to find work, disappointment with living conditions, or resentment at what was happening to their children. A popular Spanish song in the 1920s recalled the plight of a Mexican factory worker:

> Many Mexicans don't care to speak
> The language their mothers taught them
> And go about saying they are Spanish
> And denying their country's flag . . .
> My kids speak perfect English
> And have no use for Spanish,
> They call me "fadder" and don't work
> And are crazy about the Charleston.
> I am tired of all this nonsense
> I'm going back to Michogan [in Mexico].[70]

Thousands contracted disease, became victims of industrial accidents, became widows, or wanted to be with their dying parents. Still others, according to various reports by the commissioner general of immigration, returned home because they were convinced America was no longer a land of liberty. They "found it difficult to forget the race riots and how the victims went without redress; and they were positive that the naturalized citizen was adjudged inferior to the native-born, that most Americanization schemes simply were the devices of employers and politicians to assure themselves of a cheap labor supply and means of controlling the votes."[71]

Others were returned home after they had died, in keeping with provisions in their will to be transported and buried back home.[72]

Although reemigration statistics for the nineteenth century are incomplete, they are fairly clear for the twentieth century. Though slightly more than 6 million entered from 1908 to 1914, some 2 million returned home—7.14 percent of Jewish immigrants, 9.36 of the Irish, 29.10 of the Poles, 44.71 percent of southern Italians, and 57.6 percent of the Hungarians. Between 1910 and 1929, more Bulgarians returned than arrived, and from 1908 to 1943, almost twice as many Chinese left as entered America. Turks had perhaps the highest return rate, some 86 percent of the 22,000 who had come between 1899 and 1924. In contrast, almost all Germans from Russia (Volga Germans) remained, though a few returned to Germany. Groups with the highest percentage of returnees generally had the lowest percentage of naturalized citizens, which inhibited their building political power. For example, in 1920, only 28.1 percent of Polish, 28 percent of Italian, and 29.1 percent of Hungarian immigrants were naturalized, in contrast to the politically strong Irish, of whom 65.7 were naturalized. Also, more likely to remain were groups with relatively high percentages of women.[73]

Many had been in America only a few years. From 1908 to 1910, 80 percent had been here less than five years. Furthermore, during the depression years of 1931 to 1935, all groups, except Jews, had more returnees than arrivals. Such was also true of the highly acculturated English from 1931 to 1938. Nevertheless, leaving America did not exempt them from being criticized for taking wealth out of the country and, after 1913, not wanting to pay income taxes. Many employers, too, feared their leaving would diminish the availability of cheap labor, though some thought it could be solved by importing Chinese workers. There were also those who applauded their leaving because it would weed out the Little Italys, Hungarys, Syrias, and foreign quarters in general.[74]

For those not returning home, many governments sought to maintain contact with them through their consulates and by providing subsidies for foreign-language newspapers, societies, and schools. "It is the consulate, the foreign chamber of commerce, the branch of a foreign bank, the trading corporation, and similar organizations which are now taking up the protection and direction of the immigrant's affairs in America," wrote Frances Kellor in 1920. For example, the Dutch government, through the Netherlands Emigration League, sought to protect immigrants after their arrival, "to see that they reach their destination without molestation, and that they maintain the good reputation of those already here."[75]

During this time, though born in America, Blacks suffered in the South and North. Thus, while other groups were beginning to elect members to political office and forming organizations to maintain their group existence and cultural heritage, Blacks continued to be disenfranchised and discriminated against, their ancestral languages, customs, and allegiances all but destroyed. Blacks had no families "in the old country to write to or send remittances to, and no African government to speak up on their behalf. Their unequal treatment was reaffirmed by the Supreme Court in *Plessy* v. *Ferguson,* in 1896, which upheld a Louisiana law requiring railroad companies to provide "separate but equal" accommodations for Whites and Blacks, and denied "that the enforced separation of the two races stamps the colored race with a badge of inferiority." If any inferiority existed, it was not in Louisiana law, said the Court, but rather "because the colored race chooses to put that construction upon it." The lone dissenting Supreme Court justice, John Marshall Harlan, identified the real meaning of the Louisiana law—"that colored citizens are so inferior and degraded that they cannot be allowed to sit in the public coaches occupied by white citizens." To Harlan (as it was to be for the advocates of civil rights and cultural pluralism in the immediate post–World War II decades), "Our constitution is color-blind, and neither knows nor tolerates classes among citizens. In respect of civil rights, all citizens are equal before the law. . . . The law regards man as man, and takes no account of his surroundings or his color when his civil rights as guaranteed by the supreme law of the land are involved. It is therefore to be regretted that this high tribunal . . . has reached the conclusion that it is competent for a state to regulate the enjoyment by citizens of their civil rights solely upon the basis of race."[76]

The Court's decision prompted southern local and state governments to adopt or extend segregationist statutes and ordinances to parks, hospitals, theaters, transportation stations, bathrooms, residential neighborhoods, and even phone booths. Eight years later, what little integrated education existed in higher education ended when the Supreme Court in *Berea College* v. *Kentucky* ruled that the college had violated Kentucky state law prohibiting racially integrated schools. Though Justice Harlan again dissented, few other Whites protested, and by 1918 one history of suffrage claimed, "Public attention has ceased to focus upon the Negro cause; it is looked upon as lost."[77]

In desperation, many Blacks fled north, so much so that the influential *New Orleans Picayune* urged readers to consider importing millions of Chinese and Japanese farm workers. In Oklahoma alone, between 1890 and 1910, twenty-five Black communities were established. As one southern Black noted, "We as a people are oppressed and disfranchised. We are still working hard and our rights taken from us. Times are hard and getting harder every year. We as a people believe that Africa is the place but to get from under bondage we are thinking of Oklahoma as this is our nearest place of safety." Some Blacks even thought of settling in Canada, only to be told by Canadian officials that the climate would prove too difficult for them or that they could not meet the country's strict health and financial requirements—though the actual reason was their color. Loud calls now arose within the Black community to return to Africa, most prominently so by Marcus Garvey, who believed that Whites would always be racist and that God and Jesus were Black.[78]

In the very capital of America, Blacks were dehumanized. "As a colored woman," wrote Mary Church Terrell,

> I may walk . . . to the White House, ravenously hungry and abundantly supplied with money with which to purchase a meal, without finding a single restaurant in which I would be permitted to take a morsel of food, if it was patronized by white people, unless I were willing to sit behind a screen. As a colored woman I cannot visit the tomb of the Father of this country which owes its very existence to the love of freedom in the human heart and which stands for equal opportunity to all, without being forced to sit in the Jim Crow section of an electric car which starts from the very heart of the city. . . . If I refuse thus to be humiliated, I am cast into jail and forced to pay a fine. . . . Unless I am willing to engage in a few menial occupations, in which the pay

for my services would be very poor, there is no way for me to earn an honest living. . . . It matters not what my intellectual attainments may be or how great is the need of the services of a competent person, if I try to enter many of the numerous vocations in which my white sisters are allowed to engage, the door is shut in my face.[79]

Even in hospitals that admitted both races invidious distinctions were made, with Blacks assigned the least desirable accommodations, including the attic or basement. Writing in 1907, an authority on racial problems in hospitals explained that "the Negro department" was always kept as far from the White and executive departments as possible and that supplies for each group be marked with different colors—cream and White blankets for White wards and slate-colored blankets for Black ones.[80]

Social segregation reinforced employment and union exclusion, which further eroded the ability of Blacks to maintain or pass on their skills to their children. Organized labor often justified its racist practices by claiming Blacks were unsuitable for unionism. A major article in the AFL's (American Federation of Labor) official publication in 1898 said they had an "abandoned and reckless disposition" and lacked "those peculiarities of temperament such as patriotism, sympathy, sacrifice, etc., which are peculiar to most of the Caucasian race." The *Social Democratic Herald,* in 1901, described them as inferior and depraved, "raping women and children"; and the following year, a national leader of the Socialist Party wrote, "there can be no doubt that the Negroes and mulattos constitute a lower race."[81]

Nevertheless, when cheap European labor was unavailable or when Blacks were wanted to intimidate White workers, industry relaxed its racist policies. Thus, with the need in World War I to fill European orders for supplies and the drop in foreign immigration from more than 1 million to some 300,000 in 1915, northern industrial companies sent labor recruiters throughout the South, offering high-paying jobs and free transportation to Black workers. By 1918's end, as many as 1 million southern Blacks had moved north. "To die from the bite of frost is far more glorious than at the hands of a mob," explained the *Chicago Defender*. The Black migration northward continued into the 1920s, after which it slowed down, to be renewed with World War II and the postwar years.[82]

Though northern racism was similar in thought, act, and effect to that of the South, clear differences existed in degree and structure. Southern racism was pervasive, with segregation legally established to maintain White social and economic dominance. Even opposition to the theory of evolution and any racial linkage between the two races was stronger there.[83]

In the North, segregation was both racial and ethnic, more the result of intergroup distrust and withdrawal than of legislative regulations. Society was also more pluralistic, with Blacks one of the many groups discriminated against. Even then, they were generally subjected to preferential exploitations, at times ironically so. One large New York City real estate firm said in 1889 that it "would rather have negro tenants in our poorest class of tenements than the lower grades of foreign white people. We find the former cleaner than the latter, and they do not destroy the property so much. We also get higher prices."[84]

The differential reaction of native-born Americans to Blacks and immigrants was not unnoticed by some Black leaders. "Americans! ... You invite to your shores fugitives of oppression from abroad, honor them with banquets, greet them with ovations, cheer them, toast them, salute them, protect them, and pour out your money to them like water," declaimed Frederick Douglass in 1852, "but the fugitives from your own land, you advertise, hunt, arrest, shoot and kill. ... You profess to believe 'that, of one blood, God made all nations of men to dwell on the face of all the earth,' and hath commanded all men, everywhere, to love one another; yet you notoriously hate (and glory in your hatred), all men whose skins are not colored like your own."[85]

Being looked down upon by White native- and foreign-born residents did not stop some Blacks from doing the same to others, including Black immigrants. At times, Black newspapers portrayed the "Chinese as idolatrous opium smokers, Japanese as disloyal, Mexicans as lazy, and Italians as bomb-throwing anarchists." Concern over losing jobs to European and Asian immigrants led the Black *Topeka Weekly Call,* in 1894, to claim that America was being "flooded with a foreign element to whom peace is a total stranger and who knows no satisfaction no matter how favorable the wages nor how short the duration of time of labor."[86]

Neither did Caribbean Islanders escape criticism. By 1920, some 50,000 foreign-born West Indians were in America, mostly in New York City. Those from former Spanish colonies spoke Spanish; from Haiti and Guadeloupe, French or Creole; and from Jamaica and the Virgin Islands, English. Most of the Puerto Ricans in New York City in 1920 lived in Harlem, where they confronted both White and Black prejudice. To the NAACP's head, Walter White, Harlem reflected a "strange mixture of reactions not only to prejudice from without but to equally potent prejudices from within."[87]

Although White Americans considered Black immigrants no different from American Blacks, the latter deemed them undesirable because of their ethnicity, language, and relative industriousness, and it was commonly said that if a West Indian "got ten cents above a beggar, he opened a business." English-speaking Jamaicans were taunted as "Jew-maicans" or "cockneys," and were resented for being able to avoid discrimination by claiming they were British citizens, who could call upon their homeland consul for protection.

In turn, many Black immigrants viewed their American racial counterparts as lazy and lacking in ambition and pride. Some Haitians declared themselves "White" on censuses and deliberately spoke French or Creole in public to avoid being taken for Black Americans. To Jamaican-born Marcus Garvey, the immediate enemy of the Black people was not the White man, but "tan-skinned," middle-class Blacks who controlled the NAACP, which he called the "National Association for the Advancement of Certain People."[88]

The Racial Perils

For all the bigotry European immigrants, Indians, and Blacks were experiencing, Asians, Pacific Islanders, Mexican Americans, and to a lesser extent Armenians on the West Coast were also being victimized by assorted nativists, political parties, unions, and other immigrant workers. When an immigrant group had relatively few members and accepted lower wages, it was welcomed—and exploited—by native-born Americans. When it resisted ill treatment, it was scorned and feared, leading to a succession and pecking order of victimization. "Oriental immigration on a large scale, whether Chinese, Japanese, Korean or Hindu, will place American institutions in grave danger of disintegration," wrote an early-twentieth-century scholar. In Canada also, fears arose of being "overrun" and "dominated by an alien race."[89]

Distinctions were made between American and Asiatic civilizations. To one senator, "Personal freedom, the home, education, Christian ideals, respect for law and order, are found on one side; and on the other, traffic in human flesh, domestic life which renders a home impossible, a desire for only that knowledge which may be at once coined into dollars, a contempt for our religion as new, novel and without substantial basis, and no idea of the meaning of law other than a regulation to be evaded by cunning or by bribery."[90]

Such attitudes did not preclude American businessmen, adventurers, and missionaries from entering the homelands of immigrants, transplanting both high ideals and low prejudices. Nor did settling in America put an end to the distrust, dislike, and discrimination that various Asian groups had for each other.

The Chinese

In the sixteenth and seventeenth centuries, small Chinese settlements existed in Mexico, from where some settlers entered New Mexico and California, including one of the founders of Los Angeles, Antonio Rodriguez, who was Chinese. In the late eighteenth century, more than a hundred Chinese lived on the northwest Pacific coast. By 1850, their numbers grew to some 7,500. At first, they were admired as "most orderly and industrious citizens," "the best immigrants to California," "inoffensive" and "tractable." In San Francisco, civil leaders and clergy honored them, and the *California Courier* editorialized that "we have never seen a finer-looking body of men collected together . . . in fact, this portion of our population is a pattern for sobriety, order and obedience to laws, not only to other foreign residents, but to Americans themselves." In Hawaii, too, where they had been brought to work on sugar plantations, they were admired. "We shall find Coolie labor to be far more certain, systematic, and economic than that of the native," said the president of the newly formed Royal Hawaiian Agricultural Society in 1850. "They are prompt at the call of the bell, steady in their work, quick to learn, and will accomplish more. . . ."[91]

As their numbers and competition for jobs grew with native-born and immigrant workers, however, they were accused of being "dangerous, deceitful and vicious," "inferior from a mental and moral view," and unsuited for citizenship. All kinds of anti-Chinese laws were enacted. In San Francisco, having pigtails or carrying baskets from poles across the shoulders were forbidden, and in a Montana town it was a crime for Whites to be seen dining in Chinese restaurants. In 1854, the California Supreme Court actually reversed a murder conviction of a White man because the witness was Chinese: "To let Chinese testify in a court of law would admit them to all the equal rights of citizenship. And we might soon see them at the polls, in the jury box, upon the bench and in our legislative hall." Samuel Bowles, writing in the late 1860s, said that "to abuse and cheat a Chinaman; to rob him; to kick him and cuff him; even to kill him have been things done not only with impunity by mean and wicked men" but also by highly respected citizens.[92]

The need for cheap labor prevailed, with the support of employers, and steamship and railroad lines, and a profitable traffic in bringing Chinese to America and the Caribbean developed, which our consul in China said was "replete with illegalities, immoralities, and revolting and inhuman atrocities, strongly resembling those of the African slave trade in former years, some of whom exceeding the horrors of the 'middle passage.' "[93]

Chinese women were believed prostitutes, who corrupted the morals of American youth. The Page Act of 1875 specifically excluded Chinese prostitutes from entering the country. That and the 1882 Exclusion Act led to an overwhelming dominance of Chinese males and "a century of bachelorhood."[94]

So intense were anti-Chinese feelings that when California voters in 1879 were asked whether they were "for" or "against" unrestricted immigration of Chinese, a mere 883 out of 161,405 voted in the affirmative.[95] "Anti-Coolie Clubs" and mass anti-Chinese demonstrations, supported by political parties and unions, demanded, "The Chinese Must Go." California's Republican and Democratic parties adopted planks favoring the exclusion of all Asians, particularly Chinese, Japanese, and Koreans.

Not surprisingly, youngsters too attacked Chinese. As the *Flagstaff Champion* reported, "All boys that have been in the habit of throwing stones and clubs at Chinamen will take notice that hereafter they will be promptly arrested for an unnecessary assault on Chinamen." In describing what was happening about him, Lee Chew, a laundryman, said, "Irish fill the almshouses and prisons and orphan asylums, Italians are among the most dangerous of men, Jews are unclean and ignorant. Yet they are all let in, while Chinese, who are sober, or duly law abiding, clean, educated and industrious, are shut out."[96]

Among those favoring Chinese exclusion were many immigrants and Blacks, including Norwegians on the West Coast, who found themselves competing with Chinese for jobs. O.B. Iverson said that the Chinese "are so industrious and thrifty and have such a physique that they can live where a European or American would starve to death. . . . They have no families to care for. . . . Therefore they can work for just as much as the American worker absolutely must have if his family is to live, and then can send out of the country as much as the support of a family requires, or they can also compel American workers to let their wives and children starve to death." Many Black newspapers were equally critical. The *San Francisco Vindicator* said the Chinese were "polluting the air and everything else," and the *Washington Colored American* proclaimed that "there is no room in this land for the disease-breeding, miserly, clannish and heathen Chinese." In vain, the Chinese minister in Washington complained of press abuse. "Why can't you be fair? Would you talk like that if mine was not a weak nation? Would you say it if Chinese had votes?"[97]

All too often, bigoted attitudes turned to murderous behaviors. In 1871, a mob of 1,000 hanged some 22 Chinese in Los Angeles, prompting the American government to apologize officially to the Chinese government. In Alaska, mobs attacked Chinese, dynamited their homes, and forced many to leave the territory. No wonder an English-Chinese phrase book at the time had such phrases as "He took it from me by violence," "He cheated me out of my wages," and "They were lying in ambush."[98]

The passions behind such actions were well reflected in the testimony of a San Francisco official before a congressional committee in 1877:

> The burden of our accusation against them is that they come in conflict with our labor interest; that they can never assimilate with us; that they are a perpetual, unchanging, and unchangeable alien element that can never become homogeneous; that their civilization is demoralizing and degrading to our people; that they degrade and dishonor labor; that they can never become citizens, and that an alien, degraded labor class, without desire of citizenship, without education, and without interests in the country it inhabits, is an element both demoralizing and dangerous to the community within which it exists.[99]

The tragic situation that the Chinese faced was well described by Mark Twain:

> They are a harmless race when white men either let them alone or treat them no worse than dogs; in fact, they are almost entirely harmless anyhow, for they seldom think of resenting the vilest insults or the cruelest injuries. They are quiet, peaceable, tractable, free from drunkenness, and they are as industrious as the day is long. A disorderly Chinaman is rare and a lazy one does not exist. . . . He is a great convenience to everybody—even the worst class of white men, for he bears most of their sins, suffering fines for their petty thefts, imprisonment for their robberies, and death for their murders. Any white man can swear a Chinaman's life away in the courts, but no Chinaman can testify against a

white man. Ours is "the land of the free"—nobody denies that—nobody challenges it. (Maybe it is because we won't let other people testify.) As I write, news comes that in broad daylight in San Francisco, some boys have stoned an inoffensive Chinaman to death, and that although a large crowd witnessed the shameful deed, no one interfered.[100]

It is not surprising that during this period "a Chinaman's chance" came to be an expression of absolute helplessness.[101]

At times, the Chinese were compared to Indians, Blacks, Irish, Italians, and even Basques, who were sometimes viewed with equal if not greater disdain. While campaigning for president in 1868, New York's governor Horatio Seymour declared, "We did not let the Indian stand in the way of civilization, so why let the Chinese barbarian?" To an 1860 writer, though the Chinese lived close together, they were "not coarsely filthy like ignorant and besotted Irish." In Idaho, the *Caldwell Tribune* acknowledged that while Basque living and business standards were similar to those of Chinese, they were nevertheless "filthy, treacherous and meddlesome."[102]

In all, between 1882 (when the Chinese Exclusion Act suspended immigration for ten years) and 1902 (when the act was made permanent), Congress passed more than a dozen laws against the Chinese, whose population was but a fraction of 1 percent of the country. Particularly galling was the Scott Act of 1888, which prohibited the return of some 22,000 Chinese laborers and miners who had gone to visit their homelands, though having valid return certificates and family and property in America.

To the Chinese go the lamentable distinction of being the first ethnic group to be specifically banned by law from freely immigrating to America. As one Congressman from Minnesota said, there "is no nation on the continent of Europe, however feeble, that we would have enacted this legislation against, however undesirable their laboring people as immigrants."[103]

Chinese in northern Mexico also suffered discrimination and violence. As in California, segregation laws were passed, restricting where they could live and prohibiting marriage or concubinage with Mexicans. In Torreon, in 1910, over 300 Chinese were killed. As Mexico underwent successive revolutions, some 500 Chinese, fearful for their lives, left for America with General Pershing's expedition, which had been pursuing "Pancho" Villa. Two decades later, when Mexican laborers in America returned home because of the Great Depression, anti-Chinese prejudice increased, culminating in the legal expulsion of thousands of Chinese residents from Sonora, who then sailed for China or California.[104]

The Japanese

In 1870, Japanese in mainland America numbered a mere 55, and a decade later, 148.[105] It was after 1885, when the "Chinese problem" was believed solved, that large numbers of Japanese began arriving on the West Coast, as well as in Hawaii. In 1900, some 10,000 lived in California, and over the next decade, their numbers quadrupled. As with European immigrants, many came to remain a few years, but unlike them, they were comparatively better educated, averaging about eight years of schooling.[106]

At first they were welcomed, but within a few years became victims of racism, economic exploitation, and invidious inter-Asian comparisons, but without being subjected to the massacres that Chinese were. In California, all kinds of petty to major laws were passed to restrict the rights of Japanese, such as forbidding them to use or own power engines, employ White girls, or inherit land. The *San Francisco Chronicle* blamed them for their mistreatment, saying that if the Japanese laborer had "throttled his ambition to progress along the lines of American citizenship and industrial development, he probably would have attracted small attention of the public mind. Japanese ambition is to progress beyond mere servility to the plane of the better class of American workmen and to own a home with him."[107]

The Asiatic Exclusion League, formed in 1905, argued that the Japanese must leave because

1. We cannot assimilate them without injury to ourselves.
2. No large community of foreigners, so cocky, with such distinct racial, social and religious prejudices, can abide long in this country without serious friction.
3. We cannot compete with a people having a low standard of civilization, living and wages.
4. It should be against public policy to permit our women to intermarry with Asiatics.
5. We cannot extend citizenship to Asiatics.[108]

Two years later, a similar league was formed in Canada, where following a mass protest meeting (addressed by an officer of the Seattle Oriental Exclusion League), participants marched through Vancouver's Chinese and Japanese sections, hurling stones and singing "Rule Britannia."[109]

Japanese-Chinese and Japanese-Black comparisons were made to the discredit of all. A *Sacramento Bee* writer noted that before the Japanese had come, "we had cheap Chinese labor—'bout seven dollars a week, a Chink would work for—but the Skippies (the name they call the Japanese in the West) took the same jobs for 75 cents a day and pig-tails had to go." To Oregon's *Portland Times,* in 1919, "the Japanese question is a curse in the West like the Negro question in the South."[110]

American fears of Japanese increased with the Russo-Japanese War of 1905, which marked "the first conquest in modern times of a . . . white people by a colored one." Captain Richmond Hobson, who had distinguished himself during the Spanish-American War, warned that Japan "has an army of soldiers in the Hawaiian Islands. They made the invasion, quietly as coolies, and now we know that they are soldiers organized into companies, regiments, and brigades." Ironically, though many American Blacks saw the Japanese as competitors for jobs, Japan's victory proved to them that "white is not always the conqueror when pitted against other races."[111]

A total break in relations was avoided only by the famous—or infamous— Gentlemen's Agreement of 1907–08, wherein Japan agreed to restrict emigration of her laborers. Nevertheless, thousands continued to enter California, either surreptitiously from Mexico or legally through the practice of picture brides, whereby Japan allowed women to join their mail-ordering husbands. To prevent further misunderstandings with America, the Japanese government in 1920 voluntarily abandoned the practice.

Just as Americans feared a "Yellow Peril," Japanese back home feared a "White Peril," which expanded in the decades that followed. "How can the white races have the face to demand equal opportunities in the Far East when they have denied them to the Far East in the West," asked a Tokyo professor in 1913. "If the white races truly love peace and wish to deserve the name of Christian nations, they will practice what they preach and will soon restore to us the rights so long withheld. They will rise to the generosity of welcoming our citizens among them as heartily as we do theirs among us."[112]

The Filipinos

Unlike other European or Asian immigrants, the first Filipinos were students, who started arriving in 1903 and who hoped to learn a profession and return home to teach their compatriots the virtues of American democracy. After them, Filipino agricultural workers immigrated to Hawaii, where sugarcane and pineapple industries readily hired them at lower wages than given to Chinese and Japanese. From there, some Filipinos moved to California. By 1910, only some 3,000 Filipinos lived in United States territories (outside of the Philippines), mostly in Hawaii. Unlike other Asians, they were not defined as *aliens,* but as nationals who could enter Hawaii or America with American passports.

Such relative freedom did not preclude their being stereotyped or abused. For example, during the 1900 congressional debates over how to deal with the territories taken from Spain because of the Spanish-American War, Senator William Bate declared, "Let us beware of those mongrels of the East, with breath of pestilence and touch of leprosy. Do not let them become a part of us with their idolatry, polygamous creeds, and harem habits." To West Coast nativists, they were "by inheritance servile, treacherous, possessed of low-cunning, and entirely devoid of the sturdy manhood of the Anglo-Saxon."[113]

With their increasing numbers went native American criticism of their being prolific, lustful of Western women, and causing meningitis and "Oriental diseases." Barred from hotels, cafes, swimming pools, barber shops, and apartments, Filipinos were compelled to "gang up" and lived ten to twelve in a single room. To some employers, however, they were a boon, because they worked for lower wages than Chinese and Japanese and could be hired as strikebreakers, both in Hawaii and on the West Coast. Predominantly young, single, male, and with some knowledge of English, they resided mainly in California, Washington, and Oregon by 1930, with Stockton, California becoming known as "the Manila of California."[114]

California and Washington became the loci of anti-Filipino demonstrations and clashes between Filipino and White American workers, who competed for work as fruit and vegetable harvesters and packers. Carlos Bulosan, a Filipino immigrant and trade union organizer, recalled how "the public streets were not free to my people: we were stopped each time these vigilant patrolmen saw us driving a car. We were suspect each time we were seen with a white woman."[115]

As with Blacks, mulattoes, and Mongolians, Filipinos were legally banned from marrying a White American, who in turn was subject to being socially ostracized. When in 1931 the California Supreme Court ruled in *Roldan* v. *Los Angeles County* that Filipinos were not Mongolian, California quickly amended its law to ban marriages between Whites and those of the Malay race. Nearby states followed suit, so that until 1941 the nearest area in which they could intermarry was New Mexico.

Racism also manifested itself in nativist support for Philippine independence, because it would render Filipinos in America as aliens. With the passage of the Tydings-McDuffie Act in 1934, granting commonwealth status to the Philippines and independence ten years later, immigration all but stopped, and the new country was given an annual quota of fifty. As Senator Millard Tydings explained, it was "absolutely illogical to have an immigration policy to exclude Japanese and Chinese and permit Filipinos en masse to come into the country . . . come in conflict with white labor . . . and increase the opportunity for more racial prejudice and bad feeling of all kinds." Shortly afterward, in 1935, President Roosevelt signed the Repatriation Act, which provided free transportation back home to all Filipinos on condition they not return to America. "In effect, the Repatriation Act was a deportation act or intended as such," wrote Carlos Bulosan. About 2,000 Filipinos accepted.[116]

The outbreak of World War II led to America's granting citizenship to some resident Filipinos, particularly those joining our military and serving in an all-Filipino regiment. Immigration increased sharply after the 1965 Immigration Act, when exclusionary national origins quotas were abolished.

Other Asians

Two smaller West Coast immigrant groups who were discriminated against came from India and Korea. Though the former were of varying religious affiliations—Sikh, Hindu, and Moslem—they were all called *Hindus*. In the post–Civil War South, some plantation owners and entrepreneurs considered importing "Hindoo coolies," who were admired for their hard work and docility, and who, like the Chinese, would serve as good role models for the newly freed Black slaves.[117] Predominantly male and Sikh, mainly from the Punjab region, they came like so many other immigrants to remain temporarily, working in agricultural or industry. Until 1910, yearly immigration numbers ranged from a few hundred to less than 2,000, and then increased to almost 2,000 per year, but never exceeded 6,000 at any one time.

Considered slow in understanding instructions, and living in squalid conditions, they could be hired for low wages in preference to those who wanted higher ones, whether native-born or immigrant. Their complexion, full beards, and turbans marked them for ridicule as "ragheads" and as *black* White men. "We don't care whether the Hindu was born under the flag or not," editorialized one monthly publication. "If he could peroxide himself white it would not make any difference. He would still be an Oriental—smooth, insinuating, sinuous, saponaceous, unctuous, and several other things expressed by adjectives more picturesque and easier to pronounce." On a more scholarly note, a 1913 study said that East Indians "are not readily assimilated, and there seem to be practically none of the people on the Pacific Coast who are not opposed to their immigration, even more strongly opposed to them than to the Chinese, and possibly than to the Japanese."[118]

In one area, an Asian Exclusion League member blamed them for causing typhoid fever, and a State Bureau of Labor Statistics official described them as "unfit for association with American people."[119] Mobs frequently attacked them. In Bellingham, Washington, where some 250 lived in 1907, some 400 to 500 men (including some Filipinos) assaulted them and destroyed their living quarters.

Although "any good citizen might be opposed" to such lawlessness, a local newspaper said "from every standpoint it is most undesirable that these Asians should be permitted to remain in the United States. They are repulsive in appearance and disgusting in their manners. . . . They contribute nothing to the growth and upbuilding of the city as the result of their labors. They work for small wages and do not put their money into circulation. They build no homes, and while they numerically swell the population, it is of a class that we may well spare."[120] In the weeks that followed, other attacks took place in the cities of Everett, Vancouver, Aberdeen, and Seattle, Washington; Live Oak, California; and Saint John, Oregon.

The strict interpretation of immigration laws was applied, and East Indian immigration dropped from almost 2,000 in 1910 to only 517 in 1911. In Canada, in 1914, a ship carrying 376 of them was denied docking permission, and after remaining off the coast for two months, departed.[121]

As in the case of the Japanese, East Indians were not allowed to purchase or lease land, and after 1917, totally excluded from immigrating. Those already here were denied the right of citizenship, and some who had become naturalized lost their citizenship. Though an Indian scholar argued that his Asian kinsmen were legally eligible for citizenship as Aryans and were "as pure Caucasians as the German," the courts held "a high-caste Hindu is not a 'white person' " according to the laws of the land.[122] Not until 1946 did Congress restore their naturalization rights and establish a small quota for Indian immigration.

Though much fewer in number, Koreans experienced similar bigotry on the West Coast and in Hawaii, where from 1902 to 1905 some 7,000 (most bachelors) had immigrated to work on plantations. The relative few who followed were mainly political refugees from Japanese rule, students, and merchants, as well as about 1,000 picture brides.[123] As a result of the 1924 Oriental Exclusion Act, only those attending universities for advanced studies were allowed to enter.

By 1930, only slightly more than 1,000 Koreans lived in California, where they were mistaken for Japanese (whom they resented) and discriminated against in restaurants, recreational areas, and housing. Their life, wrote Dr. Chang Lee-wook, former ambassador to Washington, D.C., was "loneliness, hardship and fatigue. . . . Nobody cared for and looked after them." Though mostly Christian by conversion, they soon learned that American Christians could be restrictive in their love. "I first thought when I came to the United States that everyone was a fine Christian," recalled one immigrant, "but I soon learned better. I found out there are several kinds of Christians and you have to be careful."[124]

The very smallness of their numbers prevented their creating the kinds of businesses, churches, schools, and associations that the Chinese and Japanese created. That would occur later, particularly after the Korean War when thousands of immigrants came to America, especially women who had married American servicemen, Peace Corps volunteers, or other Americans.[125]

Armenians

Some 1,500 Armenians had immigrated to America by the late 1880s, mainly men in search of better economic conditions. After that, larger numbers arrived, fleeing from oppression and massacre in Turkey, with smaller numbers from the Soviet Union seeking a better life. Many were young, literate, and skilled as tailors, shoemakers, carpenters, or clerks, which facilitated their adjustment— and success.

Between 1899 and 1914, some 52,000 arrived, mostly to the West Coast, where as with the above groups, they were barred from social and fraternal organizations like the YMCA, Elks, and Lions. To Richard Campbell, chief of the United States Naturalization Division, Armenians were of "the yellow race" and polygamists, and therefore not eligible for citizenship. Their hard-working ways also evoked envy and resentment. As one nativist explained, "The Armenian, who is generally a superior person, is unpopular because his success is for himself, in his own business." A Japanese farmer in Fresno saw similarities in their work ethic, but "I think they learned a little bit more English than the Japanese did and they looked more American and I think it helped them a lot."[126]

In Fresno County, where some 3,000 lived in 1908, a common put-down said that only 300 Turks were needed to massacre half of the Armenian population, because the other half would be killed by Americans. Restrictive racial covenants there stipulated: "Neither said premises, nor any part thereof, shall be used in any manner whatsoever or occupied by any Negro, Chinese, Japanese, Hindu, Armenian, Asiatic or native of the Turkish Empire, or descendant of the above named persons, or anyone not of the white or Caucasian race." On the East Coast, they and Syrians and Lebanese were often defamed as the "scum of the Levant," and denounced for becoming strikebreakers in Massachusetts, New Hampshire, and Pennsylvania.[127]

Mexican Americans

A series of bloody revolutions in Mexico not only strained relations with America but also between Mexican Americans and native-born Americans, particularly after "Pancho" Villa initiated a campaign of terror against Americans in Mexico and New Mexico. In response, in 1916, President Wilson ordered the army to capture him dead or alive. As thousands of American soldiers entered Mexico, Texas Rangers harassed and oppressed Mexican Americans, who subsequently referred to the actions as the *Hora de Sangre*. One Anglo recalled that "all the Rangers had to do was get a suspicion on somebody, any little thing, and they would take 'em out and shoot 'em down."[128] With the darkening of war clouds over Europe, Wilson withdrew the troops.

Throughout the World War I period, thousands of Mexican laborers were induced to immigrate to America, though in violation of the contract labor law. As with the Chinese and Japanese, some employers at first welcomed cheap and dependable Mexican workers, particularly when White or Black ones were not available. Virtually imprisoned on specific ranches, they were forbidden to seek higher wages or employment elsewhere, lest they be arrested and deported.

By 1920, some 50,000 Mexican laborers were imported. In urging their continued use, W.B. Mandeville of the American Beet Sugar Company reported that up to the war practically no Mexican labor was used in northern Colorado, Wyoming, and Montana, but mostly Bohemians, Russians, and Belgians, practically all of whom "vanished during the war and are still going"; moreover, he noted that in northern and central Texas, Black labor had moved to the cities, "so that each year there is constantly increasing demand for Mexican labor."[129]

Then as now, escape from poverty was more important than avoidance of bigotry, and more than a million Mexicans moved to America from the 1920s to the 1940s. By 1925, Los Angeles had the largest Mexican population in the world outside of Mexico City, with increasing demands to "Keep out the Mongrel Mexicans" and to "Lock the Back Door," because they were "the most

undesirable of all of the peoples" and were "lowering the standard of our population as far north as Wyoming." Still, cheap Mexican muscle power was needed.
A California fact-finding committee reported in 1928 that the Mexican laborer "does
tasks that white workers will not or cannot do. He works under climatic and working
conditions, such as excessive heat, dust, and temporary employment . . . that are
often too trying for white workers. He will work in gangs. He will work under
direction, taking orders." Fears of severe restrictions on importing Mexican
workers prompted California farmers to seek Filipino workers, who were "being
rushed in as the Mexicans are being rushed out," said the *Pacific Rural Press*.[130]

As Mexican laborers began organizing and striking for decent wages, they
met with large-scale violence, mass deportations, and everyday harassments. In
the Southwest, between 1865 and 1920, more Mexican Americans than Blacks
were lynched. In 1932 alone, over 11,000 Mexicans from the Los Angeles area
were repatriated. In 1942 and 1943, police, military personnel, and hoodlums
terrorized Mexican Americans, culminating in the "zoot suit" riots, wherein they
and Blacks were attacked in the streets. As in present times, some Mexican
Americans resented the legal or illegal importation of cheap labor, and in 1928
the newly formed Confederation of Mexican Labor Unions supported the restriction of Mexican immigration and repatriation of resident alien Mexicans.[131]

In short, to have emigrated from the transoceanic East or West or to have
been born Black or Mexican in America was a sure invitation to being a target of
prejudice and discrimination. The causes, tenacity, and immorality of bigotry
were well noted by an 1881 observer:

> I know of no people who have seemed to me to have so many prejudices of
> race as ourselves. Whether it is due to our long contests with tribes of savages,
> the natives of the vast territory which we have occupied; or to the institution of
> slavery which took upon itself among us, the very worst features which slavery
> has ever exhibited; whether it is pride of stock stimulated by our successful
> conquests over the many difficulties attending the settlement of a new, and in
> some respects, an inhospitable region; or whether all these have combined to
> produce the result, it would seem that a Negro . . . or a Chinaman . . . meets
> with a less ready reception from us than in any of the European nations. . . .
> And all the while we cry out, with what to Heaven must appear the grossest
> delusion and hypocrisy, that these other races resist our influence—they will
> not assimilate. We hold them all at arms length and then throttle them because
> they will not approach nearer to us. This is our boasted liberality and generosity.[132]

The Destruction of the Indians in the West

Just as Catholics were the most hated religious group in American history,
Blacks the most racially dehumanized, Asians the most unwelcomed, eastern and
southern Europeans the most scorned ethnic groups, Indians were the most oppressed and destroyed. Whereas it had taken White Europeans and Americans

some 300 years to suppress Indian independence in the East, it took only thirty years after the Civil War to do the same to those in the West.

Via a combination of military might, trespassing, the sale of liquor, the spread of disease, the fraudulent purchase of land, and a racist social policy, Indian tribes impeding American expansion were overwhelmed, relocated, and urged by the government, religious leaders, and "friends of the Indians" to adopt the behaviors, values, thinking, and prayers of their self-imposed rulers and guardians. National destiny and racial superiority to Americans were equivalent to blatant land-stealing, mass murder, and cultural genocide to Indians. When not the lure of land, then that of gold propelled the movement West. Major General John Pope wrote of how people, "incredible numbers, continue to throng across the great plains to these rich mining territories, undeterred by the seasons, by hardships and privation, or by the constant and relentless hostility of the Indian tribes." In Colorado, in 1858, the discovery of gold resulted in the further relocation of Cheyenne Indians, who had been earlier given the land by treaty.[133]

Continually pressured to relocate by the army, White settlers and hostile Indians, the Modocs, decided to fight back in the early 1870s. In a war lasting six months, a group of poorly armed warriors held out against howitzers and mortars in "the most expensive war, per capita of the enemy, ever fought by U.S. troops." At its end, their leaders were tried and publicly hanged as a lesson to Indian agitators, and their severed heads shipped to the United States Army Medical Museum, in Washington, D.C. The army's victories over Indians were often facilitated by employing other Indians as guides, scouts, trackers, and even combat soldiers.[134]

Legal and illegal plans were ever afoot to obtain Indian lands. Though the Dawes Allotment Act of 1887 was designed to integrate Indians into American society by dividing reservations, giving each member a specific amount of land and conferring citizenship on those who maintained their allotment, it was also motivated by land-hungry settlers and speculators who, by connivance, pay-offs, or use of local courts, hoped to dispossess Indians. Of the 136 million acres that Indians owned before the Dawes Act, only half remained thirteen years later.[135]

If White might made White right, it also contributed to White fear and guilt. General Pope questioned the right of settlers to occupy Montana and large parts of Utah, Colorado, and Nebraska. "What right, under our treaties with Indians, have we to be roaming over the whole mining territories, as well as the plains to the east of them, molesting the Indian in every foot of his country, drawing off or destroying the game upon which he depends for subsistence, and dispossessing him of the abiding places his tribes has occupied for centuries?"[136]

While settlers oppressed Indians, missionaries increased their activities. President Grant initiated a "Peace Policy" in 1869, which expanded church control of Indian reservations and provided federal aid for Indian education and missions. For the first time, an Indian, Ely S. Parker (who had been denied membership in the New York Bar Association because of his race), was appointed a commissioner of Indian affairs.[137] Religious denominations were also allowed to nominate federal agents for more than seventy reservations, though such actions were contrary to constitutional church-state separation principles.

To the government and missionaries, heathen Indian prayers, ceremonies, hallowed sites, feasts, and dancing had to be eliminated, which Christianity could best do with government support. "Under the benign influence of the Christian denominations," said Senator Joseph Brown, "we shall see Sunday schools and churches planted among them; and instead of roving bands without fixed habitations, goaded to desperation by injustice and wrong, spreading death and destruction in their pathway, we shall find them in the comfortable homes of civilized man, not only a Christian people but many of them cultivated and honorable citizens." Thus, Presbyterian missionaries among Alaskan Tlingits outlawed use of native language in their schools and urged students to reject the ways of their parents. To rally greater support for their missions, Catholics established a special Bureau of Catholic Indian Missions in 1874.[138]

Christian education and missionizing were not without their own interfaith bigotries. Not only did governmental policy discriminate against Catholics, Mormons, Jews, and southern churches, while favoring Methodists, Episcopalians, and northern churches, but Catholics and Protestants continually suspected each other of trying to establish dominance. Protestant religious leaders readily denounced each other. Congregationalists still feared an Episcopal state church, and other Protestants resented Methodists, calling each other "bed bugs" and "children of the Devil."[139]

As in colonial days, Indian-Indian conflicts paralleled those of White-Indian, facilitating Indian defeat and loss of tribal independence. The Pawnee, wrote an observer in 1848, "are in danger of losing their scalps as soon as they put their heads outside their mud hovels. . . . The Platte River, the headwaters of the Kansas, and even southwest to the Arkansas were formerly the great hunting grounds of the Pawnee; but [are] now those of the Sioux, Cheyennes, and Arapahoes, who are all gradually nearing the Pawnees, with a full determination of wiping them out." Just as European nations displayed little compassion toward each other in battle, so with Indians. In battle, Osages scalped and beheaded their enemies, chiefly Comanches and Kiowas. Some tribes took their Indian captives as slaves or as exchanges for goods or bounties. In the 1860s, Pima and Papago Indians sold captured Apache and Yuma Indians as slaves to Mexicans in Arizona. Navajo women and children were enslaved in New Mexico settlements; and Comanches, Kiowas, Cheyennes, and Arapahoes frequently traded slaves, horses, and other valuables.[140]

Within tribes there were sharp differences among members over whether to make peace or war with the encroaching White settlers. Historian Stan Hoig claims more Indian leaders were probably killed working for peace than in battle with their enemies, if not by treacherous Whites then by own tribal members who felt they were helping Whites and wrongfully giving up tribal land.[141]

Nevertheless, White Americans were the most violent and successful enemies of the Indians. A favorite United States military tactic against the Plains Indians was to attack a village without warning, regardless of guilt, killing all inhabitants, regardless of age or sex. Indians reciprocated with equal fierceness but unequal success. "I give you some of the facts as to my men, whose bodies I found just at dark," wrote Colonel Henry Carrington in 1866, after an Indian attack: "Eyes torn out and laid on rocks; noses cut off; chins hewn off; teeth chopped out; joints of fingers, brains taken out and placed on rocks with other members of the body (private parts severed and indecently placed on the person); entrails taken out and exposed; hands cut off; feet cut off; arms taken out from sockets."[142]

In spite of such bloody behavior, General George Cook told a West Point graduating class that "with all his faults, and he has many, the American Indian is not half so black as he has been painted. He is cruel in war, treacherous at times, and not over cleanly. But so were our forefathers. His nature, however, is responsive to treatment which assures him that it is based upon justice, truth, honesty, and common sense."[143]

Perhaps the most morally damning judgment about American brutality was made by President Johnson's own Peace Commission, which had been appointed in 1867 to make peace with the warring tribes of the Plains area. To its rhetorical question whether the United States had been "uniformly unjust," the commission answered, "unhesitatingly yes. . . . Nobody pays any attention to Indian matters. This is a deplorable fact. Members of Congress understand the negro question, and talk learnedly of finance and other problems of political economy, but when the progress of settlement reaches the Indian's home, the only question considered is 'how best to get his lands.' When they are obtained, the Indian is lost sight of." Then, in 1871, contrary to centuries-old international opinion and practice, the Congress formally stopped making any treaties with Indians as if they were sovereign nations. "In our intercourse with the Indians," said the secretary of interior the following year, "it must always be borne in mind that we are the most powerful party . . . we assume that it is our duty to coerce them, if necessary, into the adoption and practice of our habits and customs."[144]

Throughout the nineteenth century, the only Indians considered citizens were those who had become so by treaty, statute, or the 1887 Dawes Act bestowing citizenship on those leaving reservations to become independent farmers. Otherwise, even if they had one White parent, they were ineligible for citizenship. In an 1880 case, an Indian male born of a White father and Indian mother in British Columbia was denied citizenship because he was "as much an Indian as a white person" and therefore belonged to neither.[145]

By 1900, the Indian population had dropped to a low of 237,196, and ten years later, the basic coin of the country, the Indian-head penny, was no longer minted. According to one estimate, from 1500 to 1900 some 75 million Indians were killed in the Americas. After being rendered powerless, dispossessed, and relocated, the Indians were granted full citizenship in 1924.[146]

Manifest Destiny, Imperialism, and Racial Triumphalism

By the 1890s, the settling of the West and the building of the major railroads of America had been largely completed. Railroad trackage had increased from some 35,000 miles in 1865 to about 200,000. Foreign exports, too, had rocketed, from $71 million in 1800 to more than $800 million. The Census Bureau began using the word "Black" to describe residents three-fourths or more Black; "mulatto" for those three-eights to five-eights Black; "quadroon" for those one-fourth Black, and "octoroon" for those one-eighth Black. Indians were either "full" or "mixed" blood.[147] About one-third of the nation was of foreign White stock, and demands escalated for the ending of immigration to all who wished to enter. The federal government had taken over regulation of immigration and for the first time began excluding convicts, lunatics, idiots, paupers, epileptics, anarchists, revolutionaries, and new immigrants from Asia and Europe. Protestant self-confidence was high, and the Supreme Court in 1892, for the first time, held America to be "a Christian nation."

As the *Overland Monthly* observed, "Now that the continent is subdued, we are looking for fresh worlds to conquer." If European powers could carve up Africa, pledging to "educate the natives and to teach them to understand and appreciate the benefits of civilization," why could not and should not America do the same? *Jingoism* as a word and deed came into being, reflecting not only an expanding foreign policy, but a renewed determination to make other countries, particularly England, conform to the Monroe Doctrine and keep Canada subservient to American interests. "God has not been preparing the English-speaking and Teutonic peoples for a thousand years for nothing but vain and idle self-admiration," declared Senator Beveridge. "He has made us the master organizers of the world to establish system where chaos reigns. . . . He has made us adept in government that we may administer government among savages and senile peoples."[148]

Whereas the Puritans and Pilgrims had been parochial in their triumphalism, their latter-day counterparts were global, believing they could save the entire world. As during the Civil War, Protestants compared their dying "to make men free" with Christ's dying "to make men holy."[149] In the Pacific and Atlantic, America took the Midway Islands; annexed Hawaii; divided the Samoan Islands with Germany; acquired Puerto Rico, the Philippines, Guam, and Wake Islands; established a protectorate over Cuba; and occupied Haiti and Santo Domingo, while ever transplanting anti-Black and anti-Asian views, behaviors, and laws. The takeovers of the Samoans, Hawaii, and the Philippines are good examples.

For many years the Samoan Islands had been coveted by England, America, and Germany, each obtaining treaty rights, distrusting the others, and plotting to obtain further land and concessions. Remorsefully, the Samoan king noted, "The civilization which had been introduced by foreign governments . . . was inferior to that which its inhabitants previously possessed." Finally, in 1899, the islands were divided between America and Germany, without any discussion or concurrence of the natives. "We blot out, then, a sovereign nation," said South Dakota's Senator R.F. Pettigrew, "a people with whom we have treaty obligations, and divide the spoils."[150]

More duplicitous were actions in Hawaii. Fearful of a French or English takeover, Americans started calling for the islands' annexation in the 1850s. American missionaries and sugar interests sought to overthrow Queen Liliuokalani. When she proclaimed "Hawaii for the Hawaiians," revolution broke out, with the sub rosa help of the American foreign minister in Honolulu, who landed American troops from a nearby ship, allegedly to protect American property. Within two weeks, on 1 February 1893, America's minister proclaimed Hawaii a protectorate and immediately informed the State Department that "the Hawaiian pear is now full ripe, and this is the golden hour for the United States to pluck it." However, President Harrison could not do so because of congressional opposition; and President Cleveland would not, because of the questionable morality involved, particularly after an investigation showed that our minister had helped bring about the Hawaiian revolution and that most Hawaiians opposed American annexation. If such actions were not repudiated, editorialized the *New York Times,* our minister's intrigue "would sully the honor and blacken the fair name of the United States."[151]

It was not until 1898 that Hawaiian monarchy and independence were ended, as President McKinley formally annexed the island. "Annexation is not change," he declared, "it is consummation." And indeed it was, but of greed, intrigue, religious hubris, and expanding imperialism, resulting in the transplantation of American racist views and policies. "There shall be no further immigration of Chinese into the Hawaiian Island[s]," said the Congress, "except upon such conditions as now are or may hereafter be allowed by the laws of the United States; and no Chinese, by reason of anything herein contained, shall be allowed to enter the United States from the Hawaiian Island[s]."[152] Then, in 1924, Congress formally excluded Japanese from America and all its possessions.

No less opportunistic was how America obtained Cuba, Puerto Rico, Guam, and the Philippines as a result of the Spanish-American War of 1898. As President McKinley told a group of Methodist ministers why he annexed the Philippines:

> I went down on my knees and prayed God Almighty for light and guidance more than one night. And one night late it came to me this way—I don't know how it was, but it came: (1) That we could not give them back to Spain—that would be cowardly and dishonorable; (2) that we could not turn them over to France or Germany—our commercial rivals in the Orient—that would be bad business and discreditable; (3) that we could not leave them to themselves— they were unfit for self-government—and they would soon have anarchy and misrule over there worse than Spain's was; and (4) that there was nothing left for us to do but to take them all, and to educate the Filipinos, and uplift and civilize and Christianize them, and by God's grace do the very best we could

by them, as our fellow men for whom Christ also died. And then I went to bed and went to sleep and slept soundly.[153]

Generally, Protestant groups applauded expansionism as a sign of "the Kingdom of God coming," as an opportunity to end Spanish Catholic superstition and despotism, and even as a way of winning converts. Though in the minority, some clergy recognized the evils of overseas expansionism. To the Reverend Charles H. Parkhurst, it was ironic that "the reign of Jesus is to be widened in the world under the protection of shells and dynamite." The Anti-Imperialist League, formed in 1899, opposed our becoming the new masters of others, with "commercial gain and false philanthropy" placed above America's founding principles.[154]

For many peace advocates, Anglo-Saxon virtues should not triumph through war, but by extending Christianity, trade, business, arbitration, and American governmental structures and processes. Andrew Carnegie, an immigrant from Scotland, believed in a benevolent "race imperialism," based on an alliance of English-speaking countries, which would "compel peace" by raising its arm.[155]

In opposing American expansionism, racist arguments were frequently used. Fearful that Hawaii's annexation would lead to statehood, the franchise, and bloc voting by Chinese residents, Congressman Champ Clark asked, "How can we endure our shame when a Chinese Senator from Hawaii, with his pigtail hanging down his back, with his pagan joss in his hand, shall from his curule chair in pigeon English proceed to chop logic with George Frisbie Hoar or Henry Cabot Lodge?" Others feared that with the annexation of foreign territories, alien and inferior races living in America would become citizens. The only good that Senator Francis Newlands saw in taking over Haiti and the Dominican Republic would be colonizing them with Blacks and thereby preserving America "for all time for the white races."[156]

As America took control of the Philippines from Spain, native rebels, who had previously been our allies, rebelled, hoping to achieve national independence. To many of our troops, the natives were " 'niggers,' not better than Indians and were to be treated as such." One soldier told how after capturing a town and discovering a brutally killed comrade, "orders were received . . . to burn the town and kill every native in sight, which was done to a finish. . . . I am growing hard-hearted, for I am in my glory when I can sight my gun on some dark-skin and pull the trigger." Just as during American colonial wars and those with Indians, Americans enlisted the support of some Filipino mercenaries.[157]

As in the case when United States Black volunteer and regular army soldiers had been sent to Cuba, so in the Philippines, where it was believed they had a natural immunity to tropical climate and disease. Having become familiar with American racism, Filipino insurgents distributed flyers to our Black troops, reminding them of conditions in America and encouraging them not to cooperate in oppressing another "people of color." Some Black soldiers deserted and fought alongside the Filipinos, and most of the Black press was critical of

McKinley's policies. Lewis H. Douglass, son of Frederick Douglass, bitterly claimed that President McKinley could not be blind to the "race and color prejudice that dominates the greater percentage of the soldiers who are killing Filipinos in the name of freedom and civilization."[158]

To add insult to injury, America denied citizenship and equal legal rights to the very people she sought to civilize. Senator Henry Cabot Lodge defiantly reminded antiexpansionist critics that Filipinos, like American Indians, could be treated as subjects and not as citizens. After all, he stated, "this Republic not only has held subjects from the beginning, in the persons of those whom we euphemistically call the 'wards of the nation' " but that America acquired subjects through purchase, as in the case of Alaska, which by treaty with Russia "denied to the Indian tribes even the right to choose their allegiance, or to become citizens."[159]

In the famous *Insular* cases of the early 1900s, the Supreme Court decided that the Constitution and its provisions for citizenship, voting rights, and representation in the Congress do not necessarily follow the American flag of conquest or occupation. America had in fact become an imperial and colonial power. Thus, over and over in the early twentieth century, Congress denied Puerto Rico statehood. The American-appointed governor considered Puerto Ricans "an alien people, speaking a foreign tongue, separated by geographical, traditional, and racial barriers from the American continent."[160] Though progressively allowed to elect their own officials, they could not participate in mainland elections or be represented in Congress.

In other matters, too, islanders were denied equal treatment. The Supreme Court ruled that Puerto Rican and Filipino imports to America could be treated differently in the levy of tariffs than American goods, until the Congress decided otherwise. The Court also held, in *Hawaii* v. *Mankichi,* that full constitutional protections of jury trial and grand jury indictment need not be extended to Hawaiians. In short, the very prejudice and brutality inflicted on various minorities in America were readily transferred abroad by brazen nationalism, military might, and Christian triumphalism. However oppressive, these qualities were deemed national virtues in the civilizing of inferior people.

Continuing Violence, Inflated Patriotism, and Rampant Nativism

At home, Americans were somewhat less self-righteous but no less bigoted toward immigrants and their offspring, who were accused of lacking patriotism, having dual loyalty, bloc voting, and undermining America's political system. Such attitudes anguished new immigrants and shocked foreign visitors. The newcomer in America, noted a turn-of-the-century visitor, "is of no use except to help to fill the money-bags of the insatiable millionaires, by the sweat of his brow, by his blood and sinew—aye, even by his life itself. After all these depressing experiences comes the saddest one of all—absolute unappreciation, callous ingratitude; he is despised for the very pains with which he has filled his task-master's coffers."[161]

Though widespread, violence against minorities was rarely prosecuted, and when it was, few perpetrators were found guilty. Being a minority, and a foreign one at that, was sufficient justification for abuse, with no group knowing when and in what form it would be singled out.

In New Orleans, in 1881, some eleven Italian Americans were indiscriminately arrested and tried for allegedly killing a police superintendent. When found not guilty, a mob assaulted the prison and shot and beat the prisoners to death. Though a grand jury investigation failed to identify the culprits, the jury said they consisted of "several thousand of the first, best and even most law abiding citizens." Fearful for their lives, 700 Italians fled the city. Fifty percent of the country's major newspapers supported the lynchings, with the *Baltimore Sun* writing that "the Italian immigrant would be no more objectionable than some others were it not for his singularly blood thirsty disposition and frightful temper and vindictiveness."[162]

When Italy protested the killings, anti-Italian sentiments escalated to talk of war, and both governments recalled their ambassadors; a year later, to ease the tensions, President Harrison sent $25,000 to Italy for the victims' families, saying his doing so was "an act of justice, and from motives of comity," but not in "recognition of any claim of indemnity."[163]

One of the bloodiest assaults on ethnics occurred in 1897 when a police posse opened fire on some 150 immigrant Polish and Hungarian striking miners marching from Hazelton, Pennsylvania, to a neighboring town to enlist others. Twenty-one were killed and forty wounded, though if they had been native-born, admitted some mine foremen, no bloodshed would have occurred. In Jasonville, Indiana, in 1909, Hungarian immigrants were besieged by armed native-born residents, who compelled them to leave town and abandon their possessions.[164]

Greek workers in California, Colorado, and Utah were resented and abused. In Virginia, their stores were set upon by angry residents. In Rhode Island, legislation was proposed to ban noncitizens (meaning Greeks) from lobster fishing. In Chicago, native-born merchants so resented Greek street peddlers and lunch-wagon operators that city officials increased license fees and arrests for alleged violations of city ordinances. The most flagrant assault on Greeks took place in 1909 in South Omaha, Nebraska, where after a wild rumor that a Greek male escorting a "loose" woman had killed a policeman, a mob launched a half-day rampage against Greek stores and citizens, driving some 1,200 out of town. Against such hostility, plus that of the KKK (Ku Klux Klan), two Greek salesmen working out of Atlanta, Georgia, initiated the formation in 1922 of the fraternal and benevolent organization AHEPA (American Hellenic Educational Progressive Association).[165]

French Canadian immigrants moving to Augusta, Maine, in the 1880s, were confronted with KKK cross burnings. Finns were scorned as drunkards and Asians. "Like the drunken Magyar and Lithuanian," said sociologist E.A. Ross, in 1914, "the 'loaded' Finn is a terrible fellow," and, a few years later, a study showed that only 16 percent approved of a close relative marrying a Finn and only 27 percent approved of having a Finn as a close friend.[166]

In rural America, a vigilante White Cap movement punished violators of "traditional moral values"; Whites and Blacks were attacked in southern Indiana; Blacks in Mississippi, South Carolina, and northern Texas; Mexicans in southern Texas; and Mexicans and Anglos in northern New Mexico. In Mississippi, Jewish merchants hiring Blacks were attacked and accused of conspiring to increase prices and take over White farms.[167]

Revolutionary activities abroad and domestic urban and labor violence intensified hostility to European immigrants. Fears of "red" revolutionaries arose, particularly after the formation of the insurrectionary Paris Commune in 1871, which the *New York Times* feared might inspire the "toiling ignorant and impoverished multitude, demanding an equal share in the wealth of the rich." The 1877 railroad strike, which spread to some seventeen states, was blamed on "ragged commune wretches" and French communism. Also feared were Irish Molly Maguires, Russian nihilists, and socialists of any stripe.

Germans, Bohemians, Hungarians, Poles, and Italians were accused of reinforcing the ranks of radical labor and preparing "the way for a new revolution, or attempt at revolution." A congressional committee report charged that anarchists from Germany via England "have proven a lawless, turbulent class, and the whole country is familiar with their recent acts of violence."[168] The 1886 Chicago Haymarket Square riot was triggered by a bomb explosion at a labor rally where German anarchists called for an eight-hour workday; sixty-four policemen and more than a dozen workers were wounded, and seven policemen and two workers killed. The resultant "Great Anarchist Trial" initiated America's first big "red scare," in which socialists, communists, and anarchists—particularly German ones—were denounced. All eight men were found guilty, and eventually four were hanged, two sentenced to life imprisonment, one to a long prison term, and another committed suicide.

To combat the discrimination and to ensure their rights as American citizens, some groups formed or reformed their social, religious, and fraternal organizations. The Sons of Italy was established in 1905, the Anti-Defamation League in 1913, the Commission on Religious Prejudice of the Knights of Columbus in 1915, the Steuben Society of America in 1919, the Japanese American Citizens League in the early 1920s, and the League of United Latin American Citizens in 1929.

As in contemporary times, ethnic groups often expressed affection for their homeland. Much to Irish American resentment, Sir Lionel Sackville-West, the British minister to Washington, undiplomatically responded to a letter from an American, saying that President Cleveland liked England and that in effect a vote for Cleveland was good for England. Because the Irish had helped the 1884

election of Democrat Grover Cleveland instead of James Blaine, who had allegedly accepted charges that Irish Catholics were disloyal and that the Democratic
Party was one of "rum, Romanism and rebellion," Cleveland now feared alienating their vote and had Sackville-West return to England.

The Republican *New York Tribune* immediately published a jingle, wherein
Cleveland addressed John Bull as follows:

> Believe me that I made him go
> For nothing that he wrote,
> But just because, as well you know,
> I feared the Irish vote.[169]

In the same year, desires to retain the Irish vote led to the defeat of an
Anglo-American Arbitration Treaty relating to fishing rights, prompting
Boston's Catholic *Pilot* to editorialize proudly: "Had Irish-Americans anything
to do with the failure of the English Arbitration Treaty? We trust so, and believe
so. We should be very much ashamed of our fellow citizens of Irish blood if they
had not done their utmost to baffle this attempt to place this great Republic
before the world as a mere colony of Great Britain."[170]

German Americans also opposed any Anglo-American alliances. "It is really
not surprising," wrote Hugo Munsterberg at the time, "that the Germans in
America dislike every approach to England, because they feel instinctively that
an Anglo-American union reinforces the feeling that the Americans are an
Anglo-Saxon nation in which other Teutonic elements are strangers." As Germany, Britain, and America differed over the administration of Samoa, German
Americans spoke up strongly against American foreign policy. In fact,
Cleveland's defeat in the 1888 election has been credited to German American
dissatisfaction with the tripartite Samoan settlement.[171]

When Irish and German groups opposed American cooperation with England,
Secretary of State John Hay exclaimed that for America to "be compelled to
refuse the assistance of the greatest power in the world, *in carrying out our own
policy,* because all Irishmen are Democrats and some Germans are fools—is
enough to drive a man mad." During the Boer War, too, Irish American leaders
denounced England in rallies across the country. In Chicago, the United Irish
Societies sent some fifty volunteers, in the guise of a Red Cross contingent, to
fight alongside the Boers against the British.[172]

When Norway dissolved its union with Sweden in 1905, declaring itself an
independent nation, Norwegian Americans held rallies and futilely petitioned
President Roosevelt to recognize the action immediately. From Chicago alone,
some 20,000 signatures were sent to Washington. Such actions prompted the
New York Times to criticize Norwegians for trying to influence the government,
reminding those who had been naturalized that they no longer were politically
Norwegians.[173]

The assassinations of France's president, Spain's prime minister, Austria's empress, Italy's king, and then President McKinley intensified fears of foreigners and particularly anarchists. Reminiscent of the 1780 Alien and Sedition Acts, Congress in 1903 proceeded to exclude all who "believe in or advocate the overthrow by force and violence of the government of the United States . . . or the assassination of public officials."[174] Anarchists, socialists, and communists began being arrested, whether or not they believed in or practiced violence, and calls were made to expel them. To become a naturalized citizen, immigrants were now required not only to swear allegiance to the Constitution but also to protect the country against all enemies, foreign as well as domestic, while also affirming that they were not polygamists or anarchists.

Congressional attempts continued to institute a literacy test, which President Taft and then President Wilson vetoed in 1915 and 1917, claiming it ignored the character, quality, and personal fitness of immigrants and would "operate in most cases merely as a penalty for the lack of opportunity in the country from which the alien seeking admission came."[175]

Nevertheless, Wilson's veto was overridden, with the strong support of labor, economists, political scientists, and newspapers. In addition to a test requiring immigrants to prove they could read forty words in any language, a "barred zone" was established that virtually excluded Asians not covered by earlier laws, such as Hindu and East Indian laborers. Increased fines were set for steamship companies bringing immigrants subject to exclusion. In the same year, however, after some two decades of debate, Congress granted American citizenship and greater self-rule (but not independence) to Puerto Ricans, and then, ten years later, to Virgin Islanders.

More extensive was the violence against Blacks, some 1,000 of whom were lynched between 1900 and 1917, often accompanied by torture. "It might have been believed," wrote one sociologist in 1907, "that torture could not be employed under the jurisdiction of the United States, and that, if it was employed, there would be a unanimous outburst of indignant reprobation against those who had so disgraced us." Such did not occur, not even in the country's churches, particularly in the South. "It is no accident that in these states with the greatest number of lynchings to their discredit," wrote Walter White, "the great majority of the church members are Protestant and of the evangelical wing of Protestantism as well."[176]

Even where law prevailed, there were violations of justice for Blacks, as exemplified in Brownsville, Texas, in 1906, where 167 Black soldiers from a nearby post were accused of shooting up the town and killing a barkeeper. Without a trial or hearing, or a scintilla of credible evidence, they were dishonorably discharged from the army—though many had served with distinction on the frontier, in Cuba, and in the Philippines, and though six of them had won a Medal of Honor.[177]

Against such a setting, the NAACP formed to end lynchings, secure greater police protection for southern Blacks, widen job opportunities, and further equal opportunity and treatment for all citizens. As stated in 1910, the NAACP sought "to promote equality of rights and eradicate caste or race prejudice ... ; to advance the interest of colored citizens; to secure for them impartial suffrage; and to increase their opportunities for securing justice in the courts, education for their children, employment according to their ability, and complete equality before the law." In those pre–World War I years, differences in the brutalization of Black and ethnic minorities were of degree, extent, and duration, with Blacks being the main victims.[178]

World War I , Post-war Isolationism, and Minority Relations

With the coming of World War I in Europe, intergroup passions intensified in America, not only between native-born and foreign-born, who were accused of being more interested in the well-being of their former homelands than that of America, but also between and among the foreign-born, who differed sharply over what was occurring in Europe. About one-third of the population was foreign-born or first generation—some 32 million out of 92 million. In addition to some 11 million from Italy, America was home to 8 percent of all Finns, Czechs, and Poles; 15 percent of all Danes and Swedes; 20 percent of all Norwegians; and 24 percent of all Jews. These and other groups had created some 300 national cultural and fraternal ethnic societies, with 42,000 locals and branches, representing 30 different ethnic groupings, serviced by more than 137 daily newspapers and countless other publications.[179]

Politicians could no longer be indifferent to the ethnic vote, as Woodrow Wilson quickly learned. Prior to his presidential ambitions, he characterized Italian, Hungarian, and Polish immigrants as "men of the lowest class from the South of Italy and men of the meaner sort out of Hungary and Poland, men out of the ranks where there was neither skill nor energy, nor any initiative which increased from year to year, as if the countries of the south of Europe are disburdening themselves of the more sordid and hapless elements of their population." Somewhat less objectionable were the Chinese—"as workmen if not as citizens." Blacks were in a special category. As president of Princeton, Wilson had prevented them from enrolling, believing that their chief oppressors, the KKK, simply sought "to protect their people from indignities and wrongs ... and defend the constitution of the United States and all laws passed in conformity thereto."[180]

By 1912, however, while running for president, he had a change of rhetoric, if not of mind. The Democratic Party now included many immigrants, whose votes he needed to overcome the Republican Party, which continued to include New England Yankees, nativists, and anti-immigration advocates. When asked by an Italian American editor about his earlier views, he replied that he had merely deplored "the coming to this country of certain lawless elements which I had supposed all thoughtful Italians themselves deplored. . . . Certainly the Italians I have known . . . have constituted one of the most interesting and admirable elements in our American life." To offended Hungarians, he apologized for having been "so awkward in my way of expressing what I had to say as to bring injustice to a people whom I admire and respect." He also assured Blacks of his opposition to lynching and that as president he "would know no differences of race or creed or section."[181]

Chinese and Japanese immigrants continued to earn his scorn. "I stand for the national policy of exclusion. . . . We cannot make a homogeneous population of a people who do not blend with the Caucasian race. . . . Oriental coolieism will give us another race problem to solve and surely we had had our lesson."[182]

After election, in spite of prior avowals of good intentions, he instituted a plethora of segregationist policies, whereby Black governmental employees were to have curtained-off desks and separate bathrooms, cafeteria tables, and congressional gallery seats. Wilson believed such measures "not humiliating but a benefit," which made Blacks "more safe in their possession of office and less likely to be discriminated against."[183] He also replaced the few Black diplomats with White ones and refused to appoint Blacks to governmental positions in the South. In vain, Black leaders protested, as they did his sending military troops to occupy Haiti and Santo Domingo, where they remained for nineteen and twenty-four years respectively, denying the natives the very right of self-determination he wanted for European countries.

As hostilities abroad intensified, so did American ethnic support for their respective homelands. "Today there were processions of the various nationalities in the chief avenues of the city," noted a 1914 tourist in New York City. "The French gathered in groups in front of their consulate and at the office of the Compagnie Generale Transatlantique. . . . A hundred yards away a noisy mob of Germans are thronging in front of the North German Lloyd building. Farther off is a band of Austro-Hungarians who have evidently been scarcely denationalized by their stay in America."[184]

Groups sympathetic to England or wanting their homelands independent from Austria-Hungary, the Ottoman Empire, or Russia accused those who differed with them of fostering tyranny abroad and unfaithfulness to America. There were also pacifists who opposed the war for religious and philosophic reasons, as well as radical groups that believed the war had been started and supported by munitions manufacturers, bankers, and capitalists.

Germans and foreigners generally became prime targets. "The Hun within our gates," said Theodore Roosevelt, "masquerades in many disguises . . . and should be hunted down without mercy." Anti-German passions led to a mob lynching in Illinois of a young German baker, Robert Prager, who was falsely accused of being a spy.[185] Across the country, German symbols were ridiculed, the German language excluded from public schools, German newspapers censored, and Germany stereotyped as a swinish, untamed, and barbarian land.

Religious leaders joined in the damning. To Courtland Meyers, at Boston's Tremont Temple, "If the Kaiser is a Christian, the devil in hell is a Christian, and I am an atheist." Another believed Christ "would take bayonet and grenade and bomb and rifle and do the work of deadliness against that which is the most deadly enemy of his Father's Kingdom in a thousand years."[186]

German Americans and Austrian Americans responded in kind, with one paper claiming that the war in Europe "was a battle to the bitter end between German civilization and the pan-Slavic, half-Asiatic, and thinly veneered barbarism of Russia." A widely circulated German American editorial asked, "What have the Russians, Poles, Bulgarians, and Serbs ever done for civilization? . . . Their specialties are massacres, crucifixion of the helpless."[187]

Swedish Americans were almost as fiercely antiwar. Most Swedish-language press and Lutheran clergy praised Germany as a champion of Protestant and Teutonic civilization and criticized Russia as their traditional enemy. In Chicago, Swedes were termed disloyal, particularly after several Swedish youths were arrested for demonstrating against the draft. To Judge John F. McGee, a member of the Minnesota Commission of Public Safety, "The disloyal element in Minnesota is largely among the German-Swedish people. The nation blundered at the start of the war in not dealing severely with these vipers." For a time, the Norwegian Lutheran Church in America considered dropping "Norwegian" from its official name. Some Puerto Ricans, too, opposed being drafted because, as noncitizens, they felt they had no military obligations to the United States.[188]

Much to Italy's disappointment, Italian Americans remained largely indifferent to its declaration of war on the Austro-Hungarian Empire in 1915. Though some sent contributions, and many newspapers and societies supported the Italian war effort, few returned home to defend "the graves of their fathers." Italian socialist and anarchist immigrants opposed both Italy's and America's involvement in the war.[189]

In contrast, thousands of Polish Americans sailed to join Polish military forces in France to help fight the Germans who had occupied their homeland. Basques in the western states were divided, depending on whether they had come from France or Spain; many French Basques returned home to fight Germany, while others from Spain, which had declared neutrality, refused to enlist in the United States military, claiming they too were neutral. Some 400 Asian Indians returned to India to help gain independence from England.[190]

As the Turkish government expanded its massacre of some 1.5 million Armenians, rallies were held across the country by American church, synagogue, and political leaders, who raised millions of dollars to help the "starving Armenians." On the West Coast, a small group of Asian Indian revolutionaries and German government officials (morally supported by some Irish American extremists) were found guilty of violating America's neutrality by plotting to overthrow British rule in India. Chinese in California, inspired by Dr. Sun Yat-sen's visits, advocated the overthrow of the Manchu Dynasty in China.[191]

Such activities angered many native-born Americans, who had abandoned old anti-British feelings and now viewed England as a friend and ally. Most supportive of England were American church groups with English origins (Scotch Presbyterians, Wesleyan Methodists, Congregationalists, Baptists, Universalists).[192] Invidious questions were raised about the foreign-born: why had they not become Americanized, why was America not first in their loyalties, why were they so vociferous in supporting foreign lands they had willingly left, and why did some return to serve in the armies of their homelands?

John Callan O'Laughlin, a former assistant secretary of state, denounced Irish politicians for helping "unpatriotic Americans of German birth" and complained that "our Jews compelled diplomatic intervention in behalf of their coreligionists in Russia and the Balkan States; our Hungarians brought us into strained relations with Austria; our Armenians, supported by well-meaning missionaries, almost precipitated war between the United States and Turkey." Irish political influence moved English officials to consider having "loyal Irishmen" give interviews and write articles to counter Irish American critics "who exude poison from every spore."[193]

Relatively unconcerned with Europe's problems, Blacks had more than enough of their own in America: expanding segregation, lynchings, violations of civil rights and liberties; increasing competition for jobs by immigrants; and declining federal employment, which because of Wilson's policies went from almost 6 percent in 1910 to about 4.9 percent in 1918.[194]

Meanwhile, after his election, Wilson began attracting greater support of central and eastern European immigrant groups, particularly Poles, whom he had earlier scorned and whose calls for an independent Poland he now favored. He also endeared himself with other eastern Europeans by advocating humanitarian relief for their war-ravaged homelands and designating special nationality days for groups like Syrians, Lithuanians, Armenians, and Ukrainians. With congressional approval, he proclaimed a national Ukrainian Day in recognition of their "terrible plight" and "dire need of food, clothing and shelter."[195]

His obvious sympathy for England, however, further alienated Irish, Swedish, and German groups. In his proclamation of war, which Congress overwhelmingly approved, only German aliens were declared enemies, though Hungarians, Austro-Hungarians, Turks, and Bulgarians were fighting alongside Germany. America's foreign-born were pressured to buy war bonds and subjected to harassment, job dismissal, business boycotts, and tar and featherings. "If we made any excuse for not buying [Liberty Bonds] we were called 'traitors,' 'cowards' and other worse words," complained some Russians. The Espionage Act of 1917 (outlawing obstructing military enlistments or interference with military or industrial operations) and the Sedition Act the next year (barring language disrespectful of the Constitution or aiding our country's enemies) led to some 2,000 prosecutions and more than 1,000 convictions, even for saying that the military draft was unconstitutional, that the sinking of merchant ships was legal, that a referendum should have preceded our declaration of war, or that the war was contrary to the teachings of Christ. Ellis Island became a prison, where thousands of Germans, Austrians, and Hungarians were taken without trial, though innocent of any act of disloyalty. The postmaster general was enabled to refuse handling magazines deemed unpatriotic, including some that quoted Thomas Jefferson's belief that Ireland should be an independent country.[196]

In contrast to the American Revolution and Civil War, no one could buy his way out of military service. Religious conscientious objectors were reviled, particularly Quakers, Mennonites, Jehovah's Witnesses, Hutterites, and Seventh-Day Adventists. In South Dakota, anti-Hutterite feelings became so intense that all but one of their seventeen communities closed down and moved to Canada. When the Jehovah's Witnesses opposed the war and conscription, eight principal officers were tried for "unlawfully, feloniously, and willfully causing insubordination, disloyalty and refusal of duty in the military and naval forces of the United States of America"; seven were sentenced to eighty years and one to forty years of imprisonment. This was reversed after the war when a judge held that they had not had "the temperate and impartial trial to which they were entitled."[197]

Similar animosities were directed toward other war opponents, such as radicals, socialists, atheists, pacifists, and assorted humanists. For voting against the declaration of war, Republican Congresswoman Jeanette Rankin, of Montana (the first and lone woman in Congress), had her district redrawn by Democratic politicians, forcing her not to run in 1918. Senator Robert La Follette, of Wisconsin, an outspoken pacifist, was burned in effigy in his hometown and targeted for expulsion by a Senate investigating committee. Exaggerated charges were made about immigrants refusing to serve in the military or, if already inducted, demanding discharge because they did not want to fight against their homeland kinsmen or were not citizens.

In spite of public scorn, America's foreign-born and descendants served in the military, 10 to 15 percent of which were of German birth or origin. Some 20 percent were Irish and 5 percent Jewish. Rather than return home, as the Italian government had urged, Italian Americans joined America's armed forces; though only about 4 percent of the whole population, said George Creel, chairman of the United States Committee on Public Information, "the list of casualties shows a full 10 percent of Italian names." Polish American losses were more than three times their percentage of the population. In all, approximately one-third of the men in the American army were foreign-born.[198]

Though Indians were generally not legal citizens and therefore exempt from the draft, over 10,000 entered the armed forces, 85 percent as volunteers. To one Indian newsletter, "Indians—men and women alike—are doing their bit to help make the world safe for democracy." The old negative stereotypes of Indians as savages were reversed, with the hope that they "do as much killing in khaki as their fathers did in blankets and war paint."[199]

Close to 370,000 Blacks served, though segregated and ridiculed as "coons," "niggers," and "darkies." They were excluded from the marines, but could serve in the navy, but as messboys. YMCA recreation units at army camps ignored their needs. Though the League of Nations was high on the ethnic agenda, for Blacks—as the *Chicago Defender* editorialized—"the More Important Issue" was lynching, as reflected in an accompanying cartoon of two political leaders arguing over the League, while in the background a Black hung from a telephone pole.[200]

As tens of thousands of southern Blacks moved from rural areas to the north, residential, educational and political segregation and exclusion intensified. Restrictive covenants grew, as did segregated schools and entry into restaurants and hotels. Some established northern Blacks blamed such increased bigotry on the backwardness of the newly arrived southern Blacks. Violence against Blacks also continued, with at least thirty-eight lynched in 1917 and fifty-eight in the following year. The NAACP's publication *The Crisis* denounced "the hundreds of thousands of white murderers, rapists, and scoundrels who have oppressed, killed, ruined, robbed, and debased their black fellow men and fellow women, and yet, today, walk scot-free, unwhipped of justice, uncondemned by millions of their white fellow citizens, and unrebuked by the President of the United States."[201] Such criticisms were considered unpatriotic by government officials, who threatened to revoke the mailing privileges of Black newspapers.

In what came to be called the "Red Summer" of Chicago, in 1919, a riot triggered by a Black youth's entering a part of Lake Michigan customarily used by Whites ended thirteen days later with 23 Blacks and 15 Whites killed, 342 Blacks and 178 Whites injured, and more than 1,000 mostly Black families left homeless.

By year's end, some two dozen race riots had taken place across the country, some by Blacks in retaliation for White attacks. Newspapers carried wild headlines like "REDS TRY TO STIR NEGROES TO REVOLT," and the *New York Times* declared, "Bolshevist agitation has been extended among the Negroes." The irony of such criticism was noted by the *Pittsburgh Courier:* "As long as the Negro submits to lynchings, burnings and oppressions—and says nothing—he is a loyal American citizen. But when he decides that lynchings and burnings shall cease even at the cost of some bloodshed in America, he is a Bolshevist." More militant Black leaders began advocating armed resistance to White attacks, and W.E.B. Du Bois predicted a race war in which Blacks and Asians would win out over White people. To Professors Richard Hofstadter and Michael Wallace, the 1935 riot in Harlem marked "a turning point in racial violence," with Blacks being the initiators of violence against White property.[202]

Intergroup hostility became part of the growing postwar political isolationism, patriotic xenophobia, religious fundamentalism, and revolutions abroad, all aggravated by inflation, labor strikes, renewed immigration, and calls for Prohibition. At the same time, ethnic opposition intensified to President Wilson, the Versailles Treaty, and the League of Nations.

Irish Americans wanted an independent Ireland. American Lithuanians resented the ceding of land to Poland. Italian Americans were angered that Fiume was given Yugoslavia. German Americans damned Wilson as an Anglophile, responsible for the anti-German agitation during the war. Armenian Americans were bitterly disappointed by the denial of an independent Armenia. Syrian Americans were incensed that Syria was made a mandate of France. Greek Americans felt Greece should have been given more land. Estonian Americans organized aid for their war-torn homeland and urged diplomatic recognition of the newly proclaimed Estonian republic. Ukrainian Americans charged President Wilson with "shamelessly" violating his promise "that all subjugated nations would get their freedom and independence." Korean Americans wanted independence for Korea or at least trusteeship under the League of Nations—rather than continued rule by Japan. Marcus Garvey and his Universal Negro Improvement Association excoriated the Allies at Versailles for denying Africa self-determination, saying they "gave to the Jew, Palestine . . . to the Irish, Home Rule Government and Dominion status . . . the Poles, a new Government of their own."[203]

Republicans readily exploited such resentments. Senator Henry Cabot Lodge, who had previously criticized immigrants, now eagerly sought their support and invited them to testify before his Foreign Relations Committee, where Slovaks, Czechs, Estonians, Lithuanians, Greeks, Hungarians, Irish, Slovenes, Serbs, Croats, Latvians, Koreans, Albanians, Swedes, and Scots pleaded their particular cause. Elsewhere, American Egyptians protested Britain's attempt to make "Egypt a pendant to Britain's red circle of the globe." Fiorello La Guardia argued the case for Fiume being Italian rather than Yugoslavian. Some forty-four Americans, including congressmen from Nebraska, Massachusetts, and Pennsylvania, sent a Christmas message to the "people of India," declaring their sympathy with them and for "Ireland and Egypt who are struggling for the right of self-determination."[204]

Foreign revolutionaries were blamed for causing labor strikes, urban race riots, and revolution abroad. Inflation, job shortages, bombings, and threat of bombings led to an expansion of laws against aliens advocating or belonging to groups advocating revolution or assassination of public officials. Red, the color of the flag of international socialism, became an epithet, in contrast to the red, white, and blue of American democracy. The association of "Reds" with foreigners and conspiracies, wrote Louis Post, assistant secretary of labor from 1913 to 1921, was intensified "by sensational reports of revolutionary horrors in Soviet Russia where the 'red' flag waved."[205]

Adding fuel to the political hysteria were many Protestant fundamentalists, who damned Bolshevism, atheism, modernism, and evolution. *Moody's Monthly,* in 1923, declared that "evolution is Bolshevism in the long run. . . . It eliminates the idea of a personal God, and with that goes all authority in government, all law and order." Other religious leaders also denounced Russian Bolshevist repression of religion, with one Episcopalian saying that the world owed nothing to

Russians but "sufficient voltage to rid the earth of them." Catholic priests frequently held prayers for Russian conversion. And business leaders, patriotic organizations, and even some labor groups also denounced Russia, with the AFL repudiating "bolshevism, IWWism and red flagism in general."[206]

The linking of immigrants with revolutionaries had been in the making for some time, though the peasant origins of many immigrants bred a conservatism, which remained even when joining labor unions. Only a small fraction of the immigrant-worker population was attracted to socialism, which many ethnic, religious, and communal leaders denounced as antireligious. Although the first convention of the Socialist Labor Party in 1877 had representatives from seventeen German sections, seven English, three Bohemian, and one French, the overwhelming majority of Socialist Party members in the early twentieth century were native Americans. By 1912, some 1,200 Socialists had been elected in 340 municipalities across the country, including seventy-nine mayors in twenty-four states. In fact, the deeper one went into the heartland of America, wrote Gerald Rosenblum, "the more radical the left-wing movement became. It was not in the East, with its large immigrant population, but in the West that the radical Industrial Workers of the World was conceived." Though Blacks, too, were linked with communists, particularly during riots or fear of such, and though the Communist Party made concerted efforts to win their support, relatively few did, never exceeding 10 percent of the party's membership.[207]

Nevertheless, fiction proved stronger than fact. A Russian American newspaper despaired in 1919 that "the average American knows little about the foreign-born. He considers every Italian a member of the 'Black Hand' Society. He thinks that every Russian is a Bolshevik, every German an admirer of the Kaiser." Not satisfied with federal laws, various states passed their own to expel and bar socialists from public office, to require teachers to take a loyalty oath, and to establish legislative committees for investigating the loyalty of private citizens. Suspicion extended to would-be citizens and led in 1923 to the first major change in the "Pledge of Allegiance," wherein instead of swearing to "my flag" (which allegedly allowed immigrants and their children to think privately of their ancestral homeland), the words were changed "to the flag of the United States of America."[208]

Across the country, foreign languages were banned in private and public schools, and in public places. Though the teaching of German was the target of much legislation in the Midwest, it was French in New England's parochial schools. Between 1919 and 1925, more than 1,000 people were found guilty of using subversive speech and sentenced to jail. Furthermore, state laws and city ordinances multiplied in restricting jobs and landowning opportunities to Americans only. Anti-British feelings resurfaced as some patriotic organizations accused England of having tricked America into the war and having bribed American scholars to write pro-British propaganda. Some cities initiated investigations of "Anglicized" books, while some states passed "pure-history" laws.[209]

In Michigan, aliens could not obtain a barber's license; in New York, they were disqualified from becoming motion picture machine operators, master pilots, or marine engineers; in Florida, Oregon, Texas, and Washington, they were prohibited from catching and selling fish and oysters; in Arizona, California, and Idaho, fishing and hunting license fees were two and a half to ten times higher than for citizens; in Delaware, aliens had to pay an extra $100 for a peddler's license. Cities like Baltimore, Providence, Philadelphia, and Pittsburgh completely forbade hiring aliens for public works.[210]

Against such a setting, Attorney General A. Mitchell Palmer, whose own home had been bombed, launched a nationwide roundup of suspected alien radicals. America had to be protected against revolution, he said: "Like a prairie fire . . . it was eating its way into the home of the American workman, its sharp tongues of revolutionary heat were licking the altars of the churches, leaping into the belfry of the school bell, crawling into the sacred corners of American homes, seeking to replace marriage vows with libertine laws, burning up the foundations of society."[211]

Russian organizations, clubs, schools, labor associations, and political meetings were raided. After being arrested with some friends in a restaurant and then imprisoned at Ellis Island, one young man said:

> In Russia I was frequently maltreated and had a difficult life as a peasant, but I never did anything against the government. In the United States I am not opposed to your form of government and have never favored the use of force. I believe all the Russians here are treated unjustly, their jobs are taken away, they are arrested; at the same time they are denied passports to return to Russia. The Czar's regime, bad as it was, never treated its subjects as the Russians are being treated at the present time in America.[212]

Others, fearful of being arrested, losing their jobs, or being denied employment, shaved their beards or Americanized their names.[213]

In late 1919, 249 "radicals" were deported to Russia, including the anarchists Emma Goldman and Alexander Berkman, who attempted to murder steel tycoon Henry Clay Frick. "While many native born were also engaged in spreading Bolshevist doctrine," wrote Frances Kellor at the time, "aliens alone were raided and arrested, because the Attorney General could secure convictions only under the deportation law and not in the courts."[214]

Intergroup tensions were further aggravated by national elections and the issue of Prohibition, which was supported not only by Republicans, evangelical Protestants, rural residents suspicious of urban areas, and anti-Catholics, but also by many labor, business, and education leaders, who considered liquor destructive to societal well-being. Americans were reminded that Presidents Lincoln, Garfield, and McKinley had been assassinated by heavy drinkers and that President Theodore Roosevelt had almost been killed by a saloonkeeper. Abolish the saloon, "and the task of Americanizing the conglomerate foreign population would be lightened 50 percent."[215]

To many ethnic groups, however, Prohibition was seen as a malicious assault on them. In a 1919 referendum on whether Chicago should become "dry," Czechs, Germans, Lithuanians, and Italians opposed it by a vote of 90 percent or more; Yugoslavs and Poles, by over 80 percent; Jews, by 77 percent; Blacks, by 75 percent; and Swedes, by 64 percent. Representative Fiorello La Guardia sarcastically told Congress that neither his constituents, immigrant parents, nor ancestors were given to overly drinking: "I traced it way back and the only one of my ancestors I could find who drank to excess was a certain Nero, and he got the habit from his mother who was born on the Rhine."[216] Nevertheless, the Congress and then the states overwhelmingly enacted the Eighteenth Amendment, prohibiting the manufacture, sale, or transportation of intoxicating liquor.

Warren G. Harding's 1920 Republican landslide victory was abetted by Democratic voters whom Wilson had alienated during the war. "You may be assured that I will strive to do my just part to further the righteous cause of the Greek nation and the splendid element of citizenship it has contributed to this country," Harding wrote to a Greek society. Other Republicans issued supporting—but contradictory—statements on the Fiume question. For Italians, they said, "Fiume is not a mere name but a pledge, a symbol of triumph of Italian right over international aggression." For Yugoslavs, they attacked the League of Nations, where the "voice of Italy and her political and military influence and power will always stand against the just demands of Yugo-Slavia."[217]

In contrast, the Democratic presidential candidate, James M. Cox, accused ethnic groups of "un-American hyphenism" and charged an Afro-American party with "hyphenated activity" in order to "stir up troubles among Negroes upon false claims that it can bring social equality." His running mate for the vice-presidency, Franklin Delano Roosevelt, questioned the loyalty of German Americans and described Italians as people with "half-consciences and fifty-fifty citizens." Recalling his loss, Cox wrote that the "leaders of three racial groups, Germans, Irish and Italians, had gone over to the Republican side. The Germans were angry with Wilson because of the war. The Irish were inflamed because Wilson did not make the independence of Ireland part of the Versailles Treaty. The Italians were enraged because Fiume had been taken from Italy."[218]

The prosperity and "red-baiting" of the Harding years continued with Calvin Coolidge, who succeeded Harding when he suddenly died. Coolidge easily won the 1924 election, in which Robert La Follette ran as an independent, attracting much German and Irish support for his opposition to America's having entered the war, advocacy of an independent Ireland, and criticism of the KKK.

Anti-Catholicism peaked during the 1928 presidential election as Protestant religious leaders, Prohibitionists, anti-immigrationists, KKK members, and street bigots denounced "Al(cohol)" Smith, leading to the defection of much of the solid South from the national Democratic Party, but the return to it of those immigrant, Jewish, and Catholic voters who had gone Republican in 1920. Cheap anti-Catholic pamphlets and books, many of which were reprints of the Know-Nothing years, once again warned of Catholic plots to close the public schools, burn Protestant Bibles, and take over the country.[219]

As reputable a journal as the *Christian Century* said the "reasons why Catholics wish to elect Smith are the reasons why Protestant-minded Americans do not wish him elected. They cannot look with unconcern upon the seating of a representative of an alien culture, of a medieval Latin mentality, of an undemocratic hierarchy and of a foreign potentate." To a much lesser degree, Herbert Hoover was denounced for his Quaker religion, which would allegedly prevent him from serving as commander in chief of the armed forces.[220]

Believing Prohibition a noble social and economic experiment, Hoover overwhelmingly defeated Smith, who managed to win only six southern states, plus Massachusetts and Rhode Island. Hoover's vice-presidential running mate was Charles Curtis, who had a distant partial Kaw and Osage Indian ancestry, which his opponents demeaned by referring to him as "the Injun" and "the Noble Red Man of the Forest."[221] Although many factors were at work during the election—chiefly the prosperity of the times—Smith's Catholicism had caused many people, particularly rural Protestants, to vote for Hoover, reinforcing the belief that a Catholic could not win the presidency, but that a Quaker could—the first ever. Thirty-two years were to pass before another Catholic would run for the highest office of the land—and win.

The KKK and the Intensification of Bigotry

The post–World War I intensification of intergroup bigotry was epitomized by the rebirth of the KKK, which not only generated but also reflected the racism, anti-Catholicism, anti-Semitism, and xenophobia of the times. In April 1913, a thirteen-year-old girl, Mary Phegan, was murdered in an Atlanta pencil factory owned by Leo Frank, a former northern Jewish businessman, who was charged with the crime. In a trial reminiscent of the Dreyfus Affair in France for its anti-Semitism, Frank was found guilty and sentenced to death, though no credible evidence existed against him. Believing him innocent, Georgia's governor, John M. Slaton, commuted the sentence to life imprisonment in June 1915.

Nativists and anti-Semites damned Slaton as "King of the Jews and Georgia's Traitor Forever," burned his effigy, and intimidated Jews to leave the state. Calling themselves the Knights of Mary Phegan, a group of 150 men swore vengeance, and a mob abducted Frank from prison and hanged him. That autumn, some thirty-three Knights met on a mountaintop outside Atlanta and brought the KKK back into being.[222] Nearly seventy years later, an eyewitness at the scene of Mary Phegan's murder confessed Frank had not committed the crime, but rather the factory's janitor, who had threatened to kill him if he had spoken up at the time. Even then, it took another four years before Frank was given a posthumous pardon, not because he was believed innocent, but because the state had failed to protect him and it was believed the time had arrived to heal past animosities.

By the early 1920s, the KKK became a powerful national and local force of some 5 million members, attracting Protestants across the country, including many ministers and preachers who served as organizational leaders and lecturers. In the Northeast and Midwest, the KKK associated itself closely with the Republican Party.[223] Now urban Catholics, Jews, Asians, and the foreign-born, as well as rural Blacks, were targets.

The KKK's imperial wizard, William Simmons, boasted that Jews were excluded "because they do not believe in the Christian religion. We exclude Catholics because they owe allegiance to an institution that is foreign to the government of the United States. To assure supremacy of the white race, we believe in the exclusion of the yellow race and in the disfranchisement of the Negro." To Oregon's grand dragon, Fred Gifford, "The rapid growth of the Japanese population and the great influx of foreign laborers, mostly Greeks, is threatening our American institutions." The KKK also promoted itself as a guardian of morality, motherhood, chastity, and temperance, as well as the enemy of "every criminal, every gambler, every thug, every libertine, every girl ruiner, every home wrecker, every wife beater, every dope peddler, every moonshiner, every crooked politician, every pagan Papist priest, every shyster lawyer, every K. [night] of C. [olumbus], every white slaver, every brothel madam, every Rome controlled newspaper . . ."[224]

Theirs was no mere rhetoric. Ku Klux Klan members harassed, threatened, and attacked immigrants: ordering all Syrians and Lebanese to leave Marietta, Georgia; agitating against French in Vermont; flogging a Greek in Florida for dating a White woman, and urging that Greeks and Mexicans in Washington State be sent back to where they came from; ordering a boycott of all Italian storekeepers in East Frankfort, Illinois; and distributing thousands of copies of the contrived "Knights of Columbus Oath." The KKK biweekly, the *American Standard,* accused Rome and American Catholics of trying to take over the government, claiming that 61 percent of State Department employees and 70 percent of Treasury Department employees were Catholic.[225]

Lest anyone accuse the KKK or its leaders of being bigoted or un-Christian, the imperial wizard told a congressional committee in 1921, "I am a churchman and proud of it. . . . I am a member of two churches—the Congregational Church and a full-fledged associate member of the Missionary Baptist Church, given me as an honor." He also told of being a member of various fraternal organizations, including one believing in the "fraternity of nations, so that all people might know something of the great doctrine—the fatherhood of God and brotherhood of man." Unfortunately, he had many admiring Protestant clergymen, particularly Baptists, Methodists, and Disciples of Christ.[226]

As with the Know-Nothings of the 1850s, the KKK achieved striking election victories before becoming rent with factionalism and loss of power. Internal corruption forced the retirement of Simmons and elevation of Hiram W. Evans, who was no less bigoted, though he denied it. The KKK, Evans said, was committed to three great racial instincts: "race, pride and loyalty . . . to the white race, to the traditions of America and to the spirit of Protestantism," all reflected in its slogan of "Native, white, Protestant supremacy!"[227]

The KKK was not without respectable defenders and apologists, who saw it as a truly patriotic organization committed to improving the public schools, law enforcement, traditional morality, and Christian idealism. Paul Winter attacked "the melting pot" and "tolerance" as "anesthetics employed to stupefy the American people . . . to hide the establishing of foreign institutions, behind which alienism in all its forms might advance its lines in quest of power." More focused was Morrison I. Swift, who, while stressing the need for science and intelligence, said the KKK was "born of the blind apathy . . . to the growth of political Catholicism and kindred phenomena. Stolid Americans, over-rich, over-fed and religious, have allowed an international political church to reach vast proportions here in the deceptive guise of religion, not only splitting the American school system, but projecting other anti-democratic conquests." Some contemporary writers have also noted the all-too-human nature of KKK members. Kenneth T. Jackson, in his *The Ku Klux Klan in the City 1915–1930,* reminds us that "virtually every" Protestant denomination denounced the KKK, and that most KKK members were not "innately depraved or anxious to subvert American institutions," but rather saw their membership in keeping with "one hundred percent Americanism" and Christian morality.[228]

By the time of the Great Depression, KKK membership had dropped to some 100,000, and their enemies now included all who believed in communism, the New Deal, and organized labor. "The CIO is a subversive, radical and Red organization," declared one Klansman, "and we'll fight fire with fire."[229] And they did, attacking labor organizers and supporters in the South and West.

As with Catholics, fake and forged documents denouncing Jews were widely distributed. One alleged that Benjamin Franklin had urged that Jews be barred from entering the country. *The Protocols of the Elders of Zion* charged Jews with conspiring to control the world by building subways to blow up at a designated time and with promoting Greek and Latin in order to undermine American values. Its most prominent American distributor, Henry Ford, held Jews responsible for the Civil War, Lincoln's assassination, and a "nasty Orientalism" that was causing a deterioration of literature, amusements, and social conduct.[230]

Even among those repudiating anti-Semitism, a snobbish conviction existed that Jews were socially and genetically inferior. Believing himself not anti-Semitic, H.H. Marlin, a weekly writer in the *United Presbyterian,* said that wherever the Jew "predominates in a community he is said to be as a rule intolerable as a neighbor. He is offensive in his almost total lack of thoughtfulness and consideration of the rights of others. His children are as a rule utterly lawless."[231]

Moreover, Jews were said to be overly individualistic, good as entrepreneurs, but not as organizers and administrators of high finance or corporate business, in which Anglo-Saxons excelled. Though clearly "the ablest folk the world has ever known," wrote Nathaniel Shaler, they lacked an "imitative quality," making them "the most incapable of subjection, being in this regard even more obdurate than the American Indian or the Chinese." That Jews excelled disproportionately in some sports was noted to their discredit. In college basketball almost half of the players in the American Basketball League in the late 1930s were Jewish, and in professional boxing Jews had more fighters in the eight weight divisions than any other ethnic group. To Ed Sullivan, however, then a sports columnist for the *New York Daily News,* Jews excelled in basketball because "the Jew is a natural gambler and will take chances." Another well-known sportswriter of the time, Frederick Lieb, claimed that though a Jew could become a skillful boxer and ring strategist, "he did not have the background to stand out in a sport which is so essentially a team game as baseball."[232]

Such feelings of contempt, fear, and admiration were carried over into higher education, where anti-Jewish quotas were initiated, with rationalizations made that the Christian character of institutions had to be maintained and the spread of anti-Semitism prevented. Jewish students were believed too anxious to acculturate and too studious in classes, thereby alienating nice Protestant students. "While many of these Hebrew boys are fine students," said Yale's Dean Frederick Jones in 1922, "I think the general effect on the scholastic standing is bad. Some men [Christians] say that they are not disposed to compete with Jews for first honors; they do not care to be a minority in a group of men of higher scholarship record, most of whom are Jews."[233]

Lest they be accused of brazen anti-Semitism, some colleges adopted a number of seemingly innocent admission policies, such as increasing the number of Christian applicants (particularly those of alumni), screening out Jewish applicants by requiring their photographs and mother's maiden name on application forms, and interviewing applicants by selected alumni. Dartmouth adopted admissions quotas in 1921 to prevent being "overrun racially." At fashionable Sarah Lawrence College, a quota system was started in 1928–29, which kept records on the number of Jews admitted and enrolled in each class and counted those of mixed parentage as full Jews.[234]

Desperate for professional training, some Jewish students applied to schools abroad or to Black ones. For example, more than 10 percent of the students in ten medical schools in Canada in 1934–35 were Jewish. In America, Howard University's medical school had twice as many Jewish applicants as Black ones in 1935.[235]

Jews themselves were often blamed for the rise of anti-Semitism. In a 1923 *Nation* magazine article "Is America Anti-Semitic?" Lewis B. Gannett argued that the Jews' appreciation of "the opportunities of America is a cause of prejudice; he sends his children to college a generation or two sooner than other stocks, and as a result there are in fact more dirty Jews and tactless Jews in college than dirty and tactless Italians, Armenians, or Slovaks."[236]

Blaming the victims was not limited to the victimizers. Some Jews, too, believed that anti-Semitism would be reduced if other Jews were dispersed into various professions. For example, the *B'nai B'rith Magazine,* in 1933, recommended that Jewish students enter fields other than law and medicine, which they were entering in large numbers.[237]

As with Jews, some other groups were believed too given to study and too lacking in talent for sports. In recalling those days, Henry Seidel Canby told of how Jewish, Italian, Armenian, and Chinese students usually restrained themselves in classroom discussions, but occasionally "some Chinese boy, caught off his guard, and forgetting the convention of the classroom, which was to answer a question and sit down, would give a precis of the entire lesson, and perhaps the previous one and the next, which only a French intellectual could have equalled."[238]

As late as 1936, the secretary of the Association of American Medical Colleges complained that Italians were "flocking into medicine at an alarmingly rapid rate." Outside the ivied walls, they were treated worse. In 1920, after the bodies of two murdered boys were found in West Frankfurt, Illinois, a mob of some 3,000 to 4,000 attacked the Italian section, burning homes, assaulting residents, and demanding they leave; after three days of mayhem and the calling in of 500 state troopers, order was restored.[239]

Anti-Italian hostility climaxed in the Sacco and Vanzetti case, where in spite of more than a dozen witnesses testifying that both men were not at the scene of the crime, they were found guilty, damned as anarchists and "dagoes." After seven years of futile appeals for a retrial, including Professor Felix Frankfurter's analysis that the trial was unfair, the men were electrocuted, but not before Vanzetti told the sentencing judge that "I have had to suffer for things that I am not guilty of. I am suffering because I am a radical, and indeed I am a radical; I have suffered because I was an Italian, and indeed I am an Italian."[240]

Though large-scale violence had ended against Indians, the prejudice lingered. In the mid-1920s, Indians were denied jobs and some even deported to Canada. Highly skilled Mohawk ironworkers from Canada were declared illegal aliens, though by the Jay Treaty and Treaty of Ghent they had been assured free passage across the border, which the courts soon upheld. Nevertheless, during the depression, Mohawk ironworkers were barred from government WPA (Works Progress Administration) construction jobs because they were not citizens.[241] Also, Arizona and New Mexico continued to deny Indians the franchise until ordered to do so by the courts in 1948.

While thousands of native-born seamen were unemployed during the Great Depression, shipping companies frequently hired nonunion foreign crews who could be paid lower wages than those given to Americans. Chinese seamen were required to sign contracts withholding 50 percent of their wages until they were discharged, post a $500 bond promising contract compliance, and agree with "the captain that we will not join any association of any kind, or attempt to form any associations while around the vessel; if any such association should be founded, it is hereby understood that such men will be returned to Hong Kong at their own expense." Puerto Ricans, too, were victims of the depression. Though relatively small in number and living mainly in New York City, they were accused of being uncivilized, crime prone, disease ridden, and uneducable. Newspapers frequently carried stories on their impoverished conditions in Harlem and in Puerto Rico, warning readers against associating with them lest they contract a disease, particularly tuberculosis. Whereas, back home, racial intermarriage was taken for granted, in America Puerto Ricans quickly learned that not being White was a sure obstacle to socioeconomic advancement.[242]

Some intellectuals, in their opposition to prejudice, adopted a blame-the-victim mindset in urging a total ban on further immigration. "There is only one way in which the United States can be protected from the anti-Semitism which so grievously afflicts the eastern sections of Europe," wrote journalist and historian Burton Hendrick. "That is by putting up the bars against these immigrants until the day comes when those already here are absorbed." To Edward Lewis, Catholics were "desirable citizens and delightful friends," but "the proportion of Catholics in our population should not be increased. If it is increased, this alien psychology may seriously modify and damage our institutions." At Ohio State University, a group of social scientists agreed that "in view of the high degree of race prejudice which prevails . . . it is doubtless desirable that the immigration of Orientals should be prevented. Until we can learn to be more tolerant of racial differences it does not appear desirable that we should admit increasing numbers of those whose presence would only add to our present manifestation of racial discrimination."[243]

Such feelings and behaviors were not without critics, as reflected in a 1920 article in *Russkoye Slovo*.

> Foreigners having to bear all this cannot write home very enthusiastic letters about America, and, of course, they want to leave, the sooner the better. If the work of the foreigner is appreciated, if he is needed in the mines, in the construction of subways, and for the work in the factories and farms, one must give him human rights, and one must not offend him at every step.

Even President Harding acknowledged that "the person of foreign birth is more a victim in this country than a conspirator."[244]

On the West Coast in the 1930s, bigotry extended along class lines to White, native-born Protestant Americans fleeing drought and poverty in Oklahoma, Texas, Missouri, and Arkansas. They were exploited, maligned, and shunned by their racial and religious counterparts in California, who pejoratively called them "Okies," "Texies," or "Arkies," and invidiously compared them to Mexicans, Blacks, Filipinos, and Asians.

One California health official warned farmers not to build cabins with more than one room for "a people whose cultural and environmental background is so bad that for a period of more than 300 years no advances have been made in living conditions among them and ethically they are as far removed from a desire to attain the privileges which present day culture and environment offers."[245]

Immigration Restrictions and Exclusions

The 1920s were rife with demands to exclude or at least restrict southern, central, and eastern European, Mexican, and Filipino immigrants. False and contradictory accusations abounded about immigrants having no skills, lowering wage standards, weakening unions, causing industrial accidents, contributing to unemployment, spreading diseases, and being viewed as another step in the "Asiatic-Slavic-Semitic" onslaught against Anglo-Saxon America and England.[246]

Post–World War I disillusionment with European politics, rising nationalism, and alleged scientific evidence further inflamed opposition to immigration. Arguments were made that foreign laborers were not really needed because the war had proven that American industry could function without them. The newly formed American Legion urged a stop to all immigration from Germany and countries neutral during the war, as well as the deportation of aliens who had given up their first citizenship papers to avoid being drafted.[247] After advocating a two-year ban on all immigration, the AFL sought total exclusion, claiming that wage standards and jobs for returning veterans had to be protected.

"Immigration should not only be restrictive but highly selective," proclaimed the widely read *A Study of American Intelligence,* and Calvin Coolidge wrote, "Biological laws tell us that certain divergent people will not mix or blend. The Nordics propagate themselves successfully. With other races, the outcome shows deterioration on both sides. Quality of mind and body suggests that observance of ethnic law is as great a necessity as immigration law."[248]

Though President Wilson had pocket-vetoed an almost identical bill, President Harding signed the Emergency Quota Act of 1921 into law. For the first time, the number of European immigrants from each nation was limited to 3 percent of the foreign-born in America as of the 1910 census, with a maximum of some 350,000 a year from outside the Western Hemisphere and a clear preference for northwestern Europeans, who would constitute 55 percent in comparison to 45 percent for southeastern Europeans. No limitations were put on Western Hemisphere nations, not only because of diplomatic desires to maintain good relations with them, but also in response to pressures from southern and western agricultural interests who wanted the continuation of cheap farm-labor immigrants.[249] Within a year of its enactment, total immigration dropped from 805,028 to 309,556. Still, greater restriction was demanded, with racial theorizing applied to White Europeans, as it had been to Indians, Blacks, Chinese, and Japanese.

Senator Johnson argued that the "day of unalloyed welcome to all peoples, the day of indiscriminate acceptance of all races, has definitely ended." Senator Reed was no less vehement: "I think most of us are reconciled to the ideal of discrimination. I think the American people want us to discriminate; and I don't think discrimination is unfair."[250]

In contrast, as never before, business and ethnic groups opposed immigration restrictions. The president of the Rural Land Owners Association, in Texas, believed that if farmers were deprived of needed Mexican laborers, "the agricultural development of that section of the country will be absolutely done for." Florida cigar makers defended Cuban immigrants because Americans would not do their kind of work. "The Cubans are of small physique and they like that kind of work because it does not require much exertion."[251]

Ethnic opposition to restrictions was broad and intense. The Chicago Bohemian paper, the *Daily Svornest,* said that if all immigrants left America, disaster would befall industry and commerce, "and all the large cities would practically be wiped out, for there are very few Americans whose grandparents or remote ancestors came to this country, who are employed at manual labor." Rabbi Stephen Wise warned a congressional committee that it was creating among Hungarians, Czechoslovakians, Serbians, and Jews of eastern Europe a sense of inferiority "which is essentially and instinctively felt when a man is proscribed against, as if, later on, he will not be helpful and serviceable to America."[252]

In spite of such protests, but much to the delight of racists, nativists, patrician exclusionists, labor leaders, and many Black newspapers, Congress once again in 1924 overwhelmingly passed restrictive legislation—the Johnson-Reed Bill, which President Coolidge, like his predecessor, had no qualms about signing into law. Annual immigration was limited to 165,000 and quotas were established for eligible countries to 2 percent of its foreign-born in the 1890 census, when there were comparatively fewer Italian, Jewish, Greek, Hungarian, Polish, and Russian immigrants. The long-time exclusion of Chinese and many Asians was affirmed, and a "National Origins Plan" was incorporated, which in 1927 would further reduce the maximum number of immigrants to 150,000, with each eligible country's yearly quota based on the foreign-born of the 1920 census. A midwestern congressman bluntly admitted that the rationale behind the legislation was to exclude "Bolshevik Wops, Dagoes, Kikes and Hunkies."[253]

No longer was America a land of opportunity for all daring or determined individuals, nor an unrestricted asylum for the oppressed, nor a land willing to acculturate all who aspired to citizenship. Just as for racial reasons America had barred the Chinese in 1882, excluded the Japanese in 1907, and then Asians from countries in the "barred zone" in 1917, so now Europeans were restricted. Instead of individual ability or potential, a person's group affiliation became the deciding criterion for admission.

Those targeted fully recognized the implications of the law. Catholics generally criticized it as an attack on them, since most new immigrants from southern and eastern Europe were of their faith. In Japan, the bill was seen as an additional insult to the 1907 Gentlemen's Agreement, and anti-American demonstrations erupted and a day of mourning was declared. Many Blacks welcomed immigration restriction, however. The *Philadelphia Tribune* said, "restricted immigration is fundamentally sound and will help keep the workers with full dinner pails. The laws were not even passed to help Negroes but that they benefit from them no reasonable person can deny."[254]

When government statisticians announced exact quotas for each country, groups that had thought they would benefit by the law discovered that with the exception of England their homeland quotas were actually curtailed—Germans and Irish by almost half and Scandinavians by almost two-thirds. Protests immediately ensued by the German-American Citizens League, the Steuben Society, the Sons of Norway, the Danish Brotherhood of America, (the Swedish) Vasa Order of America, and the American Irish Historical Society. To the German-American Citizens League, "The modus employed in figuring these quotas is a gross violation of the admitted intent of the new law to further the immigration of descendants of the Nordic races while lowering the numbers of newcomers of less desirable races."[255]

Although the law's restrictive aspects were directed at White non-Anglo-Saxons, its exclusionary aspects continued to be directed at Asians. Regardless of their complexion, some groups were deemed racially inferior and therefore unwanted. As early as the 1890s, the Supreme Court had ruled that though American-born Chinese children could become citizens, their foreign-born parents could not, because they "have never been allowed, by our law, to acquire our nationality." In the 1920s, a Michigan federal court revoked the citizenship of an Arab from India who pleaded that his ancestors had not intermarried with any Indians, but had "kept their Arabian blood line clear and pure." The Supreme Court also denied citizenship to Takao Ozawa, a Japanese male who had lived most of his life in America and Hawaii and had graduated from an American high school; while acknowledging that he was "well qualified by character and education," the Court nevertheless held that citizenship was limited to "free white persons and aliens of African nativity." In 1925, the government sought to cancel an Armenian's certificate of naturalization because the defendant, Tatos O. Cartozian, was "not a free white person within the meaning of the naturalization laws of the Congress." The government, however, lost the case for equally racial reasoning because the United States District Court in Oregon held that Armenians were "of Alpine stock, of European persuasion" and "amalgamate readily with the white races."[256]

Citizenship was also denied Burmese, Malaysian, Thai, Indian, and Korean alien applicants because they were deemed non-White, while Syrians, Palestinians, Persians, and Turks were excluded because they were Asiatics. Mixed parentage, too, was sufficient cause for denial, as in the 1912 court cases of a "half-breed German and Japanese" and a "quarter-breed Spaniard and Filipino."[257]

In contrast to Europe and Asia, the absence of quotas for Western Hemisphere countries was not due to altruism: some had relatively few nationals in America in 1890 upon which a quota could be based; Canadians and Mexicans could not be easily prevented from crossing the border; and, most important, economic interests demanded that Pan-American goodwill be maintained, that foreign investments and trade be protected, and that Mexican "stoop labor" in the Southwest be continued. As a result, immigrants from Canada, the West Indies, and Mexico assumed a larger proportion of the total immigration than ever before.

Nevertheless, in the latter 1920s, patriotic organizations, labor unions, congressmen, and eugenicists continued to demand that America's "back door" be closed to Mexicans and Filipinos. Legislation was long debated to restrict Mexicans, who Representative John Box of Texas said were creating "the most insidious and general mixture of white, Indian, and negro blood strains ever produced in America." Economic reasons and those of international affairs, however, prevented the imposition of any quota, marking "the first permanent defeat" for restrictionists.[258]

Demands increased for preventing a Filipino "invasion." Here, too, the imposition of a quota or exclusion was prevented largely because it was felt unjust to restrict those whose homeland America had annexed in 1898. As one Filipino official stated: "If we are to be treated as a foreign people for purposes of immigration, we must first be given the category of a free and independent nation."[259] Such was finally done in 1934, and a quota of a mere fifty was given the Philippines, believing it was better to give their residents freedom than admission to America.

Such restrictions intensified the desperation of those who could no longer legally enter. Illegal immigrants, wrote Professor Constantine Panunzio in 1927, "sail in little schooners and fishing smacks; cross rivers in fragile boats; make their way over snowbound passes, over ice covered rivers and lonely deserts. They swim, crawl on hands and knees or 'fly.' They pay fabulous sums—doubtless the savings of years—to be carried across. Thousands enter as seamen, hundreds as stowaways. Some even travel half around the globe, enduring unheard of hardships in the hope of entering America."[260]

With the Great Depression, immigration from all countries dropped sharply, far below established quotas. Jobs became few and unemployment high, rising from 8.7 percent in 1930 to 15.9 percent in 1931, and then to 23.6 percent in 1932. In fact, during the depression years of 1931 to 1936, some 240,000 more aliens left than entered America.

The 1920s also witnessed the decline of Protestant power, especially in the large cities, not only because of increased immigration, of differing ethnicities and religions, but also because of internal Protestant differences over Darwinian evolution, scholarly criticism of the Bible, and the rise of comparative religious studies. The Scopes Trial of 1925 (reprovingly called the "Monkey Trial") dramatized the growing split between Protestant fundamentalists and liberals, wherein the former had succeeded in having a number of states pass laws prohibiting the teaching of evolution in the public schools and universities.

Because of the depression, which began six months after President Hoover took office, industrial production and national income fell drastically, resulting in fewer people wanting to immigrate here, far below established quotas for different countries. As severe as economic conditions were, there was no replay of the patriotic paranoia, labor violence, and class conflict that had characterized the 1880s and the immediate post–World War I years. Certainly, racial, ethnic, and religious bigotry remained and a few new hate groups came into being, such as the American Patriots, the Paul Reveres, and the Black Shirts. Instead of labor unions, radicals, or immigrants being the chief targets of the discontented, they were laissez-faire economics, big-business greed, and an indifferent government.[261]

Chapter 4

The Expansion of Democratic Pluralism

Although the nineteenth and early twentieth centuries were replete with simultaneous racial, religious, and ethnic prejudices, they also reflected a determination to end them, expand individual rights, foster toleration of human differences, and allow continued immigration, though in restricted numbers. Separation of church and state remained firm, and the idea of the country as a Protestant nation was rejected. Though not fought to end racism, the Civil War facilitated its slow but progressive erosion. Occupied foreign lands in the Atlantic and Pacific were not to be free of American laws, however cruel. Whatever the issue of civil or human rights, its advocates grew in numbers and political power.

Both the hope and actuality of a better life continued to attract the world's oppressed or discontented, whether religiously, politically, or economically. Just as there were Americans opposing immigration and diversity of people, so were there those welcoming both. Theirs was a benign vision of America as a refuge, asylum, melting pot, haven, and "federation of cultures," where old and new residents would blend and possibly amalgamate (except for Blacks and Asians), making the country a still better one. Even the frontier was seen by Frederick Jackson Turner as a "crucible," in which "immigrants were Americanized, liberated, and fused into a mixed race."[1]

With the approach of the twentieth century, political, social, and economic reformers gained positions on many levels of government. Political corruption, big-business influence on government, and abuse of workers, farmers, women, children, and consumers were reduced, if not ended. To curtail federal patronage in employment, the Pendleton Act of 1883 insisted on individual merit as a criterion for hiring, based on open, fair, impartial, and competitive examinations. A new generation of Protestant theologians and clergymen, particularly in the North, began applying the Bible to social reality, stressing "the deliverance of human society from disease, poverty, crime, and misery; the development and perfection of the institutions of men's associated life; and the construction of a social order that is the city of God on earth."[2]

179

Adding force to such goals was an expanding corps of educators, intellectuals, and professional social workers, who denounced religious, ethnic, and racial prejudice. They argued that America had always absorbed immigrants without harming its ideals and institutions, that exclusivity and homogeneity were greater dangers than diversity, that the deplorable living conditions of many immigrants had preceded their arrival, that society had an obligation to help immigrants become good citizens, and that there was no conflict between holding on to one's ancestral ties and being a good American.

Louis Dembitz Brandeis, of Supreme Court fame, believed "a man is a better citizen of the United States for being also a loyal citizen of his state, and of his city; for being loyal to his family and to his profession or trade; for being loyal to his college or his lodge. Every Irish American who contributed toward advancing home rule was a better man and a better American for the sacrifice he made. Every American Jew who aids in advancing the Jewish settlement in Palestine, though he feels that neither he nor his descendants will ever live there, will likewise be a better man and a better American for doing so."[3]

Most foreign-born Americans felt likewise, particularly those with families still living abroad. After all, they had willingly come to America and knew they could freely leave. They paid taxes, obeyed laws, took pride in their children's acculturation, and were no less ready than native-born citizens to defend America in war or peace. As a Ukrainian group said in 1930, "The United States is the only country in the world where when one becomes a citizen one does not betray his own nation . . . and that is because the American nation is composed of many nations which have joined together to form a common state."[4]

Philosophically and intellectually, too, cultural pluralism and the relativity of cultures and religions gained acceptance, together with deeper awareness of the economic, social, and psychological difficulties confronting immigrants. Newly emerging religious, racial, and ethnic leaders and organizations called for an America free of bigotry, such as the Anti-Defamation League, the American Jewish Committee, the Urban League, the National Association for the Advancement of Colored People, and the National Conference of Christians and Jews.

The Roosevelt Years and Intergroup Relations

With the election of Franklin Delano Roosevelt, domestic economic reform, cultural pluralism, and ethnic power assumed new heights, while cynicism about European politics, the League of Nations, and debt defaults by World War I allies intensified calls for avoiding foreign entanglements. A 1933 poll of some 20,000 students in sixty-five colleges revealed that 72 percent opposed serving in the military even during wartime and almost 50 percent would refuse to bear arms even if America were invaded.[5] Nevertheless, Roosevelt's domestic program won broad ethnic and racial support, even from those who had previously voted Republican, such as Blacks, Norwegians, and Swedes. To be elected, political aspirants could no longer view the foreign-born as hyphenated Americans stubbornly resisting the nation's melting pot, but rather as essential ingredients whose votes were to be nurtured. With the passage of the Twenty-first Amendment in 1933, Prohibition (which had infuriated many ethnic groups) was repealed and Protestant domination of national morality suffered another setback.

Political coalitions and "balanced tickets" led to more and more minorities being elected or appointed to government positions. For example, in the early 1930s, in New York City and San Francisco, Fiorello La Guardia and Angelo Rossi, respectively, became the first Italian American mayors of major cities; in Buffalo, Joseph Mruc was elected the first Polish American mayor; and in Chicago, Anton Cermak became the first Bohemian American mayor.

In cities with heavy ethnic concentrations, minorities demanded a greater share of political power and public positions. In New York City, in the 1930s, the *Brooklyn Jewish Center Review* sadly noted that only 11 percent of the borough's public officials were Jews, though they were 47 percent of the population. In Staten Island, an Italian American political leader complained that "the Congressman, the Senator and one of two Assemblymen were Irish. The other Assemblyman and the City Councilman were of German extraction. All the judges were Irish. No judge was of Italian descent. No Italian-American was considered for public office, although the Italian-Americans constituted about 25 percent of the Staten Island population."[6]

As a result of such pressures, ethnic groups began succeeding the Irish, just as the latter had native Protestants in the late nineteenth century, prompting an officer of the Federation of Irish Societies to complain of kinsmen "being pushed aside to make room for other more aggressive and better organized races." Before La Guardia, cabinet appointments of Irish by Mayors James J. Walker and John P. O'Brien were 25 and 41 percent, respectively; with La Guardia, Irish appointments declined to 5 percent, while those of Jews and Italians doubled. Nationally, though Presidents Harding, Coolidge, and Hoover appointed only 8 Catholics as federal judges out of 207, during the administrations of Presidents Roosevelt and Truman one-fourth of judicial appointments were Catholic, and the first Black and Polish American appointments were made as well.[7]

As war clouds spread over Europe, American intergroup and interfaith relations worsened. Although many Americans had admired Mussolini's domestic policies, Italy's invasion of Ethiopia started a change of mind. In New York and Chicago, Blacks began boycotting Italian American merchants. In Harlem, the United Aid for Ethiopia coordinated anti-Mussolini protests and became the area's official fund-raising and publicity agency for the Ethiopian government in exile. The NAACP's official publication *Crisis* called the war "a sad spectacle of 'white' civilization," and *Opportunity,* published by the National Urban League, suggested that English and French efforts to prevent the war were motivated by concerns for worldwide White supremacy and their own imperialistic colonies.

Many Black newspapers praised Japan, saying it had a natural interest in Asia and that America should not get involved. A poll of Harlem residents in 1942 asked, if America lost the war, would they be treated better, worse, or the same under German or Japanese rule. While 1 percent felt that under German rule they would be treated better, 22 percent the same, and 63 percent worse, under Japanese rule 18 percent felt they would be treated better, 31 percent the same, and only 28 percent worse.[8]

On the other hand, many Italian Americans gloried in Mussolini's Ethiopian victories. When a group of young Italian Fascists arrived on a propaganda cruise in New York City, local Italian Americans enthusiastically feted and showered them with gifts. As one Italian American explained the exuberant reaction, Mussolini "enabled four million Italians in America to hold up their heads. . . . If you had been branded undesirable by a quota law, you would understand how much that means." Still, only a minority of Italians supported fascism and only a few hundred heeded Mussolini's call for volunteers to return and fight in the war.[9]

The Spanish Civil War also provoked strong intergroup differences. Generally, Catholics supported Franco. Lay organizations like the National Council of Catholic Men and the National Council of Catholic Women held rallies and letter-writing campaigns. The Catholic press reported stories of nuns raped, clergy shot, churches burned, and communism's evils in Mexico and the Soviet Union. To them, the Spanish Civil War was twixt the forces of good and evil, God and anti-God, atheists and Christians, and democracy and communism. To many American Protestants and liberals, however, American Catholics were trying to influence the government along fascist lines.[10]

Charges of being pro-Communist greatly disturbed American Basques, who, though devoutly Catholic, opposed Franco and his suppression of Basque independence. While sending overseas relief aid to their kinsmen, they denounced Russia for fomenting the Spanish Civil War, which "kept our people in a blood bath for three long years."[11]

Still remembering the World War I animosity against them, German Americans hesitated to support Hitler, though some formed outright Nazi organizations. Most German Americans, in keeping with public opinion, advocated nonintervention. In response to Germany's increasing anti-Semitism, American Jews held protest demonstrations and boycotted German products, which often ignited Jewish and German street fights. As Mussolini sided with Hitler and adopted some of his anti-Semitic policies, splits intensified between anti- and pro-Mussolini Italian Americans and between the latter and Jews. Repugnant as Mussolini had become, many Italian Americans resented Roosevelt's characterization of Italy's attacking France as "the hand that held the dagger has struck it into the back of its neighbor." Irish Catholic extremists hated England more than Germany, and also engaged in street fights with Jews, at times joining Italian American Black Shirts and Nazi Bundists in denouncing Roosevelt, England, Communists, and Jews.

Even after the Nazis attacked Sweden and Denmark, most Scandinavian Americans opposed intervention, though wishing their homeland liberated. For example, Swedish Americans were conflicted by a desire for neutrality, opposition to Russian communism, traditional suspicion of France and England, feelings of religious kinship with German Lutheranism, and fears that anti-Swedish prejudice might be resurrected. Before and after Russia invaded Finland in 1939, American Finns—like kinsmen at home—were politically divided between siding with Russia or Germany; and when Finland allied herself with Germany against Russia and England, they were distressed by Finland's drop in public opinion support and America's closing all Finnish consulates.[12]

Within ethnic groups sharp differences grew over who should govern their ancestral lands. Albanian Americans had a "Free Albania" group opposing a monarchy and a Pan-Albanian Federation of America favoring one. Armenian Americans could join a liberal, anti-Soviet, procommunist or nonpolitical organization. Austrian Americans had socialist, nationalist, and communist organizations. Carpathian Russians had communist and anticommunist ones. Czech Americans had organizations supporting or opposing the Czech government in exile. German Americans had twenty organizations, ranging from anti-Nazi to pro-Nazi, the most extreme being the German-American Bund, with a self-proclaimed membership of 20,000, almost half of which lived in greater New York City and most of its leaders being post–World War I immigrants. Such differences did not preclude many ethnic Americans from initiating war relief programs. In 1939, some 151 groups raised funds for Poland; 54, for France; 23, for England; 9, for Germany; 4, for Palestine; and 1 each, for India, Canada, Bohemia-Moravia, Australia, and New Zealand.[13]

Most Americans wanted no part of Europe's problems or wars, even though sensing they would eventually have to fight Germany. A June 1940 Gallup poll revealed that though 65 percent believed that if England and France fell, America would soon be attacked and that though another 75 percent believed America was not sufficiently helping the Allies, only some 7 percent favored a declaration of war against Germany.[14]

In keeping with such ambivalence, Congress overwhelmingly passed a series of Neutrality Acts, as well as the first peacetime draft in 1940. The following year, it extended the draft by a single vote—203 to 202—with Democrats supporting it by almost three to one and Republicans opposing it by about six to one. As late as March 1941, Americans were opposing involvement by a ratio of eight to one.

From a religious perspective, many Irish Catholics were isolationist. As during the Spanish Civil War, they feared communism more than fascism, though disliking both. "The youth of America must never be called upon to fight, suffer and die for the triumph of Red Democracy and world Atheism," declared the national chairman of the Catholic Students Peace Federation in 1939. When Germany attacked Russia, a poll of Catholic clergy showed that 90 percent opposed aid to the Soviet Union and close to 92 percent opposed American involvement in any overseas war, causing one Catholic writer to warn that should America actually enter the war, Catholics would be suspected of disloyalty.[15]

Prewar Protestant reactions were more varied. Pacifism was strong, and many denominational leaders grappled with the dilemma of wanting to stay out of the war and yet not wanting totalitarianism to win. "Victory will spell fascism for such a victor," wrote the editor of the *Christian Century*. "And defeat will spell either communism or fascism; if indeed it does not spell slavery or anarchy." A commission of the Methodist church, in 1939, declared that war "cannot achieve any good end but can only accentuate every evil it aims to correct." Almost alone among Christian thinkers, Reinhold Niebuhr denounced Germany, its anti-Semitism, and American church indifference. To him, pacifism was no realistic response to Nazi brutality, and he rejected Catholic thinking that "fascism does not intend to destroy the Church while Communism does."[16]

Most church groups, particularly those with English origins, supported aid to England and the need for an Allied victory. In voting for total aid to England, speedy rearmament, and an arms embargo for Japan, southern Baptists formally declared their "belief that some things are worth dying for . . . and worth defending to the death." Americans of Anglo-Saxon descent, as well as "internationalists" who viewed Nazism and Fascism as threats to American democracy, particularly those living in the Northeast and Southeast, also favored helping the British. Concerned with their coreligionists abroad, American Jews, too, supported increased aid to England and France.[17]

Against such a setting, America became the target of intensive propaganda efforts by foreign and domestic groups. Germany and Italy not only directed appeals to their expatriates but also to the Black community, though in vain, for many remembered what Italy had done to Ethiopia. Only a few cultists believed those countries would end their imperialism and racism. Hundreds of American hate, Fascist, and Nazi organizations cloaked their messages in patriotism and Christianity, such as the Ku Klux Klan, the Knights of the White Camellia, the Crusader White Shirts, the Silver Shirts of America, the Russian National Fascist Revolutionary party, the Italian American Black Shirts, Latin American Falangists and Sinarquists, the Japanese American Chamber of Commerce, the Ukrainian United Hetmans Organization, and so forth. Between 1933 and 1940, there were some 121 anti-Semitic organizations.[18]

Active in such groups were many people whose religious and ethnic background were anathema in prior times. Catholic Father Charles Coughlin, the famed "radio priest" and mentor of the Christian Front, saw treason in government and admired Mussolini. Fritz Kuhn, leader of the German-American Bund, was an immigrant, who eagerly lashed out at "all Atheistic teachings and . . . all racial intermixture between Asiatics, Africans, or non-Aryans; all Subversive Internationalism."[19]

Fears of such groups led Congress in 1938 to establish the Special Committee to Investigate un-American Activities, headed by Representative Martin Dies. Though accused of being more interested in exposing communism in New Deal agencies than fascism in society, it did report that the German-American Bund's programs and activities were "similar to Nazi organizations in Germany and other countries" and that some Ukrainian American organizations were "nothing in the world but agencies of foreign powers." Italian American anti-Fascists also testified that there were some 10,000 Black Shirts in the country, with some 100,000 sympathizers. In 1940, Congress passed a peacetime sedition law—the Alien Registration Act—which led to the registration and fingerprinting of over 5 million aliens, loyalty tests and oaths for government employees, and state investigations of subversives. Soon afterward, the Voorhis Act required all organizations subject to foreign control or believing in the violent overthrow of government to register. "We have a distinct spy menace," said FBI chief J. Edgar Hoover. "Hundreds upon hundreds of foreign agents are busily engaged upon a program of peering, peeking, eavesdropping, propaganda, subversiveness, and actual sabotage."[20]

World War II represented the greatest test ever of America's intergroup unity because of the unprecedented number and variety of people, many of whose familial and cultural, if not political, homeland attachments conflicted with each other and with American national interests. Would they replay Old Country war passions and fight each other—and would they refuse to support America in its fight against their homeland? In 1940, 8.5 percent of the population were foreign-born Whites, and more than 25 percent were first- or second-generation. In large cities, the percentages were higher. *Fortune* magazine warned of "dynamite on our shores." After the Japanese attacked Pearl Harbor, however, the entire Congress supported Roosevelt's call for a declaration of war, with only one dissent—again by Congresswoman Jeanette Rankin, who had returned to office the prior year. "As a woman I can't go to war, and I refuse to send anyone else," she explained.[21]

Once America entered the war, ethnic, religious, and racial groups rallied in support, even those whose ancestral homelands were Axis members, such as Germans, Italians, Austrians, Romanians, Bulgarians, Finns, Hungarians, and Japanese. Pro-Hitler and pro-Mussolini organizations and newspapers overwhelmingly switched positions or disbanded. The Japanese United Citizens Federation wrote Roosevelt: "We reaffirm our absolute allegiance to the United States of America, pledge all-out energy to defeat Japan and the Axis, place complete faith and confidence in your leadership as commander-in-chief of our armed forces, appeal to you to call upon us that we may do our part for our country." American Asians whose countries were attacked, threatened, or occupied by the Japanese also supported the war. Though declared enemy aliens, Korean immigrants in Hawaii and California supported America, and many took to wearing native Korean clothes and carrying badges, "I am Korean." Some Filipinos and Chinese did likewise. Discrimination and immigration restrictions did not stop Filipino support or the forming of two regiments. Defying the physical attacks on their youthful "Zoot Suiters" in Los Angeles (which German and Japanese propagandists exploited), large numbers of Mexican Americans served in the armed forces, earning seventeen Congressional Medals of Honor. Also, despite the prevailing anti-Semitism, some 550,000 Jewish men and women entered the military, with over 80 percent in the army or air force.[22]

The most discriminated against were Blacks, who had to confront racism in most private enterprises and war plants, near which many Blacks moved to work. For example, while the total populations of the ten largest war production centers increased by 19 percent from 1940 to 1944, the Black population increased by 49 percent, leading to further competition and tension between White and Black workers. The National Labor Relations Act of 1935, which had been hailed as labor's "Bill of Rights," continued to do little for Blacks, who had criticized its framers for not including a nondiscrimination clause. Only after A. Philip Randolph, president of the Brotherhood of Sleeping Car Porters, threatened a march on Washington in 1941 did Roosevelt issue Executive Order 8802 forbidding employment discrimination in "defense industries or Government because of race, creed, color, or national origin. . . ."[23] Racism, however, did not stop some million Blacks serving in segregated ranks, about half of them overseas. For the first time, however, Blacks were admitted to the air corps, marines, and naval ranks above messmen. Just as Mexico had encouraged American Catholic soldiers to desert during the Mexican American War, so did Germany with the Black soldiers of the 92nd Division in Europe, asking them:

> What is Democracy? Personal freedom, all citizens enjoying the same rights socially and before the law. Do you enjoy the same rights as the white people do in America, the land of Freedom and Democracy, or are you rather not treated there as second-class citizens? Can you go into a restaurant where white people dine? Can you get a seat in the theater where white people sit?[24]

Contrary to German propaganda hopes of Indians' rebelling rather than bearing "arms for their exploiters," Indians overwhelmingly rushed to the colors. The Six Nations of the Iroquois League declared that "it is the unanimous sentiment among the Indian people that the atrocities of the Axis nations are violently repulsive to all sense of righteousness of our people." Nevertheless, many Florida Seminoles refused to register for the draft, remembering the brutal wars against them in the early nineteenth century and claiming they were still an independent nation, not American citizens. Overall, according to the commissioner of the Bureau of Indian Affairs, Indians constituted "a larger proportion than any other element of our population" in the armed forces.[25]

Respectable isolationists and nativists (like Charles Lindbergh) and disreputable ones (like Father Coughlin), as well as dozens of fascist and nazi leaders in America, faded from prominence. Even the Communist Party (after Germany invaded the Soviet Union) switched sloganizing from "The Yanks Are *Not* Coming" to "Open Up The Second Front Now." To Americans generally, the enemy had become Nazi Germans instead of international bankers, Jews, Communists, and secret Washington cabals.[26]

Though the war did not ignite the hysteria of World War I, Italian Americans and German Americans met with job discrimination, particularly in war-related occupations. Anti-Chinese discrimination still lingered in California, where though the aircraft industry needed skilled and unskilled workers, university-educated Chinese were not hired. Japanese Americans suffered most, with more than 100,000 (two-thirds of whom were born in America) placed in detention camps, including some 1,400 who had married non-Japanese spouses, such as Blacks, Filipinos, and Caucasians. A number of South American countries, particularly Peru, also deported some 2,200 Japanese for internment in America at separate facilities controlled by the Immigration and Naturalization Service. In defending such actions, General John Dewitt said, "the Japanese race is an enemy race and while many second and third generation Japanese born on United States soil, possessed of United States citizenship, have become 'Americanized,' the racial strains are undiluted. . . . There were no grounds for assuming that Japanese-Americans will not turn against the United States."[27]

Nevertheless, Japanese Americans from Hawaii and the mainland readily served in the military in both Europe and the Pacific. "Why can't all Americans see that blood isn't as thick as the principles of democracy," said one volunteer. "Every single one of us, Americans of Japanese ancestry in the 442nd Infantry Regiment, would rather fight the 'Japs' than the Germans to prove our loyalty."[28]

In Alaska, where substantial anti-Eskimo prejudice existed, close to 1,000 Aleuts were summarily relocated from their island homes in the Bering Sea and sent to detention camps without adequate shelter, medical support, or clothing, resulting in epidemics and scores of deaths. Military censorship prevented the outside world from knowing what was happening and that no evidence existed to indicate that Aleuts were a security risk.[29]

In addition, some 200 Italian and 5,000 German aliens, as well as several hundred Italian and German seamen, were interned. Nearly 600,000 foreign-born and unnaturalized Italians were declared enemy aliens and put under surveillance. Ten months later, however, the United States attorney general said the need for internment was true of "only 228 or fewer than one-twentieth of 1 percent" and that all others would be "free to travel and to go about their lives as any other person." Henceforward, they were reclassified as "aliens of enemy nationality." Likewise, no drastic actions were taken against German Americans, whom Roosevelt thought possibly more dangerous, but whose political support he valued. In 1944, he praised German Americans as "loyal, freedom-loving, and peace-loving citizens."[30]

As in World War I, intolerance of conscientious objectors surfaced, and some 5,000 were imprisoned, mostly Jehovah's Witnesses, who futilely claimed exemption as ministers. Some 200 Catholics declared themselves conscientious objectors, largely members of Dorothy Day's Catholic Worker movement. In New York City and Chicago, dozens of Blacks were arrested and charged with violating the draft and encouraging others to do likewise. Though the Roosevelt administration had promised to increase the percentage of Blacks in the army and among commissioned officers, the War Department's policy remained "not to intermingle colored and white enlisted personnel in the same regimental organizations." Gays were not wanted in the military, and some 9,000 who had managed to enter were discharged.[31]

It should be stressed that with few exceptions, during the greatest challenge to America's security and unity, which involved close to 12 million citizens in the armed forces, our native- and foreign-born remained loyal.

World War II and Immigration

Before and during World War II, anti-immigration sentiments remained strong, with most National Origins Act quotas unfilled, though many Americans were sympathetic to the plight of Europeans. To be sure, thousands of immigrants were admitted, but in numbers far less than could and should have been.

Right after the infamous Kristallnacht in November 1938, when Nazis brutally attacked Jews and their synagogues and buildings, 77 percent of Gallup poll respondents opposed increased Jewish immigration, though a month later 94 percent disapproved of Germany's anti-Jewish activities. Similarly, addressing the debate over foreign affairs, a 1939 poll asked, "If you were a member of Congress, would you vote yes or no on a bill to open the doors of the U.S. to a larger number of European refugees than now are admitted under our immigration quotas?" Eighty-three percent answered in total opposition.[32]

American callousness toward Jewish refugees in particular peaked in May 1939 when the *SS St. Louis,* sailing from Nazi Germany with 936 passengers, most of them Jews, was denied admission to Cuba and then to America, only to return to Europe and death for many of its passengers. "The Cruise of the *St. Louis,*" editorialized the *New York Times,* "cries to high heaven of man's inhumanity to man."[33] At the same time, the Congress refused to pass the Wagner-Rogers Bill, which would have allowed in a two-year period 20,000 German Jewish refugee children to enter the United States—an action in keeping with two-thirds of the polled population.

Also, proposals to resettle nonquota European immigrants in Alaska were rejected, with invidious distinctions made between German Jews, who were the wrong kind of people, and Finns, Norwegians, and Balts, who were praised for being Christian, sturdy, and adaptable. To oppose immigration, declared Senator Lewis C. Schwellenbach, was "perhaps the best vote-getting argument in present-day politics. The politician can beat his breast and proclaim his loyalty to America. He can tell the unemployed man that he is out of work because some alien has a job."[34]

Even after America entered the war, the administration's attitudes toward Jewish refugees remained hostile. In early 1944, Rudolph E. Paul, general counsel of the Treasury Department, wrote to his superior, Henry M. Morganthau Jr., charging governmental acquiescence in the murder of European Jews, in which some State Department officials were "guilty not only of gross procrastination and wilful failure to act, but even of wilful attempts to prevent action from being taken to rescue Jews from Hitler."[35] In vain, Jewish organizations urged Roosevelt and the Congress to admit more refugees, pressure England to open Palestine for additional immigrants, and initiate relief and rescue actions on behalf of besieged Jewry.

Governmental lack of response was not inconsistent with public opinion polls, which generally opposed immigration and specifically believed that Jews were more of a threat to the nation than Blacks, Catholics, Germans, and Japanese, except for 1942 when the latter two groups were rated more so. By April 1945, pollster Elmo Roper warned that "anti-Semitism has spread all over the nation and is particularly virulent in urban centers."[36]

In Canada, between 1933 and 1945, only 5,000 Jewish refugees were admitted, largely because of anti-Semitic governmental officials, fear of fomenting an "anti-Semitic problem," and a desire to appease Quebec's widespread anti-Semitism. In all, from 1940 to 1945, less than 100,000 were admitted to America, which was much less relative to our population than allowed to enter Great Britain, France, or the Netherlands. Even then, groups like the American Legion urged continued immigration restrictions and when the war ended a complete ban until all veterans had a chance for employment and until "all foreign labor battalions, refugees, war prisoners and those given temporary sanctuary had returned to the lands of their origin."[37]

And yet, for mixed reasons of humanitarianism, economic necessity, international credibility, domestic morale, and goodwill to our wartime allies, some immigration reforms took place. The Nationality Act of 1940 liberalized naturalization for all descendants of people indigenous to the Western Hemisphere, such as Aleuts and Eskimos, and within a few years, for Chinese, Filipinos, and East Indians. As Dr. Taranknath Das told a congressional committee, "If this war is for world unity and world freedom, then the United States cannot practice double standards of international morality—one for whites and the other for Asiatics."[38]

Wartime shortages of farm workers led to an agreement with Mexico in 1942 to allow thousands of *braceros* to enter for short-term periods. Also admitted for temporary work were 21,000 Jamaicans and 6,000 Bahamians.[39] At the insistence of the sheep and wool industry, a series of "Sheepherder Laws" and special exemptions to Spain's quota were enacted, granting permanent residency to Basques and allowing greater numbers to immigrate to the West's sheep ranges. To counter Japanese propaganda about American racism, the 1882 Chinese Exclusion Act was repealed in 1943, allowing instead a token 105 Chinese to enter per year, as well as allowing permanent-resident aliens to become naturalized citizens. The 1945 War Brides Act and an amendment to it two years later led to an increase in women immigrants, whose numbers for the first time began exceeding that of men. Though Filipino nationals were at first barred from volunteering for military service, the irony of America fighting for Philippine liberation while denying their nationals American citizenship moved the Congress to allow citizenship to those joining the armed forces; however, when as many as 250,000 in the Philippines applied, the offer of citizenship for service was revoked.

A few months after the war ended in 1945, public opinion still strongly opposed admitting more immigrants—32 percent favoring present levels, 37 percent favoring a decrease, 5 percent favoring an increase, and the remainder undecided. Congress nevertheless widened the door somewhat for foreign war brides of American personnel, which included some 6,000 to 7,000 from China and Japan and, in 1951, for some 10,000 Canadian woodsmen, who were needed in Maine, Vermont, New Hampshire, and New York.[40]

More far reaching was the passage of several acts to relieve the plight of millions of homeless Europeans, concentration camp victims, escapees from communist-controlled nations, anti-Nazi Germans, nationals of countries overrun by Germany, and former slave laborers in Germany who refused to return to their lands taken over by communists. Humanitarianism was now joined by anti-Soviet feelings and the need to prove that we would accept displaced and distressed people just as we were urging other countries to do. Between 1945 and 1950, nearly 350,000 such people were admitted.

Their admission differed from earlier and much larger immigrant movements in several ways: it consisted of unparalleled numbers of people in extreme distress, it was highly organized by government and private organizations guaranteeing financial support, and it was predominantly middle class and supported by political parties, who, in addition to their humanitarian motivations, sought the favor of domestic ethnic groups, which also were calling for more immigration.

Nevertheless, anti-Semitism and invidious ethnic distinctions continued to be made. The Displaced Persons Act of 1948, which allowed 220,000 people entry over a two-year period as long as they resided in Germany by 22 December 1945, adversely affected Jewish and ethnic Catholic "DPs" who had fled west after that time. President Truman reluctantly signed the bill, and in an accompanying message said it reflected "a pattern of discrimination and intolerance wholly inconsistent with the American sense of justice." Meanwhile, rising concern about the Soviet Union, China, and Korea led Congress to pass legislation fostering defections among anti-Soviet residents behind the Iron Curtain and to conduct covert intelligence operations in China and Korea.[41]

Elsewhere, Pacific Islanders began entering, particularly from Hawaii and the West Coast. In 1950, Congress conferred citizenship on Guam's native residents, enabling them unrestricted immigration. As United States nationals, Samoans moved to Hawaii and from there to the mainland. Tongan Islanders started arriving in the 1950s, with the help of the Mormon church. Other Pacific Island immigrants included Tahitians and Fijians.[42]

The 1950 Displaced Persons Act eliminated those provisions that worked against Jews and Catholics and established a new two-year ceiling of 415,000. Still excluded from consideration were Near and Far East wartime refugees, though Senator James Eastland tried to stop the act's passage by speciously asking why special consideration should not be given them. "No one can deny the compelling humanitarian reasons which will be advanced to obtain special consideration for millions of unfortunate displaced victims of the war in China, or approximately 10 million Pakistanian persons displaced in the partition of India, or approximately 1 million Palestinian displaced persons in the Palestine war."[43]

However grudgingly and discriminatorily, immigration policies and politics had moved from almost total exclusion and severe restrictions to more openness.

Expansion of Civil Rights and Civil Liberties

In contrast to pre–World War II decades, the need to improve domestic intergroup relations was supported by the public generally and returning veterans in particular. What GIs most wanted, wrote *Yank*'s army editor, was "wiping out racial and religious discrimination."[44] At the same time, pressures for reform came from "old" and "new" Black leaders, executive orders, court cases, demonstrations, sit-ins, boycotts, and so forth. No longer did Blacks accede passively to being confined to a back seat in a bus, denied a place at a lunch counter, barred from a park, refused a hotel room, excluded from a job, prevented from voting, or called a "boy." They wanted their constitutional rights and they wanted—indeed, demanded—them *now*. As they gained rights long denied them, other groups—ethnic, religious, and sexual—insisted upon a fuller achievement of their rights.

"The protection of civil rights is a national problem which affects everyone," said the president's Committee on Civil Rights in 1947. "We need to guarantee the same rights to every person regardless of who he is, where he lives, or what his racial, religious, or national origins are." In 1948, President Truman issued an executive order abolishing segregation in the armed forces, thereby ending the confinement of Blacks to the labor and supply departments. In the same year, the Supreme Court outlawed restrictive covenants that denied "any person other than of the Caucasian race," "Negro descent," "African, Chinese or Japanese descent," or of the "Negro and African races," the right to rent or purchase homes or property. Americans were also becoming increasingly aware of foreign criticism and the need to improve their image, especially in Asia and Africa.[45]

For nativists and bigots, the post–World War II period became a psychological, social, and political nightmare as the racially excluded were included and as more immigrants entered the country. Jefferson's "wall of separation between Church and State" rose higher when the Supreme Court in 1947 agreed that the First Amendment's "establishment of religion" clause meant at least: "neither a state nor the Federal Government can set up a church. Neither can pass laws which aid one religion, aid all religions, or prefer one religion over another."[46]

Slowly, but decidedly, interreligious tolerance and cooperation kept replacing religious triumphalism and exclusiveness, inspired mainly by liberal Protestants, Jews, and Pope John XXIII, all of whom viewed pluralism not as a menace to their respective faiths but as a societal good. Ecumenism was sought among Christian groups, and interfaith understanding and cooperation between all American religious groups. Religious and political leaders increasingly spoke of our country's *Judeo-Christian* rather than solely *Christian* traditions and values. Being religious was deemed a private matter, to be respected and tolerated, but not imposed on others, particularly by government. No longer was patriotism automatically equated with Protestantism, at least not by major church and civic leaders. "Our government," said President Eisenhower in 1954, "makes no sense unless it is founded on a deeply felt religious faith—and I don't care what it is."[47] Seven years later, the Supreme Court, in *Torcaso* v. *Watkins,* unanimously ended a Maryland constitutional provision requiring a belief in God's existence as a prerequisite for holding public office.

More dramatic were the changes in race relations. In *Brown* v. *Board of Education,* the Supreme Court in 1954 declared the 1896 doctrine of "separate but equal" unconstitutional and separate educational facilities "inherently un-equal," generating feelings of inferiority among Black children. In arguing for desegregated schools, civil rights advocates claimed that race, ancestry, and color should not serve as a basis for legislative action. Government had to be color-blind. As a result, desegregated and then integrated schools became the order—and disorder—of the day, as various states, communities, and citizen groups differed over the compulsory busing of schoolchildren.

At the same time, civil rights organizations began changing their tactics and goals, with calls made for stressing group rights rather than individual rights; self-interest politics rather than coalitional politics; color-conscious justice rather than blindfolded justice; and preferential treatment rather than equal opportunity. The collapse of colonialism in Africa also spurred a new sense of pride, power, and urgency among American Blacks.

Cold War and McCarthyism

The 1950s and 1960s were not free of intergroup prejudice, superpatriotism, spy trials, and paranoia about domestic and foreign relations. In late 1949, a Gallup poll reported that 68 percent of the population believed the Communist Party should be outlawed, and some years later, 57 percent of the population believed we were "actually in World War III." In a burst of national piety, the words *under God* were added in 1954 to the Pledge of Allegiance, and the following year *In God We Trust* on all new currency. The Cold War and Korean War intensified concerns about national security, communists in government, "godless" Soviet Union, "Red" China, and communists entering the country in the guise of immigrants.

The pro-Soviet and pro-Chinese feelings of World War II years soured over Soviet policies in Europe and Chinese actions in the Korean War. American Chinese feared that what had been done to American Japanese during World War II would be done to them. They were forbidden to send remittances to families back in China, and their businesses were raided in search of illegal immigrants. Wild stories circulated of an international Mafia, with connections to the Soviet Union, having infiltrated the White House. Civil rights protests were seen as part of an international communist conspiracy to destabilize the country. Political extremists and professional racists exploited anticommunist passions and called for ending the United Nations and deporting "Zionists" and Blacks. Homophobia became part of the hysteria, with the chairman of the Republican National Committee warning that "perhaps as dangerous as the actual communists are the sexual perverts who have infiltrated our Government." Government agencies escalated the firing of gays, not only because of their alleged "sexual perversity," but also their being "easy prey" to blackmailers and foreign agents. In fact, rumors had it that Hitler had compiled a worldwide list of homosexuals who could be forced to engage in espionage and sabotage.[48]

Senator Joseph McCarthy led a call to expose communists in high office and charged the Democratic Party with "twenty years of treason." Unlike in the 1920s, the menace was not foreigners, but prestigious, native-born public and governmental figures who were deemed either communists, communist sympathizers, or communist dupes. Ironically, some of the charges were made by members of groups that were once similarly accused.

Senator McCarthy was a Catholic and two of his chief aides (Roy Cohn and David Shine) were Jewish. "It is not the less fortunate," said McCarthy, "or members of minority groups who have been selling this nation out, but rather those who have had all the benefits the wealthiest nation on earth has had to offer—the finest homes, the finest college education, and the finest jobs in the government that we can give." Also, Robert Welch, the founder of the John Birch Society, acknowledged the existence of millions of devout Catholics and faithful Jews, but singled out President Eisenhower and many of his key appointees as being Kremlin agents. Religious leaders, too, joined the anticommunist rage, with the Reverend Billy Graham praising the exposure of "the pinks, the lavenders, and the reds," and New York City's Francis Cardinal Spellman decrying "the Communist flooding of our own land."[49]

In the early 1950s, patriotic triumphalism and determination to combat the world communist movement led Congress to pass the Internal Security Act (over President Truman's veto), and a Subversive Activities Control Board was established. All communists and communist-front organizations had to register with the Justice Department. Educational institutions, business and industry, unions, and Hollywood became foci of governmental and private group accusations and investigations. Almost immediately, any immigrant who was a communist or suspected of such was denied admission, so that between September 1950 and March 1951 more than 100,000 refugees were adversely affected.[50]

Again over Truman's veto, the McCarran-Walter Act, in 1952, not only barred communists from entering but facilitated the deportation of those already here. Immigrants and visitors could be barred for more than thirty reasons, ranging from being former or actual members of anarchist, communist, or totalitarian organizations to those whose activities here would be "prejudicial to the public interest," as happened to Pablo Picasso and the dean of Canterbury, the Reverend Hewlett Johnson. Conversely, in the name of national security and combating communism, passports were denied Americans wanting to travel to Russia or China.

The new law restated the National Origins Act and set a limit of 154,000 immigrants per year, with various countries given a quota based on the 1920 census. Though favoring Europeans, an "Asia-Pacific Triangle" was established, granting countries therein a small annual quota not to exceed 2,000 for all combined. Although outright exclusion of Asian immigrants was repealed, those half-Asian, no matter where they were born, were credited to the small quota given Asian countries.

Truman denounced the act as repressive and inhumane and, like the 1924 legislation, deliberately and intentionally discriminatory, implying that "Americans with English or Irish names were better people and better citizens than Americans with Italian or Greek or Polish names." As for the clause on half-Asians, he said, "The countries of Asia are told in one breath that they shall have quotas for their nationals, and in the next that the nationals of the other countries, if their ancestry is as much as 50 percent Asian, shall be charged to these quotas. It is only with respect to persons of oriental ancestry that this invidious discrimination applies." For propaganda purposes in Asian countries, the Soviet Union also criticized the act, saying it was "very similar to the Nazi theory of racial superiority" and another example of "the contempt of the American ruling circles . . . which spread racial prejudice among the people of the United States against the Asian people."[51]

In or out of government, those opposing the act were called "communists" or "pinks and sincere but misguided and uninformed liberals who are captivated by the emotional Communist slogan." America was the last hope of Western civilization, declared Senator McCarran, "and if this oasis of the world shall be overrun, perverted, contaminated, or destroyed, then the last flickering light of humanity will be extinguished."[52] To immigration restrictionists, it mattered not that desirable immigrants were excluded and that recently naturalized citizens could be deprived of citizenship and deported for actions naturalized citizens could commit with impunity. On the positive side, provision was made for the attorney general to grant parole status in special cases, which in succeeding years was liberally defined.

Pressures for immigration reform nevertheless continued, and Truman established a special commission on immigration and naturalization, which called for a total revision of immigration legislation. With the presidency of Eisenhower, immigration policy became markedly influenced by foreign relations. In 1953, Congress passed the Refugee Relief Act, which had a three-year term. Some 200,000 nonquota immigrants, largely German, Italian, and Greek anticommunist emigrés or victims, were allowed to enter, including several thousand orphans and Dutch nationals expelled from Indonesia. The definition of *refugee* now included "any person in a country or area which is neither Communist nor Communist dominated, who because of persecution, fear of persecution, natural calamity, or military operations is out of his usual place of abode and unable to return thereto, who has not been firmly resettled, and who is in urgent need of assistance for the essentials of life."[53]

Soon after, from 1955 to 1964, some 4,000 Chinese came per year, though their yearly quota was only 105. Greece's quota was 308, but some 5,000 came yearly. Italy's quota was 5,666 per year, but more than 20,000 came yearly. With a quota of less than 200 per year, close to 5,000 nonquota Japanese arrived per year. Nonquota and above-quota immigrants included several thousand Portuguese refugees from the Azore Islands after a volcano and earthquake. The largest group was Hungarians fleeing from the Russian-quashed 1956 uprising, which America favored publicly and covertly. Though Hungary had a quota of 865 per year, some 38,000—mostly young, educated males—were allowed to enter, much to the disapproval of 32 percent of the population who thought they would be "a bad influence" on the country versus the 26 percent who thought the reverse.[54]

The Intensification of Democratic Pluralism

With Senator McCarthy's increasing loss of credibility and Earl Warren becoming the Supreme Court's chief justice, actions against alleged and real communists abated. In a series of Supreme Court decisions in the late 1950s, particularly *Yates* v. *United States,* many state sedition laws were overturned, presidential power to dismiss governmental employees summarily was reduced, the right of defendants to have access to information supplied to the government by informers was upheld, and a distinction was made between "the abstract doctrine of overthrow of the government" and action-incitement to do so.[55]

In the years to follow, congressional civil rights acts, city and state statutes, and court rulings increasingly mandated equal opportunities in private and public jobs, education, and public accommodations. The first Catholic ever was elected president, John F. Kennedy; the first Black since the Reconstruction was elected a United States senator, Edward Brooke; the first Jew was appointed secretary of state, Henry Kissinger; and the first Black was appointed to the Supreme Court, Thurgood Marshall. As never before, officials of varying ethnic and religious backgrounds were elected across the country, and statutes were enacted outlawing verbal and physical intimidation of individuals because of their racial, religious, ethnic, or sexual backgrounds. Being a minority was slowly becoming a badge of pride rather than a mark of shame.

Starting with *Baker* v. *Carr,* in 1962, the Supreme Court affirmed the principle of "one person, one vote," with equal representation for equal numbers of people, "without regard to race, sex, economic status, or place of residence within a State." Poll taxes in federal elections ended with the Twenty-fourth Amendment to the Constitution in 1964. The following year, the Voting Rights Act abolished White primaries, grandfather clauses, property qualifications, literacy tests, and other forms of racial discrimination in voting.

During this period, civil rights activists sought only an equal opportunity and right to be treated like everyone else. The NAACP's executive director, Roy Wilkins, argued against any quota system for Blacks or Whites, because "people ought to be hired because of their ability, irrespective of their color." The emphasis on the individual was reinforced by the 1964 Civil Rights Act, which opposed employers giving preferential treatment to any group because of any imbalance in the workforce, and banned "the assignment of students to public schools in order to overcome racial imbalance." As originally used in President Kennedy's executive order 10925, "affirmative action" was race neutral, specifying that government agencies treat all job applicants and employees "without regard to race, creed, color or national origin."[56]

In 1965, an unprecedented change in thinking about ending racism was initiated by President Johnson, who declared it insufficient just to open the gates of opportunity. "All our citizens must have the ability to walk through those gates. We seek not just legal equity but human ability, not just equality as a right and a theory but equality as a fact and equality as a result." Toward that goal, presidential orders, court decisions, and state and federal regulations not only prohibited government contractors from discriminating because of race, creed, color, religion, sex, or national origin, but affirmative action and preferential treatment programs were initiated in the recruiting, hiring, promotion, pay, and training of minorities. In everyday life, segregation and separate facilities steadily ended in restaurants, movie houses, hotels, department stores, restrooms, buses, and lunch counters. With the Nixon administration, racial quotas and timetables were established, particularly in its Philadelphia Plan, requiring a given workforce proportionately reflect the minority population of the surrounding community.[57]

Then, in 1967, the Supreme Court in *Loving* v. *Virginia* declared all antimiscegenation laws unconstitutional, thereby permitting marriages by Whites with Blacks, American Indians, Chinese, Japanese, Filipinos, or any other "race." Under our Constitution, said the Court, "the freedom to marry a person of another race resides with the individual and cannot be infringed by the State."

Remedies, however, were not immediately operationalized, and justice delayed was deemed justice denied. Within the Black community the nonviolent tactics and strategies of Martin Luther King Jr. were criticized by younger, more militant Black leaders, who demanded that all forms of racism be ended "now," and when it wasn't, their anger and impatience sometimes erupted in rioting. Calls and demonstrations increased for "Black power," as well as criticism of White liberals and coalitional politics. To them, Black power, Black nationalism, and even racial separation were preferable to integration. As Malcolm X said, before breaking with the Black Muslims of Elijah Muhammed, "No *sane* black man really wants integration! No *sane* white man really wants integration! No sane black man really believes that the white man will ever give the black man anything more than token integration. . . . The only solution is complete *separation* from the white man." Similarly to Stokely Carmichael and Charles V. Hamilton in their book, *Black Power,* the goal of Blacks "must *not* be to assimilate into middle-class America," which "is without a viable conscience as regards humanity." To Black power militants, observed Stephen Carter, affirmative action "represented an effort by a terrified white power structure to buy off the victims of racist oppression by offering the same old integrationist strategy in a new and unpersuasive guise."[58]

As Blacks organized, demonstrated, and made advances, other minority groups, especially women, adopted Black rhetoric and tactics, insisting on the ending of all discrimination against them, as well as demanding their share of jobs and federal funds. Title VII of the 1964 Civil Rights Act not only outlawed employment discrimination because of race and national origin but also because of sex. Six years later, the Office of Federal Contract Compliance issued guidelines banning such discrimination by federal contractors. As more women entered the job market in the 1970s, additional legislation came into being, so that by the mid-1970s women were said to be benefiting more from affirmative action programs than racial minorities. Less striking, but symbolically important, were the American Psychiatric Association's decision in 1973 no longer to classify homosexuality as a mental illness, the U.S. Civil Service Commission's decision in 1975 no longer to exclude gays from government employment, and the 1974 election of an openly gay woman, Elaine Nobel of Massachusetts, to a state legislature.[59]

Meanwhile, new immigrants were accorded benefits prior immigrants never received. In public schools, ethnic pluralism and bilingualism were mandated by federal and local governments and courts. The Supreme Court, in 1974, in *Lau* v. *Nichols,* said public schools were obliged to educate non-English-speaking children, even if it meant special funding. "Where inability to speak and understand the English language excludes national origin-minority group children from effective participation in the educational programs offered by a school district, the district must take affirmative steps to rectify the language deficiency."

Though belatedly, government attitudes changed toward the "forgotten Americans." In 1971, the Congress finally settled Alaskan Indian and Eskimo claims, providing them with compensation of $1 billion over a twenty-year period and over 40 million acres of land. Seven years later, Congress passed legislation granting American Indians, Alaskan natives, and native Hawaiians the right to believe, express, and exercise their traditional religions, including access to sites and use and possession of sacred objects. A decade later, Congress apologized for the forced internment of Japanese Americans and relocation of Aleuts during World War II, and authorized payments to each surviving Japanese American internee of $20,000 tax-free and to each Aleut $12,000.

No less belatedly, some Protestant and Catholic religious leaders apologized for their churches' historic participation in the destruction of traditional Native American spiritual practices. While on a pilgrimage to America in 1987, Pope John Paul II told a group of Indians that not all Christians had lived up to their responsibilities in dealing with their ancestors: "The cultural oppression, the injustices, the disruption of your life and of your traditional societies must be acknowledged." Similarly, some Catholic and Protestant church organizations began decrying anti-Semitism as "a sin against God and human life," and started repudiating the theological concept of "Christian supersessionism" toward Jews, wherein God's biblical covenant with Jews was believed a preparation for the coming of Jesus.[60]

Because of two Supreme Court decisions in 1987, one involving a naturalized Iraqi who had been denied tenure in a college (*St. Francis College* v. *Al-Khazraji*), and the other, a synagogue vandalized by anti-Semites (*Shaare Tifila Congregation* v. *Cobb*), ethnic-group members could sue under the provisions of the 1866 Civil Rights Act and its 1870 amendment, and like Blacks, seek punitive damages and compensation, have a trial by a jury, and not have their lawsuits restricted to job discrimination. Writing for a unanimous Court in both cases, Justice Byron R. White said that intentional discrimination based on ancestry or ethnicity constitutes racial discrimination "whether or not it would be classified as racial in terms of modern scientific theory." The federal government also enacted "hate crime" legislation in 1988, mandating heavy fines and long prison sentences for those vandalizing religious institutions. Two years later, Congress passed the Hate Crimes Statistics Act, requiring the Justice Department to collect and publish statistics on crimes motivated by racial, religious, ethnic, or sexually oriented prejudice. By 1998, forty states and the District of Columbia had some forms of hate crimes, though only twenty-one states included those based on sexual orientation. The Americans with Disabilities Act of 1991 outlawed discrimination in employment and workplace conditions against the blind, deaf, mentally retarded, HIV positive, physically impaired, or those with cancer or epilepsy. Federal legislation was also extended in 1994 to interracial adoptions, outlawing the delay or prevention of adoptions because of racial and ethnic differences between would-be adoptees and adopters.[61]

In short, cultural pluralism, antidiscrimination laws, and affirmative action were more and more becoming integral parts of American reform life. Though not dead, ethnic, racial, and religious discrimination had suffered major setbacks, and no longer was being victimized a sure invitation to further victimization.

End of Ethnic Immigration Discrimination

The advances in civil rights in the 1960s inspired similar ones in immigration policy, which increasingly reflected the principles of nondiscrimination, equal opportunity, and greater compassion toward the oppressed, all advocated with a new militancy by a variety of minority groups and political leaders. Anglo-Saxon chauvinism in the upper echelons of government all but disappeared. At the same time, anticommunist foreign policy considerations led to an unprecedented admission of tens of thousands of above-quota Caribbean Islanders and Asians, particularly Cubans and Vietnamese, whose presence generated nativist feelings among American-born residents, including minorities. To a far less extent were the special admissions of thousands of Czechs fleeing Soviet occupation of their homeland, Jews from the Soviet Union, Chinese from Hong Kong, as well as small numbers of South and Central Americans and Iranians. Relatively few Black Africans were admitted, though refugee problems in Africa equaled that of Europe.

Cubans leaving Castro's government were the first large-scale beneficiaries of our anticommunist policy. By boat and plane, some 125,000 legal and illegal Cuban immigrants arrived between January 1959 and April 1961, settling mostly in Florida and overwhelming its education and social services. So large were the numbers and deep the American hostility to Castro that standard admission procedures were waived or ignored. President Kennedy instituted an asylum policy of financial aid, job counseling, education, and food allowances, while criticizing existing immigration policy for not satisfying national or international purposes. "In an age of interdependence among nations, such a system is an anachronism for it discriminates among applicants for admission . . . on the basis of accident of birth."[62] As relations worsened between America and Cuba during President Carter's administration, Castro, to spite America and relieve himself of discontents and imprisoned criminals, allowed all who wished to leave to do so, resulting in an additional 200,000 entering America by 1983.

Earlier, the Hart-Cellar Act of 1965, which President Johnson signed into law at the base of the Statue of Liberty, ended the invidious national origin and Asia–Pacific Triangle criteria, as well as discrimination against half-Asian immigrants. A maximum of 170,000 immigrants per year was established for the Eastern Hemisphere, with a limit of 20,000 from any one country, and another 120,000 from the Western Hemisphere. Excluded from limitations were immediate relatives of United States citizens. Entry was on a priority procedure, with the highest going to those with close relatives in America; being a scientist, artist, professional, or skilled worker; or being a political refugee or escapee from natural calamity. The law also increased the power of the government to grant people parole visas in special cases, without specific numerical limitation. Thus began the unprecedented admission of Asians, who soon outnumbered immigrants coming from Europe.

Such reforms were soon rendered ineffectual. Thousands of Czechs fleeing Soviet occupation and Jews emigrating from the Soviet Union, as well as East Asians expelled from Uganda, were given special permission to enter. Overshadowing these movements was Saigon's fall in 1975 and American withdrawal from Vietnam, which led to the massive above-quota program for Vietnamese military and civilian allies. As with Cubans, anticommunism prompted the admission of Vietnamese, which totaled some 750,000, who settled mainly on the West Coast. Unlike the Cubans, however, they for the most part had to have American sponsors to provide shelter and sustenance until they became self-supporting. Both private industry and religious organizations helped enormously, though—as with prior immigrant groups—a majority of Americans opposed their admission by 54 percent to 36 percent.[63] Then, the invasion of Cambodia by Vietnam and the collapse of the royal Laotian government (both of which America had helped militarily) led to the admission of some 130,000 Cambodians, Laotians, and Hmong, none of whom their neighboring countries of Malaysia and Thailand wanted.

In the 1970s, some 30,000 Haitians were allowed to enter, though with great reluctance, for unlike the Cuban and eastern European immigrants, most were not fleeing from communism but men in search of economic opportunity. They arrived in small and often unsafe boats, without American approval, sympathy (at first), or eligibility for aid given other groups. Also, mainland China was given its own quota of 20,000, which together with Taiwan's 20,000 quota, made the once despised "coolies" the highest ethnic recipients.

Reflecting Congress's concern about the overuse of paroles and a desire for a more humanitarian approach, particularly when human rights were violated, the Refugee Act of 1980 abolished the parole procedure and broadened the definition of refugees to include the persecuted or threatened in communist or noncommunist countries because of "race, religion, nationality, membership in a particular group, or political opinion." Now, refugees from any country could enter under a special quota or receive help in settling elsewhere.

These reforms, like previous ones, were almost immediately undermined by additional large-scale immigrations of Cubans, Vietnamese, Ethiopians, Nicaraguans, Iranians, Salvadorans, and Jews and Armenians from Russia. In the very year the Refugee Act was passed, 800,000 immigrants entered the country.[64]

Totally unanticipated by immigration reformers were the reactions of some domestic ethnic groups (especially Irish, Italian, and Greek), who in the 1970s began claiming that the Hart-Cellar Act's priority system was having an adverse, if not discriminatory, impact, pointing out that while most of their immediate families abroad had already come, thousands of others wanted to. Worse yet, the State Department refused after 1978 to issue any "nonpreference" visas, making it impossible for the unskilled and those without family in America to enter legally. This was in stark contrast to Asian Americans and Hispanics who still had many close family members abroad entitled to a higher priority than Europeans without such connections. As a Boston city official said, though the Irish "hold the greatest number of Congressional Medal of Honor winners for any single ethnic group in the history of this republic," they are "apparently not remembered at all."[65]

Unresponded to were the reactions of most Americans and America's first inhabitants. In mid-1980, 80 percent of the population favored reducing the number of aliens entering the country. More pointed was the National Congress of American Indians, which opposed "the free access and open immigration of refugees" to the "aboriginal lands of the Native people" and their use of facilities controlled by the Bureau of Indian Affairs and the Indian Health Service.[66]

While such developments were taking place, the courts were strengthening the rights of Americans abroad and extending new ones to legal and illegal aliens. Historic charges of "dual loyalty" were undermined when the Supreme Court in 1967 upheld the right of American citizens to serve in foreign armies and vote in other countries. As Justice Hugo Black wrote in *Afroyim* v. *Rusk,* the Fourteenth Amendment assured every citizen "a constitutional right to remain a citizen in a free country unless he voluntarily relinquished that citizenship."[67]

In 1982, for the first time ever, the Court explicitly held that the Fourteenth Amendment's equal protection clause applied "to anyone, citizen or stranger," assuring children of illegal aliens the same right to a free public school education as native-born ones. Henceforward, no state could deny such children an education or charge them special tuition fees. In the same year, President Reagan signed legislation facilitating the entry of thousands of Asian children fathered and abandoned by American servicemen since 1950 in Korea, Vietnam, Laos, Thailand, and Cambodia. Similarly, Congress in 1987 passed the Amerasian Homecoming Act, allowing Vietnamese children fathered by Americans as well as their families to enter the country, with full rights of refugee benefits and without their numbers being charged against refugee admission ceilings.

With these actions, the government, the courts, and political leaders were helping relocate, house, clothe, feed, employ, and educate immigrants from practically all parts of the world, often from the moment of their arrival. If not by intent then by deed, inclusion and diversity of people became more prevalent than exclusion and selectivity. Not only was a national diversification taking place, but also within groups. Being Asian no longer primarily meant being Chinese, Japanese, or Filipino, but coming from any of the Asian countries. Likewise, being Hispanic now included people from any of the South and Central American countries, as well as the Caribbean.

By the late 1970s, 42 percent of immigrants came from Latin America and 39 percent from Asia, while those from southern, central, or eastern Europe had declined to 8 percent and those from northern and western Europe to a mere 5 percent. For the next decade, 1981 to 1990, only 10 percent came from all of Europe, and by that decade's end minorities represented at least one-fourth of the population, or twice that in the 1970s—when 75 percent of the population had European origin, 12 percent Black, 9 percent Hispanic, 3 percent Asian, and 1 percent American Indian. More specifically, while from 1960 to 1990 the percentage of Asians among the foreign-born zoomed from 5 to 25 percent and for Latin Americans from 9 to 43 percent, the percentage for Europeans dropped from 67 to 20 percent. Then, four years later, the Census Bureau reported that the foreign-born had risen to 8.7 percent of the population.[68]

The proliferation of minority-group organizations, their increasing political activism, and their support by civil rights and religious groups discouraged governmental and political calls for racial, religious, or ethnic discriminatory policies. Bigotry in immigration debates and policy had become unacceptable, particularly since the ethnic vote was now a significant force in local and federal government, where descendants of once restricted or despised groups were helping make public policy and legislation. How could they deny others what had been denied their parents or grandparents?

Whether of old or new immigration stock, minority groups were wooed by political leaders and aspirants, many of whom were proud of their ethnic roots. Attracting rather than condemning "the ethnic vote" had become an accepted way of political life. Both the Democratic and Republican parties formed special minority advisory committees, and their platform committees eagerly sought to endorse the agendas of ethnic groups. Rare was the group that could not obtain a favorable statement from political leaders supporting its activities and congratulating its contributions to America. Even the formation of minority political clubs was encouraged, with the West Coast having a Filipino-American Republican Council, an Asian-American Republican Association, and some Japanese and Chinese Democratic clubs.[69]

Echoes of Neonativism

Advances in civil rights, cultural pluralism, ethnic power, and affirmative action were not without tensions between and among American-born and foreign-born residents, particularly in areas where large numbers of immigrants had moved or were suffering from unemployment or economic decline. As the population grew more diverse, so did the targets of bigotry. Across the country, bitter feelings, words, and confrontations flared over jobs, reciprocal xenophobia, group social behavior, immigration policies, minority business practices, public use of foreign language, and actual or alleged local and federal preferential policies.

Not uncommon was the stereotyping by minorities of each other, often more negative than that of the dominant White society about them. A 1993 Louis Harris poll found:

- 46 percent of Hispanics and 42 percent of African Americans polled agreed with a description of Asians as "unscrupulous, crafty and devious in business"—in contrast to 27 percent of the Whites;
- 68 percent of Asians and 49 percent of African Americans agreed that Hispanics tend "to have bigger families than they are able to support"—in contrast to 50 percent of the Whites;
- 33 percent of Hispanics and 22 percent of Asians believed that African Americans, "even if given a chance, aren't capable of getting ahead"—in contrast to 12 percent of the Whites;
- 54 percent of African Americans, 43 percent of Hispanics, and 35 percent of Asians agreed, "When it comes to choosing between people and money, Jews will choose money"—in contrast to 12 percent of non-Jewish Whites;
- 58 percent of non-Catholic Hispanics, 57 percent of Asians, and 49 percent of African Americans believed that Catholics are "narrow-minded because they are too controlled by their church"—in contrast to 34 percent of non-Catholic Whites;
- 48 percent of Hispanics, 39 percent of African Americans, and 30 percent of Asians believed that Moslems belong "to a religion that condones or supports terrorism"—to which, in contrast to the above, non-Moslem Whites were in large agreement by 41 percent.[70]

Worse yet were the behaviors.

Haitian Americans complained of the immigration criteria for admission used against them, saying that if they were applied to the Vietnamese or Soviet Jews, "then we would have to turn back perhaps up to 80 percent of them." After several hundred Mennonites from Mexico entered Texas in the early 1980s to join a prior group, some Mexican Americans complained that border guards had allowed them to do so because they were light-skinned and did not fit the stereotype of the "wetback." With the establishment of martial law in Poland in 1982, Polish Americans complained that fleeing Poles were discriminated against by American immigration rules because they were "not jumping on boats and going into the ocean and risking their lives like the Vietnamese." In 1984, eighteen American Indian groups protested United States military sales to the Guatemala government, which was oppressing Mayan natives, and accused President Reagan of speaking of freedom and human rights when Poland was involved, but not when Mayans were, whom they demanded be given political asylum in America.[71]

Immigrants, particularly illegal ones, were viewed as economic threats. More Blacks than Whites in 1979 believed illegal immigrants deprived them of jobs—

55 percent to 34 percent respectively. As a Black Floridian journalist wrote: "Blacks have lost 35 percent of hotel and banking jobs, etc., to Cubans. Most of these Cubans are White and the regular American tourist seems to feel better in being served by a White Cuban or waiter than by Blacks." Tensions also erupted in Florida between Cubans and Haitians, who believed that "the government gives the Cubans financial assistance to get started, while we get deported." In Hawaii, Filipinos, Puerto Ricans, Koreans, Samoans, and native Hawaiians complained about Japanese being overly represented in government and education.[72]

In other areas, such as New York City's Harlem and Washington, D.C., Blacks accused Koreans of not hiring their youth, taking profits out of the neighborhood, and receiving financial aid denied them. Similar charges by Blacks were directed at Arab businessmen in Detroit and at Asian Indians in Jersey City. In West Philadelphia, in the early 1980s, Black students assaulted Asian ones for allegedly receiving preferential treatment in schools. In Denver, Mexican Americans reacted violently to Vietnamese obtaining apartments in a housing project for which they were on the waiting list. In Puerto Rico, when the United States government said it would resettle some 2,000 Cuban and Haitian refugees, fears arose they would displace Puerto Rican workers, bring crime and homosexuality, and cause malaria, dengue fever, and leprosy. In Long Beach, California, resentments and gang wars took place between Mexicans and Cambodians. "Our government gives them everything," complained one Mexican American. "The rest of us have been living here all our lives and the government is not giving us anything." In Boston, in 1996, it was Asian Americans who resented being excluded from the city's racial quotas for admission to its elite schools, saying that some of their children had higher test scores than many Hispanics and Blacks admitted.[73]

According to the Southern Poverty Law Center, hate crimes in 1992 involving mainly race, religion, ethnicity, and sexual orientation resulted in at least 31 killings and 322 acts of vandalism. The year before, Arab Americans suffered 119 attacks, and then experienced many more within just a few days after the bombing of a federal building in Oklahoma in 1995, though no members of their community were involved. Incidents of violence against Asian Americans rose from 335 in 1993 to 452 in 1994, motivated largely by anti-immigration sentiments. In Michigan, a Chinese American was beaten to death by two White men who believed him Japanese and therefore responsible for the auto industry layoff. In New York City, a Chinese American woman was pushed in front of a subway train by a man claiming he had a "phobia about Asians." Violence against gays and lesbians in 1992–94 resulted in 151 deaths, nearly half of which were motivated by antigay bias or suspicion of such. On some 79 campuses, hate incidents against Jews increased in 1994 to 143—compared to 54 in 1988. Other studies showed that anti-Catholic views are more likely held by educated people, including faculty members, than by the poor and less educated. Teenage crime, in particular, rose, and alarmingly so. According to a national survey of tenth, eleventh, and twelfth grade students in 1990, racially motivated crime sky-rocketed 149 percent in two years. Most recently, in 1997, close to 10,000 "hate crimes" were reported, most motivated by racial bias (5,898), followed by religious bias (1,483), sexual-orientation bias (1,375), ethnic bias (1,083), disability bias (12), and multiple bias offenses (10).[74]

Traditional hate groups and publications were also at work. Dedicated to "God, Truth, Freedom, Morality, Capitalism and Constitutional Government," *Straight Talk* denounced legal and illegal immigration, asking, "why don't the Blacks, Asiatics and Hispanics develop an environment in their native countries which will give them a good standard of living, responsible self-government, and freedom? There has never been a black nation which achieved, without the leadership of whites, a high degree of democracy. . . . As for Hispanics, look at Central and South America. Starvation, terrorism. . . . The same is true for Asiatics." By 1997, some 500 "hate" groups existed across the country, including Alaska, all to varying degrees believing in racial superiority, distrusting government, preparing for a race war in the year 2000, and some even plotting to destroy government buildings, refineries, utilities, clinics, and certain politicians, judges, and civil rights leaders. Eighty-one of the groups—including a few Black ones—established Internet web sites to spread their beliefs, such as the Christian White Knights of the Ku Klux Klan, Aryan Nations, Blood and Honor, Bible Restoration Ministries, and the Nation of Islam.[75]

As in prior centuries, the educated and uneducated criticized ethnic political power and foreign language usage by immigrants. In 1975, Senator Mike Mansfield complained of American Jewish and American Greek respective pressure on behalf of Israel and Greece, proclaiming himself loyal only to America. "My father and mother were immigrants from Ireland, but my loyalty is not to Ireland, it is to this country—unquestioned." Blacks, too, were accused of exercising narrow political power. Their voting patterns of 90 percent-plus for Jesse Jackson in 1984 and 1988 led the *National Review,* a conservative journal, to say, "Those Jackson voters considered being black more important than being intelligent or even being American. This type of loyalty is unprecedented in our politics."[76]

New immigrants were once again belabored for not speaking or wanting to learn English, for using their foreign language in public places, for insisting that public schools provide them with bilingual programs, and for demanding that local governments publish materials and post signs in their tongue. To many Americans, including pre–World War immigrants, such requests seemed socially regressive, un-American, and destructive of national unity.

In 1981, Senator S.I. Hayakawa of California proposed a constitutional amendment making English the country's official language and prohibiting federal and state governments from requiring any other language in laws, ordinances, regulations, orders, programs, and policies. Two years later, "US English" was formed to lobby for such requirements, which the public generally favored. A *New York Times*/CBS News poll, in 1986, found that 60 percent of the public believed that state and local governments should conduct business only in English—60 percent of Whites, 50 percent of Blacks, and 34 percent of Hispanics. Most supportive were sixty-five or more year olds (72 percent), college students (72 percent), and Republicans (70 percent).[77]

By late 1988, seventeen states had passed some form of "English Only" legislation, while some others futilely tried or considered doing so. Two years later in Arizona, a federal judge declared such an amendment to the state's constitution unconstitutional. In 1998, a half-dozen bills were introduced in the Congress that would not only declare English the country's official language but also ban citizenship ceremonies from using any foreign language, ban bilingual ballots, require all government business be carried on in English, and end bilingual education in the public schools. Nevertheless, a few states with large numbers of foreign-speaking residents have officialized non-English languages. New Mexico did it with Spanish; and Hawaii, with Hawaiian. Louisiana's constitution provided for the "Preservation of Linguistic and Cultural Origins," whereby French continued to be used in schools and courts. Though Georgia had approved "English Only" legislation, the city of Atlanta passed a resolution declaring itself multicultural and multilingual.

"Welcome All"

In spite of the lingering echoes of nativism and xenophobia, it was clear that the forces of reform, humanitarianism, tolerance of diversity, and ethnic political power were in the ascendance in all major arenas of society. Many Protestant church leaders, whose predecessors had opposed immigration, now supported cultural pluralism within their churches and in many cases offered illegal aliens (especially Salvadorans, Guatemalans, and Haitians) sanctuary against arrest and deportation. In 1985, the Supreme Court eased the plight of illegal immigrants by barring racial and national-origin discrimination in regulations governing their detention and the granting of parole status.

Even among Americans who opposed immigration, ambivalence rather than rigidity prevailed, with different attitudes toward immigrants, refugees, and illegal aliens, and with most sympathy for those fleeing natural disaster or persecution—as long as their numbers were relatively few. A 1985 poll showed that though only 27 percent agreed that "America should keep its doors open to people who wish to immigrate to the U.S. because that is what our heritage is all about," 66 percent approved admitting those fleeing homeland persecution. Fears of job competition also softened, at least in areas where there was little or none. Although 61 percent of those polled believed immigrants took jobs away from American workers, 80 percent agreed they were taking jobs that Americans did not want.[78]

More persistent was opposition to illegal immigrants. Most Americans wanted penalties imposed on employers hiring them. In a 1980 poll in nine cities, only 21 percent of the respondents believed Indochinese should be encouraged to move into their communities; nearly 50 percent preferred their settling in other Asian countries, and 25 percent believed that "America has too many Asians in its population."[79]

Even then, reactions depended on how, who, where, and when polls were taken—whether during war or peace, recession or boom, urban unrest or quiet, little or big city. For example, in the above nine-city poll, only 8 percent in Dothan, Alabama, favored immigrants moving in, while in San Francisco 31 percent did. Responses also depended on the racial and ethnic character of those questioned. A 1986 *New York Times*/CBS News poll revealed that 52 percent of Whites favored reduced immigration, as did 39 percent of Blacks, and 31 percent of Hispanics; conversely, 25 percent of the Hispanics polled favored an increase, compared to 11 percent for Blacks and 5 percent for Whites. Usually the poor and those with little education were most likely to favor immigration restriction.[80]

With, or as a result of, such opposition, negative attitudes toward prior European immigrant groups eased. A 1982 Roper poll asking people whether "on balance" certain ethnic groups had been "a good or bad thing for this country," no European ones received lower than a favorable 53 percent response and no Asian group (Japanese, Chinese, Korean, and Vietnamese) received higher than a favorable 47 percent. Two years later, 51 percent of Americans believed there were too many Latin American immigrants, compared to 26 percent for European ones. Even opposition to African immigrants was lower, 31 percent.[81]

Whatever the public opposition, it was not sufficient to deter political leaders from easing immigration laws. They knew that the general public simply did not consider the issue a major one, at least not enough to affect their being elected or reelected. For example, a 1984 Gallup poll reported that though 84 percent of the respondents thought unemployment a "very important" problem, 73 percent inflation, and 70 percent the threat of nuclear war, only 55 percent felt that way about illegal immigration. In California, where pro-English-language sentiment was growing, only 3 percent of those polled in 1985 cited illegal immigration as the most pressing problem facing the state and its communities.[82]

Except for a few outright racist groups, no major public figures, political leaders, social commentators, or academics deplored any erosion of Anglo-Saxon or Teutonic roots or called for exclusion of Asian, Spanish, Catholic, Jewish, or other group because of its genetic or cultural makeup. Rather, as never before, politicians (many of whom had minority roots) supported increased immigration. Some respected individuals and organizations did raise some critical questions: Were there no limits to how many people America should admit—and could absorb? Are not immigrants receiving jobs and social benefits denied Americans and native-born minorities? Must America be a haven to all who wish to leave their homeland, whether for political, economic, or natural-disaster reasons?

In 1978, the Sierra Club expressed concern about the impact of mass immigration on the environment, but when it polled its members in 1998 on whether to adopt officially a policy recommending reduced immigration, it was defeated. Other prominent opposition came from the Federation for American Immigration Reform (FAIR) and from Negative Population Growth, Inc. Organized in 1979, FAIR sought to educate the public and to lobby federal and state governments to stop illegal immigration, as well as to reform immigration policies, which it said was exacerbating domestic problems, such as unemployment and social service costs. Negative Population Growth, founded in 1972, believes that in any given year total immigration should not exceed emigration.

A member of FAIR, Governor Richard D. Lamm of Colorado, said in 1986 that immigration must be restricted because the country could not absorb and assimilate all who wanted to come.

> We have not adequately integrated blacks into our economy or our society. We have an education system rightly described as a "rising tide of mediocrity." Fifty percent of our Hispanic students never graduate from high school; we have the most violent society of the industrialized world; we have startling high rates of illiteracy, illegitimacy, and welfare. It takes an incredible hubris to madly rush, with these unfinished social agendas, into blindly accepting more immigrants and refugees than all of the world put together, and still hope that we can keep a common agenda.[83]

In spite of negative feelings toward increased legal and illegal immigration, as well as the use of foreign languages in conducting business or official matters, Congress passed the 1986 Immigration Reform and Control Act, offering legal status to millions of illegal aliens who had entered before January 1982 and were residents for five continuous years. Those who had worked in agriculture for at least ninety days between 1 May 1985 and 1 May 1986 could become legal temporary residents. Lest they be fined, employers were required to ask prospective employees for documents substantiating their citizenship or legal alien status. To reimburse the anticipated state costs for public assistance, health care, and education, the government set aside $1 billion a year for four years. The rights of legal aliens were expanded to protect them against job discrimination by employers who thought they were not citizens. By the end of the filing period in May 1988, some 1.6 million aliens had applied for amnesty, most of whom were Mexicans residing in Texas and California.

Then, in response to growing criticism that Western European applicants were being discriminated against, the State Department in early 1987 issued regulations for a two-year period, allowing 5,000 visas for each year above the 270,000 limit established in 1965, with the proviso that mailed applications arrive in Washington between 21 and 27 January. The reaction was overwhelming, with many people sending multiple applications. More than 400,000 arrived from around the world before the stipulated time and were therefore disqualified, while another 500,000 reached Washington on 21 January, with the largest number mailed from Ireland and Canada. A similar procedure was adopted in 1989, but the two-year number was raised to 20,000 and no applicant could file more than once. This time some 3.2 million filed.[84]

Meanwhile, the Supreme Court in 1987 ruled that the government's attitude toward aliens seeking asylum was too rigid. Instead of having to prove a "clear probability" that if returned home they would be persecuted, tortured, or killed because of their "race, religion, nationality, membership in a particular social group, or political opinion," aliens needed prove only "a reasonable possibility" of such occurring.[85] Some two years later, the Morrison/Lautenberg law eased the entry of immigrants (chiefly Jews, Pentecostal Christians, and Ukrainians) as "refugees," making them eligible for federal aid. To prove fear of persecution, they needed only to adduce a "credible basis" for such happening by pointing to past persecution, discrimination, or prejudice, if not against themselves then against similar group individuals in their geographic area. Such liberalization aroused little criticism. In fact, legal or illegal immigration did not become an issue of contention in the 1988 presidential election, where candidates boasted of their immigrant roots (Michael Dukakis) or having family members of immigrant roots (George Bush).

In short, from the 1960s onward, a number of domestic and foreign relations influences helped widen the doors of immigration and provide immigrants with financial and social service aid: a renewed humanitarianism, the civil rights movement, the election of ethnic Americans to high office, opposition to communism abroad, the growth of ethnic and racial political action groups, the need for unskilled and semiskilled workers, Supreme Court decisions expanding the rights of aliens and immigrants, and a media that sympathetically projected the plight of would-be and illegal immigrants. The almost 100 years of successive attempts to reduce or exclude the poor, Asians, illiterates, political radicals, and people from southern, central and eastern Europe had failed, as had attempts to establish permanent quotas, deport all illegal aliens, and make our borders entry-proof.

Continuing pressures for reform led to the Immigration Act of 1990, wherein for three years the annual immigration admission ceiling was raised to 700,000, after which it would be 675,000. Among its key provisions were granting special preferences to applicants possessing needed work skills, such as scientists, engineers, and artists. The spouses and children of Hispanics who had gained legal status in 1986 received 55,000 visas for each of the next three years. A new "diversity" visa category was established to admit people disadvantaged by previous legislation, such as those from Western Europe and Ireland. Illegal Salvadoran immigrants in America were granted a special temporary protected status. Filipinos who had served in American World War II armed forces or had helped them became immediately eligible for naturalization. Also, some of the exclusionary provisions of the 1952 McCarran-Walter Act were eased.[86]

However ajar the immigration doors, people from more and more countries passed through them, and in spite of periods of xenophobia, nativism, racism, anti-Catholicism, and anti-Semitism, America became the most immigrant-accepting and linguistically diverse country in the world. Still more changes are in the making. Census predictions are that out of an estimated total American population of 383 million in the year 2050, Asians and Pacific Islanders will grow from 9 million in 1992 (3 percent of the total population) to 41 million (11 percent of the population; Hispanics from 24 million in 1992 (9 percent) to 81 million (21 percent of the population), making them the nation's largest minority group; Blacks from 32 million (12 percent) to 62 million (16 percent); and American Indians, Eskimos and Aleuts will double to 4.6 million (1.2 percent). In contrast, while the non-Hispanic White population will grow from 191 million to 202 million, its percentage of the total population is expected to decline from 75 percent to 53 percent.[87]

Summary

Before and after the coming of the White man, prejudice and discrimination existed in some form within and between religious, ethnic, and racial groups. As more and different people arrived, and as more Americans moved westward and into the Atlantic and Pacific Islands, bigotry proliferated, and profitably so: whether in the selling and owning of slaves, the transporting and hiring of immigrant laborers, the dispossession of Indians and Mexicans, the polarizing of native- and foreign-born workers, the paying of lower wages to immigrants, or the establishing of exploitative commercial bases abroad.

The forms of bigotry differed in degrees, durations, and motivations. Blacks, Indians, and Mexicans were more vulnerable than other groups to physical abuse and property expropriations. Anti-Catholicism, anti-Mormonism, and Anti-Semitism generally exceeded Anglophobia and Francophobia in intensity and time. By the end of the nineteenth century, the earlier prejudice against Scotch-Irish, British, Quakers, Baptists, and Huguenots became a dim memory.

Throughout most of the nineteenth century, bitter wars were waged against Indians, whose homes were destroyed, lands occupied, and survivors relocated to smaller areas. By creeping annexation and force of arms, Mexicans in the Southwest were rendered strangers in their land of birth. Differences between Northern and Southern Whites over the Constitution and slavery erupted in a bitter war, which though holding the Union together freed the slaves largely in name only. Regardless of the feelings of the native residents, the Louisiana Territory was purchased from France and Alaska from Russia, and our military and missionaries moved into the Caribbean and Pacific. Intense as hostility to German Americans and Italian Americans was during

World Wars I and II, it remained less violent than that directed at Chinese and Japanese Americans.

Whatever the decade, some groups—White Protestants and Anglo-Saxons—were preferred to others; and some groups—Asians and Africans—were not wanted at all. In the process, a continuing pecking order and succession of targets evolved, motivated by religious triumphalism, racial superiority, national destiny, economic necessity, or any combination thereof.

The inconsistency of democratic preachments and undemocratic practices was sadly epitomized during both world wars. While fighting to make the world safe for democracy, our military services maintained segregated ranks, and during the second war, the Congress denied refuge to large numbers of Europe's homeless and persecuted, while interning thousands of Japanese Americans.

In the post–World War II years, public opinion, civil protests, riots, Supreme Court decisions, presidential orders, and laws and legislation led to massive changes in minority-group relations. "Now," or with "all deliberate speed," the rights of every citizen had to be equal. No more could discrimination, segregation, or exclusion be legally allowed because of race, religion, or national origin. To hasten the process, the War on Poverty was declared.

Progress in civil, political, and religious rights and liberties had now become significantly measurable by comparing years or decades rather than centuries. Clearly, the contradictions between the realities of minority-group life and the ideals of the Constitution and Bill of Rights had eased, and clearly also, today's generation of minorities confront less personal and institutional bigotry than did their parents and grandparents.

Being *American* has come to embrace a pluralistic dimension that validates foreign languages, customs, and heritages as never imagined by the Founding Fathers. By the 1970s, our views on relating to other countries changed from the eighteenth-century desire to avoid all foreign entanglements and the nineteenth-century belief in Manifest Destiny to defending and promoting human rights almost everywhere in the world, as well as rescuing or helping victims of tyranny or natural catastrophes. As American economic and military power increased in the decades that followed and as that of the Soviet Union declined, fears of communist and radical subversion at home and Soviet expansionism abroad weakened, so much so that by the late 1990s America was in the forefront in supporting financial aide to Russia and some of her former republics.

In short, from our beginning as a nation to the present, freedom, justice, religious diversity, and cultural pluralism proved stronger than geocentrism, ethnocentrism, intergroup intolerance, and Anglo-Saxon superiority. To no other country in the world did so many different people come (and still want to come), knowing that it is safer and more self-satisfying to be of an ethnic, racial, or religious minority here than being of a majority back home. And no other countries—larger, older, or even wealthier in natural resources—have developed and expanded such a benign government of socioeconomic opportunities, civility, and laws.

The result has been a mixture of new and old worlds, adding reality to the vision of *e pluribus unum*.

Before exploring the future of American intergroup relations, and the basis for both optimism and pessimism, the role of education in intergroup relations is examined.

Chapter 5

The Teaching of Contempt

Religious, racial, and ethnic prejudice in America cannot be fully understood without probing their connections to the personnel, processes, politics, and institutions of education, which reflected and validated society's attitudes and behaviors toward the native-born, immigrant, and foreigner.

Unfortunately, throughout most of American history relatively few schools and educators defied the xenophobia, geocentrism, ethnocentrism, and bigotry of the surrounding society. They were unable, if not unwilling, to recognize the educational needs and aspirations of groups other than their own or to respond to the immediate and future needs of ever-increasing numbers of people from more and more countries.

In many ways such inactivity was understandable, for what and how what was being taught were believed beneficial to students and society. No experience existed in America or elsewhere in educating so varied a population. Education was decentralized, and not until the mid-nineteenth century did a professional corps of educators and teacher-training centers begin emerging. Least of all, no one in the seventeenth or eighteenth century could have predicted that America would become the world's leading refuge.

Only in recent decades did the field of education recognize its responsibility for teaching respect for minority groups and combating intergroup bigotry. Even then, progress was slow, largely due to local political and minority-group pressures rather than educational or societal foresight. At best, the educational network was reactive rather than initiatory.

Newly arrived immigrants had to adjust to contradictory forces in the host society and their own group. On one hand, they entered a country about which they knew little, but which offered them and their children an opportunity for an education not usually available in their ancestral lands. At the same time, they were denied full acceptance by public and private institutions, whose leaders insisted they learn English, reject past allegiances, and become totally assimilated. Only in their own groups and neighborhoods could they feel a sense of security and surcease of rejection; even then, depending on their success or failure in the larger society, they could be told by prior immigrants that they were too foreign or too American, too servile or too ambitious, too forgetful of their past or too critical of their own people.

Early American Education

American education, like American government, did not evolve in a vacuum free of foreign influence or unaffected by local conditions. Each immigrant group brought its own religious suspicions and intolerances. Lutherans and Catholics did not tolerate Anabaptists. Baptists and Quakers were resented by all. Protestants generally could not stand Catholics, and vice versa. Their separate communities "became bastions of one faith or another . . . punishing or even expelling nonbelievers."[1] At the same time, the growing diversity of people, geographic distance from Europe, enormous natural resources, and vast availability of land for settlement facilitated the development of a variety of new private and public educational models and philosophies.

"Educated" citizens were those who adhered to the "true religion" of the established church in their area, whether it was the Dutch Reformed church in New Netherland, the Anglican Church of England in Virginia and the Carolinas, the Swedish Lutheran church in the Delaware area, or the Puritan Congregational churches in New England. The French, Dutch, Spanish, and Swedes also set up schools, but none as extensively or successfully as the English.

Colonial schools emphasized preaching, catechizing, and prayers, which asked deliverance from "the delusion of the Devil, the malice of the heathen, the invasions of our enemies, and mutinies and dissensions of our own people."[2] Preachers, teachers, and funds were always scarce, so much so that King James I initiated a fund-raising campaign in England to help the Virginia colonists establish "some churches and schools for the education of the children of those barbarians."[3]

In both elementary and secondary schools, reading, writing, and arithmetic were taught mainly through the Bible and biblically related textbooks. Religion and state were indivisible. As the first Massachusetts school law stated in 1642, children should be taught "to read and understand the principle of religion and the capital laws of this country."[4]

Females were considered responsible for man's downfall and mentally inferior to males. Their place was in the kitchen, and various New England communities refused to spend money on female education. As late as 1782, the Reverend John Eliot wrote that "we don't pretend to teach ye female part of ye town anything more than dancing, or a little music perhaps . . . except ye private schools for writing, which enables them to write a copy, sign their name &c, which they might not be able to do without such a privilege."[5]

The poor attended elementary schools and were apprenticed at an early age to learn a trade. In school and home, discipline was strict, and children could be convicted of "stubborn or rebellious carriage against their parents or governors," which could result in imprisonment or even death. Puritans taught the horrors of infant damnation, and Pilgrims held that "there is in all children (though not alike) a stubbornness and stoutness of mind which must in the first place be broken and beaten down that so the foundation of their education being laid in humility and tractableness other virtues may in their time be built thereon."[6]

Secondary schools taught Latin and Greek and were for the wealthy, some of whom sent their sons to England to be educated. Colleges such as Harvard, Yale, and William and Mary represented separate scholastic worlds for the religious and wealthy. William and Mary was established in 1693 primarily to train clergy and community leaders. Eight years later, because Harvard was believed lax in Puritan orthodoxy, Yale was established to ensure that "places of learning should not be places of riot and pride," but prepare students "for public service, and . . . be under the oversight of wise and holy men." Hebrew and Aramaic were taught at many of the early colleges. At Harvard, whose first two presidents were scholars of Hebrew, all students were required to study Hebrew, and graduation exercises featured an oration in that language.[7]

Religious denominational conformity—and intolerance—pervaded academia and community. "I thank God there are no free schools or printing," said the governor of Virginia, "and I hope we shall not have them these hundred years. For learning has brought heresy and disobedience and sects into the world, and printing has divulged them, and libels against the best government." In New England, the very concept of toleration of other beliefs was considered an evil. "Toleration made the world anti-Christian," declared John Cotton.[8]

Academic witch hunts and purifications were common. Harvard's first president, the Reverend Henry Dunster, was forced to resign in 1654 because he had become a Baptist. At Yale, in the 1720s, the president and entire teaching staff were dismissed because they had become Episcopalians. Though lacking trained scientists, Yale's Timothy Dwight opposed hiring Europeans because "a foreigner, with his peculiar habits and prejudices, would not feel and act in union with us, and that however able he might be in point of science, he would not understand our college system, and might therefore not act in harmony with his colleagues."[9]

On lower levels of education, teachers generally had little or no preparation for their duties. As a 1773 clergyman wrote, "Not a ship arrives either with redemptioners or convicts, in which schoolmasters are not as regularly advertised for sale . . . at least two thirds of the little education we receive are derived from instructors, who are either INDENTED SERVANTS, OR TRANSPORTED FELONS."[10]

As to worldly knowledge, both teachers and students had little contact with the larger society about them. Seventeenth-century colonies were separated by large stretches of uninhabited wilderness, with few local newspapers or passable roads and no regular postal service. "Wee are here att the end of the World," wrote William Byrd of Virginia in 1690, "and Europe may bee turned topsy turvy ere wee can hear a Word of itt, but when news come [by the tobacco fleet once a year] we have it by whole Sale, very often much more than truth; therefore I beg the favour to hear from you as frequently as may bee."[11]

In backcountry areas, illiteracy was widespread, and in New England at the time of the Revolution, Horace Mann estimated that perhaps one out of ten youngsters attended a school. About one-third of the Founding Fathers had some formal education and only the upper fourth had graduated from college. Educational backgrounds were somewhat better in the first Congress, where 48 percent of House members and 56 percent of those in the Senate were college graduates. In spite of early colonial intergroup differences and sexism, Puritan commitment to reading and understanding the Bible made New Englanders one of the most literate populations of the time.[12]

French, Spanish, and English colonizers established schools for Indians. The French, mainly Jesuits, sought to teach Christianity and French culture, or as Louis XIV said, to "educate the children of the Indians in the French manner." In Florida, by 1655, some seventy Spanish friars in thirty-eight missions were at work converting the Indians. At first, in the Southwest, more emphasis was put on teaching trades and ending Indian languages than on Spanish culture, but in the 1790s, the Spanish Crown ordered its mission schools to teach Indians to speak, read, and write in Spanish only.[13]

The English taught Christianity and Western culture. Hoping to convert Indians, John Eliot translated the Bible into the Algonquin language, but at the same time urged them to cut their hair, adopt European clothes, and live like other Englishmen. Philanthropists in England also helped. In the later seventeenth century, Thomas Coram initiated efforts to send books to New England missionaries working among the Indians; similarly, the Anglican Society for the Propagation of the Gospel in Foreign Parts maintained missionaries and provided books and schools for Indians, Blacks, and poor Whites. In 1754, a special and short-lived London effort was made to reach German settlers by the establishment of the Society for Propagating Christian Knowledge Among the Germans in America.[14]

As early as 1645, some Indians attended integrated schools; a decade later, Harvard actually established a college to train Indian teachers and ministers. Out of the less than a dozen who enrolled, however, only one graduated. At William and Mary, an early program for converted Indians to become missionaries failed to produce any graduates. Generally, efforts to educate Indians proved feeble, and were often unwelcomed by the supposedly unenlightened. As Benjamin Franklin recorded the reply of some Indian leaders:

> But you, who are wise, must know that different Nations have different Conceptions of things, and you will therefore not take it amiss, if our Ideas of this kind of Education happen not to be the same with yours. We have had some Experience of it; Several of our young people were formerly brought up at the

Colleges of the Northern Provinces; they were instructed in all your Sciences; but, when they came back to us, they were bad Runners, ignorant of every means of living in the Woods, unable to bear either Cold or Hunger, knew neither how to build a Cabin, take a Deer, or kill an Enemy, spoke our Language imperfectly, were therefore neither fit for Hunters, Warriors, nor Counsellors; they were totally good for nothing. We are however not the less oblig'd by your kind Offer, tho' we decline accepting it; and, to show our grateful Sense of it, if the Gentlemen of Virginia will send us a Dozen of their Sons, we will take great Care of their Education, instruct them in all we know, and make *Men* of them.[15]

Free or slave, Blacks were generally denied schooling, especially in the South, where laws provided heavy fines and bodily punishment to anyone educating them. Not only was education unnecessary "for the performance of those duties which are required of our slaves," said the Charleston City Council in 1826 but it was "incompatible with the public safety" because it would enable slaves to "carry on illicit traffic, to communicate privately among themselves, and to evade those regulations that are intended to prevent confederation among them." Some colonists, however, gave religious instruction to slaves and free Blacks, and some schools were set up for them in Georgia, South Carolina, Kentucky, Virginia, Florida, Tennessee, and Louisiana.[16]

In the northern colonies conditions were only a little less unfavorable, where some church groups and slave owners provided religious education. Cotton Mather in 1717 established a school for Blacks and Indians, and in 1728 a school was established in New England "for the Instruction of Negro's in reading, Catechizing, & Writing if required."[17]

Not only were Blacks and Indians usually excluded or severely restricted but so were the children of White indentured servants and convicts from England, a practice in keeping with the British view that laborers should be kept ignorant and poor and be made to work rather than allowed to think.[18]

Emergence of State Control of Education

After the Revolution, family and church control of schooling began being replaced by community and state, and to some extent by the national government, particularly as more and more calls arose for secularism, science, and humanism in education. Schooling and the need for higher education began being seen as a sectionally unifying and nationally homogenizing force. The Senate in 1789 affirmed that "Literature and Science are essential to the preservation of a free constitution." Washington, in 1796, told Congress that "the assimilation of principles, opinions, and manners of our countrymen, by the common education of a portion of our youth from every quarter, well deserves our attention. The more homogeneous our citizens can be made in these particulars, the greater will be our prospect of permanent union."[19]

In Massachusetts, in 1821, the first public high school was established, and six years later, the state passed the first law requiring public high schools in towns having more than 500 families. By the mid-1830s, female teachers were replacing male ones in public schools because they could be paid as much as 60 percent less. Trade schools, too, were established for the development of navigators, surveyors, and bookkeepers. Colleges multiplied, though remaining small, exclusive, sexist, racist, and usually affiliated with some denomination headed by a minister. Full-time scientists began being hired, not to conduct research or develop new technologies, but to teach that nature revealed God's perfection and sovereignty. Mount Holyoke became the first college for women in 1837, followed by Vassar in 1865, Smith in 1872, Wellesley in 1875, and Bryn Mawr in 1866. Likewise, Oberlin became the first coeducational college in 1833, followed by Cornell and the University of Michigan in the 1870s.[20]

Though English had not been mandated by the Constitution as the national or official language, in some areas, private schools and state legislatures utilized foreign languages. For many decades after Louisiana became a state, laws were published in English and French, which were spoken in legislative debates and court cases. In California and New Mexico, and later in Texas, early laws were printed in English and Spanish.[21]

As state control over education grew, it met with heated opposition. Schools for the public assumed a negative image of being for the poor. In many towns and rural districts only the children of declared paupers were allowed free schooling. Throughout the 1820s, suspected or convicted delinquents, orphans, and impoverished children were committed to newly established asylums, reform schools, and orphanages, in which, isolated from parents and with clocklike supervision, it was hoped they would learn self-discipline and law-abiding and productive ways of citizenship.[22]

Early-nineteenth-century educational reforms in the Northeast and Midwest began enunciating a social philosophy that eventually swept the country. Though focusing mainly on White Anglo-Saxons, they believed that universal schooling would hasten social harmony and, as Horace Mann said, protect "society against the giant vices which now invade and torment it—against intemperance, avarice, war, slavery, bigotry, the woes of want and the wickedness of waste."[23]

Some historians have argued that such reformers would not have succeeded without the support of the business world, which helped them with needed funds and political power. Reformers like Mann and Caleb Mills in Indiana continually sought their support, saying that educated workers were more productive, docile, clean, frugal, law-abiding, and reliable than uneducated ones. To Mills, the diffusion of knowledge benefited prosperity. Such reasoning was irrelevant to the South, with its slave plantations and small rural farmers. Wealthy Southerners preferred educating their children privately and saw no benefit to themselves in educating Blacks, free or slave.[24]

Even then, many citizens, clergy, and private schools opposed public schools and believed they should not be taxed for educating others. There were also employers who feared free schooling would end child labor and parents who argued that compulsory education laws infringed upon their rights. As in the present, some minority groups, particularly Catholics, wanted to control their children's education and thereby ensure their ethnic or religious survival.

Moreover, differences existed over which and how much religious education should be conducted in public schools, what teacher qualifications should be, what kinds of school books should be used, and even what languages should be taught in classrooms, as with the Dutch in New York and the Germans in Pennsylvania, who respectively considered learning Dutch and German essential to group existence.

Nevertheless, more and more ethnic immigrants turned to the public schools, largely because they did not want to pay double tuition—taxes for public schools and fees for private ones. For example, in New York City, the number of private schools declined from 430 in 1829 to 138 in 1850. In New England, from 1840 to 1850, private school attendance declined by 6 percent while public school enrollment increased by 10 percent.[25] The structure and contents that the educational reformers established both socialized and Americanized successive waves of European immigrants, but excluded Indians, Blacks, Mexican Americans, and Asians, who when admitted to the public schools were segregated.

The Immigrant Challenge

Increasing numbers of immigrants from increasingly diverse countries arrived at a time when American education was expanding and becoming more professionalized. By the time of the Civil War, state school systems were firmly established, with over 200 colleges and universities. Just as in the North the government established the army's West Point (1802) and the navy's Annapolis (1845), in the South, private and publicly funded military schools were founded, such as Virginia Military Institute in 1839 and the Citadel three years later. In the Midwest, particularly in Ohio, Protestant denominations rushed to establish theological and liberal arts colleges, such as Oberlin, Beloit, and Wabash (Congregational); Ohio Western (Methodist); Wooster (Presbyterian); and Denison (Baptist).

Teacher organizations and periodicals appeared, and teachers were expected to inspire students with patriotism and Protestantism, which resulted in excluding Catholics and Jews from teaching in public schools and a similar exclusion of deists and Unitarians in many places.[26] Public evening school classes began being established in the larger cities for teaching vocational skills, providing education for those who had not received one, and for Americanizing immigrants. Whether foreign- or native-born, English was to be used, taught, and learned in the nation's classrooms.

Many early-nineteenth-century political leaders and educators viewed immigrant children with a mixture of contempt, prejudice, and yet cautious optimism. In America, they should learn, think, and act like Americans, and the faster they did, the better off they and the country would be. To Edward Everett, in 1820, it was an "inconceivable perversity" for immigrants "to speak a language which your neighbor cannot understand, to be ignorant of the language in which the laws of the land you live in are made and administered, and to shut yourself out . . . from half the social privileges of life."[27]

The *Massachusetts Teacher,* in 1851, advocated coercive education, together with laws closing bars, outlawing street beggars, and imprisoning drunkards, particularly among the Irish. The hope for the future was with immigrant children rather than their parents, lamented the publication.

> The rising generation must be taught as our own children are taught. We say *must be,* because in many cases this can only be accomplished by coercion. In too many instances the parents are unfit guardians of their own children. If left to their direction the young will be brought up in idle, dissolute, vagrant habits, which will make them worse members of society than their parents are; instead of filling our public schools, they will find their way into our prisons, houses of correction, and almshouses. Nothing can operate effectively here but stringent legislation, thoroughly carried out by an efficient police; the children must be gathered up and forced into school, and those who resist or impede this plan, whether parents or *priests,* must be held accountable and punished.[28]

Throughout the Southwest, as more and more Anglos, as well as Catholic and Protestant missionaries, settled after the Mexican War, using Spanish in schools was increasingly banned. In California, in 1852, fiscal support for private Spanish-language schools ended, and three years later, the state's Bureau of Public Instruction required all teaching to be in English.[29]

The Indiana superintendent of instruction was kinder when, in 1853, he wrote, "our policy as a state is to make of all of the varieties of population amongst us, differing as they do in origin, language, habits of thought, modes of action, and social custom, one people with one common interest." Such goals were easier stated than fulfilled, particularly among the poor and the immigrants in large cities, where truancy was high. For example, in Boston, in 1849, of 1,066 children sent to reform schools for the crime of truancy and vagrancy, 90 percent were "of foreign parents." In 1850, more than half the children in New York's reformatories were Irish; and in Cincinnati, over half were Irish or German. Similar percentages were found across the country.[30]

Catholics

In the second quarter of the nineteenth century, the problem of educating immigrant children was compounded by anti-Catholicism. The connection between the two was well recognized by Governor Seward of New York, who in 1840 told the state legislature:

The children of foreigners . . . are too often deprived of the advantages of our system of public education, in consequence of prejudices arising from difference of language or religion. It ought never to be forgotten that the public welfare is as deeply concerned in their education as in that of our own children. I do not hesitate, therefore, to recommend the establishment of schools in which they may be instructed by teachers speaking the same language with themselves and professing the same faith.[31]

Underlying Catholic-Protestant differences were profound psychosocial hostilities. The average Protestant from birth on learned to be suspicious, if not hateful, of Catholics. In the 1850s, anti-Catholicism permeated schools, books, popular periodicals, and newspapers, and parents warned children of papal plots, conspiracies, and licentiousness. At church, Protestant ministers denounced Catholics for believing in a prostituted religion and demanded that the Protestant Bible be read, lest America become a nation of godless citizens.[32]

When not maligned, Catholics, whether immigrant or native-born, were sought out by Protestant missionaries. To the publisher of the *American Protestant Vindicator,* it was better to save Catholics than destroy them. "I do persecute them in the same manner as I would persecute my neighbor, who is fast asleep in his bed, and his house on fire. I persecute him by rushing in through the flames, and dragging him, his wife and little ones out of the door, to a place of safety."[33] In the Southwest, when missionizing efforts failed to convert Mexicans and Indians, Protestants established free schools for them. The Presbyterian Reverend D. McFarland, in 1867, urged his supporters to send him a "Christian lady" to teach in such a school, which would "effect more for the evangelization of the Spanish population than a direct attempt to introduce the Scriptures among the people generally."[34]

As in contemporary times, Catholics complained of "double taxation," only to be told that they had brought it upon themselves by building parochial schools, that religious instruction should be given at home and church, that public schools cannot accommodate the self-defined needs of every ethnic and religious group, and that only in the public schools could students learn the common culture of America.[35]

Generally, Catholics formed their own schools to ensure their faith's survival, and in the case of Catholic ethnics, to preserve their cultural heritage as well. Every rector and curate knows, wrote one observer, "that the children in the parochial school are the *hope* of the parish; that it is they and not the children educated in public schools, who will be the most exemplary, practical, devout members of the church."[36] Particularly resented were public school use of the Protestant Bible, anti-Catholic and Protestant-slanted textbooks, Protestant prayers and hymns, and exclusion of positive doctrinal religion, which Catholics felt fostered godlessness, infidelity, secularism, and indifferentism.

An eloquent and stinging criticism of Protestant domination of the public schools was made by Archbishop Hughes of New York City when, in 1840, he

asked for public funds for Catholic schools from the New York Board of Alder-
men. After discussing the inaccuracies, biases, and prejudices of public school
materials and lessons, he said:

> Suppose the Presbyterians were in the minority, and Catholics were numeri-
> cally what Protestants are now, and therefore able to decide what lessons these
> children should read in the schools, I ask if the gentlemen would not conceive
> they had reasonable objections if they [Catholics] forced upon them a system
> of education which taught that their denomination, past, present and to come,
> was deceitful. Now take up these books which teach that all is infamous in our
> history. . . . If such a practice were reversed . . . would not Presbyterians have a
> right to complain . . . if we spread before *their* children lessons on the burning
> of Servetus by Calvin, and on the hanging of members of the Society of
> Friends by those who held Calvinistic doctrines? . . . How was it that after the
> Protestant Bible, "without note or comment" came into use, every denomina-
> tion of Protestants in *the whole world* that had the misfortune to be yoked to
> civil power, wielded the sword of persecution, and derived their authority for
> so doing from the naked text.[37]

Though generally supporting the public schools, Protestants did so for varying
reasons: traditional control of educational institutions, anti-Catholicism, opposition to Catholic parochial schools, possession of their own Sunday schools,
differences over the purposes of religious education, and failures of some denominations to establish their own parochial school systems, like Presbyterians
and Episcopalians. To Richard Ognibene, "It was the inability of the denominations to achieve their goals rather than their enthusiastic support that helped to
insure growth and eventual dominance of secular public school systems during
the last third of the nineteenth century."[38]

From the mid-1840s on, increasing numbers of states enacted legislation or
constitutional amendments banning state expenditures for parochial schools,
which affected not only Catholics but also Episcopalians, Lutherans, German
Reformed, Friends, Mennonites, Jews, Methodists, Congregationalists, and Presbyterians who had or tried to establish their own parochial school systems. In the
decades before and after the Civil War, a majority of states had taken steps to
ban such financial aid.[39]

Inherent in these differences was a competition for status. "In my judgment,
the contest is not about religious education at all," noted a lawyer in an 1870
court case initiated by "a temporary coalition of Jews, Catholics, free thinkers,
and a few strong mind[ed] Protestants" who challenged Bible use in the Cincinnati schools, but it is "about denominational supremacy, the right to be higher, to
be better, to be more powerful than your neighbor; the right to say to one: 'You
are nothing but an unbelieving Jew,' and to another, 'You are the slave of a
Roman bishop,' and to both, 'What rights of conscience that a Protestant need to
respect have you?' "[40]

Nevertheless, Catholic leaders and organizations continued to assert their devotion to America, the legality of parochial schools, and the need for public funds to maintain them. To Thomas H. Cummings, a prominent Catholic layman and lecturer, "the best American is he who best exemplifies in his own life, that this is not a Protestant country, nor a Catholic country, nor a Hebrew country, any more than it is an Anglo-Saxon or a Latin country, but a country of all races and all creeds, with one great, broad, unmolturable [sic] creed of fair play and equal rights for all."[41]

To prove they were no less patriotic than Protestants, Catholic parochial schools emphasized the teaching of civic values and Catholic contributions to creating America. "That the Stars and Stripes has not received its glories from Protestants alone," observed the Pittsburgh *Catholic News*, "is a fact that will be duly emphasized in this diocese by the uprearing of the national standard over the parochial schools." America's very discovery was credited to Catholicism, for "it was a Catholic monk who inspired Columbus with hope; it was a Catholic and Catholic crew that first crossed the trackless main; . . . that it was a Catholic queen who rendered the expedition possible; and . . . it was a Catholic whose name has been given to the entire continent."[42]

There were, however, some Catholics who favored the public schools, either for philosophic or economic reasons. Orestes Brownson argued that parochial schools tended to reinforce a separatist mentality, while others claimed that churches and not parochial schools were needed. The Catholic position was not free of its own biases. Association with "Protestants, Jews and Infidels" was opposed. To "sit on the same bench with them and meet them on the playground" would make Catholics lose their sense of piety and become "ashamed of their faith." Parents were told to keep their children away from the public schools. To one Slovak priest, the public schools made "loafers of all girls who attended them," and trade schools were places from which cities got "their vagabonds, suburbs their tramps and murderers and the gallows their offspring."[43]

Catholic nationality churches, too, feared contact with other groups, whether Protestant or Catholic. German immigrants were warned against settling in English-speaking parishes because where no German-speaking priests were present "German Catholics will become indifferent to the Church within a short time and in due course will be even worse than Protestants and pagans."[44]

Many Catholic writers blamed Protestantism for abortion, divorce, women's suffrage, and family breakdowns. The Boston Irish weekly, the *Pilot,* compared "Puritan Massachusetts" with "Catholic Maryland," noting the latter did not have "the blood stained codes, the diabolical treachery, and the savage cruelty which characterized . . . the infamous Puritans . . . whose vices would put the demons to the blush." Were it not for recent immigrants, the paper said, "witches would still be burning on Boston Common."[45]

More pervasive, however, were public school insensitivity and hostility to Catholic educational needs, which contributed to the hierarchy's adopting a policy in 1884 of "every Catholic child in a Catholic school" and the creation of a separate school system. More than ever before, parents in many areas who sent their children to public schools were threatened with denial of the sacraments.[46] To Protestant nativists, such actions were seen as deliberate attempts to weaken the public schools in order to gain more students, and in Boston a coalition of Canadians and native Protestant evangelists sought to purge the public school committee of all Irish Catholics.

With good reasons, Cardinal Gibbons, of Baltimore, wrote Pope Leo XIII that because of the Catholic educational system, Americans had become convinced that "the Catholic Church is opposed by principle to the institutions of the country and that a sincere Catholic cannot be a loyal citizen of the United States."[47]

Jews

Much less heated was the problem of Jews and public education. Numbering less than 25,000 in the 1840s and certainly more secure socially and politically than their kinsmen in Europe, Jews were nevertheless not fully accepted by other Americans and felt uncertain about their children's religious identity, which, like Catholics, they believed was threatened by the public schools' Protestant or secularizing influences. As early as 1843, Jews in New York City futilely objected to the use of the New Testament and other religious textbooks in the public schools.[48]

In Philadelphia, Rabbi Isaac Leeser wrote in the early 1850s that the state should not and could not teach religious morals because of the diversity of beliefs that existed, rejecting any right of the majority to dictate what minorities should believe: "No minority, however insignificant, can fairly be coerced to set aside its own convictions, without submitting thereby to the most galling tyranny. . . . You will then . . . have to conclude, that no State can be required to educate the morals of its members, notwithstanding the great interest it has at stake in the matter. . . . If there were no other party chargeable with this duty, mankind would speedily degenerate."[49]

Jews were also disturbed by Protestant organizational missionizing, which between 1816 and 1820 was largely carried on by the Female Society of Boston and Vicinity for Promoting Christianity amongst the Jews, the American Society for Evangelizing the Jews, and the American Society for Meliorating the Condition of the Jews. From 1870 to 1900, more than 5,000 Jewish baptisms took place, according to one missionary group. To counteract such missionizing among children, the Hebrew Free School Association was spurred into being in 1864.[50] With the beginning of large-scale Jewish immigration, the late-nineteenth-century missionizing efforts were abetted by Jewish converts, who were occasionally attacked by other Jews who recalled the bitter experiences of forced conversions in Europe.

As in the Catholic community, some Jews viewed Christian or Jewish paro-chial school education with disfavor. Isidore Bush, in 1849, urged coreligionists to support as much as possible the public schools and "lend no help whatever to sectarian institutions: *do not send* your children, neither your sons nor your daughters, to such, and don't complain about heavy school taxes; establish no Jewish schools except only the one branch of your religion, history and Hebrew language." Six years later, a Cleveland conference of rabbis formally opposed all-day Jewish schools.[51]

Nevertheless, to growing numbers of Jews, the public schools reflected Amer-ican democracy, bringing together "the children of the rich and poor, high and low, putting the Teuton and the Celt, the Aryan and Semitic, the believer and the unbeliever on the same footing . . . merit alone to win."[52]

Blacks

During the second half of the nineteenth century, Black aspirations for education rose sharply in the North and South, only to be frustrated and suppressed by White society. Free Blacks in the South established schools, funded by contribu-tions, White philanthropy, and Black self-help organizations. The few Protestant missionary educational efforts focused more on convincing slaves to be obedient and trustworthy workers rather than enlightened free Christians. To the *Southern Literary Messenger,* in 1851, "To prevent the general instruction of negroes in the arts of reading and writing" became "a measure of policy essential to the tranquility, nay to the existence of Southern society."[53]

In the North, segregation by law or custom prevailed, with the public schools receiving no or little funding. As the *New York Tribune,* in 1859, editorialized, in schools for Whites "no expenditure is spared to make them commodius and elegant. . . . The schools for the blacks, on the contrary, are nearly all, if not all, old buildings, generally in filthy and degraded neighborhoods, dark, damp, small, and cheerless, safe neither for the morals nor the health of those who are compelled to go to them." More often than not, Black protests about school segregation failed, and by the time of the Civil War most Blacks attended segre-gated public schools. On a college level only a few schools admitted Blacks. Two all-Black colleges were created in the 1850s by church groups—Presbyteri-ans created Ashmun Institute in Pennsylvania for the training of Blacks to be missionaries in Africa and Methodist Episcopal Church North created Wilberforce University in Ohio.[54]

While such segregation and exclusion were taking place, so were vast educa-tional innovations: the rise of land-grant colleges for women, growth of tax-sup-ported high schools and higher education, Indian reservation day schools and off-reservation high schools, separate private and land-grant colleges for Blacks, segregated schools for Asians, and perhaps most significant, compulsory school attendance laws and legislation. The latter were supported by educational reformers as well as bigoted nativists, with the former believing compulsory regulations necessary for the development of loyal, moral, intelligent, and democratic citizens, while nativists viewed them as a way of civilizing inferior immigrants and undermining parochial schools.

After the Civil War, Blacks—young and old—rushed to schools, day, evening, and Sunday. In 1860, there had been only about 4,000 Blacks in slave state schools and about 23,000 in the free state schools. As one Reconstruction-period observer described the educational hunger of Louisiana Blacks:

> When the collection of the general tax for colored schools was suspended in Louisiana by military order, the consternation of the colored population was intense. Petitions began to pour in. I saw one from the plantations across the river, at least thirty feet in length, representing ten thousand negroes. It was affecting to examine it, and note the names and marks (x) of such a long list of parents, ignorant themselves, but begging that their children might be educated; promising that from beneath their present burdens and out of their extreme poverty, they would pay for it.[55]

By 1877, some 600,000 were attending southern elementary and secondary schools, while young adults were enrolling in such colleges and institutions as Fisk, Howard, Hampton, and Atlanta. In some southern areas, more Blacks than Whites attended school. In Florida, not until 1888 did White enrollment exceed that of Blacks, though the latter constituted only 30 percent of the state population. By 1900, Black daily school attendance in Alabama and South Carolina averaged some 62 percent of their total enrollment, in comparison to 66 percent for White children.[56]

As with European immigrants, Blacks in the North and border states utilized and created religious and fraternal organizations to promote the education of their children. One Black minister exhorted a conference in 1884: "We 'who once were not a people' are now a people. The fetters of our captivity have been sundered . . . and education is the necessity of the hour. . . . Ye mothers! Send your boys to school. God wants them there. No matter what your circumstances or conditions, send your children to schools; send them there if they go in rags."[57]

Unfortunately, education was easier wished for than obtained, and when obtained, was not respected. One of the White founders of Hampton Institute believed that though a Black child acquired knowledge just as readily as a White one, "the Negro matures sooner than the white, but does not have his steady development of mental strength up to advanced years. He is a child of the tropics, and the differentiation of races goes deeper than the skin."[58]

Reporting from the South in 1866, Carl Schurz wrote that "the popular prejudice is almost as bitter set against Negro's having the advantage of education as it was when he was a slave. . . . Hundreds of times I have heard the old assertion repeated . . . 'learning will spoil the nigger for work.' Another most singular notion still holds a potent sway over the minds of the masses—it is, that the elevation of the blacks will be the degradation of the whites."[59]

Schoolteachers, particularly northern ones who had gone South to help with the Reconstruction, were subjected to scorn, terror, and violence. One such teacher wrote home, "I habitually received the polite salutation of 'damned Yankee bitch of a nigger teacher,' with the occasional admonition to take up my abode in the infernal regions." The newly formed Ku Klux Klan raged that schoolteachers were teaching political insurrection, integration, and disrespect for Whites. The result was a "veritable reign of terror which saw schools burned and teachers whipped, tortured, murdered and driven out of the state."[60]

With the end of the Reconstruction period, the educational situation of Blacks began declining, as did their newly gained political power. If not by the state legislation, then by local school policy, segregated schools became the norm throughout the South. Moreover, fewer funds were spent on Black schools and colleges than on white ones, and differential pay scales for White and Black teachers came into being.

In the North, anti-Black feelings were less intense, but no less exclusionary. Of greater concern to northern educators and political leaders was the Americanization of immigrants and their children. Blacks were not oblivious to the inferior and invidious treatment they received. When Black parents futilely petitioned the Boston School Committee in 1849 to abolish a fifty-year-old segregated school that they held was a racist "barrier" and "obstacle" to common rights, they pointed out that, though native-born, they were denied privileges granted foreigners.[61]

Anti-Black attitudes and behaviors inevitably resulted in the Supreme Court's enthronement of segregation. First, under the banner of "separate but equal," the Court, in *Plessy* v. *Ferguson,* declared that state legislatures could legally enforce racial segregation because they were "at liberty to act with reference to the established usages, customs, and traditions of the people . . . and the preservation of the public peace and good order."[62] Then, in 1904, in *Berea College* v. *Kentucky,* the Supreme Court ruled that the college had violated the state's law prohibiting racially integrated public or private schools.

Indians

While immigrants were grudgingly Americanized and Blacks firmly segregated, Indians were forcibly Americanized and segregated through relocation, reservation day schools, and off-reservation boarding schools. In 1819, the Congress voted $10,000 annually to hire "capable persons of good moral character" to teach Indians reading, writing, arithmetic, and farming.[63] At the same time, government officials, religious leaders, and assorted humanitarians believed Indians could be civilized by undermining their language, culture, and tribal identities and by teaching them the Protestant ethic of work and profit.

"Instruction of Indians in the vernacular is not only of no use to them," ruled the Bureau of Indian Affairs in 1887, "but is detrimental to the cause of education and civilization and will not be permitted in any Indian school over which the government has any control. . . . This language which is good enough for a white man or a black man ought to be good enough for the red man . . . teaching an Indian youth in his own barbarous dialect is a positive detriment to him. The impracticability, if not impossibility of civilizing Indians . . . in any other tongue but our own would seem obvious."[64]

Such views were reinforced by missionaries. Just as the Spanish in the Southwest, the French in the Northwest, and the Russians in Alaska, Christian missionaries rushed to convert the Indians. "The greatest problem of the missionary," wrote Fermín F. Lasuén in 1801, in California, "was how to transform a savage race such as these into a society that is human, Christian, civil, and industrious."[65]

Indian mission schools were established as far as possible from tribal homelands, and family members were forbidden to visit their children lest they again contaminate them with heathen ways. From 1837 to 1893, the Board of Foreign Missions of the Presbyterian Church in the United States sent more than 400 missionaries to some seventeen different Indian tribes believed depraved, ignorant, and heathen. "*As tribes and nationals the Indians must perish and live only as men!*" wrote a mid-nineteenth-century missionary, who believed Indians should "fall in with *Christian civilization* that is destined to cover the earth."[66]

With equal hubris, missionaries divided Alaska, with Presbyterians on the north coast, Catholics in the Yukon River area, Moravians in the Bethel region, and other groups elsewhere. At the same time, government began issuing laws banning all Indian ceremonies believed pagan and detrimental to the spread of Christianity.[67]

From an Indian perspective, the actual behaviors of the White men were more evident than their avowed ethics. One Alaskan Tlingit Indian chief noted that "the missionaries and teachers tell us that no one but God make[s] the people. We know that the same God made us. And the God placed us here. White people are smart; our people are not as smart as white people. . . . They have the power. They have men of wars. It is not right for such powerful people as you are to take away from poor people like we are, our creeks and hunting grounds."[68]

Chinese, Japanese, and Other Asians

Totally unwanted were the Chinese and Japanese, particularly on the West Coast, where most of them lived. It was not enough to stop their immigration to America and to deny resident Asians citizenship, but their children, as with Blacks, were not allowed to attend schools with Caucasian children. In 1885, the California legislature empowered school boards to "exclude all children of filthy or vicious habits, children suffering from contagious diseases, and also to establish separate schools for Indian children, and for the children of Mongolian [Japanese] and Chinese descent. When such separate schools are established children must not be admitted into any other schools." In the same year, the Supreme Court upheld Mississippi's right to prohibit a Chinese student from attending an all-White school. The Court ruled that just as the establishment of schools for Whites and Blacks were within the discretion of the state and not violative of the Fourteenth Amendment so for "white pupils and the pupils of the yellow race."[69]

When in 1906 the San Francisco Board of Education ordered all Japanese and Korean pupils to join Chinese ones in one Asian school, it almost caused an international scandal. The order was revoked only through the intercession of President Roosevelt, who feared a possible diplomatic break with Japan, though he favored restricting Japanese immigration. The school board's rationale was that "our children should not be placed in any position where their youthful impressions may be affected by association with pupils of the Mongolian race." A connection between anti-Asian and anti-Black feeling was made clear when the Congress discussed the school board's order. Southern senators and representatives generally supported it. "I stand with the State of California in opposition to mixed schools," said one Mississippi legislator. "I stand with Californians in favor of the proposition that we want a homogeneous and assimilable population of the white people in the Republic."[70] Although Indian children were allowed to attend any school they wanted in 1921, just as Blacks had been some years earlier, Chinese and Japanese schoolchildren had to wait until 1929, when the California school system ended its discriminatory practices.

On the college level, subtler forms of discrimination continued. As small numbers of Asian and Filipino students came to further their education and then return home, they were frequently denied rental rooms in private homes and YMCA dormitories. Some students from India were even denied cafeteria service at the University of California at Berkeley. As late as the 1930s, Japanese and Chinese college students, though they had excellent records, were advised by counselors not to enter certain professions, such as teaching, because prevailing racist policies excluded their being hired.[71]

The Pains of Immigrant Acculturation

By the end of the nineteenth century, some thirty-one states had adopted compulsory attendance laws, swelling school enrollments, which went from some 6.5 million in 1870 to 15.5 million in 1880 and then to some 21.5 million. Almost all the states that had not passed compulsory attendance laws were southern, border, or southwestern. "There is no doubt that in the Southern States," wrote Frank Ross, "the presence of Negroes in large numbers was a strong deterrent to the enactment of compulsory education laws in those States. It is not due purely to chance that of the 16 States (excluding the District of Columbia) popularly considered Southern, none had enacted such legislation prior to 1893 and only 3 prior to 1905."[72]

The typical child attended school for five years, and strange as it may seem today, America was considered the world's leader in mass education. By 1911, 57.5 percent of children in the public schools of thirty-seven of the largest cities were of foreign-born parents. The task of educating new immigrants had become much more difficult than in previous decades because of their increasing numbers and diverse religious, ethnic, and national backgrounds. According to the 1910 census figures, nearly 3 million of the almost 13 million foreign-born residents over ten years of age could not speak English.[73]

Immigration statistics beclouded the existence of ethnic groups that had more children than others, with varying ratios of children to adults. For example, from 1899 to 1910, the average percentage of children below fourteen years of age for Jewish immigrants was 24.9 percent, for Poles 9.5 percent, Magyars 8.8 percent, Russians 7.5 percent, and Romanians 2.2 percent. Such differences were not solely due to differential reproduction rates but also to emigration patterns, in which some immigrants came as families while others (usually males) came as advance settlers who eventually brought over their wives, children, or parents. For instance, in the 1820s, 80 percent of all immigrants were males. More specifically, in 1920, there were more than four times as many Greek male immigrants as female ones, and among Bulgarians, the ratio was higher—ten males for every female immigrant. The principal exception were the Irish, among whom for every 78 males who arrived there were 100 females.[74]

For many immigrant children, particularly those who did not have to work, the school was their first confrontation with America. As one of them later wrote in 1918:

> Although almost five years now had passed since I had started for America it was only now that I caught a glimpse of it. For though I was in America I had lived in practically the same environment which we brought from home. Of course there was a difference in our joys, our sorrows, in our hardships, for after all this was a different country; but on the whole we were still in our village in Russia. A child that came to this country and began to go to school had taken the first step into the New World. But the child that was put into the shop remained in the old environment with the old people, held back by the old traditions, held back by illiteracy. Often it was years before he could stir away from it, sometimes it would take a life time.[75]

Then, as now, a generation and culture gap developed between immigrants and their children, which presented enormous problems in the Americanizing of both groups. "Too often," wrote one educator, "we find that the cause of disrupted immigrant homes is due to the fact that the parents do not understand nor sympathize with their children who have been remolded in our public schools. Children become ashamed of their parents' ways and lose the proper respect for them. Quarrels ensue and the older boys and girls leave home to work in the mill or factory."[76]

The Norwegian author Ole Rolvaag, in 1922, noted how the children of Norwegian immigrants came to believe that "all that has grown on American earth is good, but all that can be called *foreign* is at best suspect. . . . Under such conditions how could anyone expect that young people should show only enthusiasm for their forefathers' tongue—that would be to expect the impossible." Similarly, as a ten-year-old growing up in Arizona, the famed New York City mayor Fiorello La Guardia recalled how his friends reacted to the coming of an Italian organ-grinder with a monkey: " 'A dago with a monkey! Hey Fiorello, you're a dago too. Where's your monkey?' It hurt. And what made it worse, along came Dad, and he started to chatter Neapolitan with the organ-grinder. . . . The kids taunted me for a long time after that."[77]

A few educators grasped the complexity of the strained relations between parents and children, and between both and the native-born generation of Americans. The schools, it was felt, had to somehow build bridges between the immigrant's European and American experiences. With great insight, Jane Addams in 1910 wrote that "I meditated that perhaps the power to see life as a whole, is more needed in the immigrant quarter of a large city than anywhere else, and that the lack of this power is the most fruitful source of misunderstanding between European immigrants and their children, as it is between them and their American neighbors; and why should that chasm between fathers and sons, yawning at the feet of each generation, be made so unnecessarily cruel and impassable to these bewildered immigrants?" The answer, she believed, was in operationalizing John Dewey's "continuing reconstruction of experience" and in Goethe's reverence of the past as the basis of all sound progress.[78]

Though young Abe Lincoln could be portrayed studying in front of a fireplace in a log cabin, immigrant children studied—or did not study—in much more crowded and difficult conditions. Lincoln, at the least, heard English spoken all about him. This was not so with the massive numbers of immigrants.

To an 1861 visitor to our large cities, the immigrants had created "distinct communities, almost as impervious to American sentiments and influences as are the inhabitants of Dublin or Hamburg. . . . They have their own theaters, recreations, amusements, military, and national organizations; to a great extent their own schools, churches and trade unions; their own newspapers and periodical literature." Some states, too, had a decidedly ethnic character. Norwegians, Swedes, and Danes flocked to the Dakota Territory and Minnesota, where by 1890 some 400 cities had Swedish names, and in Dakota it was said to be easier to make friends if one spoke Norwegian rather than English.[79]

It was primarily in schools and government offices that they encountered English. Though the Constitution had never mandated it as the official language of the country, Congress on four occasions required its use in public schools and legislatures as a condition for statehood—Louisiana and its large Spanish and French population, New Mexico and Arizona and their Spanish population, and Oklahoma with its large Indian population. For example, when Louisiana was admitted in 1812, the Enabling Act stipulated that its judicial and legislative proceedings be conducted "in the language in which the laws and the judicial and legislative written procedures of the United States are now published and conducted." In 1912, New Mexico's constitution required that laws be issued in both English and Spanish for twenty years and that teachers be trained in both languages.[80]

Whether in the slums of Chicago, New York, Boston, Pittsburgh, or Washington, D.C., report after report in the mid-nineteenth and early-twentieth centuries found overcrowding, unsanitary conditions, crime, disease, high death rates, and struggling immigrants. Typhoid, diarrhea, and cholera periodically erupted in cities with large immigrant populations. For example, in one Chicago neighborhood, in 1851, a cholera epidemic killed 332 Scandinavians, mostly Norwegians. In New York, in the 1850s, 85 percent of those admitted to Bellevue Hospital were Irish, and in poorhouses across the country, the foreign-born outnumbered the native-born. By 1900, two-thirds of Chicago's streets were still unpaved, as were most of Baltimore's and New Orleans'; over one-third of the streets in Philadelphia, St. Louis, and Atlanta had no underground sewers. Death rates in the cities were 20 percent higher than in rural areas.[81]

The living conditions of a few cities are worth looking at a little closer in order to appreciate the dire conditions under which immigrant children went to school and to understand how, for the most part, they far surpassed educationally their parents and, at the least, equaled the educational achievement of the children of native-born Americans. Moreover, they illustrate the hardships that eastern and southern European immigrant parents overcame in their socioeconomic rise within a single generation, even if it was mainly within the working class.[82]

In mid-nineteenth-century New York City, "Typical of overcrowded cellars was a house on Pike Street which contained a cellar ten feet square and seven feet high, with one small window and an old-fashioned inclined cellar door; here lived two families consisting of ten persons of all ages. Rain water leaked through cracks in the walls and floors and frequently flooded the cellars; refuse filtered down from the upper stories and mingled with the seepage from outdoor privies." Similarly, in one Boston neighborhood, "the situation of the Irish . . . is particularly wretched. . . . This whole district is a perfect hive of human beings, without comforts and mostly without common necessaries; in many cases, huddled together like brutes, without regard to sex, or age, or sense of decency; grown men and women sleeping together in the same apartment, and sometimes wife and husband, brothers and sisters, in the same bed."[83]

Living conditions in smaller cities were no better, according to a 1911 Immigration Commission report. "A comparison of the conditions in a great city like New York or Chicago with those in some of the smaller industrial centers such as mining and manufacturing towns shows that average conditions as regards overcrowding are very materially worse in some of the small industrial towns."[84]

Immigrants then, as many Blacks, Asians, and Spanish-speaking people today, were blamed for the conditions under which they lived, as if poverty and dilapidation had not existed before their arrival. As one early-nineteenth-century Romanian immigrant wrote: "The slums are emphatically not of our making. So far is the immigrant from being accustomed to such living that the first thing that repels him on his arrival in New York is the realization of the dreadful level of life to which his fellows have sunk. And when by sheer use he comes to accept these conditions himself, it is with something of a fantastic resignation to the idea that such is America."[85]

Whatever the conditions of the neighborhood, it was there that churches, social and fraternal organizations, political clubs, friends and family, and ethnic newspapers and leaders helped immigrants acculturate. In recording his impressions of Catholic immigration at the turn of the century, Abbé Felix Klein praised the church's numerous schools, asylums, orphanages, hospitals, clubhouses, refuges, and good works. "If the Church had not been on hand to receive them," he wrote, "to watch over them, to offer them some sort of moral refuge, to teach their children religion, and at the same time the English language and American customs, one could hardly view without dismay the possible misery and crime to come from this ignorant and abandoned multitude."[86]

The neighborhood was both a receiving station from the Old World and a transmitting station for the New World. "It was an institution of Americanization from which immigrants could begin to find their way into the political, economic, social, and educational life of the new country, not as isolated individuals but as members of a strong, supportive community, strongly committed (perhaps implicitly) to the pluralistic notion that anyone could become an American, and it was not necessary to give up one's traditional loyalties, heritage, family or church in the process."[87] In the post–World War II years, the ethnic neighborhood was to prove a "departure station," which many second and third generations left as they rose educationally, socially, and economically.

The Arrogance and Prejudice of Education

For all their differences in reproduction rates, cultural inheritances, occupational backgrounds, and attitudes toward education, significant numbers of yesteryear's immigrants and their children sought and utilized educational institutions—public and private—without the benefit of elective courses, open campus, or parental participation. More often than not, immigrant parents were unable to help their children with school lessons, unless translated into their native language, and even then, standard subjects like American history and civics were outside their experience.

That schools were insensitive and bigoted is true enough. Immigrant students had to confront the arrogance of many teachers, educators, and scholars who began differentiating between the educable (native-born, middle-class, and upper-class students) and the uneducable (immigrants, Blacks, Indians, and His-panics). The solution was to adopt a philosophy of "differential education" and "social efficiency," and to establish a system of vocational schools and courses in which students were taught subjects in keeping with their "probable destiny." For immigrants and racial minorities this meant learning how to be law abiding, tractable, unskilled laborers. For the masses of White working-class students, it meant training for supervisory and managerial positions. And for the economi-cally better off, it meant preparation for college. The desired destiny for girls was to be good housekeepers and mothers.

All students, it was believed, could not and should not be equally schooled, particularly since some seemed to prefer truancy, fighting, and vandalizing school property (which some did). As Dean James Earl Russell, of Teacher's College in New York City, asked a 1908 National Education Association sympo-sium: "How can a nation endure that deliberately seeks to rouse ambitions and aspirations in the oncoming generations which in the nature of events cannot possibly be fulfilled? If the chief object of government be to promote civil order and social stability, how can we justify our practice in schooling the masses in precisely the same manner as we do those who are to be our leaders."[88]

Invidious distinctions were made between Whites and Blacks, native- and foreign-born, and among all groups. The less Teutonic or Anglo-Saxon, the worse they were considered educationally and the more unwelcome they were to American shores and schools. Substantiating such beliefs were a profusion of pseudo-scientific books and studies. Lothrop Stoddard was not alone in believing in an "Iron Law of Inequality," whereby Americans of northern European de-scent were racially superior, while those from southern and eastern Europe were "decidedly inferior," with Blacks the most inferior of all. Psychologist and eu-genicist Henry Herbert Goddard found that "feeblemindedness" existed among 87 percent of Russians, 83 percent of Jews, 80 percent of Hungarians, and 79 percent of Italians entering Ellis Island. In Professor Lewis Terman's *The Mea-surement of Intelligence,* published in 1916, it was argued that because of their low IQ scores, Indian, Mexican, and Black children were genetically dull and should be sent to special segregated classes to learn "concrete and practical" subjects.[89]

Even American-born children of immigrants were suspect. Francis Amasa Walker, the first president of the American Economic Association, considered second-generation Irish and German Americans as "home-made foreigners." "So separate has been their social life, due alike to their clannishness and to our reserve," he wrote in the 1870s, "so strong have been the ties of race and blood and religion with them; so acute has been the jealousy of their spiritual teachers towards our popular institutions—that we speak of them, and we think of them, as foreigners."[90]

To many leading academics and intellectuals, about the only group worthy of assimilation was the British. All others were to varying degrees of lesser psychological, sociological, and biological breeds. The poverty and illiteracy of Mexican Americans were blamed on their passivity, indolence, and hatefulness. Scandinavian students—Swedish, Norwegian, and Danish—were considered "plodders." French Canadians were deemed "shiftless, unmechanical and unreliable." Though of Teutonic roots, Germans were thought to be phlegmatic and too given to drinking beer and material matters. The Irish were irresponsible, lacking seriousness, and degenerate, due to their "low stage of social development." Though Armenians and Englishmen were Christians, they were not "members of the same race and upholders of the same ideals of society." If Jewish students were doing well in school, wrote Burton Hendrick, it was only because they were "more industrious" and "work six hours at their studies where 'American' children work two or three."[91]

Students were not oblivious to such views and the behaviors they bred. Recalling his grammar school days in the early 1900s, Bagdasar Krekor Baghdigian described how a teacher asked his name and he volunteered to write it because it was "a hard name," after which she advised him to change it to "Smith, Jones or a name like that and become Americanized. Give up everything you brought with you from the Old Country. You did not bring anything worth while anyway." Victor Wong recalled how in the 1920s teachers "didn't believe in Chinese customs" and discouraged students from speaking Cantonese. "Their view of Chinese ways was that they were evil, heathen, non-Christian."[92]

Problems of schooling were compounded not only by high rates of truancy, dropouts, and shortages of classroom space and buildings, particularly in large cities, but also by the cultural values, social class, and economic pressures of parents, many of whom did not believe a high school or college education necessary or felt that the family's economic needs were more important. In the early twentieth century, though 90 percent of New York's annual school population were registered in elementary school, only 4.7 to 6.6 percent were registered on the high school level. Moreover, of all students attending high school in 1910, 30 percent dropped out before graduating.[93]

Children, particularly girls, were often kept out of school to help meet family living costs, do household chores, or care for sick family members. In New England, a 1905 study of cotton mill workers revealed that French Canadian children contributed one-third of the family income and Irish children contributed 45 percent.[94]

Many an immigrant, particularly Polish, Italian, and Jewish, believed that educating daughters beyond twelve or thirteen years old would impair their chances of getting married and, when married, serve little purpose. Among the Irish, however, more nineteenth-century girls than boys attended public and parochial schools and for longer periods (whereas in Ireland it was the opposite), thereby facilitating their entering professions, particularly schoolteaching and nursing.[95]

Differential ethnic rates of attendance, particularly for those over eleven years old, also prevailed. A study of Chicago public and nonpublic schools in 1900 revealed that almost 50 percent of Russian, Bohemian, and Polish children either attended irregularly or not at all; Irish and Germans had moderately good attendance rates, and Scandinavians and children of native-born Americans had the best rates.[96]

"We were five children at the time and my step-mother," recalled a Jewish immigrant. "We came to McKeesport in 1900 when I was sixteen years old. There was no place for me to go to school. Besides, I had to stay home and help with the work in a cigar factory. I learned how to speak a little English, very poorly. I can't write well, and I can't read the newspaper in English." Humberto Cardinal Medeiros, of Boston, remembered how as a fifteen-year-old immigrant from the Azores he, his mother, two brothers, and sister joined his father in Massachusetts. "It was the height of the depression and Fall River ... was suffering the decline of its textile industry. . . . In spite of obvious difficulties, my family believed, and I believed along with them, that this was still the land of opportunity. It was in January 1935 that my father was able to allow me to enter high school—I was almost twenty years old—so that I could begin the long preparation for the priesthood."[97]

Just as there were differences between groups, so within them. Children of laborers were more likely than those of the middle class to abort schooling. In pre–World War II decades, children of German laborers in Milwaukee had lower years of attendance than those of the total German population. Most Italian youths completing high school in Philadelphia in the 1920s had parents who were professionals—businessmen, doctors, lawyers, and so forth. Texas Hispanics organized for equal schooling in 1929 after the middle-class League of United Latin Americans was formed.[98]

Children were often absent because of illness or hunger. A 1917 study of Gary, Indiana, students revealed that Poles, Slovaks, Serbs, and Croats had the highest percentage with inadequate breakfasts and lunches, and the rate for Polish students was twice that of Blacks. Unlike today, there were no relatively quick cures for tonsillitis, adenoids, or infected teeth, which kept students out of school for extended periods. Undernourishment was common among the poor, as was school overcrowding. Those unable to speak English were put into classes with younger, native-born ones; then, as their command of English grew, they were transferred to classes with students closer to their age. At times, because of overcrowding and doubts about the educability of immigrant children, school personnel and politicians encouraged students to leave. For example, in 1912, the Chicago Board of Education opposed amending the state's compulsory education law to prohibit employment of children at fourteen years of age.[99]

Immigrant children also had to cope with teaching materials saturated with racial, religious, and ethnic stereotypes. Even immigrants from England felt demeaned, as when one student, after learning about the American Revolution, told his Yorkshire father, "You had the king's army, and we were only a lot of farmers, but *we* thrashed you!"[100]

In her study of nineteenth-century American schoolbooks, Ruth Miller Elson amply documented what was taught about various groups in America and abroad. The superiority of White people was taken for granted, not only because they were considered physically beautiful but also genetically, intellectually, and morally superior to all other groups. The darker the skin, the weaker the intellect. Ergo, Blacks were characterized as gay, thoughtless, unintelligent, subject to violent passions, and "the least of all races." Africa was a "country of monsters," where people lived in "a state of low barbarism."[101]

If American Indians were sometimes credited with being brave, they were usually faulted for being warlike, fond of cruelty, and having "little capacity for civilization." Textbooks frequently illustrated Indians mistreating Whites, particularly a fierce Indian about to tomahawk a White mother clutching her baby. Jews were portrayed as peddlers, stingy and greedy, and schoolbooks were filled with theological and social anti-Semitism. If at times Jewish monotheism was praised, it was only when compared to polytheistic societies. When compared to Christianity, Judaism was condemned for having rejected Christ and Christianity. The Irish were a threat to America because of their Catholicism, poverty, and readiness to work for low wages. One textbook portrayed them as "an ignorant, uncivilized, blundering sort of people, impatient of abuse and injury; implacable, and violent in their affections."[102]

Though Lafayette was considered a hero, the French were not well regarded because of their Catholicism and prevalence of atheists in the French Revolution. Oftentimes they were invidiously compared to the English, who were adjudged better in commerce and agriculture. With few exceptions, said one book, settlers in New France were "unprogressive peasants or reckless adventurers . . . averse to labor."[103]

Although Italy and Greece were recognized for their contributions to the arts, textbooks put a great emphasis on their decline, describing Italians as affable, superstitious, revengeful, effeminate, and immoral. Spain and Portugal were said to be in a state of decline. In Asia, human nature languished. The Chinese were deceitful and cunning: "The most dishonest, low, thieving people in the world; it is a maxim that none but the Chinese can cheat a Chinese."[104]

In spite of the above stereotypes, growing numbers of educators, social workers, clergymen, and political leaders believed in the public school's power to enlighten. "Educate the rising generation mentally, morally, physically, just as it should be done," said Senator Henry Blair in 1882, "and this nation and this world would reach the millennium within one hundred years."[105]

So confident was Professor Edward Thorndike in 1911 in the advancing "sciences of human nature and its work in the industries, professions and trades" that he predicted "the average graduate of Teachers College in 1950 ought to be able to give better advice to a high school boy about the choice of an occupation than Solomon, Socrates, and Benjamin Franklin all together could give."[106]

A deepening awareness that immigrant children required special attention also took place. As early as 1897, in an address to the National Educational Association, Jane Addams criticized the isolation of school from the realities of urban ghetto life. In speaking of the Italian child, she said:

> Too often the teacher's conception of her duty is to transform him into an American of a somewhat snug and comfortable type, and she insists that the boy's powers must at once be developed in an abstract direction, quite ignoring the fact that his parents have had to do only with tangible things. She has little idea of the development of Italian life. Her outlook is national and not racial, and she fails, therefore, not only in knowledge of, but also in respect for, the child and his parents. She quite honestly estimates the child upon an American basis. The contempt for the experiences and languages of their parents which foreign children sometimes exhibit, and which is most damaging to their moral as well as intellectual life, is doubtless due in part to the overestimation which the school places upon speaking and reading in English. This cutting into his family loyalty takes away one of the most conspicuous and valuable traits of the Italian child.[107]

Some teachers actually developed curriculums fostering intercultural understanding. In the mid-1920s, a Chicago syllabus stated "every race strain found in our citizenship has contributed much to the agricultural, artistic, commercial, industrial, material, moral, political, and scientific advancement of America"; in a Toledo junior high school, more than a dozen junior and senior high school students participated in a year-long ethnic studies project. In the Midwest, Scandinavian and Czech pressure resulted in many state universities establishing courses on their respective culture.[108]

Intellectuals and academics such as Charles W. Eliot, Emily G. Balch, William James, and Edward Everett Hale were also optimistic. Eliot stated that it was easy "for people whose forefathers came to this western world one or more generations ago to believe that the people who have just come are the source of all municipal woes," but if the "American race" was in decline, it was not the fault of immigrants, but "its own shortcomings." Emily Balch criticized many of her contemporaries for being "charity scholars—beneficiaries of those who have worked before us. That we are not dirty, cruel, stupid, cave dwellers is due to the efforts of others."[109]

Moreover, a few states passed legislation allowing the use of a foreign language in classroom instruction when requested by a given number of parents: Kansas in 1867 allowed instruction in German; Colorado in 1908 permitted it in German and Spanish; and Nebraska in 1913 did so for any European language. Some ethnic groups pressed for changes in educational materials, which they felt were too pro-British and oblivious to their own group's contributions to America and world civilization. Such beliefs led to the creation of ethnic historical organizations, such as the Huguenot Society in 1883, the Holland Society in 1885, and the Scotch-Irish History Society and the German-American Historical Society in 1897.

Immigrant Desires for Schooling

In spite of the bigotry, miserable living conditions, and difficulties in earning a living, many immigrants hungered for schooling, though to varying degrees and for various reasons: to hasten their adjustment to a new environment; to obtain, hold, or improve their jobs; to maximize chances of self-sufficiency or wealth; to gain status among kinsmen; to prove to themselves that they could learn; to take advantage of a free education; to escape the drudgery of work or home life; to learn about the country in which they now lived; to start the process of becoming a citizen; to resume studies neglected or started back home; and even to keep up with their children. For some, being strangers and ridiculed simply increased their desire to maintain their identity and to attend school. Race prejudice, said one second-generation Japanese student, "is producing an unusual phenomenon . . . an educated class . . . the like of which is not duplicated anywhere else in the world."[110]

In cities with large immigrant populations, night classes were organized, often at the request of immigrants, as when some sixty-six Lithuanians petitioned the city fathers of Melrose Park, Illinois, "to install a free night school in our locality for the purpose of the education of the Lithuanian-American citizens in the English language." In 1904, young Slavs in Pennsylvania's mining towns rushed to private night schools because the public schools would enroll only those under twenty years of age. In Chicago, during the 1907–08 school term, one out of five Greeks attended evening school, and from 1902 to 1922, Greeks were the seventh largest ethnic group enrolled in the city's evening programs.[111]

Instead of conforming to the prevailing negative stereotypes, immigrants increasingly thought of themselves and particularly their children as Americans, an identity encouraged by ethnic associations, religious groups, social reformers, assorted patriots, and business and industry. The Pittsburgh section of the National Council of Jewish Women, in 1899, inaugurated English and citizenship classes at a local synagogue, where morning and evening classes were held. Czech organizations published English grammars and dictionaries and urged community leaders to learn English and take an active part in all civic activities.[112]

For Christ, conversion, and country, religious groups reached out to the new immigrants. The Woman's Home Mission of the Methodist Episcopal Church South established an education department in 1892, opening schools for Cuban and Italian workers in Florida and night schools for Japanese and Chinese in California, where English and love of Jesus were taught. The YMCA began immigrant evening classes in 1907, and three years later, the YWCA originated International Institutes to provide English classes, recreational activities, and various other immigrant services; by the mid-1920s, there were some fifty-five Institutes across the country.[113]

Old-line patriotic organizations like the National Society of Colonial Dames of America and the National Society of the Sons of the American Revolution published tracts and educational materials for immigrants and sponsored patriotic lectures and classes. Chapters of the Daughters of the American Revolution offered foreign-language lectures on American history, utilizing stereopticon slides; in Buffalo such programs attracted audiences of nearly 600 Poles.[114]

Ethnic newspapers encouraged readers to learn English and become naturalized citizens. The editor of Chicago's *L'Italia* told readers to "make their homes and raise their children in the United States" and the sooner they became citizens, the better. To the Armenian *Gotchag,* "the key to success and leaving the factory" was by attending school and talking with "Americans, by reading papers and copying words."[115]

Stoyan Christowe, a Bulgarian, reflected the passion of many immigrants to learn English: "I never threw away a package, a can or a box without reading whatever labels were pasted upon them. . . . The words that were unfamiliar to me I wrote on small square pieces of paper in red or green pencil. These I tacked to the walls of the bunk until every available inch of space was covered. In whatever direction I looked I saw words. Every week or so I went along the walls and culled out the words that had become familiar and friendly to make room for new and strange ones."[116]

Some older immigrants sought an education after a ten-or-more-hour workday. For working women and mothers, learning meant neglecting or adding to countless household chores, such as preparing meals, cleaning dishes, and washing clothes. Their fatigue was made all the more debilitating by inadequate school facilities. A 1912 observer found in a New England town, "a Hungarian, six feet tall and weighing two hundred pounds, was put in a combination desk, suited for a child of twelve years."[117]

A New York City reform-minded evening school teacher warned in 1916 that unless improvements were made before the fall school opening, "the immigrants will be pushed into school benches intended for eight-year-old children, their knees reaching to the very desks. They will be uncomfortable and sorely puzzled. . . . After a while, the teacher will become capricious and unduly exacting. The students will lose heart. . . . One by one they will cease to come until barely a third of the original number is left."[118]

Although large numbers of adults enrolled in classes, most did not complete their courses, either because of the difficulty in learning after a long day's work, poor school conditions, or inexperienced or insensitive teachers. To Professor Alexander Petrunkevitch of Yale, in 1920, night schools for immigrants were of little help: "The Russian workman has first to learn English before he can understand instruction in other subjects; but even in this, he becomes quickly discouraged. He is a stranger to the teacher, who does not take into account his peculiar psychology. A few days, perhaps a few weeks of most strenuous work in the evening after the day's work at the factory, and the Russian workman gives up in despair."[119]

More successful were the children, who for the most part had opportunities for educational advancement and social positions denied them in their ancestral homelands. It was not unusual for parents who could not learn English to insist their children do so. With an education, particularly a high school diploma, children would earn more money than the parents did and at the least, not have to labor in difficult and dangerous jobs. White-collar jobs meant status and could be obtained in offices, stores, and civil service. Moreover, having an education meant being a real American and winning the respect of others. Without one, wrote a mid-nineteenth-century Norwegian American editor, children would continue to be "strangers and foreigners" and "hewers of wood and drawers of water all their days." Armenian parents often warned their children, "Don't be ignorant like me—get an education and be a man." Japanese parents admonished children to always "obey your teacher, she is always right."[120]

The Americanization Crusade

While many immigrants hungered for education and schools sluggishly responded, private and public group efforts to Americanize them reached an apex in the post–World War I years, motivated by a constellation of political, economic, social, and religious factors about what America is and should become. To evangelical Christians, Americanization was synonymous with Protestantization.

School-business cooperation was evident in the early 1900s. Good citizens made for good workers—and good workers, good citizens. Lowell, Massachusetts, established evening schools for immigrants under twenty-one years old who could not read or write English. Some employers distributed school attendance cards, which had to be validated weekly. "The withdrawal of this card" wrote an early scholar of Greek immigration, "is the severest punishment in vogue in the night schools, and the mere threat of such an action is usually sufficient to secure obedience."[121]

Chicago's assistant superintendent of schools, in 1919, stressed the need for help by the business world, telling a national Americanization Conference that "if the employers representing the dominant industries in any industrial city remain indifferent as to whether or not the foreign-born men in their employ know the English language, it requires extraordinary effort on the part of other agencies of the community to get them started in learning English."[122]

Industry, however, had more than a patriotic interest. Americanization was believed profitable. The more immigrants understood English, the easier they would operate factory machinery efficiently, increase production, and reduce absenteeism and industrial accidents. Thus, just before World War I, the International Harvester Corporation prepared a brochure to help Polish workers learn English, which had as its first lesson the following passage:

> I hear the whistle. I must hurry.
> I hear the five minute whistle.
> It is time to go into the shop.

> I take my check from the gate board and hang it on
> 　　the department board.
> I change my clothes and get ready to work.
> The starting whistle blows.
> I eat my lunch.
> It is forbidden to eat until then.
> The whistle blows at five minutes of starting time.
> I get ready to go to work.
> I work until the whistle blows to quit.
> I leave my place nice and clean.
> I put all my clothes in the locker.
> I must go home.[123]

Other industries established libraries and English classes, and provided medical advice on how to safeguard their health. The Goodyear Tire and Rubber Company instituted an employee representative plan in which only workers who had become citizens could vote. One of the most extensive educational efforts was by the Ford Motor Company, in which workmen representing more than fifty different nationalities spoke over a hundred different languages and dialects. "Our great aim," said one Ford official, "is to impress these men that they are, or should be, Americans, and that former racial, national, and linguistic differences are to be forgotten." Ford established a school for foreign employees, who had to attend before and after work for two days a week. The first thing taught was how to say "I am a good American."[124]

Various studies showed that those who did not know English were injured more often and more seriously than those who did. At one factory in which immigrants represented 34 percent of the workers, they were involved in 80 percent of the accidents. "We attacked this by organizing a fellowship club with over 1,000 members," said the employer. "At the meetings the men all get together and the aliens quickly learn English. Our percentage of accidents among foreign workers is steadily decreasing and we count on an even better showing in the future."[125]

Also influencing Americanization were labor unions, at least those that admitted immigrants as members. Immigrants learned that by organizing with others—immigrant or native-born—they could obtain higher wages, reduce working hours, improve safety conditions, and protect themselves from being unfairly dismissed. In 1904, the first commissioner of the Bureau of Labor wrote that when the immigrant learns that the union wants to help and protect him, he "begins to see the necessity of learning the English language, of understanding the institutions he hears talked about in the union meetings, and other matters which interest him."[126]

A few years later, a scholar praised the union's Americanization process as seeking to

> create discontent with low wages and low standards of living, and [a belief
> that] Americanization can only come to the low-standard-of-living immigrant

worker as his wages are increased and his standard of living raised. . . . The union teaches self-government. . . . The immigrant learns to remedy grievances through the use of the ballot. . . . The union gives the immigrant the sense of a common cause and of a public interest. . . . Different nationalities are thrown into a common group, and they soon adopt a common way of thinking and acting. . . . Foreigners are thrown into intimate contact with those who have partially adopted American customs and ideals. . . . Unions usually require members to be citizens . . . or to have declared their intention to become citizens. . . . The union raises the wages of the immigrant, shortens his working day, and improves his working conditions. . . . It reduces the feeling of antagonism often existing between different nationalities.[127]

After World War I, Americanization took another sharp xenophobic turn as fears grew of foreigners, revolution, ethnic reactions to the Versailles Treaty and League of Nations, and political and labor activists. If immigration could not be stopped totally, it should be restricted. Those who would not avail themselves of an American education should be compelled to do so, particularly in the large cities, where, according to the deputy commissioner of naturalization, in 1916, "Vice grows. . . . There the influence of foreign sovereignties, institutions, ideas, and ideals are strongest."[128]

Across the country, foreigners and foreign languages, particularly German, were branded un-American. Theodore Roosevelt believed it "a crime to perpetuate differences of languages in this country" and proposed that if after five years an immigrant "hadn't mastered English," he should "be sent back to the land from whence he came." Dozens of states passed laws requiring English in all public and private school instruction. Iowa's governor banned foreign languages in schools, church services, public conversations—and on the phone. In many New England parochial schools, laws were passed restricting or excluding the use of French, except in specific foreign-language classes. In one Maine town, both teachers and students were prohibited from using French even during recess periods. Hawaii's legislature imposed harsh regulations and restrictions on private schools teaching Japanese, Chinese, or Korean, including a requirement that schools pay a fee of one dollar per student for a permit to teach foreign languages.[129]

Just as many states and cities refused to hire aliens or denied them licenses for various professions and jobs, so with private employers, who hired only citizens and those who had filed to become such, or if they had to reduce personnel, fired first those who had not become citizens. The Delaware Americanization Committee, in 1921, reported being "besieged by men and women who want to become citizens, and incidentally voters, not because they have learned to love this country better than any other in the world," but because would-be patriotic employers would not otherwise employ them.[130]

Notwithstanding these conditions, the vast majority of children attended elementary schools for at least some period of time. High schools, colleges, and night schools became increasingly available, and new forms of education emerged, such as junior high schools and junior colleges. By 1918, compulsory elementary education became a right and obligation. The 1920 census reported that of children between the ages of seven and fifteen at least 67 percent of Indians, 70 percent of Blacks, and 85 percent of Chinese and Japanese were attending school and doing so for longer periods of time. Though most states required 135 days of school attendance in 1890, the amount increased to 170 days by 1930. Compulsory attendance laws, however, were not self-enforcing, as seen in the prevalence of child labor, which in 1920 involved a million children between the ages of ten and fifteen.[131]

At the same time, the courts defended the rights of parents to have their children educated in private schools, as well as study foreign languages. In 1923, the Supreme Court, in *Meyer* v. *Nebraska,* denied the constitutionality of laws and statutes banning or restricting foreign-language instruction. Four years later, in *Farnington* v. *Tokushige,* the Court unanimously declared unconstitutional Hawaii's attempts to regulate private school foreign-language instruction, saying that the Japanese parent "has the right to direct the education of his own child without unreasonable restrictions; the Constitution protects him as well as those who speak another tongue."[132]

Parochial Schools Attacked

As public schools grew in number and popularity, so did religious and ethnic all-day, late-afternoon, and weekend ones. Many ethnic traditionalists believed that only in their own schools could youngsters learn their ancestral language, group traditions, and respect for family and church, thereby becoming law-abiding and God-fearing citizens, living in stable neighborhoods and sheltered from the ridicule of the American born. What public schools and textbooks ignored or slighted, their own presented, whether it was religious beliefs or ethnic kinsmen who had helped discover or develop America, served in American wars, or distinguished themselves in the arts, government, or science.

A study of Slovak immigrants from 1870 to 1930 found that parents seemed to agree that "the chief aim of schooling was not necessarily to promote social mobility on earth, but to prepare for the afterlife. Thus, once a Slovak child had learned the 'three R's' and knew his catechism, extended schooling became superfluous. . . . It was all right to be a blue-collar worker, to drop out of school at an early age, and to live in the same neighborhood all your life."[133]

Generally, foreign-language instruction was a central part of parochial schools. "Language Saves the Faith" proclaimed a large number of midwestern German Catholic priests, who futilely petitioned Rome in the 1880s to grant their congregants greater autonomy, particularly from Irish clergy seeking to Americanize them. "In English you must count your dollars," said one priest, "but in German you speak with your children, your confessor, and your God."[134] Similar feelings about language retention were expressed by Italians, Czechs, Poles, Slovaks, and French Canadians.

Even then, immigrant support for parochial schools varied. Germans and French Canadians were most supportive, followed by Poles, and then Slovaks, Czechs, Lithuanians, and Ukrainians. Italians and Mexicans were least support-ive. The Irish, knowing English, but strongly committed to preserving the faith, ranked below Germans, French Canadians, and Poles. Catholic parochial schools were generally more concerned with educating girls than boys, and doing so in sexually segregated schools, usually staffed by nuns. By 1920, more than 5,000 Catholic parish schools existed, with enrollments in some cities exceeding those of public schools. In the same year, among Missouri Synod Lutherans, 30 per-cent of the congregations had their own schools, with nearly 50 percent of their children in attendance. By 1946, Polish Catholics had over 500 elementary schools and 86 secondary ones.[135]

Not all immigrant schools were religious. The Bohemian Free Thought Sun-day Schools were atheistic. Japanese-language schools focused on language, ethics, and values. Sholem Aleichem schools stressed Jewish secular and cultural life, as well as the Yiddish language and literature. In the 1920s, Mexico spon-sored private schools in some California communities to prevent the de-Mexicanization of youngsters through fostering the use of Spanish.[136] Nevertheless, some ethnic leaders continued to prefer public schools, believing Old Country curriculums and ways ill-suited for success in America. The result was intragroup debates between traditionalists and modernists, as well as be-tween laity and clergy.

As with nonethnics, many immigrants and particularly their children adopted the American ideal of being educated secularly, earning a great deal of money, obtaining high social status, and leaving the old neighborhood. They believed that if they did not go to school, especially a public one, and did not go on to college, they would never "make it," trigger bigotry toward themselves, and remain non-Americans.

Liberal Norwegians in the 1870s criticized their parochial schools for clan-nishness and self-destructiveness. To establish a parochial school system, as had Roman Catholics and Lutheran Germans, warned one Norwegian group, would create "Norwegian Indians," "outcasts," and "trash," as well as provoke religious wars. For their own sake, as well as that of their children, church, and America, the *Greek Star* of Chicago, in 1904, told readers that they "must accept this great American educational system which is free from any ecclesiastical domination. Church is an imperative necessity for a nation, but school is the nation's whole life, and public schools which are free from theocracy are the real bulwarks of the country."[137]

Meanwhile, throughout the nineteenth and early twentieth centuries, parochial schools were criticized for lacking the democratic, middle-class, and Puritan ethics that contributed to intellectual, professional, and educational achievement.

Morrison I. Swift accused the Catholic church of projecting "a separate school system to produce a dissonant culture, splitting the unity of the national mind." In Oregon, in 1922, the KKK almost succeeded in ending the Catholic parochial school system when it and nativists generally tried to enact a state law compelling all parents to send their children between the ages of eight and sixteen to public schools. The "mongrel hordes must be Americanized" or, if that was impossible, they should be deported, proclaimed Oregon's grand dragon.[138]

Paradoxically, nativist support of public schools was articulated in democratic terms. The KKK favored an "American public school, non-partisan, non-sectarian, efficient, democratic, for all of the children of all the people; equal educational opportunities for all." A pamphlet published by the supporters of the bill stated that "the assimilation and education of our foreign-born citizens in the principles of our government, the hopes and inspiration of our people, are best secured by and through attendance of all children in our public schools. We must now halt those coming to our country from forming groups, establishing schools, and thereby bringing up their children in an environment often antagonistic to the principles of our government."[139]

By a slight margin, the bill was enacted, then declared unconstitutional by a federal court, and appealed to the Supreme Court. By this time, not only Catholics but a large number of others opposed the Oregon law, such as Jews, Lutherans, Seventh-Day Adventists, Indians, Blacks, Unitarians, Presbyterians, and immigrants generally. The American Civil Liberties Union, the Society of the Sisters of the Holy Name of Jesus, and the Hill Military Academy also entered the legal battle, supporting the existence of private and parochial schools. In a legal brief supporting the Sisters, Louis Marshall, of the American Jewish Committee, argued that more than a few private schools were involved. "Fundamentally ... the questions in these cases are: May liberty to teach and to learn be restricted? Shall such liberty be dependent upon the will of the majority? Shall such majority be permitted to dictate to parents and to children where and by whom instruction shall be given? If such power can be asserted, then it will lead inevitably to the stifling of thought."[140]

In a landmark decision for a pluralistic school pattern, the Supreme Court declared the Oregon law unconstitutional: "The fundamental theory of liberty upon which all government in this union respose[s] excludes any general power of the state to standardize its children by forcing them to accept instruction from public teachers only. The child is not the mere creature of the state; those who nurture him and direct his destiny have the right, coupled with the high duty, to recognize and prepare him for additional obligations."[141]

Subsequent court decisions also dealt with the problem of parochial and private education and the respective rights of parents and the state. As in other areas of life, the courts maintained that the principle of religious freedom is not absolute. Even though one's religious beliefs might be violated, students had to attend school for a given time period and receive a basic secular education, either in a public or private school.

Immigrant Reactions to Super-Americanization

Regardless of the internal differences over how children should be educated and how group faith or ethnic identity should be assured, most group leaders reacted negatively to the 100 percent Americanization threats, rhetoric, and legislation demanding that immigrants learn English, revere American institutions, and abandon Old World loyalties, customs, and memories.

Chicago's *Yiddish Daily Courier* argued against World War I's increased calls for everyone "melting"; the war's most valuable lesson was that "it is not at all necessary for the liberty, security, and prosperity of America to fuse all the nationalities here to a point where they will lose their identity completely."[142] An editorial in *Dziennik dla Wszystkich,* a Polish-language newspaper in Buffalo, stated: "Poles! do not deny your mother tongue and use English only. It is deplorable that so many Americans object so much to foreign customs. It smacks decidedly of Prussianism, and it is not all in accordance with American ideals of freedom." *L'Aurora,* an Italian newspaper, published in Reading, Pennsylvania, said in 1920 that "Americanization is an ugly word. Today it means to proselytize by making the foreign-born forget his mother country and mother tongue."[143]

Similar editorials during 1919 to 1920 expressed varying degrees of disapproval of the Americanization drive, while supporting the necessity for learning English and the American way of life. After all, America and Americans were not that good or fair, otherwise why their prejudice, raids, and calls for immigrant restriction and exclusion. Why did Americans not practice what they preach? Particularly irritating was the attitude of superiority by the more extreme Americanizers, who in their advocacy of education and literacy were usually able to speak only one language, while immigrants could speak two, three, or more.

On the other hand, some immigrant spokespersons saw no danger in Americanization and argued that it was an enrichment of their ethnic heritage and destiny. For example, the editor of one Greek newspaper wrote that "Americanization corresponds neither to Turkification, Bulgarization, nor to becoming a Frenchmen. . . . America does not seek your head on a platter, like another Herod, or as a newer Mephistopheles—your soul for the Devil. America views your Americanization as the discharge of the duties of which Divine Providence entrusted you. In this endeavor it is not driven by an impressive chauvinism or an impious fanaticism."[144]

At the same time, the nonethnic liberal world of the time, at least as reflected in a 1920 national survey of some 200 respondents, viewed the Americanization process with much ambivalence. Some thought Americanization would come about through emotional contagion and singing patriotic songs, while others proposed dissolving immigrant communities, societies, press, and language, as well as making naturalization and immigration more difficult, utilizing deportation if necessary. About the only thing the respondents agreed upon was that immigrants should be required to learn English, with the help of public and private agencies.[145]

Cultural Pluralists

In the early twentieth century, many educators and writers began realizing that new and old immigrants would not and ought not totally assimilate and pointed to immigrants who contributed to America's productivity and vitality, even though retaining ethnic communities, churches, clubs, and newspapers. A social concept of "immigrant gifts" emerged, with one school superintendent urging a policy of welcoming "the best of the culture, the arts, and the crafts of the Old World, that . . . we may be enriched with this spiritual inheritance"; John Dewey pleaded for a "unity created by drawing out and composing into a harmonious whole the best, the most characteristic, which each contributing race and people has to offer."[146]

To Dewey, such phrases as Irish-American, Hebrew-American, or German-American were false and misleading.

> The genuine American, the typical American, is himself a hyphenated character . . . he is international and interracial in his makeup. He is not American plus Pole or German. But the American is himself Pole-German-English-French-Spanish-Italian-Greek-Irish-Scandinavian-Bohemian-Jew—and so on. The point is to see to it that the hyphen connects instead of separates. And this means at least that our public schools shall teach each factor to respect every other, and shall take pains to enlighten all as to the great past contributions of every strain in our composite makeup.[147]

A philosophy of *cultural pluralism* led many teachers to view ethnic students as necessary parts in the mosaic of America. To Horace Kallen, America was a federation or commonwealth of nationalities, "cooperating voluntarily and autonomously through the perfection of men according to their kind. The common language of the commonwealth . . . is English, but each nationality expresses its emotional and voluntary life in its own language . . . so in society each ethnic group is the natural instrument, its spirit and culture are its theme and melody, and the harmony and dissonances and discords of them all make the symphony of civilization."[148]

Such views were not without critics. Lothrop Stoddard, a disciple of Madison Grant, denigrated Kallen as "an arch-champion of 'hyphenism' who exemplifies the alien spirit better than any other of its spokesmen!" Stoddard believed "the disintegration of national unity into anything like a 'Pluralistic America' would mean not an orchestration of mankind, but a hellish bedlam [of a] vast nondescript mass, with no genuine loyalties, traditional roots, or cultural and idealistic standards."[149]

Fortunately, the positive views of immigrants and their children began to win out. Anthropologists like Franz Boaz and Margaret Mead helped the process by stressing the basic equality of all people and the relativity of all cultures. *Cultural pluralism* and *cultural relativism* became the guiding principles of progressive educators. Theologically, too, Reinhold Niebuhr supported the right, indeed duty, of ethnic and racial groups to maintain their identity. Society's responsibility was also emphasized. "If the foreign-born population is to be fused with the native-born," wrote William M. Leiserson in 1924, "the same freedom of opinion and action that is allowed to Americans will have to be granted to the immigrants. Equal opportunity, equal protection, equal treatment, and equal right of self-assertion are as necessary for them in the process of becoming Americans, as it is to maintain the ideal of American citizenship."[150]

Cultural Pluralism and the Race Revolution

As immigrants acculturated and rose socioeconomically, the situation of Blacks remained dismal. The segregated and usually inferior schools they attended provided little or biased attention to their past. "In their own as well as in mixed schools," wrote Carter G. Woodson in 1931, "Negroes are taught to admire the Hebrew, the Greek, the Latin and the Teuton and to despise the African. The thought of inferiority of the Negro is drilled into him in almost every class he enters." The reality of their plight—institutionalized racism—was ignored by cultural pluralists, who idealistically described America as a mosaic or symphony, but whom John Higham recently criticized for encapsulating White ethnocentrism and projecting a liberalization of America rather than Black liberation from America.[151]

As noted in an earlier chapter, as America moved closer to entering World War II, concern once again arose over communists and communist influence in government, labor unions, and schools and teaching materials. Organizations such as the American Legion and the National Association of Manufacturers denounced "treason in textbooks." Many state and city governments established committees to investigate communist infiltration into school systems. Once we entered the war, with the Soviet Union as an ally, passions and paranoia abated.[152] Just as the war proved the underlying patriotism of the immigrant-descended and native-born, so it proved that enormous numbers of working-class and ethnic Americans were capable of graduating from college if given the opportunity and financial help. Almost 2.5 million veterans took advantage of the GI Bill of Rights, which provided federal funds for tuition, books, supplies, and living expenses.

Conservative estimates indicate that about 500,000 GIs would not have attended college without such assistance and that contrary to the many negative stereotypes about their intelligence, they "earned slightly better grades relative to ability than did those who probably would have attended in any case." Moreover, when veterans are compared to nonveterans, they scored better-than-average grades and did so at better colleges and in more difficult subjects. As David Nasaw pointed out, World War II veterans represented the nation's first—and largest—generation of nontraditional college students.[153] A similar, though less generous, federal program was offered Korean War veterans in 1953.

Though it required two wars (and fears of veteran unemployment and agitation) to broaden higher education enrollment, it remained for the Supreme Court and the Congress to change the racist structure of education and society. In 1954, segregated schools and the doctrine of separate but equal education ended, at least legally. "Separate educational facilities are inherently unequal," said the Supreme Court in *Brown* v. *Board of Education*. Combining constitutional principles and social science findings, it unanimously held that racial segregation of children "generates a feeling of inferiority as to their status in the community that may affect their hearts and minds in a way unlikely to ever be undone."[154]

In addition, a simultaneity of civil rights protests, governmental regulations, strong federal and local enforcement of antidiscrimination laws, and open admissions educational policies hastened a revolution in intergroup relations, which allowed more and more Blacks, Hispanics, Asians, and women to enter college. Only grudgingly was voluntary busing replaced by court-ordered busing. With the enactment of affirmative action programs, proportional representation, and outright quotas, more minority group members obtained teaching positions. Educational admission was now greatly influenced by a group's proportion of the total population rather than by an individual's achievement, wherein low percentages of students in a school were considered prima facie evidence of probable institutional prejudice or racism.

Throughout the 1960s, the Supreme Court also continued to ban religious activities in the public schools and deny governmental financial aid to parochial schools. In 1962, nondenominational prayers in New York public schools were held unconstitutional, as were Bible reading and the Lord's Prayer in Pennsylvania's public schools in the following year. In 1985, the Court struck down an Alabama law permitting a one-minute daily period of silence or prayer in the public schools.

During this time, the Congress encouraged the rise of ethnic pride and education, especially through the 1972 Ethnic Studies Act, and authorized the United States Office of Education to promote ethnic studies. Other congressional acts provided bilingual education "to the extent necessary to allow a child to progress effectively through the educational system . . . and such instruction is given with appreciation for the cultural heritage of such children." When challenged in the courts, the Supreme Court in *Lau* v. *Nichols* upheld them in 1974, declaring that "students who do not understand English are effectively foreclosed from any meaningful education." Four years later, bilingual education was being provided in some 70 different languages and by 1990, in more than 140. Equally significant, the Supreme Court in 1982 ruled in a five-to-four decision that illegal alien children have a constitutional right to a free public school education, stating for the first time that the Fourteenth Amendment's equal protection guarantee "extends to anyone, citizen or stranger, who is subject to the laws of a state, and reaches into every corner of a state's territory." Gay and lesbian public school students also began being legislatively protected against discrimination in 1993, when Massachusetts upheld their right to form their own groups and attend proms with same-sex dates.[155]

Changes in teaching methods, material, and organizations escalated as a result of such actions, as well as the rise in group pride and lobbying, and the increased immigration from South and Central America, the Caribbean, and Asia (about whose cultures teachers knew little and whose histories American teaching materials either excluded or treated inadequately). Adult immigrants, too, sought an education, particularly English, of which a minimal understanding was required of illegal aliens seeking legal residency under the 1986 Immigration Reform and Control Act. Adult classes in English as a second language (ESL) proliferated in cities with large immigrant populations, such as Los Angeles, Chicago, Houston, and New York. In Los Angeles, in 1987, ESL classes were overenrolled with nearly 200,000 adults in attendance and some 40,000 turned away.[156] Racially, ethnically, and religiously, such changes triggered a constellation of new controversies, which not only challenged the philosophy, structure, and process of education but those of American society.

Immigrant Achievements

In looking at immigrants and education at the turn of the century, the wonder is not that so few immigrants learned English or attended school but that so many did. Moreover, this was completely contrary to nativist beliefs about their biological, intellectual, and cultural inferiority, wherein statistics for the failures of the foreign-born were highlighted while their achievements were ignored, as were the differences in educational motivation, participation, and accomplishments among and between immigrant groups and native-born Americans.[157]

The reasons for such differences are not fully known. Were immigrant achievements or failures due to American environmental conditions, cultural inheritance, Old Country socioeconomic position, biological intelligence, or any combination thereof? If so, to what extent? Experts disagree. Clearly, some immigrant groups did better educationally and economically than others; discrimination and prejudice did not automatically stop all members of a group from gaining an education. Although a high socioeconomic background facilitated educational achievement, immigrant poverty and illiteracy did not prevent many of them, particularly their children, from learning. Just as clearly, especially from the late nineteenth century onward, immigrant children had opportunities for an education not obtainable in their ancestral land or available to Blacks, most of whose forefathers had been in America for centuries. Educational facilities and reforms, as well as semiskilled and skilled job openings, multiplied.

Some groups arrived with relatively high degrees of literacy in their own language and even in English. That of immigrant Slavs was generally higher than that of the total population back home. Over 90 percent of early-twentieth-century Japanese immigrants averaged eight years of schooling, which was considerably higher than those of the average American. Ninety-nine percent of West Indian immigrants from 1911 to 1924 were able to read and write English. Some evidence exists that immigrants who traveled the greatest distances to reach America were more literate than those who remained home or traveled a short distance from it, as in the case of Swedes, Slovaks, and Irish.[158] Of course, all immigrants from the British Isles spoke but not necessarily read English.

Once in school, immigrant children generally achieved a higher literacy rate than native-born ones, even in the heavily populated Middle Atlantic and North Central states. In 1890, only 16 percent of second-generation children aged ten to fourteen were illiterate, compared to some 66 percent of White children of native parentage. Though illiteracy declined sharply by 1920, differences between the two groups continued, with 5 percent of second-generation children illiterate in contrast to 11 percent for third-generation-and-over White children.[159]

At the same time, though each immigrant group had high achievers, not all groups achieved equally. Thus, in 1908, children of Swedish and German parents in Boston, Chicago, and New York were likely to be as behind in schooling as nonimmigrant White students; those of English, Irish, and Russian Jewish parents tended to be in a middle range of achievement; and those of southern Italian, Polish, and native-born Black children were most likely to be behind in school. As late as 1935, a Welfare Council of New York study showed that Italian boys and girls had "the smallest proportion of any white group attending school." Of all the racial and ethnic groups in 1940, Asian Indians, who then lived mostly in California, had the lowest median number of completed school years: 3.7.[160]

Nevertheless, large numbers of immigrant offspring managed to go on to higher education and even become teachers. By 1910, Irish and German Catholics were equaling or exceeding the national average for college attendance. In the 1920s, Scandinavian American educational performance far exceeded other ethnic groups in the Midwest. In Cleveland, from 1890 to 1940, more than 90 percent of the sons of Romanian immigrant families finished high school and 70 percent went on to college or professional education. By 1935, children of Jewish immigrants in schools and colleges almost equaled in proportion those of native-born parents, and, more impressive yet, Jewish males were graduating from college at a rate four times greater than non-Jews. After polling seventy-seven institutions of higher learning in 1907–08, a congressional committee reported almost 400 foreign-born women of different ethnic backgrounds studying engineering, medicine, pharmacy, dentistry, law, and other professional programs.[161]

In professional education, the daughters of Irish immigrants made extraordinary advances. What domestic work had been for the first generation of Irish immigrants, teaching school became for their daughters. As early as 1870, 20 percent of New York City teachers were Irish, most of whom worked in Irish neighborhoods. In New Haven, in 1910, while close to 70 percent of public school teachers were of Anglo-Saxon descent, some 25 percent were Irish and close to 10 percent were German; by 1913, Anglo-Saxons declined to 30 percent and Irish rose to more than 40 percent, Germans to more than 10 percent, and for the first time, Russians (mostly Jews) and Italians entered the teaching professions, representing approximately 5 percent each; by 1939, 20 percent of New Haven's teachers were of Italian descent.[162]

Moreover, rather than replicate jobs held by their parents, many immigrant children entered new ones. By 1910, the sons of Austrians, Italians, Poles, and Hungarians averaged 9.9 percent laborers, while their fathers averaged 22.9 percent. In mining and quarrying, the percentages for fathers were 16.4 percent, but only 5.8 percent for their sons. On the other hand, in the skilled trades, while 2.7 percent of fathers were employed, 4.2 percent of their sons were. Though less than 1 percent of immigrant fathers worked as clerks, almost 10 percent of their children did. Percentages in professions for immigrant offspring almost tripled, rising to 3.3 percent in contrast to 1.4 percent for immigrant men. In more recent decades, while 4 percent of Japanese males in 1940 were professionals, 33.5 percent were in professional or management positions in 1980.[163]

Like economic success, educational success was not only a matter of individual determination but of a society that required school attendance, offered free elementary and secondary education, had a plenitude of jobs, and provided relatively inexpensive professional training. "Yes," wrote historian Thomas Kessner, "the myth of an open American society with opportunity for the common man 'squared with social reality.' "[164]

Whether literate or not, many immigrants (particularly economically motivated ones) willingly exchanged the gloomy certainty of their homeland life for the possibility of a brighter one, where they delayed immediate gratification for future rewards, and, time and energy willing, utilized the educational resources about them.

Recent and more disciplined research continues to show how wrong nativists were about the intelligence and educability of immigrant "stock" and children. The younger the immigrant students were and the earlier they entered school, the more they achieved educationally, with each succeeding generation doing better than the prior one—and even better than native White Americans.

For example, in 1961, five years after Hungarian refugees arrived in Cleveland, 20 percent had obtained university degrees and the majority had participated in some schooling. Among American Latvians in 1974, 55 percent had a college education, and most of them were under thirty-five years of age. According to some 1981 studies, more than 95 percent of second-generation Lebanese Americans in Hartford had graduated from a liberal arts or technical college, and among third and fourth generations, the question was "not whether they should go to college, but which college should they attend." Greeks, according to a 1959 study, scored highest in motivation achievement, and in the 1970 census of twenty-four second-generation nationality groups, they ranked first in educational attainment and second to Jews in income levels.[165] By early 1982, five Greek Americans (including one woman) were presidents of colleges or universities, including Radcliffe.

According to the 1980 census, twenty-five to thirty-four year olds of southern and eastern European descent had as a whole a larger percentage (37.7) of those who had completed college than other Whites (24.1 percent). Census data also revealed a striking increase in educational achievement between the first and second generations in these groups, wherein the latter exceeded the prior generation by four or more years of schooling, in contrast to other White groups, in which intergenerational gain was about two years. By 1997, when nearly 1 in 10 residents was foreign-born, about 25 percent of those twenty-five years old and over had completed four or more years of college.[166]

When looked at from a religious perspective, Polish, Italian, and other eastern European Catholics attending college increased so sharply after 1940 that by the 1970s, they exceeded the national average, and Irish Catholics were deemed "the most likely of any American White Gentile ethnic group to send their children to college." More extraordinary were Jewish household heads of varying ages in 1971, wherein 56 percent had some college education; and for those under thirty years of age, 87 percent of males and 60 percent of females had at least some college. By the early 1990s, 87 percent of college-age Jews were attending schools of higher education.[167]

For Blacks, long excluded, segregated, and denied access to jobs, even when educated, their future remained bleak until the civil rights movement and the establishment of equal opportunity and affirmative action programs. Since then, decade by decade, improvements were dramatic. In 1969, those twenty-five to thirty-four years old had a median education achievement of 12.1 years, almost equaling the 12.6 years of English, German, and Irish Americans. Five years later, Blacks constituted 12.3 percent of college freshman classes, though only 11.4 percent of the population. Even in historically all-White independent schools, Black enrollment rose from 2.7 percent in 1980–81 to 4 percent in 1983–84. By 1997, 86 percent of Blacks twenty-five to twenty-nine years old had graduated from high school, statistically equaling that of Whites.[168]

Hispanic American college enrollments increased from 383,000 in 1976 to 529,000 in 1984, with their graduates rising from 3 percent in 1981 to 7 percent in 1984, and those with some college education going from 12 to 15 percent, though the percentages of those completing eighth grade or less remained about

30 percent. By March 1996, the percentage of Hispanics twenty-five years and over who had graduated from high school rose somewhat to 53 percent.[169]

Asian American (mainly Chinese, Japanese, Vietnamese, Filipinos, Koreans, and East Indians) made the most impressive gains in recent decades, far beyond their almost 2 percent of the population. From 197,000 college students (1.8 percent of the college population) in 1976, their numbers climbed to 382,000 (3.1 percent of the college population) in 1984. Also, their enrollment in independent schools rose to 3.5 percent in 1985. Sexual and ethnic differences, however, existed. Except for Vietnamese, males aged twenty-five to twenty-nine did better than their White cohorts. Although 87 percent of male Whites and 74 percent of male Blacks, according to a 1980 census study, had completed high school, for Japanese it was 96 percent; Koreans and Asian Indians, 94 percent; Chinese, 90 percent; Filipinos, 89 percent; and Vietnamese, 76 percent. By 1997, Asians and Pacific Islanders aged twenty-five years and over had more college graduates proportionately than any other census group. Fifty percent had a bachelor's degree or higher—compared to 29 percent for Whites, 14 percent for Blacks, and 10 percent for Hispanics.[170]

On both high school and college levels, Asian Americans distinguished themselves. One researcher found that nationally 50 percent of Asian American high school students were never absent from classes, compared to 25 percent for White students. Almost 23 percent of Westinghouse's Science Talent awards in 1984 went to Asian Americans, and 20 percent of its top ten awards in 1985. In one Boston high school, in 1983, fifty-six of the eighty-three students on the honor roll were Vietnamese, and all of the thirty-two Vietnamese from the previous year's graduating class had gone on to college. In New York City's elite Stuyvesant High School, which stresses math and science and requires an admission test, 36 percent of the students in 1986 were Asian Americans.[171]

Of course, not all Asians or Asian groups achieved or achieved equally. Although, according to the 1980 census, 35 percent aged twenty-five and older had graduated from college, for Chinese aged twenty to twenty-four, 60 percent were in college; for Japanese, 48 percent; for Vietnamese, 42 percent; for Koreans, 40 percent; and for Filipinos, 27 percent. A 1980 study of immigrants from India reported that those living in New York had six times the national percentage of those with four or more years of higher education, and a later study showed that across the country 78 percent of Indian men and 52 percent of Indian women were college graduates. Within a multigenerational group, educational achievements differed. For example, for Japanese second generation households, according to a 1978–79 study, 44 percent of male "Nisei" had college degrees, and for third-generation "Sansei," the percentage zoomed to 88 percent.[172] At the same time, adult Asian and Spanish-speaking people, as well as other adult immigrants, like earlier European ones, flocked to special classes to learn English, and in the case of illegal immigrants, to meet the federal requirement to have a minimal understanding of English before being granted legal residency.[173]

With such advances went a revising of historical attitudes toward parochial schools and their effectiveness. No longer were they being automatically characterized as foreign outposts of a totalitarian faith, centers of educational mediocrity, and purveyors of intolerance. Historian Henry Steele Commager credited the late-nineteenth-century Catholic church as "one of the most effective of all agencies for democracy and Americanization," representing a vast cross section of the American people, ignoring distinctions of class, region, and race, and providing newcomers with both "spiritual refuge" and "social security."[174]

In the 1980s, parochial and private schools were praised in terms usually applied to public schools. In a major 1981 survey of nonpublic schools, sociologist James T. Coleman found strong evidence that Catholic schools "function much closer to the American ideal of the 'common school,' educating children from different backgrounds alike, than do the public schools." When family background factors predicting achievement were controlled, students in Catholic and other private schools were shown to achieve at a higher level than those in public schools. In 1984, a National Catholic Educational Association study revealed that 80 percent of Catholic high school students entered college, compared to 50 to 60 percent of public high school graduates. Equally impressive were the increasing numbers of non-Catholic children in parochial schools. Across the country, particularly in large urban cities, non-Catholic enrollment increased from 2.7 percent in the 1969–70 academic year to 11.7 percent in 1986–87, and with decided benefits for the students. A 1990 survey concluded that Black Catholics were more likely to complete high school and college than most other students and that only 18 percent dropped out of high school, compared to 31 percent of the total Black population and 21 percent of the general population. Similar achievements were found in a 1990 Rand study of private and public inner-city schools, in largely Black and Puerto Rican neighborhoods. Not only were the percentage of graduates higher in the Catholic schools (82 percent) than in the public schools (55 percent), but so were the SAT scores (803 compared to 642).[175]

Nevertheless, remnants of nineteenth-century anti-Catholicism were seen in the political and legislative opposition to parochial schools and proposals for tuition tax credits to inner-city parents who sent their children to private and parochial schools. When the Supreme Court, in 1985, declared one such program unconstitutional, Chief Justice Burger, in a dissenting opinion, said the ruling "exhibits nothing less than hostility towards religion and the children who attend church-sponsored schools."[176]

Summary

The education of immigrants and their own search for education were replete with successes and failures, wherein at one and the same time they were victims of bigotry and benefactors of freedom. Their successes, however, far outweighed their failures, if not for themselves then certainly for their offspring; greater numbers and percentages gained an education, leaving behind the unskilled trades and lower social positions of their parents, whether from Europe, Asia, or America.

Their impact upon American institutions and cultural diversity was unequaled by immigrants to any other country in the world because they succeeded in bridging Old World attachments and behaviors with New World opportunities and necessities. By their presence and determination, they helped challenge and broaden the concept and content of public and private education both for American- and foreign-born. Equally important, they proved that variety, difference, and even disagreement could exist in a society without endangering it.

From its early beginnings, American education underwent revolutionary changes, reflecting an ever-growing diminution of prejudice and discrimination and an ever-expanding outreach to all segments of society. Instead of remaining a private privilege for the wealthy few, elementary and secondary education became a public requirement for all, financed by public funds. Even in higher education, as noted above, enrollments for all groups keep rising, far beyond the less than 1 percent in colonial times.

Nonsectarianism and separation of church and state replaced religious educational elitism, sponsorship, control, and indoctrination. Not only was religion in the public schools declared illegal but the purposes and content of education changed radically. From curriculums limited to reading, writing, arithmetic, and religion, educational programs exploded into almost countless subjects, activities, and services.

The racial, ethnic, religious, and sexual xenophobia, and official school policies of segregation and exclusion of past decades, all but disappeared. No longer do schools and teachers—and school lessons—validate intergroup stereotypes and biases, but rather refute and condemn them. Instead of cultural superiority, cultural diversity is promoted.

In short, our private and public educational systems today are multicultural—or striving to become so—not only because of changing educational and governmental policies, as well as federal and state court decisions, but also because of minority-group demands for recognition and respect.

Chapter 6

The Future of Minority Progress

In the previous chapters I have tried to show that prejudice and discrimination existed in America long before its "discovery" by Europeans; that assorted invaders, migrants, settlers, and immigrants brought—or abandoned—Old Country biases; that minority groups experienced varying types, degrees, and durations of hostility; that a simultaneity, accretion, and pluralism of victims and victimizers took place; that being victimized did not preclude victimizing others; and that nevertheless prejudice and discrimination diminished as our population grew in numbers and variety, and as government, political and religious leaders, educational institutions, and the American public generally committed themselves to making a more democratic society.

In fact, it can be said that meliorism characterizes the evolution of American minority-group relations.

Such progress has always been debated, not only between members of a particular group, but also between them and other groups. Those affirming progress are often viewed as being blind to existing problems, or, at best, naive. Conversely, anyone denying progress is often called paranoid, or, at best, overly concerned with the darker side of life. Of course, there are also people who alternate between optimism and pessimism.

The varied reactions are due to a number of factors, which are not necessarily mutually exclusive: an eagerness for the immediate surcease of bigotry; an impatience with the slowness of progress thus far; an uncertainty about the permanency of newly gained improvements; a foreboding, anxiety, or resentment about continuing injustices; and, most recently, a belief that being recognized as a disadvantaged minority will bring group preferences and remedies—or that being denied such recognition will deprive them of just treatment.

A look at the various ways American interracial, interfaith, and interethnic relations can be measured may be helpful in understanding what has been happening—and what needs to happen to assure a truly bias-free society:

258

1. Today's American intergroup relations can be compared to those of the past. Are they better or worse?
2. American intergroup relations can be compared to those in other countries.
3. A minority group's progress or lack of progress can be compared to that of other minority groups in American society.
4. Minority-group relations can be evaluated in terms of the nation's constitutional guarantees of equal rights and opportunities for life, liberty, and the pursuit of happiness.
5. American intergroup relations can be viewed from the perspective of major religious, poetic, or political ideals. How close or far are we from an era of peace, love, and harmony among all human beings?
6. Finally, intergroup relations can be judged by the relatively new criteria of diversity and proportional representation, wherein a variety of people is sought in all arenas of public and private iife, or wherein minority groups are represented in all major areas of society according to their proportion of a given workforce or population.

The perspective of this book is based on the first approach—comparing the past to the present. After exploring that relationship, the other approaches are evaluated.

Thus, in comparing the past and present of American prejudice and discrimination, one sees the following:

A Steady Decrease in Religious, Racial, and Ethnic Violence

Buried in history are the colonial expulsions, whippings, tongue borings, and hangings of heretics, dissenters, and witches; the mob attacks on Mormons, Asians, Mexican Americans, Filipinos, and Italians; the burning down of Catholic churches; and the lynchings and shootings of Blacks and Indians. Neither among American Indians nor between Whites and Indians, Whites and Blacks, French and English, Dutch and Swedes, Russians and Americans, Catholics and Protestants, and Protestants and Protestants are there the territorial and imperial wars that once raged on American soil; nor have American ethnic groups replicated the extensive violence that existed or exists in many parts of Europe and Asia, such as between Russians and Poles, Greeks and Turks, Jews and Arabs, Spaniards and Basques, Irish and English, Japanese and Chinese, and Tibetans and Chinese.

Gone are the Anglophobes, Francophobes, Spanophobes, and Germanophobes, who believed that Britain, France, Spain, and Germany respectively were plotting to destroy our government. Also gone are the once popular beliefs that Masons, Illuminati, the pope, communists, and international Jewry had infiltrated our government and courts or that America was imperiled by Chinese and Japanese invasions.

A Growing Tolerance and Respect for
Religious Differences

Absent is the Christian triumphalism that justified slavery, poverty, and state support of religious beliefs and institutions. Rare is the prominent clergyman, intellectual, educator, or scientist who today espouses Anglo-Saxon genetic and cultural superiority over eastern Europeans, Asians, Indians, Blacks, Mormons, or Mexicans. Christian ecumenism and interreligious cooperation have become the goals, if not ideals, of practically all major religious groups, as has the reduction, if not abandonment, of aggressive missionizing of members of other religious denominations and groups.

Theologically, too, dramatic changes have occurred, particularly toward Jews. In 1963, the Catholic church rejected the belief that Christianity superseded Judaism, and in 1982, 92 percent of Catholic educators polled agreed that "Judaism still plays a unique role of its own in God's plan of salvation," while another 85 percent felt that the "Jewish covenant with God has never been revoked by God; the Jews remain 'people of God.' " Four years later, in a study of religiously conservative Protestants (most of whom considered themselves "born again" Christians), 90 percent disagreed that "Christians are justified in holding negative attitudes towards Jews since the Jews killed Christ," and 86 percent disagreed that "God does not hear the prayer of a Jew." Relations between Protestants, Catholics, and Jews improved dramatically, as the more conservative members of each faith similarly opposed strict church-state separation, abortion, and gay rights.[1]

Such developments led to interfaith socializing and marriages with less opposition than ever before. A 1979 poll showed that though in 1952, 41 percent of the nation's Protestants thought Catholics were trying to gain too much power and 35 percent thought the same about Jews, percentages had dropped to 11 percent for Catholics and 12 percent for Jews. Catholics believing that Jews were trying to gain too much power dropped from 33 percent to 13 percent, and for Protestants, from 8 percent to 6 percent. For Christians generally, the belief that Jews had too much power dropped still further in 1987. At the same time, the proportion of Americans approving of marriages between Catholics and Protestants rose from 59 percent in 1968 to 73 percent in 1978, and of those between Jews and non-Jews rose from 59 percent to 69 percent. By the 1990s, young people of one faith marrying a person of another faith had skyrocketed—about 50 percent for Jews and Catholics, 69 percent for Methodists, 70 percent for Lutherans, and 75 percent for Presbyterians.[2]

In short, religious suspicions, animosities, and feelings of superiority steadily declined, with late 1970s polls showing that 81 percent of Americans believed individuals should arrive at their religious beliefs "independent of any church or synagogue" and 78 percent believed "a person can be a good Christian or Jew without attending church or synagogue." Another poll in 1993 found that 96 percent of parents believed their children should be taught to respect those of different racial and ethnic backgrounds, 87 percent to respect people with different religions, and 50 percent to respect those of different sexual orientations.[3]

A Growing Freedom of Geographic Mobility among
Minority-Group Members

Minorities no longer need to build walls or private militias for protection against religious, ethnic, or racial group attacks, as did nineteenth-century Irish Catholics, Indians, and Mormons. Even racially segregated neighborhoods have declined. For example, while in 1970, 38.6 percent of Blacks lived in census tracts that were 90 percent Black, in 1980 the percentage dropped to 31. Conversely, in the same period, Whites living in practically all-White neighborhoods declined from 64.6 percent to 57.2 percent. Nor are minorities leaving areas in which they had been discriminated against, but rather many are returning. For example, between 1990 and 1996, the South experienced a net gain of Blacks from the Northeast, Midwest, and West. Similarly, in spite of the historic anti-Hispanic and anti-Asian passions in the West, 45 percent of the nation's Hispanics and 53 percent of its Asians live there. Moreover, minorities increasingly move into areas that once excluded them. Thus, the Black population in suburbia grew by close to 35 percent from 1980 to 1990, the Hispanic population by almost 70 percent, and the Asian population by some 126 percent.[4]

An Ending of Racial, Religious, and Ethnic
Immigration Quotas and Outright Exclusions

Historically unprecedented was the absence of significant protests by nativists or labor unions to the admissions of hundreds of thousands of Caribbeans, Central and South Americans, and Vietnamese or to the passage of the 1986 Immigration Reform and Control Act, which granted amnesty and opportunity for citizenship to more than a million illegal immigrants. As noted earlier, by 2050 our population is predicted to be 53 percent non-Hispanic White, 21 percent Hispanic, 16 percent Black, and 11 percent Asian and Pacific Islanders, in sharp contrast to 1790 when the population was overwhelmingly of White European origin.

An Increasing Lack of Support for Extreme Right- and
Left-Wing Groups or "Hate" Organizations

Neither the Communist Party, Students for a Democratic Society, Posse Comitatus, Socialist Labor Party nor the KKK has been able to muster broad political support. For example, while the KKK had millions of members in the 1920s, by 1984 its membership numbered only 6,000. Also, before World War II, some 250 to 300 pro-Fascist, pro-Nazi, anti-Semitic, or racist groups existed, with thousands of members, but by 1984, neo-Nazi groups had a combined total of no more than 500 members. Even the number of recently formed "patriotic" militia groups have declined because of government action against them, membership disaffection with their violence, and/or weariness in waiting for a revolution that did not occur.[5] Unlike pre–World War II decades, no prominent elected official jurist, police chief, editor, or clergyman admits or contributes to such organizations.

A Continuing Political Achievement by Minority-Group Members

In spite of a bitter group history of prejudice, two Quakers (Herbert Hoover and Richard Nixon), an Irish Catholic (John F. Kennedy), and a German (Dwight D. Eisenhower) became president; a Greek (Spiro Agnew), a vice president, and another (Michael Dukakis), a candidate for president; a Jew (Henry Kissinger), a woman (Madeleine Albright), and a Pole (Edmund Muskie), secretaries of state; an Italian (Antonin Scalia), a Supreme Court justice; a Mexican American (Lauro Cavazos), a secretary of education; and a Black (Edward Brooke), a Basque (Paul Laxalt), a Lebanese (James Abourzek), and a Japanese (S.I. Hayakawa), senators. In the 1980s, three Roman Catholics were on the Supreme Court. The first Armenian (George Deukmejian), the first French Acadian (Edwin Edwards), the first Black (L. Douglas Wilder), the first native Hawaiian (John D. Waihee Jr.) and the first Chinese (Gary Locke) were respectively elected governor of California, Louisiana, Virginia, Hawaii, and Washington. In Florida, Ileana Ros-Lehtinen became the first Cuban American congresswoman. As a result of the 1992 election, Ben Nighthorse Campbell became the first American Indian senator, Carol Moseley Braun the first Black woman senator, Jay Kim the first Korean representative, and Nydia Velazquez the first Puerto Rican woman representative. The election of President Clinton resulted in the appointment of two Danish Americans in his cabinet: Lloyd Bentsen as secretary of the treasury and Janet Reno as attorney general.

No less historic was the appointment of General Colin L. Powell as chairman of the Joint Chiefs of Staff, the first Black ever, who was succeeded by foreign-born General John Shalikashvili, of Polish and Russian parents.

Opposition to electing a Black or a Jew for president softened. For a Jewish candidate, it declined from 28 percent in 1958 to 10 percent in late 1987. Although 42 percent of those polled in 1958 would vote for a "well-qualified" Black, in 1996, 93 percent said they would be willing to do so.[6] In 1984, as well as in 1988, the first major Black candidate, Jesse Jackson, ran for the Democratic presidential nomination. Though he failed to win, the party in 1989 elected Ronald H. Brown as chairman of its national committee, the first Black to head a major political party.

More than token individuals were involved. With each election in recent decades, more and more minorities and women were elected to high office. In

1997, there were 38 Black congressmen, including 1 woman senator and 11 women representatives, compared to 23 a decade earlier, none of whom were women or in the Senate. Hispanic representatives totaled 18, including 3 women, compared to 14 all-male members a decade earlier. Over 2,000 Asian-Pacific Americans held elected or appointed political office in 1998, including Taiwan-born David Wu, who was elected to the Congress. More dramatic yet, women went from 23 representatives and 2 senators in 1987 to 54 representatives and 9 senators in 1998. Though a majority of Americans disapproved of homosexuality, the number of elected gay and lesbian officeholders rose from 49 in 1991 to 156 by mid-1998, including 2 congressmen, Jim Kolbe of Arizona and Barney Frank of Massachusetts.[7]

The 1997 Congress also had an impressive number of members of once-despised religious groups: 152 Roman Catholics, 62 Baptists, 35 Jews, 21 Lutherans, 15 Mormons, 6 Eastern Orthodox, 3 Unitarian Universalists, and 3 Seventh-Day Adventists. Congressional religious pluralism is also reflected in the variety of affiliations of some members, such as A.M.E. Zion, Assembly of God, Christian Missionary Alliance, Moravian, and United Brethren. What Albert J. Menendez, former research director of Americans United for Separation of Church and State, said after the 1986 elections, is no less true today: "If religious affiliations matter, then there are signs the electorate is becoming more tolerant of diversity. Candidates are being elected in areas where previously voters would have held a hostile view of their religious affiliation."[8]

An Increased National Acceptance of "Equal Employment Opportunity" and Compliance with Antidiscrimination Laws

Though in 1944 only 40 percent of Whites believed in equal job opportunity, by 1972, 97 percent did. Calls for interposition, secession, and impeachment because of the 1954 Supreme Court decision are now historical memories, as are "freedom rides," "sit-ins," and "pray-ins" to end racial segregation. No less striking has been the change of opinion by 1986 toward busing children for racial purposes, with opposition by Americans generally down to 53 percent, in contrast to 78 percent in 1976.[9]

With each passing decade, attitudes and laws supporting social, neighborhood, and fraternal discrimination decreased. Just as interfaith marriages increased sharply so with interethnic and interracial ones. For example, a 1976 study for first and fourth generations of Irish, German, French, Polish, Italian, and Eastern Europeans revealed that by the third generation, a substantial majority had married members of other groups. Racially, though only 2.2 percent of their marriages, the number of Blacks married to Whites almost quadrupled from 1970 to 1992, from 310,000 to 1,161,000. For other groups, the percentages are much greater. Some 70 percent of American Indians marry outside their groups. In California, in 1980, the rate of marriages to Whites for Chinese was 14 percent, for Vietnamese 15 percent, for Koreans 19 percent, for Asian Indians 23 percent, and for Filipinos 24 percent. By 1993, the rate of Japanese intermarriages with Whites was 65 percent. In general, interracial marriages resulted in some four million children.[10]

Socially, from the mid-1960s to 1978, White opposition to bringing a Black child home for supper went from 42 percent to 20 percent, and the belief that Blacks were trying to move ahead too fast plummeted from 71 to 37 percent. By late 1988, a national survey found that 94 percent of Black respondents and 67 percent of White ones had close friends of the other race. Private-club discrimination based on race, creed, ethnicity, and sexual preference began being outlawed by a number of cities and states. Then, in 1988, the Supreme Court unanimously upheld New York City's banning such discrimination, especially against women, in large private clubs where business dealings were carried on. Two years later, the New Jersey Supreme Court ordered two male-only Princeton University undergraduate clubs to start admitting women, stating that the clubs were not private associations but "public accommodations."[11]

An Expansion and Enforcement of the Right to Vote, to Work, to Be Educated, to Utilize Public Accommodations, and to Buy or Rent Housing

Whether due to changed employer attitudes, stricter laws against discrimination, affirmative action policies, or people simply taking advantage of opportunities not previously available, minority well-being increased dramatically. Income and homeownership in 1997 reflected impressive gains for nearly all minority households, including Blacks, Hispanics, and Asians. While an income gap still existed between White men and Black men, it was the smallest in three decades, some 20 percent. Likewise, the median family income for Black married couples declined to 13 percent below that of White married couples. Poverty and welfare rolls also declined sharply. For example, while 87 percent of Black families lived in poverty in 1940, the figure dropped to 26 percent by 1995. Similarly, in 1940, 60 percent of employed Black women were domestic servants; fifty years later, relatively few were, holding instead mostly white-collar jobs.[12]

Women, too, have been making great economic and educational strides. Though earning less than men, the gap has been narrowing, rising from 59 percent of men's earnings in 1975 to 71 percent in 1995. Educationally, in 1997, women aged 25 to 29 had a higher percentage of high school graduates (89 percent compared to 86 percent) and college graduates (29 percent compared to 26 percent). While in 1970 women constituted only one-tenth of medical and law school graduates, in 1995 they represented 40 percent. In 1996, 83 percent of *Fortune* 500 companies had at least one woman director.[13]

Though barriers against Jews in employment, housing, and public accommodations tumbled rapidly in the immediate post–World War II years, Jews were
still excluded from the executive suites of banks, public utilities, insurance companies, and heavy industry. By the mid-1980s, however, their numbers and percentages grew. Researchers no longer found evidence of discrimination against
them in being hired, confined to a specialized position, given lesser authority, or
paid less than Catholics and Protestants.[14]

Most extraordinary is the socioeconomic rise of Asian Americans. By 1980,
Chinese, Japanese, Koreans, Filipinos, and Asian Indians generally had a greater
family median income than Whites: $22,713 compared to $20,835. By 1996, the
median family income of Asian Americans rose to $43,000, some $3,000 more
than that of non-Hispanic Whites, $18,000 more than that of Hispanics, and
almost $20,000 more than that of Blacks. Asian Americans also had the highest
percentage of people working in high-skilled jobs. Males of southern European
descent also distinguished themselves, earning from 4 to 6 percent more than
non-Euroethnic White men, and those from eastern Europe earned 18 percent
more. The earnings of southern European women, as compared to non-Euroethnic White women, ranged as high as 7 percent more; and for eastern European
ones, 10 to 15 percent more.[15]

A Growing, Though Belated, Willingness of
Government Officials and Religious Organizations
to Apologize for Past Wrongdoing

On a local level, the Florida legislature in 1995 awarded compensation to nine
Black survivors of White mob attacks seven decades earlier. In that same year,
Mississippi finally ratified the Thirteenth Amendment abolishing slavery. Some
100 years after 31 Chinese gold miners in Oregon were brutally killed in 1887
were the files on what had happened first made public. On a national level, four
decades passed before Congress voted compensation for the unjust internment of
American Japanese and Aleuts during World War II, and not until 1993 did
Congress pass a resolution apologizing for the overthrow a hundred years earlier
of the Hawaiian monarchy.

Religionists, too, have increasingly acknowledged past wrongs. On almost a
hundred different occasions Pope John Paul II apologized for Catholic wrongs
against Jews, Africans, Indians, Protestants, women, and even the astronomer
Galileo. In 1995, on the 150th anniversary of its founding, the Southern Baptist
Convention overwhelmingly voted to ask forgiveness of "all African-Ameri-
cans" for past support of slavery. Two years later, Lutheran, Anglican, Catholic,
and United Methodist leaders in South Carolina issued a statement confessing
their sins of racism.

Last has been a multiplication of minority community and political action
groups, which as never before seek civic and political recognition and power. No

longer are hyphenated groups viewed as unpatriotic, and no longer are they dependent on the altruism of others to solve their problems, or, in the case of immigrants, to rely on homeland governments to speak on their behalf. Rather, much in the manner of Blacks, they hold marches, parades, demonstrations, and political forums, often with the encouragement of second- and third-generation local or federal politicians of their own group.

Both the Democratic and Republican parties have outreach programs to all major minority groups, including the solicitation of funds. On both local and national levels, political officeholders are sure to have prominent minority representatives as advisers or staff.

Facilitating all of the above were the press, radio, and television, which no longer ignored prejudice, discrimination, or violence against minorities, but portrayed such behavior as socially unacceptable and morally wrong and called upon political and public officials to take remedial action.

In short, today's minority groups have more protections, opportunities, and freedoms than their parents or grandparents had—or dreamed of possibly having—and they are demanding and taking advantage of them as never before. With time, changes for the better have taken place. Acknowledging such does not mean that there still are not victims and problems, but rather proves that change is possible and that pessimism and paranoia are unwarranted.

A second criterion is comparing intergroup relations in America to those in other countries. Here, too, America comes off very well, as is evident by what is and has been going on in other countries, as well as by the desires of so many foreigners to leave their homelands.

We simply do not have the wars, ethnic conflicts, and calls for secession, self-determination, or ethnic purification that take place in Eastern Europe, Yugoslavia, Spain, England, Northern Ireland, India, Indonesia, Rwanda—or in our border neighbors, Canada and Mexico. Few Native Americans, Hawaiians, and Alaskans want secession, and few Puerto Ricans want complete independence from America. Still fewer are the number of Americans who renounce their citizenship and leave to live in another country.

Nor do we have the intense animus toward minorities that exist in other countries, where in 1991, 54 percent of East Germans disliked Poles, 49 percent of Czechs disliked Hungarians, 44 percent of Russians disliked Azerbaijanis, 42 percent of French disliked North Africans, 39 percent of Bulgarians disliked Turks, and 21 percent of English disliked Irish—in contrast to the 13 percent of White Americans who disliked Blacks.[16]

Third, intergroup relations can be compared to the nationally cherished values of equal rights and opportunities for life, liberty, and the pursuit of happiness, where individuals are judged regardless of their race, religion, ethnicity, age, and sex. By this criterion, it is very clear—particularly to minorities—that problems still exist, that racism, anti-Catholicism, anti-Asianism, anti-Hispanicism, anti–Native Americanism, anti-Semitism, homophobia, and sexism have not disappeared.

The fourth criterion involves comparing a group's progress or lack of it to other groups. The results, of course, depend on the groups being compared. When the situation of American Blacks is compared to that of American Indians or Haitians, Blacks are doing very well, but when compared to that of Irish Catholics or Jews, they are far behind.

If being murdered and robbed of one's home are the worst that can befall a group, then Indians were the biggest victims, followed by Blacks, who were the only group brought here against their will as slaves, separated from their families, and not allowed to perpetuate their customs, languages, and even names. Mexicans throughout the Southwest were made strangers in their own land, as were native Hawaiians, both of whose lands were taken by trickery and conquest. Alaskan natives were not asked whether they wanted their land sold by Russia to America. Asians were the most unwanted groups, and Catholics the most hated religious group.

Often neglected in group comparisons are the significant numbers of minorities who, in spite of discrimination, achieved, such as Arabs, Armenians, Asians, Cubans, Greeks, Huguenots, Jews, Latvians, Mormons, Quakers, and West Indians. Also neglected are the ethnic and socioeconomic subdivisions within a specific victimized group—as with late-nineteenth- and early-twentieth-century relatively well-off northern Italians and poor southern ones, as well as with relatively poor eastern and well-off western European Jews. Today, too, noticeable differences in achievement exist between such Hispanic groups as Cubans, Mexicans, and Puerto Ricans—with Cubans generally having a much higher median income and educational attainment than the two other groups and than Whites generally.

In short, the picture that emerges from group-to-group comparisons is a mixed one, depending on which groups are being compared.

A fifth criterion is that of Utopia. All too obviously, America is not a Garden of Eden, Elysian Field, Happy Isle, Golden Land, or heaven on earth. Yes, we have come a far way from the prejudice and discrimination of early America or of Europe, Africa, and Asia, but we have a long way to go before it can be credibly said that Americans live by the Golden Rule.

The last and politically newest criteria (at least in America) are those of diversity and proportional representation. At first, the terms generally implied that if a group did not have a percentage of jobs, school admissions, positions, elections, and so on, equal to its percentage of the local or national population, or to its percentage of the workforce, it was a sign of being discriminated against. For example, since African Americans are some 12 percent of the population, or women some 50 percent, it was argued, they should have that percentage of jobs, college admissions, political appointments, and the like.

As a result of the continuing nonrepresentation or exclusion of minorities, and the growing public and court rejection of race-conscious solutions, calls began being made for establishing multiculturalism and diversity. Schools, workplaces, political offices, media, and much else, were admonished to create workforces that reflect the makeup of America, thereby assuring a greater minority inclusion than by merely calling for equal opportunity for all minorities.

By this criterion, with the exception of the armed forces, sports, and civil service jobs, few arenas of society are free of discrimination.

What does all this mean?

First, bad as bigotry was, it has been declining for all minority groups, though differentially so.

Second, how much of a decline has there been, how fast or slow has it occurred, what has caused either, and how best to escalate the speed of reform are legitimate topics of concern and debate.

Third, the absence of commonly agreed upon criteria for measuring progress distorts the reality of the progress made—and not made. Worse yet, in many cases, the absence has exacerbated intergroup relations, wherein one group's self-interests clash with those of other groups. Instead of forming coalitions to solve problems of common concern, many groups believe in focusing on their own priorities.

Without a coalitional agreement on what needs to be done, the pace of further progress will be delayed, but not stopped. Too much goodwill exists in America, and too many reforms have taken place, at too high a cost in lives and energy, to be stopped.

The proverbial glass is neither empty nor full, but being filled—and the sooner the better.

Notes

Chapter 1. The Seeds of Contempt

1. Ruth E. Sutter, *The Next Place You Come To* (Englewood Cliffs, NJ: Prentice-Hall, 1973), 73.

2. Durand Echeverria, *Mirage in the West* (Princeton: Princeton University Press, 1968), 6.

3. Henry Steele Commager and Elmo Giodanetti, *Was America a Mistake?* (New York: Harper & Row, 1967), 77.

4. Thomas Y. Canby, "The Search for the First Americans," *National Geographic,* September 1979, 333; *New York Times,* 19 June 1986, A23.

5. Kenneth Macgowan and Joseph A. Hester Jr., *Early Man in the New World* (Garden City, NY: Anchor Books, 1962), 5, 26.

6. Stan Hoig, *Tribal Wars of the Southern Plains* (Norman: University of Oklahoma Press, 1993), 32–33; Robert F. Spencer, Jesse D. Jennings, et al., *The Native Americans* (New York: Harper & Row, 1967), 186; Milton Meltzer, *Slavery: From the Rise of Western Civilization to Today* (New York: Dell, 1972), 197–200; Wilcomb E. Washburn, *The Indian in America* (New York: HarperColophon, 1975), 64; Irenaus Eibl-Eibesfeldt, *The Biology of Peace and War* (New York: Viking Press, 1979), 135.

7. Meltzer, *Slavery,* 198; *New York Times,* 19 February 1977; John Francis Bannon, *Indian Labor in the Spanish Indies* (Lexington, MA: D.C. Heath, 1966), vii.

8. Cornelius J. Jaenen, *Friend and Foe* (New York: Columbia University Press, 1976), 144.

9. Ibid., 128.

10. Nigel Davis, *Human Sacrifice* (New York: William Morrow, 1981), 250.

11. Andrew Sinclair, *The Savage* (London: Weidenfeld and Nicolson, 1977), 35.

12. Rasmus B. Anderson, *America Not Discovered by Columbus* (Chicago: S.C. Griggs, 1883), 38–39.

13. Macgowan and Hester, *Early Man in the New World,* 15; T.D. Steward, *The People of America* (New York: Charles Scribner's Sons, 1973), 60–61; Gordon Bronitsky, "Jews and Indians: Old Myths and New Realities," unpublished paper, Albuquerque, New Mexico, 1988, 1.

14. Dwight W. Hoover, *The Red and the Black* (Chicago: Rand McNally, 1976), 9–10; Ronald Sanders, *Lost Tribes and Promised Lands* (Boston: Little, Brown, 1978), 369; Edwin Wolf II and Maxwell Whiteman, *The History of the Jews of Philadelphia* (Philadelphia: Jewish Publication Society of America, 1975), 43.

15. Jaenen, *Friend and Foe,* 20; Larry L. Meyer, *Shadow of a Continent* (Palo Alto, CA: American West, 1975), 98.

16. Brian W. Dippie, *The Vanishing American* (Middletown, CT: Wesleyan Univer-

269

sity Press, 1982), 17; William Stanton, *The Leopard's Spots* (Chicago: University of Chicago Press, 1960), 11.

17. Barry Fell, *America* B.C. (New York: Quadrangle/New York Times Books, 1977), 6; "Hi, Columbus: Like the Trip?" *Newsweek,* 26 May 1975, 81–82; *New York Times,* 10 October 1982, 3.

18. Stan Steiner, *Fusang—The Chinese Who Built America* (New York: HarperColophon, 1979), 27; *Boston Globe,* 10 November 1985, 48.

19. Michael G. Michlovic and Michael W. Hughey, "Norse Blood and Indian Character: Content, Context and Transformation of Popular Mythology," *Journal of Ethnic Studies,* Fall 1982, 87; Howard F. Stein and Robert F. Hill, *The Ethnic Imperative* (University Park: Pennsylvania State University Press, 1977), 1975; Fell, *America* B.C., 7, 176; Meyer, *Shadow of a Continent,* 96; *The Jewish Encyclopedia,* vol. 12 (New York: KTAV undated reprinting), 252; Peter Caley, "Canada's Chinese Columbus," *Beaver,* Spring 1983, 6, 8.

20. Fell, *America* B.C., 7; *Bay State Banner,* 6 March 1975, 2; Anderson, *America Not Discovered by Columbus,* 150.

21. William A. Douglass and Jon Bilbao, *Amerikanuak* (Reno: University of Nevada Press, 1975), 1; Steiner, *Fusang,* 33; W.S. Kuniczak, *My Name Is Million* (Garden City, NY: Doubleday, 1978), 1; Mascarenhas Barreto, *The Portuguese Columbus* (New York: St. Martin's Press, 1992); Francis R. Walsh, "Who Spoke for Boston's Irish? The Boston Pilot in the Nineteenth Century," *Journal of Ethnic Studies,* Fall 1982, 31; Joseph Rothchild, "Introduction," in *East Central European Perceptions of Early America,* ed. Bela K. Kiraly and George Barany (Lisse: Peter DeRidder Press, 1977), 11; Andrew T. Kopan, "Greek Survival in Chicago: The Role of Ethnic Education, 1890–1980," in *Ethnic Chicago,* ed. Peter d'A. Jones and Melvin G. Holli (Grand Rapids, Mich.: William B. Eerdmans, 1981), 82.

22. Sinclair, *The Savage,* 29; Sydney E. Ahlstrom, *A Religious History of the American People* (New Haven: Yale University Press, 1972), 1; Samuel Eliot Morison, *The Oxford History of the American People* (New York: New American Library, 1972), 1: 51.

23. Louis Bertrand and Charles Perrie, *The History of Spain* (New York: Collier Books, 1971), 165; Walter Hart Blumenthal, *Brides from Bridewell—Female Felons Sent to Colonial America* (Rutland, VT: Charles E. Tuttle, 1962), 117.

24. Hans Koning, *Columbus: His Enterprise* (New York: Monthly Review Press, 1976), 21.

25. George Stimpson, *A Book about American History* (New York: Harper & Brothers, 1950), 3; William Miller, *A New History of the United States* (New York: Dell, 1967), 20.

26. Robert N. Bellah, *The Broken Covenant* (New York: Seabury Press, 1975), 5; Edwin Scott Gausted, *A Religious History of America* (New York: Harper & Row, 1966), 7.

27. *The Journal of Christopher Columbus* (New York: Clarkson N. Potter, 1960), 78.

28. Douglass and Bilbao, *Amerikanuak,* 74.

29. Jack D. Forbes, ed., *The Indians in America's Past* (Englewood Cliffs, NJ: Prentice-Hall, 1964), 88; Gianni Granzotto, *Christopher Columbus* (Norman: University of Oklahoma Press, 1987), 222, 250.

30. Sanders, *Lost Tribes and Promised Land,* 17; Meltzer, *Slavery,* 154; Sidney W. Mintz, "The Caribbean Region," *Daedalus,* Spring 1974, 49; Blumenthal, *Brides from Bridewell,* 118.

31. Judith S. Koffler, "Terror and Mutilation in the Golden Age," *Human Rights Quarterly,* May 1983, 118; Robert Royal, *1492 and All That* (Washington, DC: Ethics and Public Policy Center, 1992), 66.

32. Lewis Hanke, *The Spanish Struggle for Justice in the Conquest of America* (Boston: Little, Brown, 1965), 123.

33. Wilcomb E. Washburn, *Red Man's Land—White Man's Law* (New York: Charles Scribner's Sons, 1971), 7.

34. Ibid.

35. Magnus Morner, *Race Mixture in the History of Latin America* (Boston: Little, Brown, 1967), 25–26.

36. Meltzer, *Slavery,* 190; Frederick Bowser, "Colonial Spanish America," in *Neither Slave nor Free,* ed. David W. Cohen and Jack Greene (Baltimore: Johns Hopkins University Press, 1972), 27; Tzvetan Todorov, *The Conquest of America* (New York: Harper & Row, 1987), 136; Miller, *A New History of the United States,* 38.

37. Stephan Thernstrom, ed., *Harvard Encyclopedia of American Ethnic Groups* (Cambridge: Harvard University Press, 1980), 909.

38. Sutter, *The Next Place You Come To,* 66.

39. Michael R. Marrus, *The Unwanted—European Refugees in the Twentieth Century* (New York: Oxford University Press, 1985), 8; John Keats, *Eminent Domain* (New York: Charterhouse, 1973), 82–83; John Webster Grant, *Moon of Wintertime* (Toronto: University of Toronto Press, 1984), 7, 8.

40. Blumenthal, *Brides from Bridewell,* 80–81.

41. Bertram Wallace Korn, *The Early Jews of New Orleans* (Waltham: American Jewish Historical Society, 1969), 4; Oliver Evans, "Melting Pot in the Bayous," *American Heritage,* December 1963, 49; Blumenthal, *Brides from Bridewell,* 83.

42. George L. Smith, *Religion and Trade in New Netherland* (Ithaca: Cornell University Press, 1973), 5–6, 143.

43. Curtis Nettels, *The Roots of American Civilization* (New York: Appleton-Century-Crofts, 1963), 201.

44. Smith, *Religion and Trade in New Netherland,* 190–93; Thernstrom, *Harvard Encyclopedia of American Ethnic Groups,* 998.

45. Henri and Barbara van der Zee, *A Sweet and Alien Land* (New York: Appleton-Century-Crofts, 1963), 80; Sidney Mead, "From Coercion to Persuasion: Another Look at the Rise of Religious Liberty and the Emergence of Denominationalism," in *The National Temper,* ed. Lawrence W. Levine and Robert Middlekauff (New York: Harcourt Brace Jovanovich, 1972), 61.

46. Miller, *A New History of the United States,* 42; John E. Ferling, *A Wilderness of Miseries—War and Warriors in Early America* (Westport, CT: Greenwood Press, 1980), 32.

47. Sanders, *Lost Tribes and Promised Lands,* 230–31; James Muldoon, "The Indian as Irishman," *Essex Institute Historical Collections,* October 1975, 267–70.

48. Sanders, *Lost Tribes and Promised Lands,* 221.

49. J.H. Parry, *The Establishment of the European Hegemony: 1415–1715* (New York: Harper Torchbooks, 1966), 95.

50. D'Arcy McNickle, "Indian and European: Indian-White Relations from Discovery to 1887," in *The Emergent Native Americans,* ed. Deward E. Walker (Boston: Little, Brown, 1972), 77.

51. Ferling, *A Wilderness of Miseries,* 11; Mead, "From Coercion to Persuasion," 65; *The Encyclopedia of American Facts and Dates,* Gordon Carruth and associates, eds. (New York: Thomas Y. Crowell, 1979), 9.

52. Marchette Chute, *The First Liberty* (New York: E. Dutton, 1969), 18; Louis B. Wright, *The Cultural Life of the American Colonies* (New York: Harper Torchbooks, 1962), 46.

53. Alan Grimes, *Equality in America* (New York: Oxford University Press, 1964), 13.

54. Ahlstrom, *A Religious History of the American People,* 136.

55. Edward Potts Cheyney, *European Background of American History: 1300–1600*

(New York: Collier Books, 1961), 133; William E. Woodward, *The Way Our People Lived* (New York: Washington Square Press, 1970), 13–14.

56. Marcus Lee Hansen, *The Atlantic Migration, 1607–1860* (New York: Harper & Row, 1961), 32.

57. Carla Gardina Pestana, "The City upon a Hill under Siege: The Puritan Perception of the Quaker Threat to Massachusetts Bay, 1656–1661," *New England Quarterly,* September 1983, 324; van der Zee, *A Sweet and Alien Land,* 296; Hector Chevigny, *Russian America* (Portland, OR: Binford and Mort, 1985), 388.

58. Max Savelle, *Empires to Nations: Expansion in America, 1713–1824* (Minneapolis: University of Minnesota Press, 1974), 104.

59. Parry, *The Establishment of European Hegemony,* 123; Echeverria, *Mirage in the West,* 11.

60. Thernstrom, *Harvard Encyclopedia of American Ethnic Groups,* 487; James Oakes, *The Ruling Race* (New York: Alfred A. Knopf, 1982), 7.

61. Edwin Scott Gaustad, *A Religious History of America* (San Francisco: Harper San Francisco, 1990), 43.

62. Samuel Orth, *Our Foreigners* (New Haven: Yale University Press, 1921), 8.

63. Henry Steele Commager, *Living Ideas in America* (New York: Harper & Row, 1967), 11; Roger Daniels, *Coming to America* (New York: Harper Perennial, 1991), 47.

64. Miller, *A New History of the United States,* 81; Abbot Emerson Smith, *Colonists in Bondage* (New York: W.W. Norton, 1971), 32–33; Blumenthal, *Brides from Bridewell,* 36.

65. Michael Kraus, *Immigration, the American Mosaic* (New York: Van Nostrand Reinhold, 1966), 116; Daniels, *Coming to America,* 36.

66. V.F. Calverton, *The Awakening of America* (New York: John Day, 1939), 259.

67. Miller, *A New History of the United States,* 81; David Cressy, *Coming Over* (Cambridge, England: Cambridge University Press, 1989), 67.

68. Richard Hofstadter, *America at 1750* (New York: Vintage Books, 1973), 38.

69. Peter C. Marzio, *A Nation of Nations* (New York: Harper & Row, 1976), 59; Meltzer, *Slavery,* 186; Thernstrom, *Harvard Encyclopedia of American Ethnic Groups,* 909; Francis Parkman, *Pioneers of France in the New World* (Boston: Little, Brown, 1931), 221.

70. Smith, *Colonists in Bondage,* 125.

71. Hubertis M. Cummings, *Scots Breed and Susquehanna* (Pittsburgh: University of Pittsburgh Press, 1964), 24; Hofstadter, *American at 1750,* 48–49; Richard B. Morris, *Government and Labor in Early America* (New York: Harper Torchbooks, 1965), 326, 333.

72. Thernstrom, *Harvard Encyclopedia of American Ethnic Groups,* 486.

73. Meltzer, *Slavery,* 122–27, 144, 180.

74. Ibid., 149.

75. Marzio, *A Nation of Nations,* 89.

76. Jonathon Derrick, *Africa's Slaves Today* (London: George Allen and Unwin, 1975), 116.

77. C.R. Boxer, *Four Centuries of Portuguese Expansion, 1415–1825* (Berkeley: University of California Press, 1972), 32.

78. Melzer, *Slavery,* 184.

79. Barbara Kaye Greenleaf, *American Fever* (New York: New American Library, 1970), 18.

80. Hofstadter, *America at 1750,* 68.

81. Smith, *Religion and Trade in New Netherland,* 185; Carl Degler, "Slavery and the Genesis of American Race Prejudice," in *Essays on American Colonial History,* ed. Paul Goodman (New York: Holt, Rinehart and Winston, 1972), 190; Gary B. Nash, *The Urban Crucible* (Cambridge: Harvard University Press, 1979), 109.

82. Oakes, *The Ruling Race,* 3; Greenleaf, *American Fever,* 18.

83. Thomas Bacon, "Sermon to Negro Slaves," in *Great Issues in American History, From Settlement to Revolution, 1584–1776,* ed. Clarence L. Van Steeg and Richard Hofstadter (New York: Vintage Books, 1969), 238.

84. Fernando Henriques, *Children of Conflict* (New York: E. Dutton, 1975), 42; Jon Butler, *Awash in a Sea of Faith* (Cambridge: Harvard University Press, 1990), 134.

85. Arthur Zilbersmit, *The First Emancipation: The Abolition of Slavery in the North* (Chicago: University of Chicago Press, 1969), 20; Nathaniel Weyl and William Marina, *American Statesmen on Slavery and the Negro* (New Rochelle, NY: Arlington House, 1971), 14–15; W.J. Eccles, *France in America* (New York: Harper & Row, 1973), 244.

86. Joel Williamson, *New People—Miscegenation and Mulattoes in the United States* (New York: New York University Press, 1984), 7.

87. James Hugo Johnston, *Race Relations in Virginia and Miscegenation in the South, 1776–1860* (Amherst: University of Massachusetts Press, 1970), 184.

88. Charles M. Segal and David C. Stineback, *Puritans, Indians and Manifest Destiny* (New York: G.Putnam's Sons, 1977), 32; Frank H. Tucker, *The White Conscience* (New York: Frederick Ungar, 1968), 45.

89. Ahlstrom, *A Religious History of the American People,* 156; Gaustad, *A Religious History of America,* 17; Francis Jennings, *The Invasion of America* (New York: W.W. Norton, 1976), 48; Ahlstrom, *A Religious History of the American People,* 156; Chevigny, *Russian America,* 38.

90. Robert E. Bieder, "Scientific Attitudes toward Indian Mixed-Bloods in Early Nineteenth Century America," *Journal of Ethnic Studies,* Summer 1980, 21.

91. Grimes, *Equality in America,* 42; Johnston, *Race Relations in Virginia and Miscegenation in the South,* 170.

92. Johnston, *Race Relations in Virginia and Miscegenation in the South,* 172; Jaenen, *Friend and Foe,* 7.

93. Ferling, *A Wilderness of Miseries,* 35.

94. Segal and Stinebeck, *Puritans, Indians and Manifest Destiny,* 137; Jill Lepore, "When Deer Island Was Turned into Devil's Island," *Bostonia,* Summer 1998, 16; Nettels, *The Roots of American Civilization,* 212–13.

95. Jaenen, *Friend and Foe,* 127.

96. Stewart, *The People of America,* 37; Alfred W. Crosby Jr., *The Columbian Exchange* (Westport, CT: Greenwood Press, 1973), 36, 42.

97. Hoig, *Tribal Wars of the Southern Plains,* 53; Bruce A. Glasrud and Alan M. Smith, eds., *Race Relations in British North America, 1607–1783* (Chicago: Nelson-Hall, 1982), 85–99.

98. Todorov, *The Conquest of America,* 103; George T. Hunt, *The Wars of the Iroquois* (Madison: University of Wisconsin Press, 1960), 19.

99. Jay Dolan, *The American Catholic Experience* (Garden City, NY: Doubleday, 1985), 67; Smith, *Religion and Trade in New Netherland,* 24.

100. Jaenen, *Friend and Foe,* 147.

101. Roger Burlingame, *The American Conscience* (New York: Alfred A. Knopf, 1960), 36; Gary B. Nash, "Red, White, and Black," in *The Great Fear,* ed. Gary B. Nash and Richard Weiss (New York: Holt, Rinehart and Winston, 1970), 3.

102. Richard E. Greenleaf, "The Inquisitors and the Indians," in *History of Latin American Civilization,* ed. Lewis Hanke (Boston: Little, Brown, 1973), 325–26; Cecil Roth, *The Spanish Inquisition* (New York: W.W. Norton, 1964), 178–80; Steiner, *Fusang,* 81; Korn, *The Early Jews of New Orleans,* 32.

103. Evelyn Page, *American Genesis* (Boston: Bambit Inc., 1973), 97–98; Dolan, *The American Catholic Experience,* 26.

104. Nettels, *The Roots of American Civilization,* 386.

105. Allan Keller, "Little Sweden on the Delaware," *American History Illustrated,* January 1979, 12.

106. James Axtell, *America Perceived: A View from Abroad in the 17th Century* (West Haven: Pendulum, 1974), 185.

107. Vamberto Morais, *A Short History of Anti-Semitism* (New York: W.W. Norton, 1976), 146.

108. Boxer, *Four Centuries of Portuguese Expansion,* 51–52.

109. van der Zee, *A Sweet and Alien Land,* 9.

110. Morris U. Schappes, ed., *A Documentary History of the Jews in the United States* (New York: Schocken Books, 1971), 2.

111. Ibid., 5.

112. Smith, *Religion and Trade in New Netherland,* 201, 224; van der Zee, *A Sweet and Alien Land,* 297.

113. Smith, *Religion and Trade in New Netherland,* 230.

114. Miller, *A New History of the United States,* 48; Clifford E. Nelson, *The Lutherans in North America* (Philadelphia: Fortress, 1960), 9.

115. Calverton, *The Awakening of America,* 241; Maurity A. Hallgren, *Landscape of Freedom* (New York: Howell, Soskin, 1941), 80–81.

116. Frederick C. Drake, "Witchcraft in the American Colonies, 1647–1662," in *American Vistas, 1607–1877,* ed. Leonard Dinnerstein and Kenneth T. Jackson (New York: Oxford University Press, 1975), 37; Miller, *A New History of the United States,* 102.

117. Hofstadter, *America at 1750,* 57; *Bulletin, The Eire Society of Boston,* February 1986, 1.

118. Ray Allen Billington, *The Protestant Crusade* (Chicago: Quadrangle Paperbacks, 1964), 9; Hallgren, *Landscape of Freedom,* 26.

119. Robert Kelley, *The Cultural Pattern in American Politics* (New York: Alfred A. Knopf, 1979), 73–74.

120. Nettels, *The Roots of American Civilization,* 392; Charles H. Anderson, *White Protestant Americans* (Englewood Cliffs, NJ: Prentice-Hall, 1970), 40; Kelley, *The Cultural Pattern in American Politics,* 71–72; Thernstrom, *Harvard Encyclopedia of American Ethnic Groups,* 900; Arthur Mann, *The One and the Many* (Chicago: University of Chicago Press, 1979), 51.

121. Stanley Feldstein, *The Land That I Show You* (New York: Doubleday/Anchor, 1978), 18; Oscar Handlin and Mary F. Handlin, "The Acquisition of Political and Social Rights by the Jews in the United States," in *The Characteristics of American Jews,* ed. Joseph L. Blau, Nathan Glazer, and Oscar and Mary F. Handlin (New York: Jewish Education Committee Press, 1965), 245.

122. Louis Harap, *The Image of the Jew in American Literature* (Philadelphia: Jewish Publication Society of America, 1974), 19.

123. Gaustad, *A Religious History of America,* 69; Richard L. Bushman, *From Puritan to Yankee* (New York: W.W. Norton, 1967), 169; Robert G. Torbet, *A History of the Baptists* (Philadelphia: Judson Press, 1950), 254; Leo Pfeffer, *Church, State, and Freedom* (Boston: Beacon Press, 1953), 81.

124. Nelson, *The Lutherans in North America,* 289; Wolf and Whiteman, *The History of the Jews of Philadelphia,* 44.

125. Carl Bridenbaugh, *The Spirit of '76* (New York: Oxford University Press, 1975), 141.

126. Carl A. Brasseaux, *The Founding of New Acadia* (Baton Rouge: Louisiana State University Press, 1987), 24.

127. Ira M. Leonard and Robert D. Parmet, *American Nativism, 1830–1860* (New York: Van Nostrand Reinhold, 1971), 13; William Faulkner Rushton, *The Cajuns* (New York: Farrar, Straus & Giroux, 1979), 54–55; Olson, *The Ethnic Dimension in American History,* 128; Moses Rischin, "Creating Crevecoeur's 'New Man': He Had a Dream," *Journal of American Ethnic History,* Fall 1981, 34.

128. Peter Brock, *Pioneers of the Peaceable Kingdom* (Princeton: Princeton University Press, 1970), 3–93; Nettels, *The Roots of American Civilization,* 75–78.

129. Axtell, *America Perceived,* 197–98.

130. Smith, *Religion and Trade in New Netherland,* 226.

131. Ibid., 225; Pfeffer, *Church, State, and Freedom,* 84.

132. Nettels, *The Roots of American Civilization,* 129.

133. Thomas H. O'Connor, *The Heritage of the American People* (Boston: Allyn and Bacon, 1965), 68; Nelson, *The Lutherans in North America,* 18.

134. Miller, *A New History of the United States,* 63.

135. Grimes, *Equality in America,* 16.

136. Ibid.

137. Dolan, *The American Catholic Experience,* 85.

138. Robert T. Handy, *A Christian America* (New York: Oxford University Press, 1984), 15–19; Butler, *Awash in a Sea of Faith,* 270.

139. Miller, *A New History of the United States,* 124; Stephen Birmingham, *America's Secret Aristocracy* (Boston: Little, Brown, 1987), 56.

140. Robert Kelley, *The Shaping of the American Past to 1877* (Englewood Cliffs, NJ: Prentice-Hall, 1975), 85.

141. Claude H. Van Tyne, *England and America* (Cambridge, England: Cambridge University Press, 1927), 60; John C. Miller, *Origins of the American Revolution* (Stanford: Stanford University Press, 1959), 190.

142. Carl Bridenbaugh, *Mitre and Sceptre* (New York: Oxford University Press, 1962), 237.

143. Merle Curti, *The Roots of American Loyalty* (New York: Atheneum, 1968), 12–13; G.N.D. Evans, *Allegiance in America* (Reading, MA: Addison-Wesley, 1969), 3.

144. Mann, *The One and the Many,* 53; Ferling, *A Wilderness of Miseries,* 125.

145. Kelley, *The Shaping of the American Past to 1877,* 106; Richard L. Merritt, "Nation-Building in America: The Colonial Years," in *Nation-Building,* ed. Karl W. Deutsch and William J. Foltz (New York: Atherton Press, 1963), 66; John Phillip Reid, *The Concept of Liberty in the Age of the American Revolution* (Chicago: University of Chicago Press, 1988), 16.

146. Allison Lockwood, "The Times of Samuel Curwen," *American History Illustrated,* April 1978, 24.

147. Evans, *Allegiance in America,* 22; Wallace Brown, *The Good Americans* (New York: William Morrow, 1969), 93.

148. Evans, *Allegiance in America,* 17.

149. J.C. Furnas, *The Americans* (New York: Harper & Brothers, 1950), 1: 239; Lockwood, "The Times of Samuel Curwen," 24; Marrus, *The Unwanted,* 8–9.

150. Jack M. Sosin, *The Revolutionary Frontier, 1763–1883* (New York: Holt, Rinehart and Winston, 1967), 336; Peter S. Onuf, "State-Making in Revolutionary America: Independent Vermont as a Case Study," *Journal of American History,* March 1981, 798; Wright, *The Cultural Life of the American Colonies,* 67; Thernstrom, *Harvard Encyclopedia of American Ethnic Groups,* 528; Charles Murphy, *The Irish in the American Revolution* (Groverland, MA: Charles Murphy Publications, 1975), 52; Theresita Polzin, *The Polish Americans* (Pulaski, WI: Franciscan Publishers, 1973), 34.

151. Van Tyne, *England and America,* 75; Kelley, *The Shaping of the American Past to 1877,* 59; Kit and Frederica Konolige, *The Power of Their Glory* (New York: Wyden Books, 1978), 54.

152. Richard B. Morris, "Civil Liberties and the Jewish Tradition in Early America," in *The Jewish Experience in America—The Colonial Experience,* ed. Abraham J. Karp (New York: KTAV, 1969), 421; Dolan, *The American Catholic Experience,* 97.

153. Torbet, *A History of the Baptists,* 256; Ahlstrom, *A Religious History of the American People,* 371; Brasseaux, *The Founding of New Acadia,* 64; Van Tyne, *England and America,* 78.

154. Carl Berger, *Broadsides and Bayonets—The Propaganda War of the American Revolution* (Philadelphia: University of Pennsylvania Press, 1961), 94; Benjamin Quarles, *The Negro in the American Revolution* (New York: W.W. Norton, 1973), vii, 23, 107–8.

155. Glasrud and Smith, *Race Relations in British North America,* 328; Matthew Mellon, *Early American Views on Negro Slavery* (New York: Bergman, 1969), 43; John Sibley Butler, "Affirmative Action in the Military," *Annals of the American Academy of Political and Social Sciences,* September 1992, 199.

156. Berger, *Broadsides and Bayonets,* 52–83; Glasrud and Smith, *Race Relations in British North America,* 282.

157. David Levinson, "An Explanation for the Oneida-Colonist Alliance in the American Revolution," *Ethnohistory,* Summer 1976, 270.

158. Lillian Schlissel, *Conscience in America* (New York: E. Dutton, 1967), 30; Ferling, *A Wilderness of Miseries,* 24; Hunter James, *The Quiet People of the Land* (Chapel Hill: University of North Carolina Press, 1976), 35.

159. Ferling, *A Wilderness of Miseries,* 95; Marshall Smelser, *The Winning of Independence* (New York: New Viewpoints, 1973), 108; Robert Leckie, *The Wars of America* (New York: Harper & Row, 1968), 1: 105, 122; Ben C. Fenwich, "The Plot to Kill Washington," *American History Illustrated,* February 1987, 11–12.

160. Berger, *Broadsides and Bayonets,* 144, 147; Blumenthal, *Brides from Bridewell,* 121; Quarles, *The Negro in the American Revolution,* 147.

161. George Washington Greene, *Historical View of the American Revolution* (Boston: Ticknor and Fields, 1865), 283; Smelser, *The Winning of Independence,* 106.

162. Berger, *Broadsides and Bayonets,* 103.

163. Ibid., 114, 123.

164. Stephen T. Wagner, "America's Non-English Heritage," *Society,* November/December 1981, 37; *Franco-Americans in Vermont* (Washington, D.C.: U.S. Commission on Civil Rights, 1983), 2; Berger, *Broadsides and Bayonets,* 23.

165. John Tracy Ellis, *Documents of American Catholic History* (Chicago: Henry Regnery, 1967), 1: 136; *Franco-Americans in Vermont,* 2.

166. Berger, *Broadsides and Bayonets,* 195; Thomas A. Bailey, *A Diplomatic History of the American People* (New York: Appleton-Century-Crofts, 1950), 27; Barbara Tuchman, *The First Salute* (New York: Alfred A. Knopf, 1988), 22.

167. Jonathan R. Dull, *A Diplomatic History of the American Revolution* (New Haven: Yale University Press, 1985), 108–11; Valentine Belfiglio, "Military Participation of Italians during the American Revolution," in *The Contributions of Italians to the United States Before the Civil War,* ed. Peter Sammartino (Washington, D.C.: National Italian American Foundation, 1980), 79–80; J.J. Jusserand, *With Americans of the Past and Present Days* (New York: Charles Scribner's Sons, 1916), 211; Neil Longley York, *Mechanical Metamorphosis—Technological Change in Revolutionary America* (Westport, CT: Greenwood Press, 1985), 76.

168. Claude H. Van Tyne, *The Loyalists in the American Revolution* (New York: Peter Smith, 1929), 154–56; Berger, *Broadsides and Bayonets,* 158.

169. Peggy Robbins, "Benjamin Franklin and His Son, a Tory," *American History Illustrated,* November 1980, 45–46.

170. Levinson, "An Explanation for the Oneida-Colonist Alliance in the American Revolution," 276; Glasrud and Smith, *Race Relations in British North America,* 322.

171. Berger, *Broadsides and Bayonets,* 91; Ellen Gibson Wilson, *The Loyal Blacks* (New York: Capricorn Books, 1976), 41–42; Mellon, *Early American Views on Negro Slavery,* 60.

172. Stimpson, *A Book About American History,* 185; Ferling, *A Wilderness of Miseries,* 182; Francis Paul Prucha, *The Sword of the Republic* (Lincoln: University of Nebraska Press, 1969), 6.

173. Kelley, *The Shaping of the American Past to 1877,* 148; Nathan O. Hatch, *The Democratization of American Christianity* (New Haven: Yale University Press, 1989), 44.

174. Tuchman, *The First Salute,* 299.

175. Axtell, *America Perceived,* 192.

176. Wright, *The Cultural Life of the American Colonies,* 46; Constantine Panunzio, *Immigration Crossroads* (New York: Macmillan, 1927), 15.

177. Richard A. Bartlett, *The New Country* (New York: Oxford University Press, 1976), 28.

178. Gary B. Nash and Richard Weiss, eds., *The Great Fear—Race in the Mind of America* (New York: Holt, Rinehart and Winston, 1970), 22.

179. Leonard I. Sweet, *Black Images of America, 1784–1870* (New York: W.W. Norton, 1976), 29.

180. Meltzer, *Slavery,* 260.

181. Wilson, *The Loyal Blacks,* 3; Echeverria, *Mirage in the West,* 129.

182. William S. Willis, "Divide and Rule: Red, White, and Black in the Southwest," in *American Vistas, 1607–1877,* ed. Leonard Dinnerstein and Kenneth T. Jackson (New York: Oxford University Press, 1976), 70; Terry Eastland and William Bennett, *Counting by Race* (New York: Basic Books, 1974), 37.

183. Daniels, *Coming to America,* 59.

184. Willis, "Divide and Rule," 60.

185. Ibid., 70; R. Halliburton Jr., "Black Slave Control in the Cherokee Nation," *Journal of Ethnic Studies,* Summer 1975, 32; Earle H. West, *The Black American and Education* (Columbus, OH: Charles E. Merrill, 1972), 36; R. Halliburton Jr., "Black Slavery among the Cherokees," *American History Illustrated,* October 1976, 13; Forrest G. Wood, *The Arrogance of Faith* (New York: Alfred A. Knopf, 1990), 121.

186. Curti, *The Roots of American Loyalty,* 69.

187. Hatch, *The Democratization of American Christianity,* 3; Thomas J. Curry, *The First Freedoms* (New York: Oxford University Press, 1987), 219.

188. Morton Borden, *Jews, Turks, and Infidels* (Chapel Hill: University of North Carolina Press, 1984), 13–14; Naomi W. Cohen, *Encounter with Emancipation* (Philadelphia: Jewish Publication Society of America, 1984), 76.

189. Borden, *Jews, Turks, and Infidels,* 12.

190. Ibid., 14.

191. Dolan, *The American Catholic Experience,* 109.

192. Merle Curti, *American Philanthropy Abroad* (New Brunswick, NJ: Rutgers University Press, 1963), 9–10.

193. Curti, *The Roots of American Loyalty,* 73.

194. Kurt Rabl, Christoph Stoll, and Manfred Vasold, *From the U.S. Constitution to the Basic Law of the Federal Republic of Germany* (Grasfelfing, West Germany: Verlag Moos and Partner, 1988), 54.

195. Bertram W. Korn, "Jews and the American Revolution," *Jewish Digest,* July 1975, 10.

196. Moshe Davis, *With Eyes toward Zion* (New York: Arno Press, 1977), 4; Borden, *Jews, Turks, and Infidels,* 7.

197. Charles Boewe, *Prairie Albion—An English Settlement in Pioneer Illinois* (Carbondale: Southern Illinois University Press, 1962), 62.

198. Leo Pfeffer, *The Liberties of an American* (Boston: Beacon Press, 1956), 34; Curry, *The First Freedoms,* 197.

199. Richard W. Pointer, *Protestant Pluralism and the New York Experience* (Bloomington: Indiana University Press, 1988), 13–15; Kelley, *The Shaping of the American Past to 1877,* 91; Hansen, *The Atlantic Migration,* 72–77; Dolan, *The American Catholic Experience,* 109; John Hope Franklin, *From Slavery to Freedom* (New York: Alfred A. Knopf, 1969), 162–64.

200. Hofstadter, *America at 1750,* 181.

201. Echeverria, *Mirage in the West,* 109.

202. Frances Kellor, *Immigration and the Future* (New York: George H. Doran, 1920), 246.

203. Seymour Martin Lipsett, "Religion and Politics in the American Past and Present," in *Religion and Social Conflict,* ed. Robert Lee and Martin E. Marty (New York: Oxford University Press, 1964), 74.

204. Curti, *The Roots of American Loyalty,* 93.

205. Gerald Carson, "Watermelon Armies and Whiskey Boys," in *American Vistas, 1607–1877,* ed. Leonard Dinnerstein and Kenneth T. Jackson (New York: Oxford University Press, 1975), 115; Kelley, *The Cultural Pattern in American Politics,* 113.

206. Kelley, *The Cultural Pattern in American Politics,* 114; Schappes, *A Documentary History of the Jews in the United States,* 84–85.

207. Echeverria, *Mirage in the West,* 176.

208. Marshal Smelser, "The Federalist Era as an Age of Passion," in *Conspiracy—The Fear of Subversion in American History,* ed. Richard O. Curry and Thomas M. Brown (New York: Holt, Rinehart and Winston, 1972), 54; John C. Miller, *Crisis in Freedom* (Boston: Little, Brown, 1951), 6.

209. Smelser, "The Federalist Era as an Age of Passion," 50; Miller, *Crisis in Freedom,* 11; Echeverria, *Mirage in the West,* 188; Maldwyn Allen Jones, *American Immigration* (Chicago: University of Chicago Press, 1960), 85.

210. Seymour Martin Lipset and Earl Raab, *The Politics of Unreason* (New York: Harper & Row, 1970), 36–37.

211. Thomas I. Emerson and David M. Helfeld, "Loyalty among Government Employees," *Yale Law Journal* 58 (1948): 4; H.L. Mencken, *The American Language* (New York: Alfred A. Knopf, 1963), 144.

212. James M. Banner Jr., *To the Hartford Convention: The Federalists and the Origins of Party Politics in Massachusetts, 1789 to 1815* (New York: Alfred A. Knopf, 1970), 89, 93.

Chapter 2. The Weeds of Contempt

1. Thomas Low Nichols, *Forty Years of American Life, 1821–1861* (New York: Stackpole Sons, 1937), 38.

2. Clinton Rossiter, *The American Quest, 1790–1860* (New York: Harcourt Brace Jovanovich, 1971), 262.

3. William Preston Jr., *Aliens and Dissenters* (New York: Harper & Row, 1966), 30.

4. Richard A. Bartlett, *The New Country* (New York: Oxford University Press, 1979), 144.

5. Robert Swierenga, "Dutch International Migration Statistics, 1820–1880: An Analysis of Linked Multinational Nominal Files," *International Migration Review,* Fall 1981, 446.

6. Robert Kelley, *The Shaping of the American Past to 1877* (Englewood Cliffs, NJ: Prentice-Hall, 1975), 206–7.

7. Michael J. Piore, *Birds of Passage* (Cambridge, England: Cambridge University Press, 1979), 148.

8. Jeanette Meisel Baron, ed., *Steeled by Adversity—Essays and Addresses on American Jewish Life by Salo Wittmayer Baron* (Philadelphia: Jewish Publication Society of America, 1971), 283–84.

9. Leonard Dinnerstein and Frederic Cople Jaher, *The Aliens* (New York: Appleton-Century-Crofts, 1970), 20.

10. Wayne Charles Miller, *A Handbook of American Minorities* (New York: New York University Press, 1976), 103.

11. Francis M. Rogers, *Americans of Portuguese Descent* (Beverly Hills, CA: Sage, 1974), 26.

12. Ray Allen Billington, *The Protestant Crusade* (Chicago: Quadrangle Paperbacks, 1964), 1.

13. Victor R. Greene, *American Immigrant Leaders, 1800–1910* (Baltimore: Johns Hopkins University Press, 1987), 33.

14. Arnold Shankman, *Ambivalent Friends—Afro-Americans View the Immigrant* (Westport, CT: Greenwood Press, 1982), 84.

15. Maldwyn Allen Jones, *American Immigration* (Chicago: University of Chicago Press, 1960), 120–21.

16. Moses Rischin, ed., *Immigration and the American Tradition* (Indianapolis: Bobbs-Merrill, 1976), 48.

17. Herbert W. Schneider, ed., *Benjamin Franklin, the Autobiography and Selections from His Other Writings* (New York: Liberal Arts Press, 1953), 194.

18. James Stuart Olson, *The Ethnic Dimension in American History* (New York: St. Martin's Press, 1979), 96.

19. Alixa Naff, "Becoming American: Peddling and the Syrian Immigrants, 1880–1914," *Journal of Armenian Studies* 3 (1986–87): 63.

20. Leonard Dinnerstein and David M. Reimers, *Ethnic Americans: A History of Immigration and Assimilation* (New York: Dodd, Mead, 1975), 21–22; Alan Conway, "Welsh Emigration to the United States," in *Perspectives in American History,* vol. 7, ed. Donald Fleming and Bernard Bailyn (Cambridge: Charles Warren Center for Studies in American History, 1973), 221.

21. Edward Wakin, *Enter the Irish-American* (New York: Thomas Y. Crowell, 1976), 34; Hasia R. Diner, *Erin's Daughters in America* (Baltimore: Johns Hopkins University Press, 1983), 122.

22. Peter C. Marzio, *A Nation of Nations* (New York: Harper & Row, 1976), 131.

23. Arthur Mann, *The One and the Many* (Chicago: University of Chicago Press, 1979), 80.

24. Lucy M. Cohen, *Chinese in the Post/Civil War South* (Baton Rouge: Louisiana State University Press, 1984), 27–28.

25. Frances Wright, *Views of Society and Manners in America* (Cambridge: Belknap Press of Harvard University Press, 1963), 237.

26. Maxine Schwartz Seller, *Immigrant Women* (Philadelphia: Temple University Press, 1981), 32.

27. Theodore C. Blegen, *Grass Roots History* (Minneapolis: University of Minnesota Press, 1947), 113.

28. Durand Echeverria, *Mirage in the West* (Princeton: Princeton University Press, 1968), 210; Leo Schelbert, "On Becoming an Emigrant: A Structural View of Eighteenth- and Nineteenth-Century Swiss Data," in *Perspectives in American History*, vol. 7, ed. Donald Fleming and Bernard Bailyn (Cambridge: Charles Warren Center for Studies in American History, 1973), 442; Alan M. Kraut, *The Huddled Masses: The Immigrant in American Society, 1880–1921* (Arlington Heights, IL: Harlan Davidson, 1982), 10; Michael Kraus, *Immigration, the American Mosaic* (New York: Van Nostrand Reinhold, 1966), 31.

29. Moses Rischin, *The Promised City* (Harper Torchbooks, 1970), 75; *Christian Science Monitor*, 21 April 1986, 13.

30. John Hope Franklin, "Ethnicity in American Life: The Historical Perspective," in *Ethnicity in American Life*, ed. John Hope Franklin, Thomas F. Pettigrew, and Raymond W. Mack (New York: Anti-Defamation League of B'nai B'rith, 1971), 17.

31. Theodore Saloutos, "Causes and Patterns of Greek Emigration to the United States," in *Perspectives in American History*, vol. 7, ed. Donald Fleming and Bernard Bailyn (Cambridge: Charles Warren Center for Studies in American History, 1973), 384.

32. Marcus Lee Hansen, *The Atlantic Migration, 1607–1860* (New York: Harper & Row, 1961), 91.

33. Jones, *American Immigration*, 123; Charles Boewe, *Prairie Albion—An English Settlement in Pioneer Illinois* (Carbondale: Southern Illinois University Press, 1962), 61.

34. Rischin, *Immigration and the American Tradition*, 46.

35. Joseph W. Wieczerzak, "The Polish Boat People of 1834," *Perspectives, A Polish-American Educational and Cultural Quarterly*, September/October 1984, 363; Jones, *American Immigration*, 123; W.S. Kuniczak, *My Name Is Million* (Garden City, NY: Doubleday, 1978), 49.

36. Conway, "Welsh Emigration," 248; Nancy Eubank, *The Russians in America* (Minneapolis: Lerner Publications, 1973), 51–52.

37. Thomas A. Bailey, *A Diplomatic History of the American People* (New York: Appleton-Century-Crofts, 1946), 185.

38. Kelley, *The Shaping of the American Past*, 260.

39. Lawrence J. Friedman, *Inventors of the Promised Land* (New York: Alfred A. Knopf, 1975), 194–209; Nathaniel Weyl and William Marina, *American Statesmen on Slavery and the Negro* (New Rochelle, NY: Arlington House, 1971), 133.

40. August Meier and Elliott Rudwick, *From Plantation to Ghetto* (New York: Hill and Wang, 1970), 3, 105; Arthur and Lila Weinberg, eds., *Passport to Utopia—Great Panaceas in American History* (New York: Quadrangle Books, 1968), 50–51.

41. Weyl and Marina, *American Statesmen on Slavery and the Negro*, 84; Brian W. Dippie, *The Vanishing American* (Middletown, CT: Wesleyan University Press, 1982), 77.

42. Leonard L. Richards, "Generation of Anti-Abolitionist Violence," in *Civil Strife in America*, ed. Norman S. Cohen (Hinsdale, IL: Dryden Press, 1972), 105; Matthew Mellon, *Early American Views on Negro Slavery* (New York: Bergman, 1969), 155.

43. Leonard I. Sweet, *Black Images of America, 1784–1870* (New York: W.W. Norton, 1976), 55.

44. Meier and Rudwick, *From Plantation to Ghetto*, 117–18.

45. Dale T. Knobel, *Paddy and the Republic* (Middletown, CT: Wesleyan University Press, 1986), 104–28.

46. Hans von Hentig, *The Criminal and His Victim* (New York: Schocken Books, 1979), 263.

47. Billington, *The Protestant Crusade*, 135.

48. Charles E. Rosenberg, *The Cholera Years* (Chicago: University of Chicago Press, 1962), 63; Francis R. Walsh, "Who Spoke for Boston's Irish? The Boston Pilot in the Nineteenth Century," *Journal of Ethnic Studies,* Fall 1982, 25; Dorothy O. Johansen and Charles M. Gates, *Empire of the Columbia* (New York: Harper & Brothers, 1957), 231.

49. Francis Paul Prucha, *The Sword of the Republic* (Lincoln: University of Nebraska Press, 1969), 323–28.

50. Ira M. Leonard and Robert D. Parmet, *American Nativism, 1830–1860* (New York: Von Nostrand Reinhold, 1971), 2; Nathan Glazer, *Affirmative Discrimination* (New York: Basic Books, 1975), 14.

51. Walsh, "Who Spoke for Boston's Irish?" 24; Roger Daniels, *Coming to America* (New York: Harper Perennial, 1991), 131; Maury Klein, "A Race in Upheaval," *American History Illustrated,* January 1979, 30.

52. J. Leslie Dunstan, *A Light to the City—150 Years of the City Missionary Society of Boston, 1816–1966* (Boston: Beacon Press, 1966), 47; Walsh, "Who Spoke for Boston's Irish?" 24–25.

53. Gustavus Myers, *History of Bigotry in the United States* (New York: Capricorn Books, 1968), 81.

54. Billington, *The Protestant Crusade,* 41.

55. Richard Maxwell Brown, "Historical Patterns of Violence in America," in *Violence in America,* ed. Hugh Davis Graham and Ted Robert Gurr (New York: New American Library, 1969), 50; Ronald G. Walters, *American Reformers 1815–1860* (New York: Hill and Wang, 1978), 9–10; Dinnerstein and Jaher, *The Aliens,* 125.

56. Richard Hofstadter and Michael Wallace, *American Violence* (New York: Vintage Books, 1971), 302; Donald E. Gelfand and Russell D. Lee, *Ethnic Conflicts and Power: A Cross-National Perspective* (New York: John Wiley and Sons, 1973), 212.

57. Gelfand and Lee, *Ethnic Conflicts and Power,* 210.

58. Stephan Thernstrom, ed., *Harvard Encyclopedia of American Ethnic Groups* (Cambridge: Harvard University Press, 1980), 730; William Mulder and Russel A. Mortensen, *Among the Mormons* (New York: Alfred A. Knopf, 1958), 271.

59. Thernstrom, *Harvard Encyclopedia of American Ethnic Groups,* 721.

60. William Fraser Rae, *Westward by Rail: The New Route to the East* (New York: Promontory Press, 1974), 148; Helge Seljass, "Polygamy among the Norwegian Mormons," in *Norwegian-American Studies* (Northfield: Norwegian-American Historical Association, 1977), 27:152.

61. Ferenc Morton Szasz, *The Protestant Clergy in the Great Plains and Mountain West, 1865–1915* (Albuquerque: University of New Mexico Press, 1988), 157.

62. Nels Anderson, *Desert Saints* (Chicago: University of Chicago Press, 1966), 183–84.

63. Hofstadter and Wallace, *American Violence,* 316–17; Szasz, *The Protestant Clergy in the Great Plains and Mountain West, 1865–1915,* 170.

64. Bruce Kenney, *Mormonism—The Islam of America* (New York: Fleming H. Revell, 1912), 41.

65. Robert F. Heizer and Alan J. Almquist, *The Other Californians* (Berkeley: University of California Press, 1971), 20.

66. Melvin Steinfield, *Cracks in the Melting Pot* (New York: Glencoe Press, 1973), 82; Milton Meltzer, *Bound for the Rio Grande—The Mexican Struggle 1845–1850* (New York: Alfred A. Knopf, 1974), 227–28; Stan Steiner, *La Raza, the Mexican Americans* (New York: HarperColophon, 1970), 362–63.

67. Billington, *The Protestant Crusade,* 238; Meltzer, *Bound for the Rio Grande,* 201–3; Gladys Thum and Marcella Thum, *The Persuaders—Propaganda in War and Peace* (New York: Atheneum, 1972), 42.

68. John R. Bodo, *The Protestant Clergy and Public Issues* (Princeton: Princeton

University Press, 1954), 196–202; Robert N. Bellah, *The Broken Covenant* (New York: Seabury Press, 1975), 57; Thomas H. O'Connor, *Fitzpatrick's Boston, 1846–1866* (Boston: Northeastern University Press, 1984), 65.

69. Wilcomb E. Washburn, *Red Man's Land—White Man's Law* (New York: Charles Scribner's Sons, 1971), 165.

70. Dippie, *The Vanishing American,* 32.

71. Ibid., 71.

72. Arthur H. De Rosier Jr., *The Removal of the Choctaw Indians* (New York: Harper Torchbooks, 1970), vi.

73. Washburn, *Red Man's Land—White Man's Law,* 66.

74. Dippie, *The Vanishing American,* 66.

75. De Rosier Jr., *The Removal of the Choctaw Indians,* 4.

76. Russell Thornton, "Cherokee Population Losses during the Trail of Tears: A New Perspective and a New Estimate," *Ethnohistory* 31 (1984): 290–91.

77. Prucha, *The Sword of the Republic,* 270–71.

78. John Tebbel and Keith Jennison, *The American Indian Wars* (New York: Bonanza Books, 1960), 210; Stan Hoig, *Tribal Wars of the Southern Plains* (Norman: University of Oklahoma Press, 1993), 150, 162–63.

79. James Hugo Johnston, *Race Relations in Virginia and Miscegenation in the South, 1776–1860* (Amherst: University of Massachusetts Press, 1970), 277.

80. Michael Paul Rogin, *Fathers and Children—Andrew Jackson and the Subjugation of the American Indian* (New York: Vintage Books, 1976), 4.

81. Sydney E. Ahlstrom, *A Religious History of the American People* (New Haven: Yale University Press, 1972), 423; Robert H. Keller Jr., *American Protestantism and United States Indian Policy, 1869–1882* (Lincoln: University of Nebraska Press, 1983), 6.

82. Alexander Ross, *Adventures of the First Settlers on the Oregon* (New York: Citadel Press, 1969), 365–66; Wilcomb E. Washburn, *The Indian in America* (New York: HarperColophon, 1975), 123.

83. Albert K. Weinberg, *Manifest Destiny* (Chicago: Quadrangle Paperbacks, 1963), 23.

84. Ibid., 31; James M. Banner Jr., *To the Hartford Convention: The Federalists and the Origins of Party Politics in Massachusetts, 1789 to 1815* (New York: Alfred A. Knopf, 1970), 93.

85. Oliver Evans, "Melting Pot in the Bayous," *American Heritage,* December 1963, 50.

86. Weinberg, *Manifest Destiny,* 35; Howard R. Lamar, ed., *The Reader's Encyclopedia of the American West* (New York: Thomas Y. Crowell, 1977), 413.

87. Melvin G. Holli and Peter d'A. Jones, *The Ethnic Frontier* (Grand Rapids, Mich.: William B. Eerdmans, 1977), 82–92.

88. Thernstrom, *Harvard Encyclopedia of American Ethnic Groups,* 324; Prucha, *The Sword of the Republic,* 104; Dippie, *The Vanishing American,* 7; Jack Weatherford, *Indian Givers* (New York: Fawcett Columbine, 1988), 158.

89. John Hope Franklin, *From Slavery to Freedom—A History of Negro Americans* (New York: Alfred A. Knopf, 1969), 168–69; Weyl and Marina, *American Statesmen on Slavery and the Negro,* 120.

90. Bodo, *The Protestant Clergy and Public Issues 1812–1848,* 196–202.

91. Leonard and Parmet, *American Nativism, 1830–1860,* 27–28.

92. Don Charles Foote, "American Whalemen in Northwestern Arctic Alaska," in *The Emergent Native Americans,* ed. David E. Walker (Boston: Little, Brown, 1972), 301; Ted C. Hinckley, *The Americanization of Alaska, 1867–1897* (Palto Alto, CA: Pacific Books, 1967), 21, 78.

93. Lamar, *The Reader's Encyclopedia of the American West,* 705; Joseph W.

Wieczerzak, *A Polish Chapter in Civil War America* (New York: Twayne, 1967), 13; Bailey, *A Diplomatic History of the American People,* 285.

94. Bailey, *A Diplomatic History of the American People,* 383; Gunnar J. Malmin, ed., *America in the Forties—The Letter of Ole Munch Raeder* (Minneapolis: University of Minnesota Press, 1929), 83.

95. Winthrop S. Hudson, ed., *Nationalism and Religion in America* (New York: Harper & Row, 1970), 97; Jane Ritchie, Review of *Pilgrim Path: The First Company of Women Missionaries to Hawaii,* by Mary Zwie, *Ethnohistory,* Winter 1993, 158.

96. Naomi W. Cohen, *Encounter with Emancipation* (Philadelphia: Jewish Publication Society of America, 1984), 35; Morris U. Schappes, ed., *A Documentary History of the Jews in the United States* (New York: Schocken Books, 1971), 606; Jonathon D. Sarna, "American Christian Opposition to Missions to the Jews, 1816–1900," *Journal of Ecumenical Studies,* Spring 1986, 226–27.

97. Peter Grose, *Israel in the Mind of America* (New York: Alfred A. Knopf, 1983), 16–18.

98. Leonard Pitt, *The Decline of the Californios* (Berkeley: University of California Press, 1971), 52; JoAnn Levy, "Forgotten Forty-Niners," *American History Illustrated,* February 1992, 38–49.

99. Kenneth O. Bjork, *West of the Great Divide* (Northfield, MN: Norwegian-American Historical Association, 1958), 25; Manoel da Silveira Cardozo, ed., *The Portuguese in America 590 B.C.–1974* (Dobbs Ferry, NY: Oceana Publications, 1976), 24.

100. David McCullough, *The Path between the Seas—The Creation of the Panama Canal, 1870–1914* (New York: Simon and Schuster, 1977), 34.

101. Pitt, *The Decline of the Californios,* 52; William A. Douglass and Jon Bilbao, *Amerikanuak* (Reno: University of Nevada Press, 1975), 204; Stan Steiner, *Fusang—The Chinese Who Built America* (New York: HarperColophon, 1979), 88; Heizer and Almquist, *The Other Californians,* 89.

102. Werner Levi, *American-Australian Relations* (Minneapolis: University of Minnesota Press, 1947), 38; John Greenway, *The Last Frontier* (London: Davis-Poynter, 1972), 19; Ray Aitchison, *Americans in Australia* (New York: Charles Scribner's Sons, 1972), 11.

103. Rodman W. Paul, *California Gold* (Lincoln: University of Nebraska Press, 1965), 28; Thernstrom, *Harvard Encyclopedia of American Ethnic Groups,* 388.

104. Steiner, *Fusang,* 116; Evelyn Wells and Harry C. Peterson, *The '49ers* (Garden City, NY: Doubleday, 1949), 229–30.

105. William Loren Katz, *The Black West* (Garden City, NY: Doubleday/Anchor, 1973), 124.

106. Heizer and Almquist, *The Other Californians,* 26.

107. Henry F. Dobyns, "Brief Perspective on a Scholarly Transformation: Widowing the 'Virgin' Land," *Ethnohistory,* Spring 1976, 100; Alvin M. Josephy Jr., *The Indian Heritage of America* (New York: Alfred A. Knopf, 1969), 171.

108. Raymond H. Robinson, *The Growing of America: 1780–1848* (Boston: Allyn and Bacon, 1973), 105–7.

109. Leonard and Parmet, *American Nativism, 1830–1860,* 33; Robinson, *The Growing of America,* 107.

110. John Bodnar, *The Transplanted—A History of Immigrants in Urban America* (Bloomington: Indiana University Press, 1985), 66–67.

111. Wieczerzak, *A Polish Chapter in Civil War America,* 15; Heale, *American Anticommunism—Combating the Enemy Within, 1830–1970,* 15–16.

112. Billington, *The Protestant Crusade,* 204; Edward J. Richter and Berton Dulce, *Religion and the Presidency* (New York: Macmillan, 1962), 32–33.

113. Joel H. Silbey, *The Transformation of American Politics, 1840–1860* (Englewood Cliffs, NJ: Prentice-Hall, 1967), 47; Diner, *Erin's Daughters in America*, 107.

114. Billington, *The Protestant Crusade*, 324; Rosenberg, *The Cholera Years*, 135.

115. C.S. Griffen, *The Ferment of Reform, 1830–1860* (New York: Thomas Y. Crowell, 1967), 76; William Cobbett, *A Year's Residence in America* (London: Chapman and Dodd, undated), 159; Elliott West, "Men, Whiskey and a Place to Sit," *American History Illustrated*, July 1981, 11–19; Ian R. Tyrell, *Sobering Up—From Temperance to Prohibition in Antebellum America, 1800–1860* (Westport, CT: Greenwood Press, 1979), 13.

116. Seymour Martin Lipset, "Religion and Politics in the American Past and Present," in *Religion and Social Conflict*, ed. Robert Lee and Martin E. Marty (New York: Oxford University Press, 1964), 77–80.

117. Tyrell, *Sobering Up*, 3; Thomas H. O'Connor, *The Heritage of the American People* (Boston: Allyn and Bacon, 1965), 234; Diner, *Erin's Daughters in America*, 113; Norman H. Clark, *Deliver Us from Evil* (New York: W.W. Norton, 1976), 24.

118. Cohen, *Encounter with Emancipation*, 81.

119. Richter and Dulce, *Religion and the Presidency*, 29; Knabel, *Paddy and the Republic*, 159.

120. Russell B. Nye, "The Slave Power Conspiracy: 1830–1860," in *Conspiracy—The Fear of Subversion in American History*, ed. Richard O. Curry and Thomas M. Brown (New York: Holt, Rinehart and Winston, 1972), 82.

121. Silbey, *The Transformation of American Politics*, 44–52.

122. Christopher J. Kauffman, *Faith and Fraternalism: The History of the Knights of Columbus, 1882–1982* (New York: Harper & Row, 1982), 6–7; Brian McGinty, "Hung Be the Heavens with Black," *American History Illustrated*, February 1983, 33.

123. Terry Coleman, *Going to America* (New York: Pantheon Books, 1972), 228.

124. P.J. De Smet, *History of the Western Missions and Missionaries in the United States* (New York: P.J. Kennedy, Excelsior Catholic, 1859), 399.

125. Cohen, *Encounter with Emancipation*, 89–90.

126. Robinson, *The Growing of America*, 106.

127. Weyl and Marina, *American Statesmen on Slavery and the Negro*, 134.

128. Mellon, *Early American Views on Negro Slavery*, 131.

129. W.E.F. Ward, *The Royal Navy and the Slavers* (New York: Shocken Books, 1970), 138–39; Kelley, *The Shaping of the American Past*, 340.

130. Meier and Rudwick, *From Plantation to Ghetto*, 38.

131. Paul Lewinson, *Race, Class and Party* (New York: Grosset and Dunlap, 1965), 29; Weyl and Marina, *American Statesmen on Slavery and the Negro*, 143.

132. Eugene D. Genovese, "The Slave States of North America," in *Neither Slave nor Free*, ed. David W. Cohen and Jack Greene (Baltimore: Johns Hopkins University Press, 1972), 269–73; Dinesh D'Souza, *The End of Racism* (New York: Free Press, 1995), 77.

133. Ronald Takaki, "The Myth of Ethnicity: Scholarship of the Anti-Affirmative Action Backlash," *Journal of Ethnic Studies*, Spring 1982, 29.

134. Herman D. Bloch, *The Circle of Discrimination* (New York: New York University Press, 1969), 80–81.

135. Richards, "Generation of Anti-Abolitionist Violence," 111–14; Leonard L. Richards, "Gentlemen of Property and Standing" in *Anti-Abolition Mobs in Jacksonian America* (London: Oxford Universty Press, 1970), 5, 131.

136. Ahlstrom, *A Religious History of the American People*, 661; Wood, *The Arrogance of Faith*, 65, 82, 289.

137. Robert V. Haynes, *Blacks in America Before 1865* (New York: David McKay, 1972), 367.

138. Aileen S. Kraditor, *The Ideas of the Woman Suffrage Movement, 1890–1920* (Garden City, NY: Anchor Books, 1965), 1; Robert L. Allen, *Reluctant Reformers* (New York: Anchor Books, 1975), 144.

139. Ibid., 152–53.

140. Kelley, *The Shaping of the American Past,* 280; Donald E. Gelfand and Russell Lee, *Ethnic Conflicts and Power* (New York: John Wiley and Sons, 1973), 66.

141. Gilbert Osofsky, *The Burden of Race* (New York: Harper & Row, 1967), 78.

142. Myers, *History of Bigotry in the United States,* 146.

143. Terry Eastland and William J. Bennett, *Counting by Race* (New York: Basic Books, 1974), 53.

144. Osofsky, *The Burden of Race,* 122; David Brion Davis, *Slavery and Human Progress* (New York: Oxford University Press, 1984), 270.

145. Morton Borden, *Jews, Turks, and Infidels* (Chapel Hill: University of North Carolina Press, 1984), 61.

146. Bell Irvin Wiley, *The Life of Billy Yank—The Common Soldier of the Union* (Garden City, NY: Doubleday, 1971), 307–8; Kraut, *The Huddled Masses,* 24.

147. Wiley, *The Life of Billy Yank,* 310; Susan M. Papp, *Hungarian Americans and Their Communities of Cleveland* (Cleveland: Cleveland State University Press, 1981), 96; Pitt, *The Decline of the Californios,* 220; Kuniczak, *My Name Is Million,* 81.

148. Wiley, *The Life of Billy Yank,* 312.

149. Wakin, *Enter the Irish-American,* 128; Stanley Feldstein, *The Land That I Show You* (New York: Doubleday/Anchor, 1978), 88; Daniels, *Coming to America,* 192.

150. Ahlstrom, *A Religious History of the American People,* 670; O'Connor, *Fitzpatrick's Boston, 1846–1866,* 192.

151. James M. McPherson, *The Negro's Civil War* (New York: Vintage Books, 1965), 31; Larry Kincaid, "Two Steps Forward, One Step Back," in *The Great Fear,* ed. Gary B. Nash and Richard Weiss (New York: Holt, Rinehart and Winston, 1970), 56–57.

152. Lawrence J. Friedman, *The White Savage* (Englewood Cliffs, NJ: Prentice-Hall, 1970), 7–9; Eli N. Evans, *Judah Benjamin, The Jewish Confederate* (New York: Free Press, 1988), 289, 291; Meier and Rudwick, *From Plantation to Ghetto,* 145.

153. Forest G. Wood, *Black Scare* (Berkeley: University of California Press, 1970), 4.

154. James M. McPherson, *The Negro's Civil War* (New York: Vintage Books, 1965), 70.

155. Jose A. Cabranes, *Citizenship and the American Empire* (New Haven: Yale University Press, 1979), 16; Kraus, *Immigration, the American Mosaic,* 59; Charlotte Erickson, *Invisible Immigrants* (Worcester, England: Leicester University Press, 1972), 76.

156. Miller, *A New History of the United States,* 292; John Bach McMaster, *A History of the People of the United States during Lincoln's Administration* (New York: D. Appleton, 1927), 449–50.

157. *Franco-Americans in Vermont* (Washington, DC: U.S. Commission on Civil Rights, 1983), 4–5; Bailey, *A Diplomatic History of the American People,* 351.

158. McMaster, *A History of the People of the United States during Lincoln's Administration,* 375.

159. Andrew Greeley, *That Most Distressful Nation* (Chicago: Quadrangle Books, 1972), 174; Hofstadter and Wallace, *American Violence,* 212.

160. Meier and Rudwick, *From Plantation to Ghetto,* 144; Stephen Steinberg, *The Ethnic Myth* (New York: Atheneum, 1981), 178.

161. Kelley, *The Shaping of the American Past,* 432; Robin Brooks, "Domestic Violence and America's Wars: An Historical Interpretation," in *Violence in America,* ed. Hugh Davis Graham and Ted Robert Gurr (New York: New American Library, 1969), 508.

162. Dee Brown, *The Galvanized Yankees* (Lincoln: University of Nebraska Press, 1986), 1–10.

163. Bertram W. Korn, *American Jewry and the Civil War* (New York: Atheneum, 1970), 64.

164. Leo Pfeffer, *Church, State, and Freedom* (Boston: Beacon Press, 1953), 209–10; Borden, *Jews, Turks, and Infidels,* 74.

165. Evans, *Judah Benjamin—The Jewish Confederate,* 209.

166. Borden, *Jews, Turks, and Infidels,* 65; Schappes, *A Documentary History of the Jews in the United States, 1654–1875,* 473; Korn, *American Jewry and the Civil War,* 126; Milton R. Konvitz, "The Quest for Equality and the Jewish Experience," in *Jewish Life in America,* ed. Gladys Rosen (New York: KTAV, 1978), 30.

167. Cohen, *Encounter with Emancipation,* 142; Lloyd Lewis, *Myths After Lincoln* (New York: Press of the Readers Club, 1941), 203.

168. Lamar, *The Reader's Encyclopedia of the American West,* 217; Wiley, *The Life of Billy Yank,* 316, 319; Hoig, *Tribal Wars of the Southern Plains,* 195.

169. Bailey, *A Documentary History of the American People,* 356.

170. Ibid., 396; Wieczerzak, *A Polish Chapter in Civil War America,* 205–6.

171. Andrew F. Rolle, *The Lost Cause—The Confederate Exodus to Mexico* (Norman: University of Oklahoma Press, 1966), 8, 219; Miller, *A New History of the United States,* 270; Handy, *A Christian America,* 61–62, 235.

172. Kelley, *The Shaping of the American Past,* 459.

173. Charles J. McClain, *In Search of Equality—The Chinese Struggle Against Discrimination in Nineteenth Century America* (Berkeley: University of California Press, 1994), 40.

174. Nell Irvin Painter, *Exodusters—Black Migration to Kansas After Reconstruction* (New York: Alfred A. Knopf, 1977), 6; Richard Stiller, *The White Minority* (New York: Harcourt Brace Jovanovich, 1977), 7; Andolsen, *Daughters of Jefferson, Daughters of Bootblacks,* 36–38.

175. Painter, *Exodusters,* 8; John Sibley Butler, "Affirmative Action in the Military," *Annals of the American Academy of Political and Social Science,* September 1992, 199–200; Meier and Rudwick, *From Plantation to Ghetto,* 172; Thomas J. Noer, *Briton, Boer and Yankee* (Kent, OH: Kent State University Press, 1978), 125.

176. James F. Kirkham, Sheldon G. Levy, and William J. Crotty, *Assassination and Political Violence* (New York: Bantam Books, 1970), 216.

177. Stiller, *The White Minority,* 25.

178. Eastland and Bennett, *Counting by Race,* 73.

179. E.L. Thornbrough, ed., *Black Reconstructionists* (Englewood Cliffs, NJ: Prentice-Hall, 1972), 69.

180. Alan Grimes, *Equality in America* (New York: Oxford University Press, 1964), 58.

181. Constantine Panunzio, *Immigration Crossroads* (New York: Macmillan, 1927), 27–29.

182. Steiner, *Fusang,* 113–14; Philip Taylor, *The Distant Magnet* (New York: Harper & Row, 1971), 70–76.

183. Jeremiah W. Jenks and W. Jett Lauk, *The Immigration Problem* (New York: Funk and Wagnalls, 1913), 21–22.

184. Kraus, *Immigration, the American Mosaic,* 71; Richard C. Brown, ed., *The Human Side of American History* (Boston: Ginn, 1967), 203; J. Valerie Fifer, *American Progress* (Chester, PA: Globe Pequot Press, 1958), 1–13.

185. Miller, *A New History of the United States,* 283.

186. Brown, *The Human Side of American History,* 109.

187. Panunzio, *Immigration Crossroads,* 50–51.

188. Ellsworth Huntington, *The Pulse of Progress* (New York: Charles Scribner's Sons, 1926), 160.

189. Baron, *Steeled by Adversity,* 284–85; Charles Prudhomme and David F. Musto, "Historical Perspectives on Mental Health and Racism in the United States," in *Racism and Mental Health,* ed. Charles V. Willie, Bernard M. Kramer, and Bertram S. Brown (Pittsburgh: University of Pittsburgh Press, 1973), 36.

190. Huntington, *The Pulse of Progress,* 157; Herbert G. Gutman, *Work, Culture and Society in Industrializing America* (New York: Vintage Books, 1976), 72; Henry Pratt Fairchild, *Greek Immigrants to the United States* (New Haven: Yale University Press, 1911), 239.

191. Joel S. Ives, "The Foreigner in New England," *Connecticut Magazine,* April, May, and June 1905, 246–47.

192. Dino Cinel, "Between Change and Continuity: Regionalism among Immigrants from the Italian Northwest," *Journal of Ethnic Studies,* Fall 1981, 21; Burton J. Hendrick, *The Jews in America* (Garden City, NY: Doubleday, Page, 1923), 27.

193. Edward N. Saveth, *American Historians and European Immigrants, 1875–1925* (New York: Columbia University Press, 1948), 162–63; Bert James Loewenberg, *American History in American Thought* (New York: Simon and Schuster, 1972), 374–75; Knobel, *Paddy and the Republic,* 87.

194. Handy, *A Christian America,* 89, 92; Leo Ribuffo, *The Old Christian Right* (Philadelphia: Temple University Press, 1983), 12; *The Jewish Encyclopedia* (New York: KTAV, undated reprinting), 1: 600.

195. Michael F. Funchion, "Irish Chicago: Church, Homeland, Politics, and Class— The Shaping of an Ethnic Group, 1870–1900," in *Ethnic Chicago,* ed. Peter d'A. Jones and Melvin G. Holli (Grand Rapids, Mich.: William B. Eerdmans, 1981), 8; Diner, *Erin's Daughters in America,* 85; *Religion in the Constitution: A Delicate Balance* (Washington, D.C.: U.S. Commission on Civil Rights, 1983), 16.

196. R. Laurence Moore, *Religious Outsiders and the Making of Americans* (New York: Oxford University Press, 1987), 59.

197. Bernard A. Weisberger, *They Gathered at the River* (Boston: Little, Brown, 1958), 165–66; Salvatore J. LaGumina, *"Wop!"* (San Francisco: Straight Arrow Books, 1973), 168; Dinnerstein and Reimers, *Ethnic Americans,* 62.

198. Cohen, *Encounter with Emancipation,* 255.

199. A. David Bos, "Washington Gladden versus Anti-Catholicism," *Journal of Ecumenical Studies,* Spring 1981, 285; Dinnerstein and Reimers, *Ethnic Americans,* 62.

200. Kauffman, *Faith and Fraternalism,* 168; Myers, *History of Bigotry in the United States,* 171; Thernstrom, *Harvard Encyclopedia of American Ethnic Groups,* 906.

201. Kauffman, *Faith and Fraternalism,* 169–71.

202. Davis, *The Fear of Conspiracy,* 175; Kinney, *Mormonism,* 97–98.

203. Kinney, *Mormonism,* 9.

204. Michael N. Dobkowski, *The Tarnished Dream—The Basis of American Anti-Semitism* (Westport, CT: Greenwood Press, 1979), 6; Robert Andrew Everett, "Judaism in Nineteenth-Century American Transcendentalist and Liberal Protestant Thought," *Journal of Ecumenical Studies,* Summer 1983, 413.

205. Benny Kraut, "The Ambivalent Relations of American Reform Judaism with Unitarianism in the Last Third of the Nineteenth Century," *Journal of Ecumenical Studies,* Winter 1986, 59.

206. Steinfeld, *Cracks in the Meeting Pot,* 171; Emil Reich, *Success among Nations* (New York: Harper & Brothers, 1904), 138.

207. Egal Feldman, *The Dreyfus Affair and the American Conscience, 1895–1906* (Detroit: Wayne State University Press, 1981), 126.

208. Ibid., 131.

209. Selma Berrol, "Germans versus Russians: An Update," *American Jewish History*, December 1983, 148; Crose, *Israel in the Mind of America*, 32; Howard N. Rabinowitz, "Nativism, Bigotry and Anti-Semitism in the South," *American Jewish History*, March 1988, 449.

210. Bernard Lewis, *Semites and Anti-Semites* (New York: W.W. Norton, 1986), 107.

211. Andolsen, *Daughters of Jefferson, Daughters of Bootblacks*, 31.

212. Aileen Kraditor, *The Radical Persuasion, 1890–1917* (Baton Rouge: Louisiana State University Press, 1981), 171.

213. Milton Viorst, *Fall from Grace—The Republican Party and the Puritan Ethic* (New York: Simon and Schuster, 1971), 130; Handy, *A Christian America*, 74.

214. Barbara Miller Solomon, *Ancestors and Immigrants* (Chicago: University of Chicago Press, 1972), 137; *Wall Street Journal*, 30 August 1984, 1.

215. Viorst, *Fall from Grace*, 134.

216. Orth, *Our Foreigners*, 228.

217. Allan Chase, *The Legacy of Malthus* (Urbana: University of Illinois Press, 1980), 8; E. Digby Baltzell, *The Protestant Establishment* (New York: Random House, 1964), 198.

218. Seymour Martin Lipset, "The Radical Right: A Problem for American Democracy," in *Conspiracy*, ed. Richard O. Curry and Thomas M. Brown (New York: Holt, Rinehart and Winston, 1972), 198; Charles Reznikoff, ed., *Louis Marshall: Champion of Liberty* (Philadelphia: Jewish Publication Society of America, 1957), 12.

219. William Roscoe Thayer, *Volleys from a Non-Combatant* (Garden City, NY: Doubleday, Page, 1919), 106; Arthur Mann, *Yankee Reformers in the Urban Age* (Cambridge: Belknap Press, 1954), 7; Kelley, *The Shaping of the American Past*, 367–68.

220. Solomon, *Ancestors and Immigrants*, 9; Andolsen, *Daughters of Jefferson, Daughters of Bootblacks*, 41; Birmingham, *America's Secret Aristocracy*, 157.

221. John M. Allswang, *Bosses, Machines, and Urban Voters* (Baltimore: Johns Hopkins University Press, 1986), 38; Albert Fried, *The Rise and Fall of the Jewish Gangster in America* (New York: Holt, Rinehart and Winston, 1980), 46.

222. LaGumina, *"Wop!"* 133–34.

223. Douglass and Bilbao, *Amerikanuak*, 265.

224. Emily S. Rosenberg, *Spreading the American Dream* (New York: Hill and Wang, 1982), 29; Hypatia Bradlaugh Bonner, *Christianizing the Heathen* (London: Watts, 1922), 14.

225. Ahlstrom, *A Religious History of the American People*, 851.

Chapter 3. Proliferation of People and Problems

1. Peter Roberts, *The New Immigration* (New York: Macmillan, 1912), 362; Stanley Lieberson, *A Piece of the Pie—Blacks and White Immigrants Since 1880* (Berkeley: University of California Press, 1980), 28.

2. Frank Tracy Carlton, *The History and Problems of Organized Labor* (New York: D.C. Heath, 1911), 327.

3. Maxine Schwartz Seller, *Immigrant Women* (Philadelphia: Temple University Press, 1981), 117.

4. Hans von Hentig, *The Criminal and His Victim* (New York: Schocken Books, 1979), 415; Vay De Vaya and Luskod, *The Inner Life of the United States* (New York: Dutton, 1908), 381.

5. Ray Allen Billington, *Westward Expansion* (New York: Macmillan, 1967), 705; Stephan Thernstrom, "Urbanization, Migration, and Social Mobility in Late Nineteenth-

Century America," in *Towards a New Past: Dissenting Essays in American History,* ed. Barton J. Bernstein (New York: Vintage Books, 1969), 160.

6. Stephen Graham, *With Poor Immigrants to America* (New York: Macmillan, 1914), 190–91.

7. Rowland E. Robinson, *Vermont—A Study of Independence* (Rutland, VT: Charles E. Tuttle, 1975), 330.

8. John M. Allswang, *A House for All People* (Lexington: University Press of Kentucky, 1971), 15–20.

9. Allen F. Davis and Mark H. Haller, *The Peoples of Philadelphia* (Philadelphia: Temple University Press, 1973), 204; Arthur Mann, *The One and the Many* (Chicago: University of Chicago Press, 1979), 77.

10. Samuel Orth, *Our Foreigners* (New Haven: Yale University Press, 1921), 216; William Wokovich-Valkavicius, *Immigrants and Yankees in Nashoba Valley Massachusetts* (West Groton, CT: St. James Church, 1981), 49.

11. Marshall B. Clinard, *Slums and Community Development* (New York: Free Press, 1966), 20; Arthur Evans Wood, *Hamtramck, Then and Now* (New York: Bookman, 1955), 15–16.

12. Roberts, *The New Immigration,* 202.

13. Jay Dolan, *The American Catholic Experience* (Garden City, NY: Doubleday, 1985), 135.

14. Leonard Dinnerstein, *The Leo Frank Case* (New York: Columbia University Press, 1968), 64.

15. Milton Viorst, *Fall from Grace—The Republican Party and the Puritan Ethic* (New York: Simon and Schuster, 1971), 117; Steven Hertzberg, *Strangers within the Gate City, the Jews of Atlanta, 1845–1915* (Philadelphia: Jewish Publication Society of America, 1978), 27, 80; Luciano Iorizzo, "The Padrone and Immigrant Distribution," in *The Italian Experience in the United States,* ed. S.M. Tomasi and M.H. Engel (Staten Island, NY: Center for Migration Studies, 1970), 49–52.

16. Dinnerstein, *The Leo Frank Case,* 64; Jeremiah W. Jenks and W. Jett Lauk, *The Immigration Problem* (New York: Funk and Wagnalls, 1913), 71.

17. John Bodnar, *The Transplanted—A History of Immigrants in Urban America* (Bloomington: Indiana University Press, 1985), 69–70.

18. Maldwyn Allen Jones, *American Immigration* (Chicago: University of Chicago Press, 1960), 131; Ronald Takaki, *Strangers from a Different Shore* (New York: Penguin Books, 1990), 28.

19. William M. Leiserson, *Adjusting Immigrant and Industry* (New York: Harper & Brothers, 1924), 171; Gerald Rosenblum, *Immigrant Workers* (New York: Basic Books, 1973), 75.

20. John Hutchinson, *The Imperfect Union* (New York: Dutton, 1972), 93–94; Harvey Wish, *Society and Thought in Modern America* (New York: Longmans, Green, 1952), 245; Melvyn Dubofsky, *When Workers Organize* (Amherst: University of Massachusetts Press, 1968), 7; Patricia Ondek Laurence, "The Garden in the Mill: The Slovak Immigrant's View of Work," *Melus,* Summer 1983, 57.

21. Bodnar, *The Transplanted,* 171.

22. Stanley Aronowitz, "The Working Class: A Break with the Past," in *Divided Society—The Ethnic Experience in America,* ed. Colin Greer (New York: Basic Books, 1974), 313–16.

23. Hasia R. Diner, *Erin's Daughters in America* (Baltimore: Johns Hopkins University Press, 1983), 31; Seller, *Immigrant Women,* 8.

24. Alice Kessler-Harris, *Out of Work—A History of Wage-Earning Women in the United States* (New York: Oxford University Press, 1983), 137; Leslie Woodcock Tentler,

Wage-Earning Women (New York: Oxford University Press, 1979), 70; Diner, *Erin's Daughters in America,* 82; Stephen Steinberg, *The Ethnic Myth* (New York: Atheneum, 1981), 154.

25. Bodnar, *The Transplanted,* 75–78.

26. Thomas Monroe Pitkin and Francesco Cordasco, *The Black Hand* (Totowa, NJ: Rowman and Littlefield, 1977), 34.

27. Diner, *Erin's Daughters in America,* 115; Albert Fried, *The Rise and Fall of the Jewish Gangster in America* (New York: Holt, Rinehart and Winston, 1980), 8–9; Ruth Rosen, *The Lost Sisterhood—Prostitution in America, 1900–1918* (Baltimore: Johns Hopkins University Press, 1985), 139.

28. Fried, *The Rise and Fall of the Jewish Gangster in America,* 9–10; Rosen, *The Lost Sisterhood,* 119.

29. Jerome Davis, *The Russian Immigrant* (New York: Macmillan, 1922), 160.

30. Richard Gambino, *Vendetta* (New York: Doubleday, 1977), 51; Herman D. Bloch, *The Circle of Discrimination* (New York: New York University Press, 1969), 42.

31. Bloch, *The Circle of Discrimination,* 90.

32. Ibid., 91.

33. William Julius Wilson, *The Declining Significance of Race* (Chicago: University of Chicago Press, 1978), 74; J. Owens Smith, "The Politics of Income and Education Differences between Blacks and West Indians," *Journal of Ethnic Studies,* Fall 1985, 21; Jacob A. Riis, *How the Other Half Lives* (New York: Hill and Wang, 1957), 111; Takaki, *Strangers from a Different Shore,* 198–99.

34. Charles Leinenweber, "Socialism and Ethnicity," in *Failure of a Dream? Essays in the History of American Socialism,* ed. John H.M. Laslett and Seymour Martin Lipset (Berkeley: University of California Press, 1984), 251.

35. Richard Krickus, *Pursuing the American Dream* (Garden City, NY: Anchor Books, 1976), 134; Bodnar, *The Transplanted,* 96.

36. Irwin Yellowitz, "Jewish Immigrants and the American Labor Movement, 1900–1920," *American Jewish History,* December 1981, 213; John Rowe, *The Hard-Rock Men* (New York: Barnes and Noble, 1971), 247.

37. H. Martin Deranian, "Worcester in America," *Journal of Armenian Studies* 3 (1986–1987): 19; Robert Mirak, *Torn between Two Lands: Armenians in America, 1890 to World War I* (Cambridge: Harvard University Press, 1983), 143.

38. Rudolf Glanz, *Studies in Judaica Americana* (New York: KTAV, 1970), 317.

39. Robert F. Heizer and Alan J. Almquist, *The Other Californians* (Berkeley: University of California Press, 1971), 260.

40. Andrew T. Kopan, "Greek Survival in Chicago: The Role of Ethnic Education, 1890–1980," in *Ethnic Chicago,* ed. Peter d'A. Jones and Melvin G. Holli (Grand Rapids, MI: William B. Eerdmans, 1981), 101.

41. Paul Knaplund, *Moorings Old and New* (Madison: State Historical Society of Wisconsin, 1963), 221.

42. Thomas Sowell, *Ethnic America* (New York: Basic Books, 1981), 277; Susan M. Papp, *Hungarian Americans and Their Communities of Cleveland* (Cleveland: Cleveland State University Press, 1981), 164.

43. Edward A. Steiner, *The Immigrant Tide—Its Ebb and Flow* (London: Fleming H. Revell, 1909), 190.

44. Naomi W. Cohen, *Encounter with Emancipation* (Philadelphia: Jewish Publication Society of America, 1984), 322; Diner, *Erin's Daughters in America,* 40.

45. Carlton, *The History and Problems of Organized Labor,* 342.

46. Marcus Lee Hansen, *The Immigrant in American History* (New York: Harper & Row, 1940), 169–70; Karel D. Bicha, "Hunkies: Stereotyping the Slavic Immigrants,"

Journal of Ethnic History, Fall 1982, 31; Thomas Kessner, *The Golden Door* (New York: Oxford University Press, 1977), 62; Oscar Uribe Jr., "Measuring the Degree of Discrimination," *Agenda, a Journal of Hispanic Issues,* July/August 1979, 15; Takaki, *Strangers from a Different Shore,* 24–27.

47. Irving Howe, *World of Our Fathers* (New York: Harcourt Brace Jovanovich, 1976), 53; M.J. Heale, *American Anticommunism—Combating the Enemy Within, 1830–1970* (Baltimore: Johns Hopkins University Press, 1990), 38.

48. Krickus, *Pursuing the American Dream,* 113, 119.

49. Edward N. Saveth, *American Historians and European Immigrants, 1875–1925* (New York: Columbia University Press, 1948), 172; James F. Kirkham, Sheldon G. Levy, and William Crotty, *Assassination and Political Violence* (New York: Bantam Books, 1970), 223.

50. Marc D. Angel, *La America—The Sephardic Experience in the United States* (Philadelphia: Jewish Publication Society of America, 1982), 19; Rosenblum, *Immigrant Workers,* 123–24; Wayne Charles Miller, *A Handbook of American Minorities* (New York: New York University Press, 1976), 71.

51. Leiserson, *Adjusting Immigrant and Industry,* 41–46; Takaki, *Strangers from a Different Shore,* 93; Roger Daniels, *Coming to America* (New York: Harper Perennial, 1991), 203.

52. Kessler-Harris, *Out of Work,* 125; Deborah Dwork, "Immigrant Jews on the Lower East Side of New York: 1880–1914," in *The American Jewish Experience,* ed. Jonathon D. Sarna (New York: Holmes and Meier, 1986), 106; Daniels, *Coming to America,* 236.

53. Davis, *The Russian Immigrant,* 60–61.

54. Richard Lingeman, *Small Town America* (Boston: Houghton Mifflin, 1980), 253; James B. Allen, *The Company Town in the American West* (Norman: University of Oklahoma Press, 1966), 51.

55. Richard G. Lilliard, *Desert Challenge* (Lincoln: University of Nebraska Press, 1969), 209–10.

56. Leiserson, *Adjusting Immigrant and Industry,* 128; Dubofsky, *When Workers Organize,* 12.

57. Dubofsky, *When Workers Organize,* 8; Lucy M. Cohen, *Chinese in the Post-Civil War South* (Baton Rouge: Louisiana State University Press, 1984), 56.

58. Seller, *Immigrant Women,* 83, 87; Takaki, *Strangers from a Different Shore,* 36.

59. Dubofsky, *When Workers Organize,* 8.

60. Leiserson, *Adjusting Immigrant and Industry,* 306.

61. John Sharpless and John Rury, "The Political Economy of Women's Work," *Social Science History,* Summer 1980, 323–25.

62. Bonnie Mitelman, "Rose Schneiderman and the Triangle Fire," *American History Illustrated,* July 1981, 47.

63. Howard B. Grose, *The Incoming Millions* (New York: Fleming H. Revell, 1906), 103; Krickus, *Pursuing the American Dream,* 115.

64. John J. Bukowczyk, *And My Children Did Not Know Me—A History of Polish-Americans* (Bloomington: Indiana University Press, 1987), 26; Roberts, *The New Immigration,* 86; Thomas C. Cochran and William Miller, *A Social History of Industrial America* (New York: Harper & Row, 1961), 231.

65. Roberts, *The New Immigration,* 87–88.

66. Bodnar, *The Transplanted,* 54; Alixa Naff, "Becoming American: Peddling and the Syrian Immigrants, 1880–1914," *Journal of Armenian Studies* 3 (1986–87): 64.

67. Seller, *Immigrant Women,* 127; Michael Kraus, *Immigration, the American Mosaic* (New York: Van Nostrand Reinhold, 1966), 36, 79–80.

68. David M. Brownstone, Irene M. Franck, and Douglass L. Brownstone, *Island of Hope, Island of Tears* (New York: Rawson, Wade, 1979), 48.

69. Roberts, *The New Immigration*, 260.

70. Gutman, *Work, Culture and Society*, 8–9.

71. von Hentig, *The Criminal and His Victim*, 264; Theodore Saloutos, "Exodus U.S.A.," in *Divided Society*, ed. Colin Greer (New York: Basic Books, 1974), 154–55.

72. Stephan Thernstrom, ed., *Harvard Encyclopedia of American Ethnic Groups* (Cambridge: Harvard University Press, 1980), 676.

73. Loren W. Fessler, ed., *Chinese in America: Stereotyped Past, Changing Present* (New York: Vantage Press, 1983), 187; Thernstrom, *Harvard Encyclopedia of American Ethnic Groups*, 187, 426, 747; Daniels, *Coming to America*, 27.

74. Michael J. Piore, *Birds of Passage* (Cambridge: Cambridge University Press, 1979), 150; Jeanette Meisel Baron, ed., *Steeled by Adversity—Essays and Addresses on American Jewish Life by Salo Wittmayer Baron* (Philadelphia: Jewish Publication Society of America, 1971), 280; Thernstrom, *Harvard Encyclopedia of American Ethnic Groups*, 335; Saloutos, "Exodus U.S.A.," 151.

75. Frances Kellor, *Immigration and the Future* (New York: George H. Doran, 1920), 87–88.

76. Gilbert Osofsky, *The Burden of Race* (New York: Harper & Row, 1967), 239.

77. Marchette Chute, *The First Liberty* (New York: E. Dutton, 1969), 314.

78. Arnold Shankman, *Ambivalent Friends, Afro-Americans View the Immigrant* (Westport, CT: Greenwood Press, 1982), 39; William Loren Katz, *The Black West* (Garden City, NY: Anchor Press/Doubleday, 1973), 249–50; Robert Craig Brown and Ramsey Cook, *Canada, 1896–1921* (Toronto: McClelland and Stewart, 1981), 61–62; Meier and Rudwick, *From Plantation to Ghetto*, 226–27.

79. Beth Millstein and Jeanne Bodin, *We, the American Women* (Chicago: Science Research Associates, 1977), 162.

80. Charles E. Rosenberg, *The Care of Strangers* (New York: Basic Books, 1987).

81. Alexander Saxton, *The Indispensable Enemy* (Berkeley: University of California Press, 1971), 271–73; J.A. Parker, "Was Karl Marx a Racist?" *Lincoln Review*, Winter–Spring 1982, 53.

82. Wilson, *The Declining Significance of Race*, 67; John Hope Franklin, *From Slavery to Freedom—A History of Negro Americans* (New York: Alfred A. Knopf, 1969), 472; Piore, *Birds of Passage*, 158.

83. Ferenc Morton Szasz, *The Divided Mind of Protestant America, 1880–1930* (Tuscaloosa: University of Alabama Press, 1982), 4.

84. Riis, *How the Other Half Lives*, 113.

85. Werner Sollors, *Beyond Ethnicity* (New York: Oxford University Press, 1986), 61.

86. Shankman, *Ambivalent Friends*, xiii, 157.

87. Thernstrom, *Harvard Encyclopedia of American Ethnic Groups*, 1022–25.

88. Lawrence W. Levine, "Marcus Garvey's Movement," *New Republic*, 29 October 1984, 29.

89. Carlton, *The History and Problems of Organized Labor*, 354; Brown and Cook, *Canada, 1896–1921*, 68.

90. Sidney L. Gulick, *The American Japanese Problem* (New York: Charles Scribner's Sons, 1914), 4.

91. Stan Steiner, *Fusang—The Chinese Who Built America* (New York: HarperColophon, 1979), 79–97, 108–9; Cheng-Tsu Wu, *"Chink!"* (New York: Meridian Press, 1972), 2; Takaki, *Strangers from a Different Shore*, 24.

92. Wu, *"Chink!"* 3, 164, 176.

93. Lucy M. Cohen, *Chinese in the Post/Civil War South* (Baton Rouge: Louisiana State University Press, 1984), 32.

94. George Anthony Peffer, "Forbidden Families: Emigration Experiences of Chinese Women under the Page Law, 1875–1882," *Journal of Ethnic History,* Fall 1986, 42.

95. Rubin Francis Weston, *Racism in U.S. Imperialism* (Columbia: University of South Carolina Press, 1972), 23.

96. Ferenc Morton Szasz, *The Protestant Clergy in the Great Plains and Mountain West, 1865–1915* (Albuquerque: University of New Mexico, 1988), 201; Takaki, *Strangers from a Different Shore,* 115.

97. Kenneth O. Bjork, *West of the Great Divide* (Northfield, MN: Norwegian-American Historial Association, 1958), 590; Shankman, *Ambivalent Friends,* 12–133; Daniels, *Coming to America,* 256.

98. Steiner, *Fusang,* 174; Richard Hofstadter and Michael Wallace, *American Violence* (New York: Vintage Books, 1971), 329–30; Donald Dale Jackson, "Behave Like Your Actions Reflect on All Chinese," *Smithsonian,* February 1991, 116–17.

99. Elmer C. Sandmeyer, "Anti-Chinese Sentiment in California," in *The Underside of American History,* vol. 1, ed. Thomas R. Frazier (New York: Harcourt Brace Jovanovich, 1971).

100. Wu, *"Chink!"* 4.

101. Ibid., 5.

102. Steiner, *Fusang,* 162; Sandmeyer, "Anti-Chinese Sentiment in California," 283; William A. Douglass and Jon Bilbao, *Amerikanuak* (Reno: University of Nevada Press, 1975), 270.

103. Weston, *Racism in U.S. Imperialism,* 25.

104. Philip A. Dennis, "The Anti-Chinese Campaigns in Sonora, Mexico," *Ethnohistory,* Winter 1979, 65–79.

105. Constantine Panunzio, *Immigration Crossroads* (New York: Macmillan, 1927), 157.

106. Takaki, *Strangers from a Different Shore,* 45.

107. Harry H.L. Kitano, *Japanese Americans* (Englewood Cliffs, NJ: Prentice-Hall, 1969), 16.

108. Roger Daniels, *The Politics of Prejudice* (New York: Atheneum, 1972), 28.

109. Brown and Cook, *Canada, 1896–1921,* 69.

110. Gulick, *The American Chinese Problem,* 78; Shankman, *Ambivalent Friends,* 50.

111. Miller, *A New History of the United States,* 358; Heizer and Almquist, *The Other Californians,* 179; Shankman, *Ambivalent Friends,* 36.

112. Gulick, *The American Chinese Problem,* 238–39.

113. Jose A. Cabranes, *Citizenship and the American Empire* (New Haven: Yale University Press, 1979), 40–41; Barbara Miller Solomon, *Ancestors and Immigrants* (Chicago: University of Chicago Press, 1972), 120.

114. Miller, *A Handbook of American Minorities,* 172; Carlos Bulosan, *America Is in the Heart* (Seattle: University of Washington Press, 1973), xii.

115. Ibid., 121.

116. Ibid., xiv; Takaki, *Strangers from a Different Shore,* 332.

117. Cohen, *Chinese in the Post/Civil War South,* 48–49.

118. Jenks and Lauck, *The Immigration Problem,* 225, 257; Gulick, *The American Chinese Problem,* 275.

119. Anne Loftis, *California—Where the Twain Did Meet* (New York: Macmillan, 1973), 196.

120. Gerald Hallberg, "Bellingham, Washington's Anti-Hindu Riot," in *The North-*

west Mosaic—Minority Conflicts in Pacific Northwest History, ed. James A. Halseth and Bruce A. Glasrud (Boulder, CO: Pruett, 1977), 150.

121. Ibid., 152; Brown and Cook, *Canada, 1896–1921,* 71.

122. Loftis, *California,* 196.

123. Bong-Youn Choy, *Koreans in America* (Chicago: Nelson-Hall, 1979), 69, 89.

124. Ibid., 110; Loftis, *California,* 197.

125. Daniels, *Coming to America,* 366.

126. Mirak, *Torn between Two Lands,* 146, 282; Takaki, *Strangers from a Different Shore,* 15.

127. Mirak, *Torn between Two Lands,* 144–45, 278; Thernstrom, *Harvard Encyclopedia of American Ethnic Groups,* 142.

128. William Madsen, *The Mexican-Americans of South Texas* (New York: Holt, Rinehart and Winston, 1964), 9.

129. Panunzio, *Immigration Crossroads,* 79; Edward R. Lewis, *America: Nation or Confusion* (New York: Harper & Brothers, 1928), 32–33.

130. Stan Steiner, *La Raza, the Mexican Americans* (New York: HarperColophon, 1970), 146–47; Robert Glass Cleland, *From Wilderness to Empire—A History of California* (New York: Alfred A. Knopf, 1962), 369; Takaki, *Strangers from a Different Shore,* 30.

131. Rudolph O. de la Garza, "Mexican Americans in the United States: The Evolution of a Relationship," in *Case Studies on Human Rights and Fundamental Freedoms,* vol. 5 (The Hague: Foundation for the Study of Plural Societies, 1976), 265; Stanley Coben, "The Failure of the Melting Pot," in *The Great Fear,* ed. Gary B. Nash and Richard Weiss (New York: Holt, Rinehart and Winston, 1970), 152; Cleland, *From Wilderness to Empire,* 369.

132. Alan Grimes, *Equality in America* (New York: Oxford University Press, 1964), 61–62.

133. Donald L. Fixico, "As Long as the Grass Grows . . . The Cultural Conflicts and Political Struggles of United States-Indian Treaties," in *Ethnicity and War,* vol. 3, ed. Winston A. Van Horne (Milwaukee: University of Wisconsin System American Ethnic Studies, 1984), 138; Stan Hoig, *Tribal Wars of the Southern Plains* (Norman: University of Oklahoma Press, 1993), 117.

134. Dave Wilkinson, "The Modoc Indian War," *American History Illustrated,* August 1978, 18, 30; Hoig, *Tribal Wars of the Southern Plains,* 46–47.

135. Gary C. Anders, "A Critical Analysis of the Alaska Native Land Claims and Native Corporate Development," *Journal of Ethnic Studies,* Spring 1985, 3.

136. Fixico, "As Long as the Grass Grows," 138.

137. Robert H. Keller Jr., *American Protestantism and United States Indian Policy, 1869–1882* (Lincoln: University of Nebraska Press, 1983), 17–18.

138. Brian W. Dippie, *The Vanishing American* (Middletown, CT: Wesleyan University Press, 1982), 163; Sergei Kan, "Russian Orthodox Brotherhoods among the Tlingit," *Ethnohistory* 32 (1985): 199; Dolan, *The American Catholic Experience,* 285.

139. Keller, *American Protestantism and United States Indian Policy,* 45.

140. Robert A. Trennert, *Alternative to Extinction* (Philadelphia: Temple University Press, 1975), 133; Milton Meltzer, *Slavery: From the Rise of Western Civilization to Today* (New York: Dell, 1972), 198–99.

141. Hoig, *Tribal Wars of the Southern Plains,* 18, 177.

142. John Greenway, *The American Tradition* (New York: Mason/Charter, 1977), 12.

143. Thomas C. Leonard, "General Custer Speaks for the Indians," *The Columbia Forum* (Summer 1974): 26.

144. Wilcomb E. Washburn, *The Indian in America* (New York: HarperColophon, 1975), 205; Thernstrom, *Harvard Encyclopedia of American Ethnic Groups,* 116.

145. Mann, *The One and the Many*, 90.

146. Adeline Wanatee, "Education, Family, and the Schools," in *The War between Two Rivers*, ed. Gretchen M. Bataille, David M. Gradwohl, and Charles L.Silet (Ames: Iowa State University Press, 1978), 101.

147. Cohen, *Chinese in the Post/Civil War South*, 166.

148. Thomas A. Bailey, *A Diplomatic History of the American People* (New York: Appleton-Century-Crofts, 1946), 459; John H. Bodley, *Victims of Progress* (Menlo Park, NJ: Cummins, 1975), 13; Richard Hofstadter, *Social Darwinism in American Thought* (Boston: Beacon Press, 1955), 180.

149. Ferenc Morton Szasz, *The Divided Mind of Protestant America* (Tuscaloosa: University of Alabama Press, 1982), 11; Eldon G. Ernst, *Without Help or Hindrance* (Louisville, KY: Westminster Press, 1977), 128.

150. Robert E. Speer, *Of One Blood—A Short Study of the Race Problem* (New York: Council of Women for Home Missions and Missionary Education Movement of the United States of America, 1924), 41; Bailey, *A Diplomatic History of the American People*, 466–67.

151. Bailey, *A Diplomatic History of the American People*, 470–73.

152. Ibid., 475; Weston, *Racism in U.S. Imperialism*, 69–70.

153. Melvin Steinfield, *Cracks in the Melting Pot* (New York: Glencoe Press, 1973), 120.

154. E. Berkeley Tompkins, *Anti-Imperialism in the United States* (Philadelphia: University of Pennsylvania Press, 1972), 12, 129.

155. C. Roland Marchand, *The American Peace Movement and Social Reform, 1898–1918* (Princeton: Princeton University Press, 1972), 116.

156. Weston, *Racism in U.S. Imperialism*, 67, 214; Allen, *Reluctant Reformers*, 90.

157. Daniel B. Schirmer, *Republic or Empire* (Cambridge: Schenkman, 1972), 143; Frank Friedel, "Dissent in the Spanish-American War and the Philippine Insurrection," in *Dissent in Three American Wars*, ed. Samuel Eliot Morison, Frederick Merk, and Frank Freidel (Cambridge, MA: Harvard University Press, 1971), 88–90.

158. Willard B. Gatewood Jr., *Smoked Yankees* (Urbana: University of Illinois Press, 1971), 15; Herbert Aptheker, ed., *A Documentary History of the Negro People in the United States* (Secaucus, NJ: Citadel Press, 1972), 824–25; Daniel B. Schirmer and Stephen Rosskamm Shalom, *The Philippines Reader* (Boston: South End Press, 1987), 32.

159. Walter L. Williams, "United States Indian Policy and the Debate over Philippine Annexation: Implications for the Origins of American Imperialism," *Journal of American History*, March 1980, 819.

160. Weston, *Racism in U.S. Imperialism*, 203.

161. Vaya and Luskod, *The Inner Life of the United States*, 379.

162. Gambino, *Vendetta*, ix; Pitkin and Cordasco, *The Black Hand*, 25.

163. Gambino, *Vendetta*, 126.

164. John Higham, *Strangers in the Land* (New York: Atheneum, 1971), 90; Papp, *Hungarian Americans and Their Communities of Cleveland*, 114.

165. Kopan, "Greek Survival in Chicago," 101–2; Theodore Saloutos, *The Greeks in the United States* (Cambridge: Harvard University Press, 1964), 66–67, 248–49.

166. *New York Times*, 6 May 1983, A9; Anderson, *White Protestant Americans*, 74–75.

167. Kirkham, Levy and Crotty, *Assassination and Political Violence*, 218; William F. Holmes, "Whitecapping: Anti-Semitism in the Populist Era," *American Jewish Historical Quarterly*, March 1974, 244–49.

168. Heale, *American Anticommunism—Combating the Enemy Within, 1830–1970*, 24–26; Panunzio, *Immigration Crossroads*, 52, 54.

169. Bailey, *A Diplomatic History of the American People*, 441.

170. Lawrence H. Fuchs, ed., *American Ethnic Politics* (New York: Harper Torchbooks, 1968), 148.

171. Hugo Munsterberg, *American Traits* (Boston: Houghton Mifflin, 1901), 21; Paul Seabury, "Racial Problems and American Foreign Policy," in *Racial Influences on American Foreign Policy,* ed. George W. Shepherd Jr. (New York: Basic Books, 1970), 64.

172. Thomas F. Gossett, *Race, the History of an Idea in America* (Dallas: Southern Methodist University Press, 1963), 439; Thomas E. Hachey, "Irish Republicanism Yesterday and Today: The Dilemma of Irish Americans," in *Ethnicity and War,* vol. 3, ed. Winston A. Van Horne (Milwaukee: University of Wisconsin System American Ethnic Series, 1984), 155, 170.

173. Terje I. Leiren, "American Press Opinion and Norwegian Independence, 1905," in *Norwegian American Studies* (Northfield, MN: Norwegian-American Historical Association, 1977), 27: 233.

174. Daniels, *The Politics of Prejudice,* 94.

175. Orth, *Our Foreigners,* 231.

176. Miller, *American Protestantism and Social Issues,* 131–32.

177. Richard Young, "The Brownsville Affray," *American History Illustrated,* October 1986, 10–17.

178. Terry Eastland and William J. Bennett, *Counting by Race* (New York: Basic Books, 1974), 94.

179. Louis L. Gerson, *The Hyphenate in Recent American Politics and Diplomacy* (Lawrence: University of Kansas Press, 1964), 62; Kellor, *Immigration and the Future,* 50.

180. Richard J. Meister, *Race and Ethnicity in Modern America* (Lexington: D.C. Heath, 1974), xi-xii; Gerson, *The Hyphenate in Recent American Politics and Diplomacy,* 62; Nathaniel Weyl and William Marina, *American Statesmen on Slavery and the Negro* (New Rochelle, NY: Arlington House, 1971), 327.

181. Gossett, *Race, the History of an Idea in America,* 442; Weyl and Marina, *American Statesmen on Slavery and the Negro,* 330.

182. Weston, *Racism in U.S. Imperialism,* 32.

183. Weyl and Marina, *American Statesmen on Slavery and the Negro,* 334.

184. Andre Siegfried, *America Comes of Age* (New York: Harcourt, Brace, 1927), 11.

185. H.C. Peterson and Gilbert C. Fite, *Opponents of War 1917–1918* (Madison: University of Wisconsin Press, 1957), 81; Frederick C. Luebke, *Bonds of Loyalty* (DeKalb: Northern Illinois University, 1974), 3–4.

186. Ahlstrom, *A Religious History of the American People,* 884–85.

187. Melvin G. Holli, "The Great War Sinks Chicago's German Kultur," in *Ethnic Chicago,* ed. Peter d'A. Jones and Melvin G. Holli (Grand Rapids, MI: William B. Eerdmans, 1981), 269.

188. Finis Herbert Capps, *From Isolationism to Involvement—The Swedish Immigrant Press in America, 1949–1945* (Chicago: Swedish Pioneer Historical Society, 1966), 54; Clarence Glasrud, review of *Ethnicity Challenged: The Upper Midwest Norwegian-American Experience in World War I,* by Carl H. Chrislock, *Journal of American Ethnic History* 3 (Fall 1983): 110; Peterson and Fite, *Opponents of War,* 85.

189. Humbert S. Nelli, *The Italians in Chicago, 1880–1930* (New York: Oxford University Press, 1979), 202.

190. Douglass and Bilbao, *Amerikanuak,* 303–4; Takaki, *Strangers from a Different Shore,* 301.

191. Howard M. Sachar, *The Emergence of the Middle East: 1914–1924* (New York: Alfred A. Knopf, 1969), 343; John Price Jones and Paul Merrick Hollister, *The German Secret Service in America, 1914–1928* (Boston: Small, Maynard, 1918), 252–87; Loftis, *California,* 201.

192. J. Milton Yinger, *Religion in the Struggle for Power* (New York: Russell and Russell, 1961), 180.

193. John Callan O'Laughlin, *Imperiled America* (Chicago: Reilly and Britton, 1916), 37–38; H.C. Peterson, *Propaganda for War* (Norman: University of Oklahoma Press, 1939), 241.

194. Paul Van Riper, *History of the United States Civil Service* (Evanston, IL: Row, Peterson, 1958), 242.

195. Myron Bohdon Kuropas, "Ukrainian Chicago: The Making of a Nationality Group in America," in *Ethnic Chicago,* ed. Peter d'A. Jones and Melvin G. Holli (Grand Rapids, MI: William B. Eerdmans, 1981), 160.

196. Davis, *The Russian Immigrant,* 161; Thomas I. Emerson, David Haber, and Norman Dorsen, *Political and Civil Rights in the United States* (Boston: Little, Brown, 1967), 54; Frederic C. Howe, *The Confessions of a Reformer* (Chicago: Quadrangle Books, 1967), 272; Richard J. Barnet, *The Rockets' Red Glare* (New York: Simon and Schuster, 1990), 158–59.

197. Victor Peters, *Victor, All Things Common—The Hutterian Way of Life* (New York: Harper Torchbooks, 1971), 43–45; W.C. Stevenson, *The Inside Story of Jehovah's Witnesses* (New York: Hart, 1968), 142.

198. Ronald Fernandez, "Getting Germans to Fight Germans: The Americanization of World War I," *Journal of Ethnic Studies,* Summer 1981, 53; Panunzio, *Immigration Crossroads,* 82; Nelli, *The Italians in Chicago,* 202; Bukowczyk, *And My Children Did Not Know Me,* 49; Kellor, *Immigration and the Future,* 58.

199. Tom Holm, "Fighting a White Man's War: The Extent and Legacy of American Indian Participation in World War II," *Journal of Ethnic Studies,* Summer 1981, 69; Russell Lawrence Barsh, "American Indians in the Great War," *Ethnohistory,* Summer 1991, 289.

200. Allswang, *A House for All Peoples,* 117; Meier and Rudwick, *From Plantation to Ghetto,* 218–19.

201. Meier and Rudwick, *From Plantation to Ghetto,* 217–18; Franklin, *From Slavery to Freedom,* 474; Patrick S. Washburn, *A Question of Sedition* (New York: Oxford University Press, 1986), 18.

202. Robert K. Murray, *Red Scare* (New York: McGraw-Hill, 1964), 178; Franklin, *From Slavery to Freedom,* 485; Meier and Rudwick, *From Plantation to Ghetto,* 221–22; Richard Hofstadter and Michael Wallace, *American Violence* (New York: Vintage Books, 1971), 258.

203. Kuropas, "Ukrainian Chicago," 167; Choy, *Koreans in America,* 152; Robert G. Weisbord and Richard Kazarian Jr., *Israel in the Black American Perspective* (Westport, CT: Greenwood Press, 1985), 17.

204. John B. Duff, "German-Americans and the Peace, 1918–1920," *American Jewish Historical Quarterly,* June 1970, 434; Edward R. Lewis, *America: Nation or Confusion* (New York: Harper & Brothers, 1928), 268.

205. Louis F. Post, *The Deportations Delirium of Nineteen-Twenty* (Chicago: Charles H. Kerr, 1923), 306.

206. George M. Marsden, *Fundamentalism and American Culture* (New York: Oxford University Press, 1982), 209; R. Laurence Moore, *Religious Outsiders and the Making of Americans* (New York: Oxford University Press, 1987), 143; Heale, *American Anticommunism—Combating the Enemy Within, 1830–1970,* 66, 82, 92.

207. Oscar Handlin, "The Immigrant and American Politics," in *Foreign Influences in American Life,* ed. David F. Bowers (Princeton: Princeton University Press, 1944), 90–91; Bodnar, *The Transplanted,* 108–9; Theodore Draper, *The Roots of American Communism* (New York: Viking Press, 1944), 31; Stanley Aronowitz, *False Promises* (New York:

McGraw-Hill, 1974), 142; Sherry Gorelick, *City College and the Jewish Poor* (New Brunswick, NJ: Rutgers University Press, 1981), 54; Rosenblum, *Immigrant Workers,* 154–55; Meier and Rudwick, *From Plantation to Ghetto,* 244–45.

208. David, *The Russian Immigrant,* 195; Harold D. Langley, *So Proudly We Hail—The History of the United States Flag* (Washington, DC: Smithsonian Institute Press, 1981), 227.

209. *Franco-Americans in Vermont* (Washington, DC: U.S. Commission on Civil Rights, 1983), 9; Richard Ruiz, "Ethnic Group Interests and the Social Good: Law and Language in Education," in *Ethnicity, Law and the Social Good,* ed. Winston A. Van Horne (Milwaukee: University of Wisconsin System American Ethnic Studies, 1983) 57; Arthur M. Schlesinger Jr., *The Disuniting of America* (New York: W.W. Norton, 1993), 54.

210. Leiserson, *Adjusting Immigrant and Industry,* 249–50.

211. Laurence Veysey, *Law and Resistance* (New York: Harper & Row, 1970), 237.

212. Davis, *The Russian Immigrant,* 169.

213. Ibid., 24–25.

214. Kellor, *Immigration and the Future,* 145.

215. James H. Timberlake, *Prohibition and the Progressive Movement, 1900–1920* (New York: Atheneum, 1970), 115, 119.

216. Allswang, *A House for All Peoples,* 120; Fiorello H. La Guardia, *The Making of an Insurgent* (Philadelphia: J.B. Lippincott, 1948), 211–12.

217. Lewis, *America,* 293–94.

218. Gerson, *The Hyphenate in Recent American Politics and Diplomacy,* 106; Duff, "German-Americans and the Peace," 440; Earl Raab, *Religious Conflict in America* (Garden City, NY: Doubleday, 1964), 72–73.

219. Edmund A. Moore, *A Catholic Runs for President* (New York: Ronald Press, 1956), 90–91.

220. Allan J. Lichtman, *Prejudice and the Old Politics* (Chapel Hill: University of North Carolina Press, 1979), 61; Moore, *A Catholic Runs for President,* 150.

221. William E. Unrau "Charles Curtis, the Politics of Allotment," in *Indian Lives—Essays on Nineteenth- and Twentieth-Century Native American Leaders,* ed. L.G. Moses and Raymond Wilson (Albuquerque: University of New Mexico Press, 1985), 114, 116.

222. Dinnerstein, *The Leo Frank Case,* 130, 150.

223. Lipset, "Religion and Politics in the American Past and Present," 89.

224. Gustavus Myers, *History of Bigotry in the United States* (New York: Capricorn Books, 1968), 220; Kenneth T. Jackson, *The Ku Klux Klan in the City, 1915–1930* (New York: Oxford University Press, 1967), 207, 19.

225. David M. Chalmers, *Hooded Americanism* (New York: New Viewpoints, 1976), 71, 110–11, 218; Ashley W. Doane Jr., *Occupational and Educational Patterns for New Hampshire's Franco-Americans* (Manchester: New Hampshire Civil Liberties Union, 1979), 16; Siegfried, *American Comes of Age,* 138.

226. Myers, *History of Bigotry in the United States,* 217; Chalmers, *Hooded Americanism,* 293.

227. Hiram Wesley Evans, "The Klan's Fight for Americanism," in *Conspiracy—The Fear of Subversion in American History,* ed. Richard O. Curry and Thomas M. Brown (New York: Holt, Rinehart and Winston, 1972), 166–67; J. Joseph Huthmacher, *Massachusetts People and Politics* (New York: Atheneum, 1973), 87.

228. Davis, *The Fear of Conspiracy,* 246; Morrison I. Swift, *The Evil Religion Does* (Boston: Liberty Press, 1927), 84–85; Jackson, *The Ku Klux Klan in the City, 1915–1930,* 247, 238.

229. Chalmers, *Hooded Americanism,* 311.

230. Leon Poliakov, *The History of Anti-Semitism* (New York: Vanguard Press,

1985), 252; Henry Ford, *My Life and Work* (Garden City, NY: Garden City Publishing, 1927), 250.

231. Miller, *American Protestantism and Social Issues,* 294.

232. Nathaniel S. Shaler, *The Neighbor* (Boston: Houghton, Mifflin, 1904), 120; William M. Simons, "The Athlete as Jewish Standard Bearer: Media Images of Hank Greenberg," *Jewish Social Studies,* Spring 1982, 96; Review of *Ellis Island to Ebbets Field: Sport and the American Jewish Experience,* by Peter Levine, in *Reviews in American History* 21 (1992): 465–70.

233. Dan A. Oren, *Joining the Club—A History of Jews and Yale* (New Haven: Yale University Press, 1985), 43.

234. Tamar Buchsbaum, "A Note on Antisemitism in Admissions at Dartmouth, 1880–1914," *Jewish Social Studies,* Winter 1987, 79; Louise Blecher Rose, "The Secret Life of Sarah Lawrence," *Commentary,* May 1983, 54.

235. Marcia Graham Synnott, "Anti-Semitism and American Universities: Did Quotas Follow the Jews? in *Anti-Semitism in American History,* ed. David A. Gerber (Urbana: University of Illinois Press, 1987), 252; Roi Ottley, *"New World A-Coming"* (Boston: Houghton Mifflin, 1943), 133; Lewis S. Feuer, "The Stages in the Social History of Jewish Professors in American Colleges and Universities," *American Jewish History,* June 1982, 455.

236. Oren, *Joining the Club,* 65.

237. Ronald H. Bayor, *Neighborhoods in Conflict—The Irish, Germans, Jews, and Italians of New York City, 1929–1941* (Baltimore: Johns Hopkins University Press, 1978), 29.

238. Oren, *Joining the Club,* 21.

239. Ibid., 146; Richard Gambino, *Blood of My Blood* (Garden City, NY: Doubleday, 1974), 110.

240. Salvatore J. LaGumina, *"Wop!"* (San Francisco: Straight Arrow Books, 1973), 246.

241. David Blanchard, "High Steel! The Kahnawake Mohawk and the High Construction Trade," *Journal of Ethnic Studies,* Summer 1983, 50–51.

242. Kwong, *Chinatown, N.Y.,* 119; Cesar Andreu Iglesias, ed., *Memorias de Bernardo Vega* (Rio Piedras, Puerto Rico: Ediciones Huracan, 1988), 117–208.

243. Burton J. Hendrick, *The Jews in America* (Garden City, NY: Doubleday, Page, 1923), 171; Lewis, *America,* 352; *Democracy in Transition* (New York: D. Appleton-Century, 1937), 233.

244. Davis, *The Russian Immigrant,* 150.

245. Walter J. Stein, *California and the Dust Bowl Migration* (Westport, CT: Greenwood Press, 1976), 60–61.

246. Solomon, *Ancestors and Immigrants,* 203.

247. David A. Shannon, *Between the Wars: America, 1919–1941* (Boston: Houghton Mifflin, 1965), 74; Richard Seelye Jones, *A History of the American Legion* (Indianapolis: Bobbs-Merrill, 1946), 210.

248. Allan Chase, *The Legacy of Malthus* (Urbana: University of Illinois Press, 1980), 175, 272.

249. Norman L. Zucker and Naomi Flink Zucker, *The Guarded Gate* (New York: Harcourt Brace Jovanovich, 1987), 10.

250. Thernstrom, *Harvard Encyclopedia of American Ethnic Groups,* 493; Saul S. Friedman, *No Haven for the Oppressed* (Detroit: Wayne State University, 1973), 21.

251. Lewis, *America,* 17–22.

252. Ibid., 22; Stanley Feldstein, *The Land That I Show You* (New York: Doubleday/Anchor, 1978), 233.

253. Friedman, *No Haven for the Oppressed,* 21.

254. Dolan, *The American Catholic Experience,* 356; Shankman, *Ambivalent Friends,* 165.

255. Robert A. Divine, *American Immigration Policy, 1924–1952* (New Haven: Yale University Press, 1957), 34; Nathan C. Belth, *A Promise to Keep* (New York: Times Books, 1979), 95.

256. Mann, *The One and the Many,* 91; Thernstrom, *Harvard Encyclopedia of American Ethnic Groups,* 742; Daniels, *The Politics of Prejudice,* 98; "The Cartozian Case," *Armenian Review* 6 (1953): 125.

257. Thernstrom, *Harvard Encyclopedia of American Ethnic Groups,* 741.

258. Divine, *American Immigration Policy,* 57.

259. Ibid., 72.

260. Panunzio, *Immigration Crossroads,* 274.

261. David Nasaw, *Schooled to Order—A Social History of Public Schooling in the United States* (New York: Oxford University Press, 1981), 170; Heale, *American Anticommunism—Combating the Enemy Within, 1830–1970,* 104.

Chapter 4. The Expansion of Democratic Pluralism

1. Randolph Bourne, "Trans-National America," in *The Diversity of Modern America,* ed. David Burner (New York: Appleton-Century-Crofts, 1970), 10; Martin Marty, *A Nation of Behavers* (Chicago: University of Chicago Press, 1976), 175.

2. Ferenc Morton Szasz, *The Divided Mind of Protestant America, 1880–1930* (Tuscaloosa: University of Alabama Press, 1982), 45; Forrest G. Wood, *The Arrogance of Faith* (New York: Alfred A. Knopf, 1990), 372–73.

3. Arthur Hertzberg, *The Zionist Ideal* (New York: Doubleday and Herzel Press, 1959), 519–20.

4. Myron Bohdon Kuropas, "Ukrainian Chicago: The Making of a Nationality Group in America," in *Ethnic Chicago,* ed. Peter d'A. Jones and Melvin G. Holli (Grand Rapids, MI: William B. Eerdmans, 1981), 171.

5. Richard J. Barnet, *The Rockets' Red Glare* (New York: Simon and Schuster, 1990), 191.

6. Ronald H. Bayor, *Neighborhoods in Conflict—The Irish, Germans, Jews, and Italians of New York City, 1929–1941* (Baltimore: Johns Hopkins University Press, 1978), 31–39.

7. Ibid., 35, 39; Stanley Lieberson, *A Piece of the Pie—Blacks and White Immigrants Since 1880* (Berkeley: University of California Press, 1980), 78–95.

8. Luciano J. Iorizzo and Salvatore Mondello, *The Italian-Americans* (New York: Twayne Publishers, 1971), 206–7; Mark Naison, "Communism and Harlem Intellectuals in the Popular Front: Anti-Fascism and the Politics of Black Culture," *Journal of Ethnic Studies,* Spring 1981, 2; Brice Harris Jr., *The United States and the Italo-Ethiopian Crisis* (Stanford: Stanford University Press, 1964), 41; Patrick S. Washburn, *A Question of Sedition* (New York: Oxford University Press, 1986), 32; Richard Polenberg, *One Nation Divisible* (New York: Viking Press, 1980).

9. Dan Vittorio Segre, *Memoirs of a Fortunate Jew* (New York: Laurel Books, 1988), 65; Humbert S. Nelli, *Italians in Chicago, 1880–1930* (New York: Oxford University Press, 1970), 241; Monte S. Finkelstein, "The Johnson Act, Mussolini and Fascist Emigration Policy: 1921–1930," *Journal of American Ethnic History,* Fall 1988, 51.

10. George Q. Flynn, *Roosevelt and Romanism* (Westport, CT: Greenwood Press, 1976), 33–34, 53.

11. William A. Douglass and Jon Bilbao, *Amerikanuak* (Reno: University of Nevada Press, 1975), 362.

12. Mark Lincoln Chadwin, *The Warhawks—American Interventionists Before Pearl Harbor* (New York: W.W. Norton, 1970), 13; Finis Herbert Capps, *From Isolationism to Involvement—The Swedish Immigrant Press in America, 1914–1945* (Chicago: Swedish Pioneer Historical Society, 1966), 202; Peter Kivisto, "Finnish Americans and the Homeland, 1918–1958," *Journal of American Ethnic History,* Fall 1987, 20.

13. Louis L. Gerson, *The Hyphenate in Recent American Politics and Diplomacy* (Lawrence: University of Kansas Press, 1964), 134–35; Bayor, *Neighborhoods in Conflict,* 61–62; Francis J. Brown and Joseph Slabey Roucek, *One America* (Englewood-Cliffs, NJ: Prentice-Hall, 1945), 419.

14. Chadwin, *The Warhawks,* 30.

15. Flynn, *Roosevelt and Romanism,* 11, 168.

16. J. Milton Yinger, *Religion in the Struggle for Power* (New York: Russell and Russell, 1961), 198–200.

17. Chadwin, *The Warhawks,* 19–20.

18. Roi Ottley, *"New World A-Coming"* (Boston: Houghton Mifflin, 1943), 327–42; Gerson, *The Hyphenate in Recent American Politics and Diplomacy,* 116; Haskel Lookstein, *Were We Our Brothers' Keepers?* (New York: Hartmore House, 1985), 192.

19. Geoffrey S. Smith, *To Save a Nation* (New York: Basic Books, 1973), 94.

20. Nathan C. Belth, *A Promise to Keep* (New York: Times Books, 1979), 123; Kuropas, "Ukrainian Chicago," 177; M.J. Heale, *American Anticommunism—Combating the Enemy Within, 1830–1970* (Baltimore: Johns Hopkins University Press, 1990), 127.

21. Brian McGinty, "Jeannette Rankin: First Woman in Congress," *American History Illustrated,* May 1988, 33; Polenberg, *One Nation Divisible,* 34–35.

22. Alexander H. Leighton, *The Governing of Men* (Princeton: Princeton University Press, 1968), 29; Stephan Thernstrom, ed., *Harvard Encyclopedia of American Ethnic Groups* (Cambridge: Harvard University Press, 1973), xiv; Paul R. Ehrlich, Loy Bilderback, and Anne H. Ehrlich, *The Golden Door* (New York: Ballantine Books, 1979), 221; Belth, *A Promise to Keep,* 151–52.

23. John Hope Franklin, *From Slavery to Freedom—A History of Negro Americans* (New York: Alfred A. Knopf, 1969), 579.

24. Terry Eastland and William J. Bennett, *Counting by Race* (New York: Basic Books, 1974), 107.

25. Tom Holm, "Fighting a White Man's War: The Extent and Legacy of American Indian Participation in World War II," *Journal of Ethnic Studies,* Summer 1981, 69–70, 74; John Tebbel and Keith Jennison, *The American Indian Wars* (New York: Bonanza Books, 1960), 219.

26. Flynn, *Roosevelt and Romanism,* 8; Polenberg, *One Nation Divisible,* 73.

27. Bayor, *Neighborhoods in Conflict,* 124; Paul R. Spickard, "Injustice Compounded: Americans and Non-Japanese Americans in World War II Concentration Camps," *Journal of American Ethnic History,* Spring 1986, 6; C. Harvey Gardiner, *Pawns in a Triangle of Hate—The Peruvian Japanese and the United States* (Seattle: University of Washington Press, 1981), viii; Jacobus Ten Broek, Edward N. Barnhart, and Floyd W. Matson, "The Attack on Japanese Americans during World War II," in *Conspiracy—The Fear of Subversion in American History,* ed. Richard O. Curry and Thomas H. Brown (New York: Holt, Rinehart and Winston, 1972), 188; Roger Daniels, *Coming to America* (New York: Harper Perennial, 1991), 15, 267.

28. Brown and Roucek, *One America,* 339.

29. Thernstrom, *Harvard Encyclopedia of American Ethnic Groups,* 339; U.S. Congress, *Hearing before the Subcommittee on Administrative Law and Governmental Relations of the Committee on the Judiciary,* House of Representatives, 92d Cong., 2d sess., H.R. 5499, Serial No. 55 (Washington, DC: U.S. Government Printing Office, 1980), 127.

30. Jerre Mangione, *An Ethnic at Large* (New York: G. Putnam's Sons, 1978), 321; Brown and Roucek, *One America,* 267; Polenberg, *One Nation Divisible,* 60.

31. Mary T. Hanna, *Catholics and American Politics* (Cambridge: Harvard University Press, 1979), 41–42; Ottley, *"New World A-Coming,"* 332–33; Washburn, *A Question of Sedition,* 35; Neil Miller, *Out of the Past—Gay and Lesbian History from 1869 to Present* (New York: Vintage, 1995), 237.

32. Saul S. Friedman, *No Haven for the Oppressed* (Detroit: Wayne State University, 1973), 31; Bayor, *Neighborhoods in Conflict,* 73.

33. Irwin F. Gellman, "The St. Louis Tragedy," *American Jewish Historical Quarterly,* December 1971. Updated reprint by the Press of Maurice Jacobs, Philadelphia.

34. Gerald S. Berman, "Reaction to the Resettlement of World War II Refugees in Alaska," *Jewish Social Studies,* Summer–Fall 1982, 271–80; Lookstein, *Were We Our Brothers' Keepers?* 207.

35. Michael Mashberg, "Documents Concerning the American State Department and the Stateless European Jews, 1942–1944," *Jewish Social Studies,* Winter–Spring 1977, 164.

36. David S. Wyman, *The Abandonment of the Jews* (New York: Pantheon Books, 1984), 9, 15.

37. John Higham, *Send These to Me—Jews and Other Immigrants in Urban America* (New York: Atheneum, 1975), 58; *New York Times,* 2 January 1983, 12; Ehrlich, Bilderback, and Ehrlich, *The Golden Door,* 70; Richard Seelye Jones, *A History of the American Legion* (Indianapolis: Bobbs-Merrill, 1946), 210–11.

38. Mann, *The One and the Many,* 93.

39. *Whom We Shall Welcome,* Report of the President's Commission on Immigration and Naturalization (Washington, DC: U.S. Government Printing Office, 1952), 31.

40. Wayne A. Cornelius, *America in the Era of Limits: Nativist Reactions to the 'New' Immigration* (San Diego: University of California Press, 1982), 11; *Whom We Shall Welcome,* 32.

41. Gil Loescher and John A. Scanlan, *Calculated Kindness—Refugees and America's Half-Open Door, 1945 to Present* (New York: Free Press, 1986), 21, 31–32.

42. Thernstrom, *Harvard Encyclopedia of American Ethnic Groups,* 763–64.

43. David M. Reimers, "An Unintended Reform: The 1965 Immigration Act and Third World Immigration to the United States," *Journal of American Ethnic History,* Fall 1983, 11.

44. Leonard Dinnerstein, "Anti-Semitism Exposed and Attacked, 1945–1950," *American Jewish History,* September 1981, 145.

45. Grimes, *Equality in America,* 69; Clement E. Vose, *Caucasians Only* (Berkeley: University of California Press, 1973), 6.

46. Leo Pfeffer, *Church, State, and Freedom* (Boston: Beacon Press, 1953), 133.

47. Sydney E. Ahlstrom, *A Religious History of the American People* (New Haven: Yale University Press, 1972), 954.

48. Albert Fried, *The Rise and Fall of the Jewish Gangster in America* (New York: Holt, Rinehart and Winston, 1980), 255–57; Jim Carnes, *US and Them* (Montgomery, AL: Southern Poverty Law Center, 1995), 116; Miller, *Out of the Past—Gay and Lesbian History from 1869 to the Present,* 259.

49. Seymour Martin Lipset, "An Instrument Rather than Creator," in *McCarthyism,* ed. Thomas C. Reeves (Huntington: Robert E. Krieger, 1978), 135; Heale, *American Anticommunism—Combating the Enemy Within, 1830–1970,* 172.

50. Loescher and Scanlan, *Calculated Kindness,* 29.

51. Abba Schwartz, *The Open Society* (New York: Simon and Schuster, 1968), 105; Stephen T. Wagner, "America's Non-English Heritage," *Society,* November–December 1981, 43; U.S. Commission on Civil Rights, *Recent Activities Against Citizens and Resi-*

dents of Asian Descent, Clearing House Publication No. 88 (Washington, DC: U.S. Government Printing Office, 1986), 12; *Whom We Shall Welcome,* 52.

52. Ehrlich, Bilderback, and Ehrlich, *The Golden Door,* 74.

53. Loescher and Scanlan, *Calculated Kindness,* 46.

54. Ibid., 58.

55. Lucius J. Barker and Twiley W. Barker Jr., eds. *Civil Liberties and the Constitution* (Englewood Cliffs, NJ: Prentice-Hall, 1970), 183; Heale, *American Anticommunism—Combating the Enemy Within, 1830–1970,* 195–96.

56. Terry Eastland, "Redefining Civil Rights," *Wilson Quarterly,* Spring 1984, 64; William Bradford Reynolds, "Affirmative Action and Its Negative Repercussions," *Annals of the American Academy of Political and Social Science,* September 1992, 39.

57. Charles V. Wilson, "On Affirmative Action as Public Policy," in *Bakke, Weber, and Affirmative Action* (New York: Rockefeller Foundation, 1979), 177; Hugh Davis Graham, "The Origins of Affirmative Action: Civil Rights and the Regulatory State," *Annals of the American Academy of Political and Social Science,* September 1992, 59.

58. Malcolm X, *The Autobiography of Malcolm X* (New York: Grove Press, 1966), 245–46; Stokely Carmichael and Charles V. Hamilton, *Black Power* (New York: Vintage Books, 1967), 40; Stephen L. Carter, *Reflections of an Affirmative Action Baby* (New York: Basic Books, 1991), 134.

59. Polenberg, *One Nation Divisible,* 257; Matthew Brelis, "From Close to Campaign Trail," *Boston Globe,* 30 August 1998, E1; Miller, *Out of the Past—Gay and Lesbian History from 1869 to the Present,* 343.

60. *Christian Century,* 9 December 1987, 1115; *Origins,* National Catholic News Service, 8 October 1987, 297; *New York Times,* 24 July 1988, 26.

61. *New York Times,* 19 May 1987, A30 and 27 October 1998, A1; *Time,* 3 August 1992, 25–28.

62. John F. Kennedy, *A Nation of Immigrants* (New York: Harper & Row, 1964), 149.

63. Loescher and Scanlan, *Calculated Kindness,* 114.

64. Ibid., 180.

65. *The New Republic,* 30 March 1987, 7; *The Tab* (Boston), 26 August 1986, 27.

66. *Immigration Report,* Federation for American Immigration Reform, July 1980, 4.

67. Thernstrom, *Harvard Encyclopedia of American Ethnic Groups,* 679.

68. *Population Bulletin* 37, no. 2 (June 1982); Philip Martin and Elizabeth Midgley, "Immigration to the United States: Journey to an Uncertain Destination," *Population Bulletin* 49, no. 2 (Washington, DC: Population Reference Bureau, September 1994): 21.

69. *Washington Post,* 2 June 1984, A6.

70. National Conference of Christians and Jews, *News Release,* 2 March 1994 and 21 March 1994, 1–8.

71. *Christian Science Monitor,* 26 November 1980, 11; *Newsweek,* 5 July 1982, 14; *New York Times,* 24 January 1982, 11 and 3 January 1984, A9.

72. Cornelius, *America in the Era of Limits,* 23; *New England Black Weekly,* 5 July 1980, 10; *Boston Globe,* 15 August 1990, 4; Yen Le Espiritu, *Asian American Panethnicity* (Philadelphia: Temple University Press, 1992), 69–81.

73. *New York Times,* 13 November 1983, 72; Loescher and Scanlon, *Calculated Kindness,* 116; *Boston Globe,* 16 August 1981, 20 and 14 October 1996, B5; *New York Times,* 6 May 1991, B7.

74. Philip Perlmutter, *The Dynamics of American Ethnic, Religious, and Racial Group Life* (Westport, CT: Praeger, 1996), 159–60; *Recent Activities Against Citizens and Residents of Asian Descent,* 5; *News Release,* Federal Bureau of Investigation, 22 November 1998, 2.

75. *Left-Right Digest* 16, Publication of American Jewish Committee, Winter 1983,

23; *Intelligence Report,* Southern Poverty Law Center, Spring 1998, 2, 8, 26, and Winter 1998, 26, 29.

76. *Near East Report,* Washington weekly on American policy in the Middle East, 13 August 1975, 137; *National Review,* 30 September 1988, 15.

77. *New York Times,* 26 October 1986, E6.

78. *Time,* 8 July 1985, 27; Edwin Harwood, "American Public Opinion and U.S. Immigration Policy," *Annals of the American Academy of Political and Social Science,* September 1986, 208.

79. Harwood, "American Public Opinion and U.S. Immigration Policy," 205; *Recent Activities Aagainst Citizens and Residents of Asian Descent,* 37.

80. *Recent Activities Against Citizens and Residents of Asian Descent,* 37; *New York Times,* 1 July 1986, 1.

81. *Recent Activities Against Citizens and Residents of Asian Descent,* 37; Harwood, "American Public Opinion and U.S. Immigration Policy," 206.

82. Harwood, "American Public Opinion and U.S. Immigration Policy," 208.

83. Richard D. Lamm, Testimony before Joint Economic Committee, Washington, D.C., 29 May 1986.

84. *Boston Irish News,* February 1987, 6; *Boston Globe,* 10 May 1989, 3.

85. *New York Times,* 10 March 1987, 1.

86. *Congressional Quarterly,* 27 October 1990, 3608.

87. Andrew M. Greely, *The American Catholic* (New Tork: Basic Books, 1977), 225.

Chapter 5. The Teaching of Contempt

1. David W. Beggs and R. Bruce McQuigg, *America's Schools and Churches* (Bloomington: Indiana University Press, 1965), 37–38.

2. Lawrence A. Cremin, *American Education* (New York: Harper & Row, 1970), 10.

3. Ibid., 12.

4. Donald E. Boles, *The Bible, Religion and the Public Schools* (New York: Collier Books, 1963), 17.

5. Maurity A. Hallgren, *Landscape of Freedom* (New York: Howell, Soskin, 1941), 52; Alice Felt Tyler, *Freedom's Ferment* (New York: Harper & Row, 1962), 229.

6. Hallgren, *Landscape of Freedom,* 54–55.

7. Robert Kelley, *The Shaping of the American Past to 1877* (Englewood Cliffs, NJ: Prentice Hall, 1975), 87; Shalom Goldman, "Biblical Hebrew in Colonial America: The Case of Dartmouth," in *Hebrew and the Bible in America,* ed. Shalom Goldman (Hanover and London: University Press of New England, 1993), 201.

8. Hallgren, *Landscape of Freedom,* 79; H.C. Good, *A History of Education* (New York: Macmillan, 1956), 6.

9. Hallgren, *Landscape of Freedom,* 31, 75; Dan A. Oren, *Joining the Club—A History of Jews and Yale* (New Haven: Yale University Press, 1985), 6.

10. Howard K. Beale, *A History of Freedom of Teaching in American Schools* (New York: Octagon Books, 1966), 11.

11. Carl Bridenbaugh, *The Spirit of '76* (New York: Oxford University Press, 1975), 35.

12. Good, *A History of Education,* 7; *New York Times,* 5 January 1987, A14; Harry S. Stout, "Word and Order in Colonial New England," in *The Bible in America,* ed. Nathan O. Hatch and Mark A. Noll (New York: Oxford University Press, 1982), 19.

13. Estelle Fuchs and Robert J. Havighurst, *To Live on This Earth: American Indian Education* (Garden City, NY: Anchor Press, 1973), 2; Jay Dolan, *The American Catholic Experience* (Garden City, NY: Doubleday, 1985), 26; Meyer Weinberg, *A Chance to Learn* (Cambridge, England: Cambridge University Press, 1977), 141.

14. Merle Curti, *American Philanthropy Abroad* (New Brunswick, NJ: Rutgers Uni-

versity Press, 1963), 5; Ralph Wood, ed., *The Pennsylvania Germans* (Princeton: Princeton University Press, 1943), 111.

15. Forrest G. Wood, *The Arrogance of Faith* (New York: Alfred A. Knopf, 1990), 20; Fuchs and Havighurst, *To Live on This Earth,* 3.

16. Richard C. Wade, *Slavery in the Cities* (New York: Oxford University Press, 1967), 91; John Hope Franklin, *From Slavery to Freedom* (New York: Alfred A. Knopf, 1969), 202.

17. Arthur Zilversmit, *The First Emancipation: The Abolition of Slavery in the North* (Chicago: University of Chicago Press, 1969), 26.

18. James Frasier, "Historical Foundations of American Education," in *An Introduction to Education,* ed. Marjorie Mitchell Cann (New York: Thomas Y. Crowell, 1972), 29.

19. Peter C. Marzio, *A Nation of Nations* (New York: Harper & Row, 1976), 306.

20. David Nasaw, *Schooled to Order—A Social History of Public Schooling in the United States* (New York: Oxford University Press, 1981), 62; Herbert Hovenkamp, *Science and Religion in America, 1800–1860* (Philadelphia: University of Pennsylvania Press, 1978), x.

21. H.L. Mencken, *The American Language* (New York: Alfred A. Knopf, 1963), 87–90.

22. Nasaw, *Schooled to Order,* 11.

23. Ibid., 38.

24. Ibid., 47–48.

25. Ibid., 83.

26. Beale, *History of Freedom of Teaching in American Schools,* 104; Ferenc Morton Szasz, *The Protestant Clergy in the Great Plains and Mountain West, 1865–1915* (Albuquerque: University of New Mexico Press, 1988), 15.

27. Stephen T. Wagner, "America's Non-English Heritage," *Society* (November/December 1981): 38.

28. Michael B. Katz, ed., *School Reform: Past and Present* (Boston: Little, Brown, 1971), 170.

29. Fred G. Burke, "Bilingualism/Biculturalism in American Education: An Adventure in Wonderland," *Annals of the American Academy of Political and Social Science,* March 1981, 167.

30. Merle Curti, *The Social Ideas of American Educators* (Totowa, NJ: Littlefield, Adams, 1959), 62; Wade, *Slavery in the Cities,* 76.

31. Tyler, *Freedom's Ferment,* 378–79.

32. Vincent Lannie, "The Teaching of Values in Public, Sunday and Catholic Schools: An Historical Perspective," *Religious Education,* March–April 1975, 127.

33. Ray Allen Billington, *The Protestant Crusade* (Chicago: Quadrangle Paperbacks, 1964), 169.

34. Guadalupe San Miguel Jr., "Culture and Education in the American Southwest: Towards an Explanation of Chicano School Attendance, 1850–1940," *Journal of American Ethnic History,* Spring 1988, 13.

35. David A. Gerber, "Language Maintenance, Ethnic Group Formation, and Public Schools: Changing Patterns of German Concern, Buffalo, 1837–1874," *Journal of American Ethnic History,* Fall 1984, 42.

36. Richard Ognibene, "Catholic and Protestant Education in the Late Nineteenth Century," *Religious Education,* January–February 1982, 9.

37. Gustavus Myers, *History of Bigotry in the United States* (New York: Capricorn Books, 1968), 114.

38. Ognibene, "Catholic and Protestant Education in the Late Nineteenth Century," 16.

39. Nasaw, *Schooled to Order,* 75; R. Freeman Butts and Lawrence A. Cremin, *A History of Education in American Culture* (New York: Henry Holt, 1953).

40. Dolan, *The American Catholic Experience,* 269; David Tyack and Elisabeth Hansot, "Conflict and Consensus in American Public Education," *Daedalus,* Summer 1981, 7.

41. Christopher J. Kauffman, *Faith and Fraternalism: The History of the Knights of Columbus, 1882–1982* (New York: Harper & Row, 1982), 88.

42. Lannie, "The Teaching of Values in Public, Sunday and Catholic Schools," 128; R. Laurence Moore, *Religious Outsiders and the Making of Americans* (New York: Oxford University Press, 1986), 58.

43. Dolan, *The Immigrant Church,* 109; Lannie, "The Teaching of Values in Public, Sunday and Catholic Schools," 126; M. Mark Stolarik, "Immigration, Education, and the Social Mobility of Slovaks, 1870–1930," in *Immigrants and Religion in Urban America,* ed. Randall M. Miller and Thomas D. Marzik (Philadelphia: Temple University Press, 1977): 72.

44. Jay Dolan, "Philadelphia and the German Catholic Community," in *Immigrants and Religion in Urban America,* ed. Randall M. Miller and Thomas D. Marzik (Philadelphia: Temple University Press, 1977), 72.

45. Hasia R. Diner, *Erin's Daughters in America* (Baltimore: Johns Hopkins University Press, 1983), 146–47; Francis R. Walsh, "Who Spoke for Boston's Irish? The Boston Pilot in the Nineteenth Century," *Journal of Ethnic Studies,* Fall 1982, 24.

46. Dolan, *The American Catholic Experience,* 270.

47. Neil G. McCluskey, *Catholic Viewpoint on Education* (New York: Hanover House, 1959), 35.

48. Naomi W. Cohen, *Encounter with Emancipation* (Philadelphia: Jewish Publication Society of America, 1984), 92.

49. Eli Lazar, "Building Day Schools in America—in the 1840's," *Jewish Life,* Spring 1976, 40.

50. George L. Berlin, "Solomon Jackson's *The Jew:* An Early American Jewish Response to the Missionaries," *American Jewish History,* September 1981, 11; Robert M. Healey, "From Conversion to Dialogue: Protestant American Mission to the Jews in the Nineteenth and Twentieth Centuries," *Journal of Ecumenical Studies,* Summer 1981, 377; Benjamin Rabinowitz, *The Young Men's Hebrew Associations (1854–1913)* (New York: National Jewish Welfare Board, 1948), 67.

51. Lazar, "Building Day Schools in America," 41; Cohen, *Encounter with Emancipation,* 93.

52. Cohen, *Encounter with Emancipation,* 91.

53. Wade, *Slavery in the Cities,* 91; August Meier and Elliott Rudwick, *From Plantation to Ghetto* (New York: Hill and Wang, 1970), 95–96; Wood, *The Arrogance of Faith,* 299–300.

54. Meier and Rudwick, *From Plantation to Ghetto,* 96.

55. Earle H. West, *The Black American and Education* (Columbus: Charles E. Merrill, 1972), 4; Stanley Lieberson, *A Piece of the Pie—Blacks and White Immigrants since 1880* (Berkeley: University of California Press, 1980), 139.

56. Lieberson, *A Piece of the Pie,* 139; Timothy L. Smith, "Native Blacks and Foreign Whites: Varying Responses to Educational Opportunity in America, 1880–1950," in *Perspectives in American History,* vol. 6, ed. Donald Fleming and Bernard Bailyn (Cambridge, MA: Charles Warren Center for Studies in American History, 1972), 317.

57. Smith, "Native Blacks and Foreign Whites: Varying Responses to Educational Opportunity in America," 320.

58. Lieberson, *A Piece of the Pie,* 136.

59. Irving Werstein, *The Wounded Land* (New York: Delacorte Press, 1968), 60.

60. Harry Lee Swint, "Education and the Attitudes," in *Race, Individual and Collective Behavior,* ed. Edgar T. Thompson and Everett C. Hughes (New York: Free Press, 1958), 508; David M. Chalmers, *Hooded Americanism* (New York: New Viewpoints, 1976), 15.

61. Katz, *School Reform: Past and Present,* 178.

62. Milton R. Konvitz, *A Century of Civil Rights* (New York: Columbia University Press, 1961), 128.

63. Brian W. Dippie, *The Vanishing American* (Middletown, CT: Wesleyan University Press, 1982), 52.

64. J.L. Dilliard, *All-American English* (New York: Vantage Books, 1975), 108–9.

65. Dolan, *The American Catholic Experience,* 24.

66. Nasaw, *Schooled to Order,* 26; Michael C. Coleman, "Not Race, but Grace: Presbyterian Missionaries and American Indians, 1837–1893," *Journal of American History,* June 1980, 41–42; Murray L. Wax and Rosalie H. Wax, "Religion among American Indians," *Annals of the American Academy of Political and Social Science,* March 1978, 31–32.

67. Thernstrom, *Harvard Encyclopedia of American Ethnic Groups,* 339; Ted C. Hinckley, *The Americanization of Alaska, 1867–1897* (Palo Alto, CA: Pacific Books, 1967), 237.

68. Hinckley, *The Americanization of Alaska,* 237.

69. Roger Daniels, *The Politics of Prejudice* (New York: Antheneum, 1972), 32; Robert H. Bremmer, ed. *Children and Youth in America,* vol. 2 (Cambridge: Harvard University Press, 1971), 1338.

70. Daniels, *The Politics of Prejudice,* 32; Carey McWilliams, *Brothers under the Skin* (Boston: Little, Brown, 1951), 146.

71. Anne Loftis, *California—Where the Twain Did Meet* (New York: Macmillan, 1973), 201.

72. Lieberson, *A Piece of the Pie,* 137.

73. David B. Tyack, "Ways of Seeing: An Essay on the History of Compulsory Schooling," *Harvard Educational Review,* August 1976, 361; Francesco Cordasco, "The Children of Immigrants in the Schools," in *Education and the Many Faces of the Disadvantaged,* ed. William W. Brickman and Stanley Lehrer (New York: John Wiley and Sons, 1972), 196; Philip Taylor, *The Distant Magnet* (New York: Harper & Row, 1971), 213.

74. Jeanette Meisel Baron, ed., *Steeled by Adversity—Essays and Addresses on American Jewish Life by Salo Wittmayer Baron* (Philadelphia: Jewish Publication Society of American, 1971), 281; E.J. Kahn Jr., *The American People* (New York: Weybright and Talley, 1974), 179.

75. William M. Leiserson, *Adjusting Immigrant and Industry* (New York: Harper & Brothers, 1924), 18–19.

76. Marzio, *A Nation of Nations,* 308.

77. Roger Daniels, *Coming to America* (New York: Harper Perennial, 1991), 176; Fiorello H. La Guardia, *The Making of an Insurgent* (Philadelphia: J.B. Lippincott, 1948), 27.

78. Christopher Lasch, *The Social Thought of Jane Addams* (Indianapolis: Bobbs-Merrill, 1965), 95–96.

79. Dolan, *The American Catholic Experience,* 195; Richard G. Durnin, "The Education of Immigrants in the United States," in *Education and the Many Faces of the Disadvantaged,* ed. William W. Brickman and Stanley Lehrer (New York: John Wiley and Sons, 1972), 189; Ray Allen Billington, *Westward Expansion* (New York: Macmillan, 1967), 706.

80. *Puerto Rico's Political Future: A Divisive Issue with Many Dimensions* (Washington, DC: U.S. General Accounting Office, GGD-81-48, 2 March 1981), 91–92.

81. Leonard Dinnerstein and David M. Reimers, *Ethnic Americans: A History of Immigration and Assimilation* (New York: Dodd, Mead, 1975), 30–31; James C. Thomson Jr., Peter W. Stanley, and John Curtis Perry, *Sentimental Imperialists—The American Experience in East Asia* (New York: Harper & Row, 1981), 98–99.

82. Josef J. Barton, "Eastern and Southern Europeans," in *Ethnic Leadership in America,* ed. John Higham (Baltimore: Johns Hopkins University Press, 1979), 157–58.

83. Marshall B. Clinard, *Slums and Community Development* (New York: Free Press, 1966), 32; Oscar Handlin, *Boston's Immigrants* (New York: Atheneum, 1971), 113.

84. Thomas Kessner, *The Golden Door* (New York: Oxford University Press, 1977), 8.

85. Majorie Barstow Greenbie, *American Saga* (New York: Whittlesey House–McGraw-Hill Book, 1939), 627.

86. Abbé Felix Klein, *The Land of the Strenuous Life* (Chicago: A.C. McClurg, 1905), 28.

87. Andrew M. Greeley, *The American Catholic* (New York: Basic Books, 1977), 225.

88. Nasaw, *Schooled to Order,* 131.

89. Allan Chase, *The Legacy of Malthus* (Urbana: University of Illinois Press, 1980), 235.

90. Barbara Miller Solomon, *Ancestors and Immigrants* (Chicago: University of Chicago Press, 1972), 72.

91. Rudolph O. de la Garza, "Mexican Americans in the United States: The Evolution of a Relationship," in *Case Studies on Human Rights and Fundamental Freedoms,* vol. 5 (The Hague: Foundation for the Study of Plural Societies, 1976), 272; Solomon, *Ancestors and Immigrants,* 180–98; Burton J. Hendrick, *The Jews in America* (Garden City, NY: Doubleday, Page, 1923), 60, 93–94.

92. Scott E.W. Bedford, *Readings in Urban Sociology* (New York: D. Appleton, 1927), 820; Ronald Takaki, *Strangers from a Different Shore* (New York: Penguin Books, 1990), 257.

93. Colin Greer, *The Great School Legend* (New York: Viking Press, 1973), 121.

94. Iris Saunders Podea, "Quebec to 'Little Canada': The Coming of the French Canadians to New England in the Nineteenth Century," in *The Aliens,* ed. Leonard Dinnerstein and Frederic Cople Jaher (New York: Appleton-Century-Crofts, 1970), 209.

95. Leslie Woodcock Tentler, *Wage-Earning Women* (New York: Oxford University Press, 1979), 100–101; Diner, *Erin's Daughters in America,* 140–41.

96. Walter J. Kelly, "Education and Group Mobility," *ICEE Heritage, Newsletter of the Illinois Consultation on Ethnicity in Education,* 1 December 1980, 1, 3.

97. Pittsburgh Section, National Council of Jewish Women, *By Myself, I'm a Book* (Waltham, MA: American Jewish Historical Society, 1972), 67; Humberto Cardinal Medeiros, *Stewards of This Heritage* (Boston: Daughters of St. Paul, 1983), 5.

98. John Bodnar, *The Transplanted—A History of Immigrants in Urban America* (Bloomington: Indiana University Press, 1985), 194.

99. John Bodnar, "Schooling and the Slavic-American Family, 1900–1940," in *American Education and the European Immigrant: 1840–1940,* ed. Bernard J. Weiss (Urbana: University of Illinois Press, 1982), 81; Tentler, *Wage-Earning Women,* 98.

100. Michael Kraus, *Immigration, the American Mosaic* (New York: Van Nostrand Reinhold, 1966), 66.

101. Ruth Miller Elson, *Guardians of Tradition* (Lincoln: University of Nebraska Press, 1964), 69, 87.

102. Ibid., 69, 124.

103. *Franco-Americans in Vermont* (Washington, DC: U.S. Commission on Civil Rights, 1983), 24.

104. Elson, *Guardians of Tradition,* 151, 162.

105. Tyack and Hansot, "Conflict and Consensus in American Public Education," 4.

106. Ibid., 9.

107. Stanley Feldstein and Lawrence Costello, *The Ordeal of Assimilation* (Garden City, NY: Anchor Press, 1974), 252.

108. Nicholas V. Montalto, "The Intercultural Education Movement, 1924–41: The Growth of Tolerance as a Form of Intolerance," in *American Education and the European Immigrant, 1840–1940,* ed. Bernard J. Weiss (Urbana: University of Illinois Press, 1982), 42–43; Victor R. Greene, "Ethnic Confrontations with State Universities, 1860–1920," in *American Education and the European Immigrant, 1840–1940,* 189–203.

109. Solomon, *Ancestors and Immigrants,* 180–89.

110. Takaki, *Strangers from a Different Shore,* 218.

111. Edward George Hartmann, *The Movement to Americanize the Immigrant* (New York: Columbia University Press, 1948), 24; Feldstein and Costello, *The Ordeal of Assimilation,* 387; Andrew T. Kopan, "Greek Survival in Chicago: The Role of Ethnic Education, 1890–1980," in *Ethnic Chicago,* ed. Peter d'A. Jones and Melvin G. Holli (Grand Rapids, MI: William B. Eerdmans, 1981), 125.

112. National Council of Jewish Women, *By Myself, I'm a Book,* 66; Frances Kellor, *Immigration and the Future* (New York: George H. Doran, 1920), 42.

113. Howard B. Grose, *The Incoming Millions* (New York: Fleming H. Revell, 1906), 168–69; Raymond A. Mohl, "Cultural Pluralism in Immigrant Education: The International Institutes of Boston, Philadelphia, and San Francisco, 1920–1940," *Journal of American Ethnic History,* Spring 1982, 37.

114. Wallace Evan Davies, *Patriotism on Parade* (Cambridge: Harvard University Press, 1955), 298.

115. Humbert S. Nelli, *The Italians in Chicago, 1880–1930* (New York: Oxford University Press, 1970), 88; Robert Mirak, *Torn between Two Lands: Armenians in America 1890 to World War I* (Cambridge: Harvard University Press, 1983), 273–74.

116. Stoyan Christowe, *The Eagle and the Stork* (New York: Harper's Magazine Press, 1976), 328.

117. Peter Roberts, *The New Immigration* (New York: Macmillan, 1912), 282.

118. Selma C. Berrol, "From Compensatory Education to Adult Education: The New York City Evening Schools, 1925–1935," *Adult Education* 26 (1976): 213.

119. John F. McClymer, "The Americanization Movement and the Education of the Foreign-Born Adult, 1914–25," in *American Education and the European Immigrant: 1840–1940,* ed. Bernard J. Weiss (Urbana: University of Illinois Press, 1982), 104–5; Davis, *The Russian Immigrant* (New York: Macmillan, 1922), 111.

120. Frank C. Nelson, "Norwegian-American Attitudes toward Assimilation during Four Periods of Their History in America, 1825–1930," *Journal of Ethnic Studies,* Spring 1981, 61; Dinnerstein and Reimers, *Ethnic Americans,* 53–54; Harry H.L. Kitano, *Japanese Americans* (Englewood Cliffs, NJ: Prentice-Hall, 1969), 23–24.

121. Henry Pratt Fairchild, *Greek Immigrants to the United States* (New Haven: Yale University Press, 1911), 146–47.

122. Davis, *The Russian Immigrant,* 190.

123. Herbert G. Gutman, *Work, Culture and Society in Industrializing America* (New York: Vintage Books, 1976), 6.

124. Bodnar, *The Transplanted,* 99; Marzio, *A Nation of Nations,* 372; John Higham, *Strangers in the Land* (New York: Atheneum, 1971), 248.

125. Leiserson, *Adjusting Immigrant and Industry,* 135.

126. Susan Bliss, "A Nation of Nations," *American Educator,* Spring 1978, 19.

127. Frank Tracy Carlton, *The History and Problems of Organized Labor* (New York: D.C. Heath, 1911), 349–50.

128. McClymer, "The Americanization Movement and the Education of the Foreign-Born Adult," 99.

129. Fred G. Burke, "Bilingualism/Biculturalism in American Education: An Adventure in Wonderland," *Annals of the American Academy of Political and Social Science,* March 1981, 168; *Franco-Americans in Vermont,* 10; Milton R. Konvitz, *Fundamental Liberties of a Free People* (Ithaca: Cornell University Press, 1957), 85.

130. Leiserson, *Adjusting Immigrant and Industry,* 254.

131. James A. Johnson, Harold W. Collins, Victor L. Dupuis, and John H. Johansen, *Foundations of American Education* (Boston: Allyn and Bacon, 1973), 267; Butts and Cremin, *A History of Education in American Culture,* 145–46.

132. Konvitz, *Fundamental Liberties of a Free People,* 85–86.

133. Stolarik, "Immigration, Education, and the Social Mobility of Slovaks," 108–12.

134. Dolan, *The American Catholic Experience,* 169, 297–99.

135. Ibid., 281, 242; Clifford E. Nelson, *The Lutherans in North America* (Philadelphia: Fortress Press, 1960), 427; Bodnar, "The Slavic-American Family," 95.

136. San Miguel, "Culture and Education in the American Southwest," 15.

137. Greene, "Ethnic Confrontations with State Universities," 195; Kopan, "Greek Survival in Chicago," 98.

138. Morrison I. Swift, *The Evil Religion Does* (Boston: Liberty Press, 1927), 80; David B. Tyack, "The Perils of Pluralism: The Background of the Pierce Case," *American Historical Review,* October 1968, 79.

139. Tyack, "The Perils of Pluralism," 79; André Siegfried, *America Comes of Age* (New York: Harcourt, Brace, 1927), 65–66.

140. Tyack, "The Perils of Pluralism," 97.

141. Ibid.

142. McClymer, "The Americanization Movement and the Education of the Foreign-Born Adult," 111.

143. Hartmann, *The Movement to Americanize the Immigrant,* 256, 257.

144. Theodore Saloutos, *The Greeks in the United States* (Cambridge: Harvard University Press, 1964), 237.

145. Horace M. Kallen, *Culture and Democracy in the United States* (New York: Boni and Liveright, 1924), 145–47.

146. Higham, *Strangers in the Land,* 251.

147. Kallen, *Culture and Democracy in the United States,* 131–32.

148. Horace M. Kallen, "Democracy versus the Melting Pot," in *Race and Ethnicity in Modern America,* ed. Richard J. Meister (Lexington: D.C. Heath, 1974), 61.

149. Michael N. Dobkowski, *The Tarnished Dream—The Basis of American Anti-Semitism* (Westport, CT: Greenwood Press, 1979), 163.

150. Leiserson, *Adjusting Immigrant and Industry,* 23–24.

151. Bremmer, *Children and Youth in America,* vol. 2, 1315; Higham, *Strangers in the Land,* 260.

152. J.J. Heale, *American Anticommunism—Combating the Enemy Within, 1830–1970* (Baltimore: Johns Hopkins University Press, 1990), 129.

153. Nasaw, *Schooled to Order,* 180.

154. Charles M. Lamb, "Legal Foundations of Civil Rights and Pluralism in Amer-

ica," *Annals of the American Academy of Political and Social Science,* March 1981, 15.

155. *New York Times,* 16 June 1982, 1; Abigail M. Thernstrom, "Bilingual Mis-education," *Commentary,* February 1990, 46; Neil Miller, *Out of the Past—Gay and Lesbian History from 1869 to the Present* (New York: Vintage Books, 1995), 557.

156. *Christian Science Monitor,* 23 March 1987, 1, 6.

157. Timothy L. Smith, "Immigrant Social Aspirations and American Education, 1880–1930," in *Education in American History,* ed. Michael B. Katz (New York: Praeger, 1973), 237.

158. Ibid., 240; Thernstrom, *Harvard Encyclopedia of American Ethnic Groups,* 317, 1022; Bodnar, *The Transplanted,* 23.

159. Smith, "Immigrant Social Aspirations and American Education, 1880–1930," 237; Lieberson, *A Piece of the Pie,* 134.

160. Thermstrom, *Harvard Encyclopedia of American Ethnic Groups,* 316; Ronald H. Bayor, *Neighborhoods in Conflict—The Irish, Germans, Jews, and Italians of New York City, 1929–1941* (Baltimore: Johns Hopkins University Press, 1978), 16; Takaki, *Strangers from a Different Shore,* 314.

161. Colin Greer, "Immigrants, Negroes, and the Public Schools," in *Divided Society,* ed. Colin Greer (New York: Basic Books, 1974), 90; Josef J. Barton, *Peasants and Strangers—Italians, Romanians, and Slovaks in an American City, 1890–1950* (Cambridge: Harvard University Press, 1975), 128; Bayor, *Neighborhoods in Conflict,* 16–17; Seller, *Immigrant Women,* 85.

162. Diner, *Erin's Daughters in America,* 96–97; Robert A. Dahl, "Leaders in Public Education," in *Governing Education: A Reader on Politics, Power, and Public School Policy,* ed. Alan Rosenthal (New York: Anchor Books, 1969), 400.

163. Roberts, *The New Immigration,* 336; *Washington Post,* 15 August 1985, A26.

164. Kessner, *The Golden Door,* 176.

165. Barton, *Peasants and Strangers,* 128; Susan M. Papp, *Hungarian Americans and Their Communities of Cleveland* (Cleveland: Cleveland State University Press, 1981), 276; *Festival Bostonian Retrospective* (Boston: City of Boston, 1977), 34; Yvonne Haddad, "The Lebanese Community in Hartford," *Arab Perspectives,* February 1981, 13; Kopan, "Greek Survival in Chicago," 105.

166. *The Economic Status of Americans of Southern and Eastern European Ancestry,* U.S. Commission on Civil Rights, Clearinghouse Publication 89, October 1986, 3, 28–29; *News,* U.S. Department of Commerce, Economic and Statistics Administration, CB9B-57, 9 April 1998, 1.

167. Greeley, *The American Catholic,* 46–47; Fred Massarik and Alvin Chenkin, "United States National Jewish Population Study: A First Report," *American Jewish Yearbook* (Philadelphia: American Jewish Committee and Jewish Publication Society of America, 1973), 277; Seymour Martin Lipset and Earl Raab, *Jews and the New American Scene* (Cambridge: Harvard University Press, 1995), 27.

168. Lieberson, *A Piece of the Pie,* 125; J.A. Parks, "Editor's Comment," *Lincoln Review,* Summer 1984, 8; Phyllis Coons, "Independent Schools Report Minorities Slowly Increasing," *Boston Globe,* 10 March 1985, B25; Press-Release @ Census. Gov., CB 98–106, 29 June 1998.

169. *New York Times,* 19 April 1987, 24, and 8 October 1984, 22; Press-Release @ Census. Gov., CB97–FS. 10, 11 September 1997.

170. Ibid., 19 April 1987, 24; Coons, "Independent Schools Report Minorities Slowly Increasing," B25; *Washington Post,* 10 October 1985, A1; Press-Release @ Census. Gov., CB98–108, 29 June 1998.

171. Fox Butterfield, "Why Asians Are Going to the Head of the Class," *New York Times Educational Life,* 3 August 1986, 20–21; *Time,* 28 March 1983, 52.

172. *Washington Post,* 10 October 1985, A1; *Christian Science Monitor,* 10 October 1985, 4; Arthur W. Helweg, "Affluent Immigrants: East Indians in the United States," *Migration World* 16 (1988): 12; Masako M. Osako, "Japanese-Americans: Melting into the All-American Pot?" in *Ethnic Chicago,* ed. Peter d'A. Jones and Melvin G. Holli (Grand Rapids, Mich.: William B. Eerdmans, 1981), 330; David A. Bell, "The Triumph of Asian-Americans," *New Republic,* 15–22 July 1985, 26.

173. *Christian Science Monitor,* 23 March 1987, 1, 6.

174. Henry Steele Commager, *The American Mind* (New Haven: Yale University Press, 1970), 193.

175. *New York Times,* 12 April 1981, 22; *The Pilot* (Boston), 5 April 1985, 14; *New York Times,* 28 November 1987, 25; Vernon C. Polite, "Getting the Job Done Well: African American Students and Catholic Schools," *Journal of Negro Education,* Spring 1992, 212; Paul T. Hill, Gail E. Foster, and Tamar Gendler, *High Schools with Character* (Santa Monica: Rand Corporation, 1990), v–ix.

176. Virgil C. Blum, "The Price of Racism and Anti-Catholicism," *The Pilot* (Boston), 15 September 1989, 15.

Chapter 6. The Future of Minority Progress

1. *Educating for Unity, a Survey of Professional Roman Catholic Educators* (Wheeling, WV: National Association of Diocesan Ecumenical Officers, 1983), 22; *New York Times,* 8 January 1987, A22; James Davison Hunger and Kimon Howland Sargeant, "The Religious Roots of the Culture Wars: How Competing Moral Visions Fuel Cultural Conflict," *The Tribal Basis of American Life,* ed. Murray Friedman and Nancy Isserman (Westport, CT: Praeger, 1998), 33.

2. *New York Times,* 5 August 1979, 43; *Jewish Telegraphic Agency* news bulletin, 5 February 1988, 4; Philip Perlmutter, *The Dynamics of American Ethnic, Religious, and Racial Group Life* (Westport, CT: Praeger, 1996), 102.

3. Wade Clark Roof and William McKinney, "Denominational America and the New Religious Pluralism," *Annals of the American Academy of Political and Social Science,* July 1985, 25; Perlmutter, *The Dynamics of American Ethnic, Religious, and Racial Group Life,* 190.

4. *Boston Globe,* 8 February 1987, 2; Sam Roberts, "U.S. Census Study Reveals a Nation of Rolling Stones," *New York Times,* 12 December 1944, A14; Karen De Witt, "Wave of Suburban Growth Is Being Fed by Minorities," *New York Times,* 15 August 1994, A1; William H. Frey, "Black Migration to the South Reaches Record Highs in 1990s," *Population Today,* February 1998, 1–3.

5. *The KKK and the Neo-Nazis* (New York: Anti-Defamation League of B'nai B'rith, 1984), 1, 10; *Intelligence Report,* Southern Poverty Law Center, Spring 1998, 6.

6. *Jewish Telegraphic Agency* news bulletin, 5 February 1988, 4; *New York Times,* 1 September 1983, A17; John Perazzo, *The Myths That Divide Us* (Briarcliff Manor, NY: World Studies Books, 1998), 377.

7. Lawrence J. Goodrich, "Changing Face of Congress: More Entrepreneurs and Minorities," *Christian Science Monitor,* 27 March 1997, 3; Matthew Brelis, "From Closet to Campaign Trail," *Boston Globe,* 30 August 1998, E1, and 24 October 1998, A4.

8. *A Congressional Direction and Action Guide* (Washington, DC: General Board of Church and Society of the United Methodist Church, 1997), 51; *United Methodist Reporter,* 6 January 1989, 3.

9. *Boston Globe,* 5 January 1987, 1.

10. Perlmutter, *The Dynamics of American Ethnic, Religious, and Racial Group Life,* 102–3.

11. *A Study of Attitudes Toward Racial and Religious Minorities and Toward Women,* Louis Harris and Associates, Study No. S28229–B, November 1978, 32–34; *New York Times,* 9 August 1988, A13, 10 January 1990, A21, and 31 May 1998, A21; *Christian Science Monitor,* 12 January 1990, 18.

12. *New York Times,* 27 August 1991, A1, and 30 September 1997, A1; Stephan Thernstrom and Abigail Thernstrom, *America in Black and White* (New York: Simon and Schuster, 1990), 18.

13. *U.S. News and World Report,* 13 January 1997, 12; *Christian Science Monitor,* 12 December 1996, 9; Press-Release @ Census. Gov. CB98–105 (29 June 1998).

14. Samuel Z. Klausner, "Anti-Semitism in the Executive Suite," *Moment,* September 1988, 38.

15. *Parade Magazine,* 2 June 1985, 4; *The Economic Status of Americans of Southern and Eastern European Ancestry,* Clearing House Publication 89 (Washington, DC: U.S. Commission on Civil Rights, October 1986), 47; Sharon M. Lee, *Asian Americans: Diverse and Growing,* Population Bulletin, 53, no. 2 (Washington, DC: Population Reference Bureau, June 1998), 27–28.

16. Thernstrom and Thernstrom, *America in Black and White,* 531.

Index

DATE DUE

DEC 1 4 2001			
RJUL 2 6 2005			
GAYLORD			PRINTED IN U.S.A.